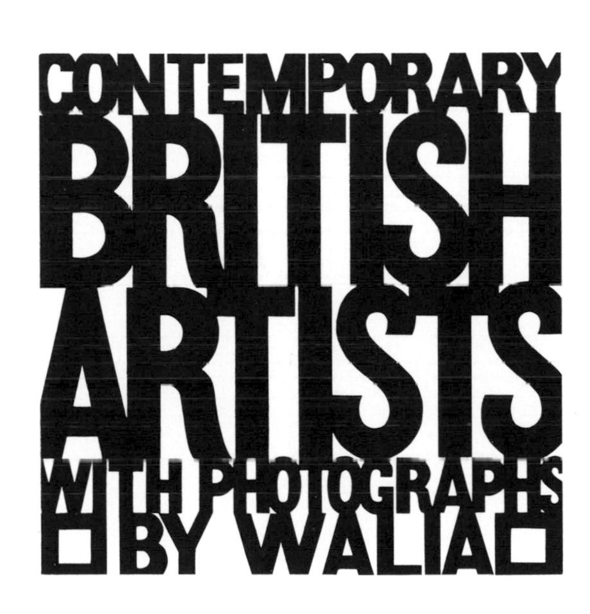
CONTEMPORARY
BRITISH
ARTISTS
WITH PHOTOGRAPHS
BY WALIA

For information write:
St Martin's Press, Inc, 175 Fifth Ave, New York, NY10010

Printed in Great Britain

ISBN 0-312-16655-9
Library of Congress Catalog Card Number: 79-87712
First published in the UK and the USA in 1979

CONTEMPORARY BRITISH ARTISTS WITH PHOTOGRAPHS BY WALIA

Edited by Charlotte Parry-Crooke
Introduction by Norbert Lynton

St Martin's Press, New York

Acknowledgments

The publishers gratefully acknowledge the extremely kind and generous help of all those who have been involved in the compilation of this book, and in particular the artists themselves and their galleries. They would especially like to thank the following:

Art Information Registry: Moira Kelly; Arts Council of Great Britain, Art Department: Sue Brandt; Bedford Typesetters: Mr Lock; Vicky Cooper; Fenella Crichton; Fieldborne Galleries: Bernard Sternfield; Fischer Fine Art: Ann Colville; Angela Flowers; Pat Gilmour; Gimpel Fils; Nigel Greenwood Inc: Nigel Greenwood, Charlotte Wynn-Parry; Annely Juda Fine Art: Annely and David Juda; Sarah Kent; James Kirkman; Knoedler Gallery: Kasmin, Ruth Kelsey; Marlborough Fine Art: The Directors; Charlotte Odgers; Anthony d'Offay: Caroline Cuthbert, Anthony d'Offay; William Packer; Padnall Printers: Tom Jobbins; Georgiana Parry-Crooke; Paul Peter Piech; Piccadilly Gallery: Christobel Briggs; Elizabeth Rees; Redfern Gallery: Harry Tatlock Miller, Maggie Thornton; Jane Ripley; Rowan Gallery: Celia Plunkett, Francie Pritchard; Royal Academy of Art; Hester van Royen Gallery: Anne Berthoud; Serpentine Gallery: Peggy Armstrong; Slade School of Fine Art: Suzanne Dumayne, Ilena Ginsburg; Waddington Galleries: Dan Cornwall-Jones, Nicola Jacobs, Sarah Tobias, Leslie Waddington; Kuldeep Walia; Whitechapel Art Gallery: Sally Williams

Publisher's Note

All the information contained in the reference section of this book (biographies and statements) was supplied by the artists concerned, their galleries or representatives, and the publishers have made every effort to ensure that this information is accurate.

The Contents list at the front of the book and the Directory, which are in alphabetical order, indicate the location of the portraits.

In the Directory all exhibition venues are in London unless otherwise indicated. The addresses of all the main dealers are included in the Gallery Addresses section at the end of the book. In the few instances where examples of an artist's work are not shown, this is at the request of the artist concerned. On the occasions where 'individual exhibition' is used instead of 'one-man exhibition', this is also at the artist's request.

A companion volume is planned, which will cover the work of contemporary British graphic artists, printmakers, illustrators and cartoonists.

Contents

Artists

The numbers refer to the position of the artist's portrait

Introduction

Art is what artists do: in the end that is the only definition that stands up. Attempt any other, try to say where art might end and other things start, and artists instantly trample it into the ground. Art's diversity was never greater than now, but what links it, what art has in common with art, is artists.

London makes one acutely aware of this. Enormous, receptive capital of a geographically small country that for some decades now has been the locus of one of the leading and most productive art worlds of our time, London houses and displays a vast concentration of British art and artists of all sorts. Native patronage is poor; public organizations do their best to compensate for some of that lack; but it is internationally that the British art world thrives, and almost all the energies and talent and agencies that put art on the international stage are focussed on London. In London art and artists are concentrated as nowhere else today. It is a special characteristic of this concentration that it is devoid of exclusive encampments. Even the Royal Academy now serves as platform for extreme diversities, whilst art schools bring into positive allegiance artists of contradictory persuasions. And those artists who live and work outside the capital, many of them notable figures, also look to London to know how the art world stands.

This book puts the British art world before your eyes and into your hands – through photographs of many of the artists that form it, through summaries of their professional lives, through a representative piece of their work and a statement indicative of their positions. The information at the back of the book is partnered by the images at the front, profoundly effective in introducing us to a broad range of artists of especial interest and value, and, taken together, telling us much of the constitution and temper of contemporary British art.

Photographing people was photography's strong suit from the start. Hardly had a way of fixing the image been found when portrait photographs began to be produced as the most convincing, the most beautiful and also the most necessary instances of the new art. Nadar, Carjat, David Octavius Hill and Julia Margaret Cameron led a swarm of talented and sometimes magnificent professionals and amateurs. The great and famous, the small, the anonymous, the near and the far, the admirable, the feared and the despicable, the beautiful, the exotic, the deformed, the damaged, the dead. Intentional portrait representations, the snapshot, the accidentally caught face at the window, the celebratory image, the mug shot, the scientific record. What all this has done to our understanding of ourselves and of each other one hesitates to say: the possibilities are as contradictory as the evidence. I opt for the belief that greater knowledge brings greater conviviality.

But the photographer is himself a positive agent in this. Though the photograph almost persuades us that it tells the truth and nothing but the truth, we know that some photographs are truer than others. Also, some photographs are more informative than others, and information need not only mean the data gathered via correct exposure and a good lens. In the upper reaches of the art, the photographic portraitist too has his particular ways. We learn to recognize an Avedon, a Cartier-Bresson, a Beaton, and we associate this recognizability with maturity and artistry. We also learn to distinguish different genres with portrait photography: the gossipy piece that seems to tell us all about the sitter's spouse, clothes, curtains and car; the ironic or sadistic epigram that pins the possibly willing sitter to the collector's tray but shows up the pinner's marksmanship more than his victim's nature; the advertising copy that eulogizes every saleable feature and forgets the rest; the map-maker's survey that notes every nook and cranny and leaves texture to tell all; the theatrical agent's handout that turns every sitter into Hamlet by dint of dramatic and unlikely angles. The portrait photograph, as opposed to the snapshot, is a conscious act and in some measure a collaboration that often turns into a con trick.

I know most of the faces in this book. In many cases I know what is behind them too. In addition, I have myself been the . . . object, target, prey? Afterwards one wonders. It all happens so quickly. Walia rings to make a date, comes punctually, works quietly and without fuss, rearranges neither you nor your surroundings, asks very little, imposes nothing, and is gone. You feel neither steam-rollered nor lionized. Walia works on the facts. He seems to invent nothing, nor 'think something up', nor least of all arrive with a preplanned strategy. You feel he has scanned everything, seen you in context, as you were before he arrived and shall be when he has left, yet he has not invaded you or in any painful sense judged you.

Yet his photographs are so much more than documentary. What is it that tells Walia when to go in close, when to go for circumstantial detail, when to have the sitter look at us, when to imply or show action, when to leave the sitter passive? As I say, I know a lot of these people; in many cases one has also seen other photographs of them. I can state that, again and again, Walia hits the nail on the head. And not just in terms of visual likeness. Not 'yes, he looks like that', but 'he *is* like that'. In some instances I feel I now know the sitter better than I did before; often I realize that no other photograph has captured him as truly, as multi-dimensionally.

Each photograph is a little essay, a brief account by an exceedingly subtle but never unfair analyst, never glorifying himself at his subject's expense. Not documentary but truth, and that means tact as well as acuity. I don't mean tact towards the sitter, though Walia does leave one feeling undamaged; I mean tact towards the medium, a sensitivity for what a photograph of so complex a thing as a human being can carry, what needs showing and what can be implied or is unnecessary. In the few cases where Walia has allowed himself a touch of humour or of staging, he has done it openly, leaving the sitter untricked. In the vast majority of cases the result is a 'straight' photograph and with it he tells us volumes.

Not about himself, though. He projects himself neither on the sitting nor on the printing. The artists who are the theme of this collection are not discoloured by the filter of an interposed personality. What characterizes these portraits is the opposite of this, a kind of transparency. Their limpidity is the product of Walia's perceptiveness, of a clairvoyant scrutiny that is as remarkable for its swiftness as for its depth. Does Walia photograph people the way he knows them or does he come to know them in photographing them? I suspect that for him, as for the best artists in any medium, seeing, knowing and making are thoroughly interdependent activities, not separable and not sequential. And the photographs before us yield a complementary unity: an artificial object called a photograph, a person portrayed, a moment representing a life, an unseen observer who selects, constructs. All that is there, and more, but here the element we most easily forget is the last of these. That, surely, is how it should be.

Norbert Lynton 1979

1 Henry Moore OM

2 Graham Sutherland OM

3 Francis Bacon

4 Ivon Hitchens

5 John Piper

6 Edward Wolfe RA

7 Anthony Gross ARA

8 Rodrigo Moynihan

9 Ruskin Spear RA

10 David McFall RA

11 Tristram Hillier RA

12 Edward Middleditch RA

13 Victor Pasmore

14 Roger de Grey RA

15 Robert Buhler RA

16 Roland Vivian Pitchforth RA

17 William Coldstream

18 Lynn Chadwick

19 Lawrence Gowing ARA

20 Mary Potter

21 James Fitton RA

22 Peter de Francia

23 Kenneth Armitage

24 Richard Eurich RA

25 Cecil Collins

26 Willi Soukop RA

27 Reg Butler

28 David Tindle RA

29 F E McWilliam

30 Peter Coker RA

31 Robert Medley

32 Donald Hamilton Fraser ARA

33 John Ward RA

34 Douglas Portway

35 Ian Hamilton Finlay

36 Bernard Dunstan RA

37 Derrick Greaves

38 Norman Blamey RA

39 Frederick Gore RA

40 Bryan Kneale RA

41 Leonard Rosoman RA

42 Jean Cooke RA

43 Carel Weight RA

44 Elizabeth Blackadder RA

45 Dennis Creffield

46 John Bratby RA

47 Ben Levene ARA

48 Josef Herman

49 Elisabeth Frink RA

50 Terry Frost

51 Harry Thubron

52 Laetitia Yhap

53 Jeffery Camp ARA

54 Kenneth Martin

55 Patrick Heron

56 Henry Mundy

57 Robert Clatworthy RA

58 William Scott ARA

59 Bernard Meadows

60 Philip Sutton ARA

61 Sandra Blow RA

62 Jack Smith

63 Norman Adams RA

64 Patrick Symons

65 Adrian Heath

66 Patrick George

67 Sheila Fell RA

68 Craigie Aitchison ARA

69 Euan Uglow

70 Anthony Eyton ARA

71 Myles Murphy

72 Gillian Ayres

73 John Copnall

74 Leon Kossoff

75 Alan Davie

76 Richard Smith

77 John Hoyland

78 John Plumb

79 Robyn Denny

80 Bridget Riley

81 Bernard Cohen

82 Anthony Caro

83 Tim Scott

84 Phillip King ARA

85 Frank Auerbach

86 William Turnbull

87 Kim Lim

88 Marc Vaux

89 Tess Jaray

90 John Walker

91 John Golding

92 Paul Huxley

93 Peter Kinley

94 Noel Forster

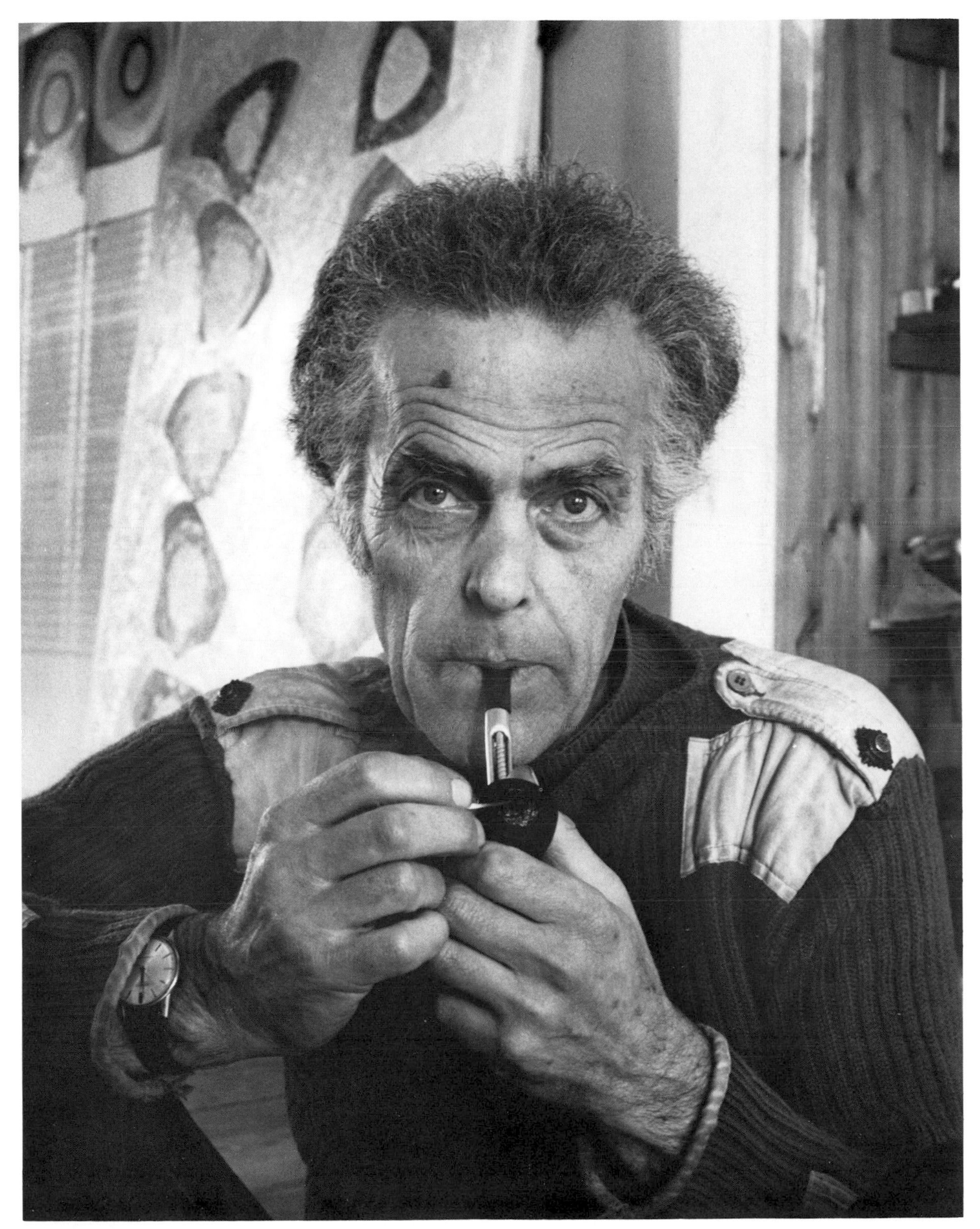

95 Michael Kidner

96 Bob Law

97 Richard Lin

98 Jean Spencer

99 Malcolm Hughes

100 Peter Lowe

101 Anthony Hill

102 Gillian Wise Ciobotaru

103 Patrick Procktor

104 Richard Hamilton

105 David Hockney

106 Joe Tilson

107 Howard Hodgkin

108 Patrick Caulfield

109 Allen Jones

110 R B Kitaj

111 Rita Donagh

112 Nicholas Monro

113 Bryan Organ

114 Patrick Hughes

115 Lucy MacKenzie

116 Peter Phillips

117 David Inshaw

118 Peter Blake ARA

119 Graham Ovenden

120 Roland Piché

121 Wendy Taylor

122 Paul Neagu

123 Phyllida Barlow

124 Garth Evans

125 John Wragg

126 Nigel Hall

127 Michael Kenny ARA

128 Raymond Arnatt

129 Nicholas Pope

130 William Pye

131 Martin Naylor

132 Katherine Gili

133 Michael Sandle

134 Ken Draper

135 Gwyther Irwin

136 Michael Andrews

137 Tom Phillips

138 Adrian Berg

139 Anthony Green RA

140 Alan Green

141 Karl Weschke

142 Peter Joseph

143 Colin Cina

144 John Lessore

145 Albert Irvin

146 Victor Newsome

147 Alan Reynolds

148 Derek Hirst

149 Knighton Hosking

150 Stephen Buckley

151 Basil Beattie

152 John McLean

153 Michael Moon

154 Maggi Hambling

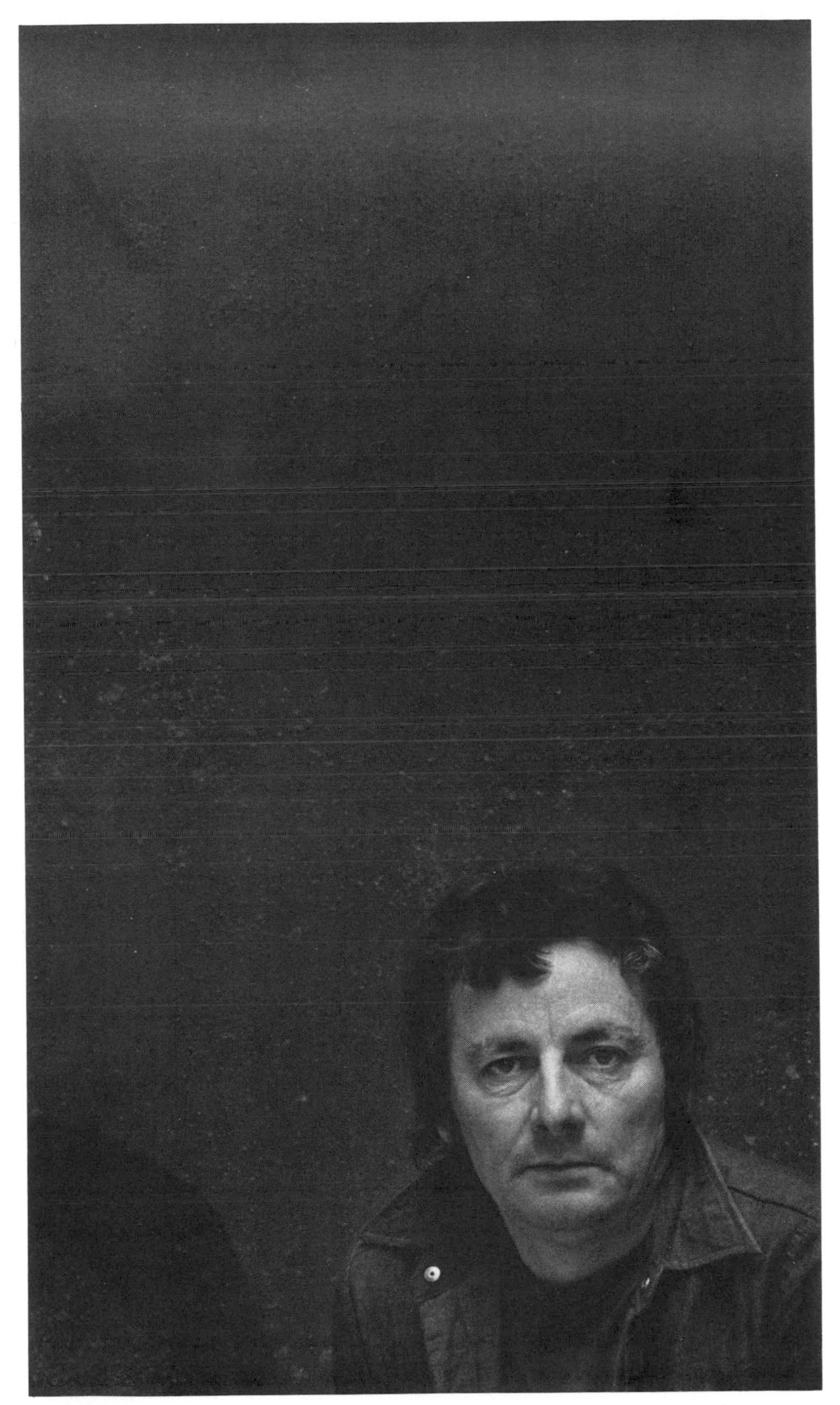

155 Anthony Whishaw

156 John Loker

157 Jennifer Durrant

158 John Edwards

159 Brian Fielding

160 William Crozier

161 John Bellany

162 Norman Stevens

163 Barry Martin

164 Ian Stephenson ARA

165 Ivor Abrahams

166 Tim Head

167 Barry Flanagan

168 Carl Plackman

169 Keith Milow

170 Terry Pope

171 Shelagh Wakely

172 Liliane Lijn

173 Peter Sedgley

174 Ian Breakwell

175 Michael Craig-Martin

176 John Hilliard

177 David Dye

178 Gilbert and George

179 Boyd and Evans

180 Cameron and Miller

181 Stuart Brisley

182 Bruce Lacey

183 Marc Camille Chaimowicz

184 Victor Burgin

185 John Stezaker

186 Conrad Atkinson

187 John Latham

188 Stephen Willats

189 Keith Arnatt

190 Susan Hiller

191 Mary Kelly

192 Brendan Neiland

193 David Hepher

194 Derek Boshier

195 Edwina Leapman

196 Bill Jacklin

197 Robert Mason

198 Garth Lewis

199 Gary Wragg

200 David Leverett

201 Michael Leonard

Ivor Abrahams

Norman Adams

Michael Andrews

paintings

drawings

Kenneth Armitage

paintings

sculpture and drawings

Keith Arnatt

Raymond Arnatt

Conrad Atkinson

Frank Auerbach

Gillian Ayres

Francis Bacon

Phyllida Barlow

Basil Beattie

John Bellany

Adrian Berg

Elizabeth Blackadder

Peter Blake

Norman Blamey

occasionally

Sandra Blow

Derek Boshier

Boyd and Evans

John Bratby

Ian Breakwell

Robert Buhler

paintings

drawings

Victor Burgin

Reg Butler

Butler '79.

Cameron and Miller

Shirley Cameron

Jeffery Camp

CAMP

Marc Camille Chaimowicz

Colin Cina

Gillian Wise Ciobotaru

Wise · Ciobotaru

Robert Clatworthy

Bernard Cohen

Peter Coker

Peter Coker P.C.

William Coldstream

W. COLDSTREAM. occasionally

Cecil Collins

Cecil Collins

Jean Cooke

JEAN COOKE

JEAN E COOKE

John Copnall

john copnall —

Michael Craig-Martin

Michael Craig-Martin

Dennis Creffield

William Crozier

William CROZIER

Alan Davie

alan Davie

Rita Donagh

Rita Donagh

Ken Draper

Bernard Dunstan

BD

Jennifer Durrant

J.A. Durrant.

JENNIFER DURRANT

Jennifer Durrant

David Dye

John Edwards

Richard Eurich

Garth Evans

Anthony Eyton

Sheila Fell

Brian Fielding

Ian Hamilton Finlay

Barry Flanagan

Noel Forster

Donald Hamilton Fraser

Elisabeth Frink

Terry Frost

Patrick George

Gilbert and George

Katherine Gili

John Golding

Frederick Gore

Lawrence Gowing

Derrick Greaves

Alan Green

drawings

paintings

Roger de Grey

Anthony Gross

etchings and engravings

Nigel Hall

Maggi Hambling

paintings drawings

Richard Hamilton

Adrian Heath

David Hepher

Josef Herman

Patrick Heron

Anthony Hill

Susan Hiller

John Hilliard

Tristram Hillier

Derek Hirst

Howard Hodgkin

Knighton Hosking

John Hoyland

Malcolm Hughes

Patrick Hughes

Paul Huxley

David Inshaw

Albert Irvin

Gwyther Irwin

Bill Jacklin

Tess Jaray

Allen Jones

Peter Joseph

Michael Kenny

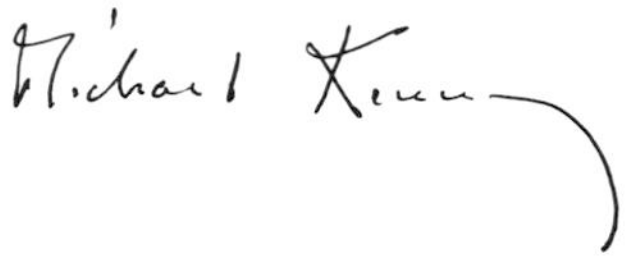

Michael Kidner

Peter Kinley

R B Kitaj

Bryan Kneale

Leon Kossoff

John Latham

Bob Law

Edwina Leapman

Michael Leonard

LEONARD.'79. paintings

ML 79 drawings

John Lessore

occasionally

Ben Levene

pre 1975

post 1975

David Leverett

Garth Lewis

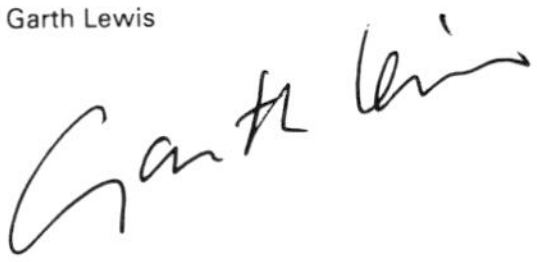

Liliane Lijn

Kim Lim

Richard Lin

John Loker

Peter Lowe

Lucy MacKenzie

Barry Martin

Kenneth Martin

Robert Mason

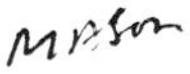

David McFall

John McLean

Bernard Meadows

Keith Milow

Nicholas Monro

Michael Moon

Henry Moore

Rodrigo Moynihan

Henry Mundy

Martin Naylor

Paul Neagu

Brendan Neiland

prints and drawings

Victor Newsome

Bryan Organ

Graham Ovenden

Eduardo Paolozzi

Victor Pasmore

Peter Phillips

Roland Piché

John Piper

Roland Vivian Pitchforth

Carl Plackman

John Plumb

Nicholas Pope

Terry Pope

Douglas Portway

Mary Potter

Patrick Procktor

William Pye

Alan Reynolds

Bridget Riley

Leonard Rosoman

Michael Sandle

William Scott

Peter Sedgley

Jack Smith

Willi Soukop

Jean Spencer

Ian Stephenson

Norman Stevens

Graham Sutherland

Philip Sutton

Patrick Symons

Wendy Taylor

Harry Thubron

Joe Tilson

David Tindle

Euan Uglow

Marc Vaux

Shelagh Wakely

John Ward

Carel Weight

Karl Weschke

Anthony Whishaw

Stephen Willats

Edward Wolfe

Gary Wragg

John Wragg

Ivor Abrahams 165

1935 Born in Wigan, Lancashire
1952-3 Studied sculpture at St Martin's School of Art
1954-5 Apprenticed to Fiorini Bronze Foundry
1954-7 Studied at Camberwell School of Art with Karl Vogel
1956-60 Worked as display artist
1960-70 Visiting Lecturer in Sculpture at Birmingham College of Art, Coventry College of Art, Hull College of Art and Goldsmiths College
1962 First one-man exhibition at Gallery One
1970 One-man exhibition at Richard Feigen Gallery, New York
Exhibited in Sao Paulo Bienal
1972 One-man exhibition at Felicity Samuel Gallery
1973 One-man exhibition at Kunstverein, Cologne
Exhibited in 'L'art anglais aujourd'hui' at Musée d'Art Moderne, Paris
1974 One-man exhibition at Van Loepper Gallery, Hamburg
1975 One-man exhibitions at Gallery Bonnier, Geneva, Galleria del Cavallino, Venice
1976 One-man exhibition at the Mayor Gallery (also 1978)
Exhibited in 'Arte inglese oggi' at Palazzo Reale, Milan
1977 One-man exhibition at Gallery Malgram, Gothenburg

Dealer Mayor Gallery

Ivor Abrahams *Tree Group* 1976 Cast latex, enamel and flock fibre 83x77x24cm (32x28x9in) Mayor Gallery

It was in the later 60s that Abrahams began to use the imagery he has made particularly his own. From the rhetoric of public sculpture he moved to that of its garden setting – the niches and alcoves, trim hedges, the alternate bands of light and dark in well-mowed lawns, the small pools and rock gardens, low walls and crazy-pavings. He is as Pope once wrote of himself 'stark mad with gardens'. But you quickly see that it is not that perceptual and sensuous passion you find in Monet for example. Nor is it the wilful exploration of natural forms for psychological ends found in much English art – for example in Sutherland and the so-called Neo-Romantics. Abrahams' work has, at its core, that manipulation of a given and accessible imagery which relates it to much recent art. We can therefore deny ourselves the pleasure of categorizing him as 'a strangely eccentric figure' and come to a more complex and satisfying estimate. His work no more concerns itself with gardens than it does with the variety of his treatment and presentation. But it does owe much to that confrontation between nature and artifice, the functional and the decorative which are central to the making of gardens – a dominant English art form.

Richard Shone 1979

Ivor Abrahams *Untitled* 1959 Bronze 44x14x85cm (17x5x33in) Mayor Gallery

Norman Adams RA 63

Norman Adams *Light, Rocks, Sea and Birds* 1974-5 Oil 192x210cm (6ft 4inx6ft 7in) Artist's Collection

1927 Born in London
1940-6 Studied at Harrow School of Art
1948-51 Studied at Royal College of Art
1951 First exhibited in 'Young Contemporaries'
1952 First one-man exhibition at Gimpel Fils Gallery (also 1953)
Designed sets and costumes for Royal Ballet production of *A Mirror of Witches* at Covent Garden
1953 Designed sets and costumes for Sadlers Wells production of *Saudades*
1954 Mural commission for Broad Lane Comprehensive School, Coventry
1955 First one-man exhibition at Roland, Browse & Delbanco Gallery (since then exhibiting there every 2-3 years)
Moved to live in Yorkshire
1959 One-man exhibition at Cartwright Hall, Bradford (also 1963)
1962-70 Head of Painting School at Manchester College of Art
1966-7 Influential visits to Italy
1967 Elected Associate of Royal Academy, exhibiting there regularly from this date
1969 Retrospective exhibition at Royal College of Art
Received Abbey Major Award for the study of mural painting
1972 Elected Royal Academician
1974 One-man exhibition at Wakefield City Art Gallery
1975-6 Commission for ceramic relief Stations of the Cross for Milton Keynes Roman Catholic church
1978- Private commission in Cumbria for large painting, and ceiling and wall mural in ceramic relief

Dealer Browse & Darby

Norman Adams *A Blueprint for the Creation* 1963 Oil 182x243cm (6x8ft) Peter Neubert Collection, Lancashire

My painting has always been about my religious beliefs – or lack of them. I don't think I am a Christian and at times even a broad religious belief has been hard work to sustain. I dislike precious aesthetic art, yet I know I am drawn to a high religion more for aesthetic reasons than for any great love of Man. My work is about these inherent contradictions in my feelings and beliefs. Fastening my blinkers on, I press forward hard, only to find in the end that I am looking back longingly the way I came. It has always been a great struggle but I wouldn't understand anything without the agony.

It seems necessary for me to live in quiet, fairly lonely places in order to work – living in Yorkshire suits me well, and the landscape has at times inspired me very much. However, art inspires me as much as nature, and as I get older I love more the work of the old masters. Music and literature also help me with ideas – my paintings are meeting places for many ideas.

I work mostly in oil paint, drawing, but particularly water colour. Recently I have been working in ceramics making reliefs of the Stations of the Cross for a church, and working on what amounts to a ceramic room, the walls and ceiling completely lined with ceramic relief. Its subject is a continuing Genesis and in it I am trying to express all I feel about creation, part-pagan, part-Christian – it is an 'everything' work.

Norman Adams 1979

Craigie Aitchison ARA 68

1926 Born in Scotland
1952-4 Studied at Slade School of Fine Art
1954 Exhibited in 'Six Young Contemporaries' at Gimpel Fils Gallery
1955 Received British Council and Italian Government Scholarship for Painting
1958 Exhibited in 'New Painting' at Arts Council Gallery (also 1959/60/61)
1959 First one-man exhibition at Beaux Arts Gallery (also 1960/64)
1962 Exhibited with London Group (also 1964/67)
1964 Exhibited in Calouste Gulbenkian International Exhibition
1967 Exhibited in 'Il tempo dell'immagine' at Bologna Biennale
1968 One-man exhibition at Marlborough Fine Art
1969 Exhibited in 'Modern British Painters' in Tokyo
1970 One-man exhibition at Compass Gallery, Glasgow
Received Edwin Austin Abbey Premier Scholarship for Painting
1971 One-man exhibition at Basil Jacobs Gallery
1974 Exhibited in John Moores Exhibition, Liverpool (awarded 3rd Prize), 'British Painting '74' at Hayward Gallery
Received Lorne Scholarship
1975 One-man exhibitions at Rutland Gallery,
Scottish Arts Council Gallery, Edinburgh
Exhibited in 23rd Salon Actualité de l'Esprit, Paris
1976 Received Arts Council Bursary
1977 One-man exhibition at Knoedler & Co
1978 Elected Associate of Royal Academy
1979 One-man exhibition at Kettle's Yard, Cambridge

Dealer Rutland Gallery

Craigie Aitchison *Model and Dog* 1974-5 Oil 213x182cm (7ft 1inx6ft 2in) David Wilkie Collection

In England one of the most notable exceptions to the general conformity is the work of Craigie Aitchison.

Aitchison is a natural. Even with good painters one can usually imagine that they have chosen to paint, but with him it is different. He may not be the greatest technician the world has ever seen, but the ease of expression is made immediately apparent by the pronounced personality of the style, the pleasure in colour, the interest in subject and variety of mood from light-hearted jokiness to profound sadness. Breadth coupled with originality is a rare combination, and it is difficult to imagine even the most world-weary spectator entirely evading the encompassing emotional net of an Aitchison exhibition.

John McEwen 1979

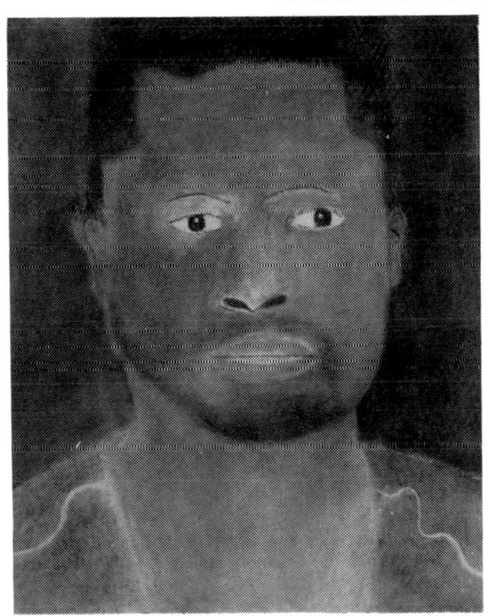

Craigie Aitchison *Georgeous Macaulay* 1972 Oil 25x30cm (10inx12in) Rory McEwen Collection

Michael Andrews 136

1928 Born in Norwich
1949-53 Studied at Slade School of Fine Art
1952 Exhibited in 'Four Young Artists' at Beaux Arts Gallery,
'Young Painters' at Institute of Contemporary Arts
1953 Received Rome scholarship in painting and Abbey scholarship
1954 Acted with Eduardo Paolozzi in Lorenza Mazzetti's film 'Together'
1955 Exhibited in '8 Painters' at Institute of Contemporary Arts
1956 Exhibited in '6 Young Painters' Arts Council exhibition

▶

1958 First one-man exhibition at Beaux Arts Gallery (also 1963)
Painted and decorated the Colony Room Club
1959 Taught at Norwich School of Art
1960 Taught at Chelsea School of Art
1960/1 Exhibited in 'Modern British Portraits' Arts Council exhibition
1961 Received Gulbenkian Purchase Award
1963 Exhibited in 'British Painting in the 60s' at Whitechapel Art Gallery
Taught at Slade School of Fine Art
1964 Exhibited in 'Painting and Sculpture of a Decade 1954-64' at Tate Gallery
1967 Exhibited in 'English Paintings 1951-67' at Norwich Castle Museum
1968 Exhibited in 'Helen Lessore and the Beaux Arts Gallery' at Marlborough Fine Art
1972 Exhibited in 'Critic's Choice' at Arthur Tooth & Sons
1974 One-man exhibition at Anthony d'Offay Gallery (also 1978)
1977 Exhibited in 'Real Life' Peter Moores Exhibition, Liverpool,
'British Painting 1952-1977' at Royal Academy

Dealer Anthony d'Offay

Michael Andrews *The Garden at Drummond from Higher Ground* 1976
Acrylic and oil on canvas 130x364cm (52x123½in) Private Collection

Left: Michael Andrews *Study of a Head* (for a Group of Figures No 6) 1967
Oil on board 22x15cm (9x6in) Private Collection

Kenneth Armitage 23

Kenneth Armitage *Fleeing Figure* 1977 Plate and cast aluminium and painted 287x187x94cm (9x6x3ft) National Museum of Art, Osaka

1916 Born in Leeds
1934-7 Studied at Leeds College of Art
1937-9 Studied at Slade School of Fine Art
1946-56 Taught at Bath Academy of Art
1952 First one-man exhibition at Gimpel Fils Gallery (also 1957)
1953-5 Gregory Fellowship in Sculpture, University of Leeds
1955 Exhibited in 'The New Decade' at Museum of Modern Art, New York
1958 One-man exhibition at Paul Rosenberg Gallery, New York (also 1962)
Exhibited in Venice Biennale
1959 Retrospective exhibition at Whitechapel Art Gallery
Exhibited in 'New Images of Man' at Museum of Modern Art, New York
1960 Film 'Kenneth Armitage' produced and directed by John Read for BBC
1962 One-man exhibition at Marlborough Fine Art (also 1965)
1963 Exhibited in 7th Tokyo Biennale
1964 Guest artist in Caracas, Venezuela, and expedition into equatorial rain forest
Exhibited in 'British Sculpture in the 60s' at Tate Gallery
1967 Exhibited in Guggenheim International Exhibition at Guggenheim Museum, New York
1967-9 Guest artist of City of Berlin Kunstlerprogram
1969 Television film 'Armitage in Berlin' made by Westdeutscher Rundfunk
1972-3 One-man Arts Council exhibition travelling to 10 English cities
1974 One-man exhibition at Hester van Royen Gallery
1975 One-man exhibition at New Art Centre
1977 Exhibited in Silver Jubilee Contemporary British Sculpture Exhibition in Battersea Park
1978 One-man travelling exhibition in Japan

Contact 22a Avonmore Road, London W14

Of statements made, I quote only from one used in an exhibition catalogue last year – notes relating to the subject matter of the exhibition, namely trees.

I had visited Richmond Park frequently throughout my life but it was not until five years' ago that I really noticed the oaks and an obsession began that still continues. Ever since, I've been in the park weekly, sometimes daily, making drawings and etchings, taking photographs – or just looking.

Kenneth Armitage *Richmond Oaks* 1977-8 Bronze 28x51cm high (11x20in)
Rickey Collection and Guirey Collection

At the time of the Jubilee Battersea Park Sculpture Exhibition in 1977 I had toyed with the idea of making a tree – showing in the park a tree that was not a real tree in relation to those that were. But having promised to contribute a piece I felt that making a tree for the first time, and large enough in scale, was too uncertain, and so instead made a piece (*Fleeing Figure*) more in keeping with my other work. But I did make some small trial trees of 11-20 inches high, in bronze, that being my normal medium. I'm now going to make a tree large enough to take its place out-of-doors.

About the Richmond Oaks I wrote: 'Out of so many trees (in the park) some became special favourites, but all are eloquent, their trunks and branches usually lopped (pollarded) adding even greater character. Partly natural, and partly due to pollarding, the strange peculiarities are well known – branches of massive girth growing out horizontally and even in places turning down in spite of normal growth direction – or branches of considerable length showing no appreciable tapering – or the jerky right-angle twists and turns as though convulsed by electric shock – and deeply fissured bark textures accentuating, like intermittent traffic markings on a highway, every bend.'

Kenneth Armitage 1979

Keith Arnatt 189

1930 Born in Oxford
1951-5 Studied at Oxford School of Art
1956-8 Studied at Royal Academy Schools
1961-4 Taught at Liverpool College of Art
1964-9 Taught at Manchester College of Art
1969 Exhibited in 'Environmental-Reversal' at Camden Arts Centre, '557,087' at Seattle Art Museum
1969- Teaching at Newport College of Art
1970 One-man exhibition '1220400 – 0000000' at Art and Project, Amsterdam
Exhibited in 'Information' at Museum of Modern Art, New York, 'Idea Structures' at Camden Arts Centre, '955,000' at Vancouver Art Gallery
1971 Exhibited in 'The British Avant-Garde' at New York Cultural Centre, 'Wall Show' at Lisson Gallery
1972 Exhibited in 'Seven Exhibitions' at Tate Gallery, London, 'The New Art' at Hayward Gallery
1973 Exhibited in Arts Council touring exhibition 'Beyond Painting and Sculpture'
1976 Exhibited in 'Arte inglese oggi' at Palazzo Reale, Milan
1977 One-man exhibition 'Looking at Me' at Whitechapel Art Gallery
Exhibited in 'British Artists of the 60s' at Tate Gallery
1979 Contributed to 'Museum of Drawers' at Institute of Contemporary Arts

Dealer Anthony D'Offay

I regard my work of the late 60s and early 70s as a commentary upon the condition of 'advanced' art of that time. Contemporary critical jargon furnished much material with which I could, partly through parody and the use of irony, reflect my ambivalent feelings towards the more extreme manifestations of recent art behaviour. In fact, it was the logic of the development of art behaviour which particularly interested me. An example of my own work, for instance, my *Self-Burial* set of photographs, might illustrate an issue relevant to the above remarks. The continual references to the disappearance of the art object suggested to me the eventual disappearance of the artist himself. The photographic sequence may be seen as a metaphor for this imagined impending condition. My work then was an oblique way of examining my own position as an artist, as well as that of others.

Having used the photograph a great deal to record my own ephemeral products and actions I became increasingly interested in the nature of the photographic act itself. My most recent work, influenced greatly by the snapshot, reflects this concern though I hope its documentary value might transcend the mere 'photography about photography' syndrome.

Keith Arnatt 1979

Keith Arnatt *Self Burial* 1969 Set of 9 photographs 152·4x152·4cm (5x5ft) Tate Gallery

Raymond Arnatt 128

1934 Born in Oxfordshire
1951-5 Studied at Oxford School of Art
1957-61 Studied at Royal College of Art
1961 Received Sainsbury Award
1962-70 Part-time teaching at various art schools
1963 Exhibited in group show at Piccadilly Gallery
1964 Exhibited in group show at Royal College of Art
1965 Exhibited in group show at Bear Lane Gallery, Oxford

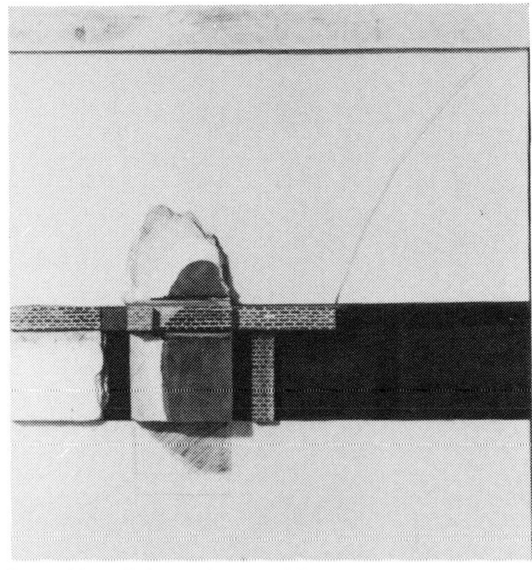

Raymond Arnatt *Perfection of the View* 1970 Mixed media 91·4x91·4cm (36x36in) Artist's Collection

1966 Bronze sculpture commissions for Stepney (LCC), Pontefract and Garforth Churches, and Queen's College, Edgbaston
1967 Exhibited in Arts Council travelling exhibition
1968 Bronze and aluminium sculpture commissions for Leeds Church and Harrogate housing complex
1969 Received prize in Sir Joseph Swan Memorial Sculpture Competition
1971 BBC TV profile 'Volumes and Voids'
1971- Senior Lecturer in Sculpture at Chelsea School of Art
1974 One-man exhibition at Park Square Gallery, Leeds
Received Herbert Baker Travelling Award, Royal Academy of Art
1975 Bronze sculpture commission for Milton Keynes
Exhibited in National Art Exhibition, Chichester
1977 Exhibited in group show at Serpentine Gallery

Contact Brook Cottage, Grazeley Green, Reading

Between 1962 and 1977 a major part of my work involved the use of bronze casting. In line with my 'Totalist' concept (my concern is to discover priorities in synthesis, throwing both synthesis and analysis into one arena, in a magnificent attempt to make the impossible work), I found that it was necessary to have control over the processes involved, and to that end, I set up my own bronze foundry. The fact that reproduction is a major element in metal casting was ▶

Raymond Arnatt *Articulated Opposites* 1970 Bronze 487·9x366cm (16x12ft 6in) Newcastle-upon-Tyne

important to me, and I found the idea that this element is invariably used solely as a means to produce editions of existing work, not only irrelevant but also destructive. I have incorporated the facility of reproduction in bronze casting into the creative process, and have made large 'unique' bronzes in the way that a painter makes 'unique' paintings. The bronzes never exist in their entirety in any material other than bronze. My sculpture *Articulated Opposites* illustrates this point.

For a short, but prolific, period in the early 70s, I made reliefs, entitled *Perfection of the View*, based on a poem by Trevor Baxter. This was a concerted effort to produce paradoxes. In a review of these works John Jones wrote 'that the adored virginity of the raw material cannot survive his passionate embrace is every artist's dilemma, and Arnatt celebrates this paradox of ends consuming means. His works savour the moment when medium and "idea" conjoin, and illusion bares its working parts'. I think that these observations express very well what these pieces are about. During the last two years I have been working predominantly in a relief format again, using gesso as my main material. This period of work has gradually evolved into a 'Cosmic Series' – of which *Polyvalue Remake* is an example.

Raymond Arnatt 1979

Conrad Atkinson 186

1940 Born in Cumbria
1957-61 Studied at Carlisle College of Art
1961-2 Studied at Liverpool College of Art
1962-5 Studied at Royal Academy Schools
1963 Exhibited in 'Young Contemporaries' (also 1964/65)
1965 Received Leverhulme Award and Abbey Minor Scholarship
1967 Two-man exhibition (with Gerald Park) at Manchester City Art Gallery
Received Granada Fellowship, Manchester
1968 Exhibited in Bicentenary Exhibition at Royal Academy
1970 Exhibited in 'Garbage Strike' at Sigi Krauss Gallery
1971 Member of Art/Science Working Party at Kings College
1972 One-man exhibition 'Strike' at Institute of Contemporary Arts
Member of British Society for Social Responsibility on Science National Committee
Received Churchill Fellowship
1973 Exhibited in 'Critic's Choice' at Arthur Tooth & Sons
1974 One-man exhibition 'Work, Wages and Prices' at Institute of Contemporary Arts
Chairman of Artists Union
1974-6 Fellow in Fine Art, Northern Arts Association, Newcastle-upon-Tyne
1975 One-man exhibition 'Northern Ireland' at Belfast Arts Council Gallery
Exhibited in Paris Biennale
1976 One-man exhibition 'Northern Ireland' at Art Net
1976- Lecturer at Slade School of Fine Art
1977 One-man exhibition 'Approaching Reality' at Northern Arts Gallery, Newcastle-upon-Tyne
1978 Exhibited in 'Art for Whom' at Serpentine Gallery,
'Art for Society' at Whitechapel Art Gallery
1979 Exhibited in 'Un certain art anglais' at Musée d'Art Moderne, Paris,
'Lives' at Hayward Gallery

Dealer Ronald Feldman Fine Arts, New York

As a member of staff of the Slade School of Fine Art I was asked along with other members to make a print for presentation to the Queen Mother on the 150th anniversary of the College's foundation. It was also (in April 1978) the 20th anniversary of the introduction of the drug thalidomide in this country by the Distillers Company (Biochemicals). In 1978 a delegation of Labour MPs went to the Royal Family and asked them to withdraw the prestigious and lucrative Royal Warrant from Distillers' products 'but their plea fell on deaf ears'. I decided to document the 20 years of actions by the Distillers Company and link it with the Royal Family's decision not to withdraw the warrant. The Arts Council of Great Britain bought a copy of the print and then refused to exhibit it as planned. They said they feared litigation – even though the print had already been exhibited several times, including once in the very gallery (the Serpentine) from which it was subsequently banned.

Conrad Atkinson 1979
(from *Writings on Art and Politics*)

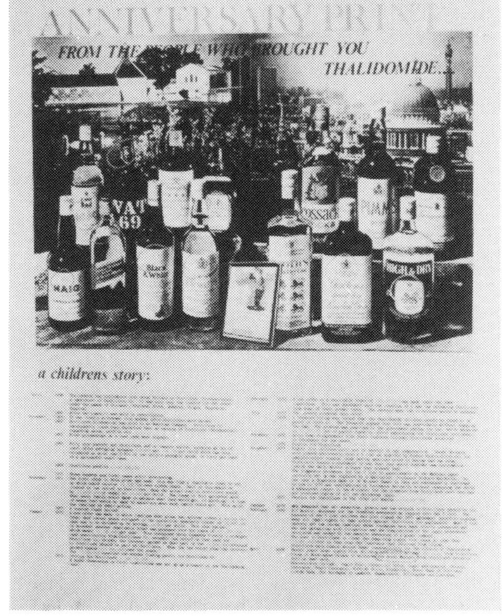

Conrad Atkinson *A Childrens Story for HM* 1978 Silk screen print hand-finished in water-colour 47x63·5cm (18½x25in)

Frank Auerbach 85

Frank Auerbach *Head of E O W VI* 1961 Oil on board 59·7x55·9cm (21½x22in) Scottish National Gallery of Modern Art, Edinburgh

1931 Born in Berlin
1939 Came to live in Britain
1948-52 Studied at St Martin's School of Art
1952-5 Studied at Royal College of Art
1956 First one-man exhibition at Beaux Arts Gallery (also 1959/61/62/63)
1956-68 Taught at art schools including Camberwell School of Art and Slade School of Fine Art

1958 Exhibited in 'Critics Choice' at Arthur Tooth & Sons (also 1963/71), Carnegie International Exhibition, Pittsburgh (also 1961)
1964 Exhibited in Gulbenkian International Exhibition
1965 One-man exhibition at Marlborough Fine Art (also 1967/71/74/75/77)
1969 One-man exhibition at Marlborough Gallery, New York
1971 One-man exhibition at Villiers Gallery, Sydney
1972 One-man exhibition at Toorak Gallery, Melbourne
1973 One-man exhibitions at University of Essex, Galleria Bergamini, Milan
1974 One-man exhibition at Municipal Art Gallery, Dublin
1976 One-man exhibition at Marlborough Gallery, Zurich
1978 Retrospective exhibition at Hayward Gallery, Fruit Market Gallery, Edinburgh

Dealer Marlborough Fine Art

Gillian Ayres 72

1930 Born in London
1946-50 Studied at Camberwell School of Art
1951-9 Worked at AIA Gallery
1956 First one-man exhibition at Gallery One
1957 One man exhibition at Gallery KB, Oslo
Exhibited in 'Tachist and Abstract Art' at Redfern Gallery
1958 One-man exhibition at Redfern Gallery
1959-65 Taught at Bath Academy of Art
1962 One-man exhibition at Molton Gallery (also 1962)
1963 One-man exhibition at Hamilton Galleries
Exhibited in 'British Painting in the 60s' at Whitechapel Art Gallery
Received Japan International Art Promotion Association Award in Tokyo Biennale
1965 One-man exhibition at Kasmin Gallery (also 1966/69)
1966-78 Taught at St Martin's School of Art
1967 Exhibited in 'Recent British Painting' at Tate Gallery (Peter Stuyvesant Foundation Collection)
1967-8 Arts Council Award
1967-9 Exhibited in 'British Paintings: The New Generation' at Museum of Modern Art, New York
1971 Exhibited in 'Large Paintings – Three Painters' at Hayward Gallery

Frank Auerbach *Head of Ken Garland* 1977-8 Black chalk on paper 57x76cm (22½x30in) Private Collection

1973 One-man exhibitions at Hoya Gallery, Oxford Gallery, Oxford
1974 Exhibited in 'British Painting '74' at Tate Gallery
1975 Arts Council Bursary
1976 One-man exhibition at William Darby, Women's Interart Centre, New York
1977 One-man exhibition at Galeria Alvarez, Porto
Exhibited in 'British Paintings in the 60s' at Tate Gallery,
'British Painting 1952-1977' at Royal Academy
1978- Head of Painting at Winchester School of Art

Dealer Knoedler Gallery

The wordless, non-literary, two-dimensional and marvellously silent medium of paint which is a pigment, and colour, which is used to make line, shape, intensity, weight, tone, structure, composition, content and area with chosen materials, are the questionable limits of painting. Through colour can be created a vision of human scale and a sense of experience of space – an art which is finally unrestrained.
Gillian Ayres 1979

Gillian Ayres *Scud* 1959 Oil on hardboard 160x305cm (60x120in) Artist's Collection

Francis Bacon 3

1909 Born in Dublin
1926-7 Lived in Berlin and Paris, designing furniture and rugs
1929 Began painting in oils
1934 First one-man exhibition at Transition Gallery
1937 Exhibited in 'Young British Painters' at Thomas Agnew & Sons
1946-50 Lived mainly in Monte Carlo
1949 One-man exhibition at Hanover Gallery (also 1950/51/52/54/57)
1950 Exhibited in Carnegie International Exhibition, Pittsburgh (also 1958/64/67 prizewinner)
1953 One-man exhibition at Durlacher Brothers, New York
1954 Exhibited in Venice Biennale
1955 First retrospective exhibition at Institute of Contemporary Arts
Exhibited in 'New Decade' at Museum of Modern Art, New York
1957 One-man exhibition at Galerie Rive Droite, Paris
1958 One-man exhibitions in Turin, Milan and Rome
1959 Retrospective exhibition at Richard Feigen Gallery, Chicago
Exhibited in Sao Paulo Bienal, 'Documenta 2' in Kassel
1960 One-man exhibition at Marlborough Fine Art (also 1963/65/67)
1962 Retrospective exhibition at Tate Gallery and travelling in Europe
1963 Retrospective exhibition at Guggenheim Museum, New York and travelling to Chicago
Two-man exhibition (with Graham Sutherland) at La Loggia, Bologna
1964 *Francis Bacon* catalogue raisonné by Sir John Rothenstein and Ronald Alley published (Thames & Hudson) ▶

Gillian Ayres *Rudra* 1977-8 Oil on canvas 228·6x366cm (7ft 6inx12ft) Artist's Collection

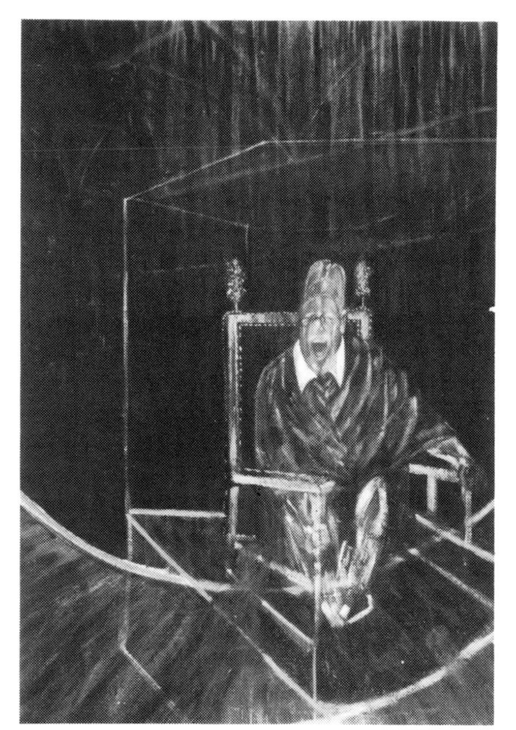

Francis Bacon *Pope II* 1951 Oil on canvas 198x137cm (6ft 4inx4ft 6in) Kunsthalle, Mannheim

Francis Bacon *Self-Portrait* 1978 Oil on canvas 198x147·5 (6ft 4inx4ft 10in) Artist's Collection

1965 Retrospective exhibition at Kunsthalle, Hamburg and travelling to Stockholm and Dublin
1966 One-man exhibition at Galerie Maeght, Paris and travelling to Rome and Milan
BBC television film 'Saturday Night – Francis Bacon' shown
1967 One-man exhibition 'Francis Bacon Rubenspreis' at Oberes Schloss, Siegen (on occasion of award of Rubens prize)
1968 One-man exhibition at Marlborough Gerson Gallery, New York
1971 Retrospective exhibition at Grand Palais, Paris and travelling to Kunsthalle, Dusseldorf
BBC television film 'Review – Francis Bacon' produced by Colin Nears
1973 Exhibited in 'Cuatro Maestros Contemporaneos – Giacometti, Dubuffet, de Kooning, Bacon' at Museo de Bellas Artes, Caracas
1975 Retrospective exhibition at Metropolitan Museum, New York
Interviews with Francis Bacon by David Sylvester published (Thames & Hudson/Pantheon Books, New York)
1976 One-man exhibition at Musée Cantini, Marseilles
1977 One-man exhibition at Galerie Claude Bernard, Paris,
Museo de Arte Moderno, Mexico and travelling to Caracas
1978 One-man exhibition at Fundacion Juan March, Madrid and travelling to Barcelona

Dealer Marlborough Fine Art

I think that great art is deeply ordered even if within the order there may be enormously instinctive and accidental things. Nevertheless, I think that they come out of a desire for ordering and for returning fact onto the nervous system in a more violent way. Why, after the great artists, do people ever try to do anything again? Only because from generation to generation, through what the great artists have done, instinct changes. And as the instinct changes, so there comes a renewal of feeling of how can I re-make this thing once again more clearly, more exactly, more violently.

Francis Bacon 1975
(From *Interviews with Francis Bacon* by David Sylvester)

Phyllida Barlow 123

1944 Born in Newcastle-upon-Tyne
1960-3 Studied at Chelsea School of Art
1963-6 Studied at Slade School of Fine Art
1965 Exhibited in 'Young Contemporaries'
1966 Exhibited with London Group (also 1975)
Exhibited in group print show at AIA Gallery,
Group show at Woodstock Gallery
1966- Teaching at Chelsea School of Art
1971 Exhibited in 'Art Spectrum' at Alexandra Palace,
Group show at Camden Arts Centre
1972 Exhibited in group show at University of Surrey
1973 One-man exhibition at Gulbenkian Gallery, Newcastle-upon-Tyne
Exhibited in group show at Warehouse Gallery
1974 Exhibited in 'British Sculpture – Attitudes to Drawing' at Sunderland Art Centre and travelling
1975 Exhibited in group shows at Camden Arts Centre,
Gallery 21
1976 Two-man exhibition (with Fabian Peake) at St Catherine's College, Oxford
1977 Exhibited in Sculpture Exhibition at Gloucester Festival
1978 Exhibited in '12 Sculptors' at West Surrey Art School

Contact 1 Woodstock Road, London N4

Francis Bacon *Seated Figure* 1961 Oil on canvas 165x142cm (65x56in) Tate Gallery

Phyllida Barlow *Corriolor* 1978 Hardboard 305x305x305cm (10x10x10ft) West Surrey College of Art Gallery

To commit myself in writing to one point of view seems to exclude the debate and argument which surrounds making sculpture. Previous statements I have written are dated, naive and an over-simplification of the facts: they have no relevance to the changeable reactions that occur in my mind.

Writing invites a predictable and corny language whereas talking, which can also be corny and predictable, is ephemeral and accommodates a flexible use of words and a greater scope for argument.

Phyllida Barlow 1979

Basil Beattie 151

1935 Born in West Hartlepool
1950-5 Studied at West Hartlepool College of Art
1957-61 Studied at Royal Academy Schools
1962- Teaching at Goldsmiths College of Art
1965 Exhibited in John Moores Exhibition, Liverpool
1967 Exhibited in 'Survey '67' at Camden Arts Centre
1968 First one-man exhibition at Greenwich Theatre Art Gallery
Exhibited in 'Four British Artists' at Gelsenkirchen,
Bicentenary Exhibition at Royal Academy
1969 Exhibited in 'Big Paintings for Public Places' at Royal Academy (also 1971 at Whitworth Art Gallery, Manchester)
1970 Exhibited in 'Large Paintings' at Hayward Gallery
1971 First one-man exhibition at Mayfair Gallery
Exhibited in 'Four Painters' at Museum of Modern Art, Oxford,
'Art Spectrum' at Alexandra Palace
1973 One-man exhibition at Consort Gallery
1974 One-man exhibition at Hoya Gallery
1976 Major Arts Council Award

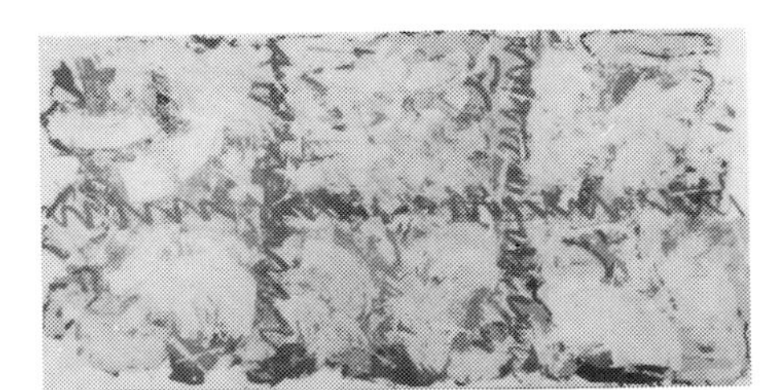

Basil Beattie *Yellow Parcel* 1972 Acrylic on canvas 213x366cm (7x14ft) Artist's Collection

Basil Beattie *Toa* 1978 Acrylic on canvas 213x305cm (7x10ft) Artist's Collection

1977 Exhibited in 'British Painting 1952-1977' at Royal Academy
1978 One-man exhibition at New 57 Gallery, Edinburgh
Exhibited in 'A Free Hand', Arts Council travelling exhibition
1979 One-man exhibition at Polytechnic Gallery, Newcastle-upon-Tyne

Contact 48 Oxford Road South, London W4

Painting, for me, has an exactitude which is directed by feeling. The means are visible but the relationships are felt. Choices are made and structured through specific interactions. We see the cause but it is the 'felt' effect towards which I obliquely strive.

Basil Beattie 1979

John Bellany 161

1942 Born in Port Seton, Scotland
1960-5 Studied at Edinburgh College of Art
1964 Exhibited in 'Young Contemporaries' (also 1966/7)
1965 Postgraduate travelling scholarship (Holland and Belgium)
First one-man exhibition at Dromidaris Gallery, Holland
1965-8 Studied at Royal College of Art
Received Burston Award
1966 Exhibited in John Moores Exhibition, Liverpool (also 1973/75)
1968 One-man exhibition at Edinburgh College of Art
Exhibited with London Group (also 1970/75/76)
1968-78 Taught at Royal College of Art
1969 Exhibited in '20 x 57' at Edinburgh Festival (also 1970/71/72)
1970 One-man exhibition at Drian Gallery (also 1971/73/74)
1971 One-man exhibition at New 57 Gallery, Edinburgh
Exhibited in 'Scottish Realism', Arts Council travelling exhibition
1972 One-man exhibition at Royal College of Art Gallery
1973 One-man exhibition at Edinburgh City Art Centre
1974 Exhibited in 'A Choice Selection' at Scottish Arts Council Gallery, Edinburgh,
'British Painting' at Hayward Gallery
1975 One-man exhibition at Aberdeen City Art Gallery
Exhibited in 'Four Scottish Realists' at Arts Council Gallery, Edinburgh
1977 Exhibited in 'British Painting 1952-1977' at Royal Academy
1978 One-man exhibitions at Acme Gallery, Third Eye Centre, Glasgow, Scottish Arts Council Gallery
1978- Lecturer in Painting at Goldsmiths College
1979 One-man exhibition at Acme Gallery
Exhibited in 'Fourteen Scottish Artists' at Amos Anderson Gallery, Helsinki

Dealer Acme Gallery

John Bellany *Totentanz* 1976 Oil on canvas 182x172cm (6ftx5ft 8in) Drian Gallery

I love art and I adore painting. But I am shy of writing about my paintings, as I would rather they stand or fall by their own visual presence. There are however two quotes from a poem by Hugh Macdiarmid which have been, for me, a perpetual guiding light:

Tae be yersel' an' tae mak' that worth bein'
Nae harder task tae mortal has been gi'en.

I'll ha'e nae hauf-way hoose
It's the only way I ken
Tae dodge the curst conceit o' bein' richt
That damns the vast majority o' men.

John Bellany 1979

Adrian Berg 138

1929 Born in London
1949-53 Studied at Caius College, Cambridge and Trinity College, Dublin
1955-61 Studied at St Martin's School of Art, Chelsea School of Art and Royal College of Art
1957 Exhibited in 'Young Contemporaries' (also 1960)
1961 Received Abbey Minor and French Government Scholarships
1961-78 Taught at various art schools
1962 Exhibited with St Pancras Artists (also 1963/64)
1963 Exhibited with London Group
1964 First one-man exhibition at Arthur Tooth & Sons (also 1967/69/72/75)
1965 Exhibited in 'Pop and Op' in Geneva
1968 Exhibited in '25 Camden Artists' at Swiss Cottage Library
1969 Exhibited in John Moores Exhibition, Liverpool (also 1974)
1970 Exhibited in Summer Exhibition at Royal Academy (also 1971/72)
1973 One-man exhibition at Galleria Vaccarino, Florence
Exhibited in 'Landscape' at Serpentine Gallery,
Florence Biennale (Gold Medal)
1974 Exhibited in 'British Painting '74' at Hayward Gallery
1976 One-man exhibition at Galerie Burg Diesdonk, Dusseldorf,
Dusseldorf Art Fair
Exhibited in 'The Human Clay' at Hayward Gallery
1977 Exhibition in Tolly Cobbold Eastern Arts National Exhibition (also 1979)
1978 One-man exhibition at Waddington & Tooth Galleries
1979 One-man exhibition at Waddington Galleries, Montreal and Toronto
Exhibited in 'The Camden Scene from the 18th Century to the present day' at Camden Arts Centre

Dealer Waddington Galleries

In 1966, Adrian Berg wrote a statement in which he claimed, 'Specialization, popular with everyone, is impoverishing'. Since that date, he has rarely painted anything other than the landscape as seen from the window of his studio in Gloucester Gate, Regents Park. However, it is only as long as one fails to distinguish between the subject matter of his painting (Regents Park), and its content ('a more truthful account of the external world') that one need assume a contradiction. In a more recent statement, Berg makes a distinction between what he calls 'critical' and 'creative' attitudes to painting, comparing them, respectively, with 'being outside looking in', and with 'being inside looking out'. Explaining his preference for the latter position, he writes: 'Here one's senses alone convey to one the significance of what one sees. This is reality, or the only reality one knows. There is a way out, however. The senses can be shamed into conveying a more truthful account of the external world. Shown a picture of that world (their product, arrived at by the skills they have developed) the senses are made to compare this artifact with nature, that is with what they now make of that same world. A process which has to be repeated: comparing, correcting. It had better be if one is to continue to paint.'

Peter Fuller 1975

Adrian Berg *Gloucester Gate, Regent's Park: February, March, April, May and June* 1977 Oil on canvas 172·7x172·7cm (70x70in) Private Collection

Elizabeth Blackadder RA 44

1931 Born in Falkirk, Stirlingshire
1949-55 Studied at Edinburgh College of Art and Edinburgh University
1957- Teaching at Edinburgh College of Art
1959 First one-man exhibition at 57 Gallery, Edinburgh
1960 Lithograph commission for Museum of Modern Art, New York
1961 One-man exhibition at Scottish Gallery, Edinburgh (also 1966/72/74)
1965 Elected member of Royal Scottish Society of Painters in Watercolours
One-man exhibition at Mercury Gallery (also 1967/69/71/73/76/78)
1967 One-man exhibition at Art Gallery, Reading
1968 One-man exhibition at Lane Gallery, Bradford
1970 One-man exhibition at Vaccarino Gallery, Florence
1971 One-man exhibition at Loomshop Gallery, Lower Largo (also 1974/76)
1972 Elected member of Royal Scottish Academy
1975 Exhibited in '10 Edinburgh Artists' Scottish Arts Council travelling exhibition
1976 Elected Royal Academician
1976- Member of Board of Trustees for National Galleries of Scotland
1977 One-man exhibition at Middlesbrough Art Gallery
Exhibited in 'British Painting 1952-1977' at Royal Academy
1978 One-man exhibition at Yehudi Menuhin School, Sussex

Dealer Mercury Gallery

I work in oil and watercolour with no particular preference – although much of my work in the last few years has been in watercolour. I like to paint either on a big scale, as large as the sheets of paper permit, or on a very small scale and in small sketchbooks. I like using different surfaces of paper, handmade Japanese papers for example, and I try to incorporate the texture into the painting.

My work is all based on some point of reference although it may move away greatly from the starting off point before it is finished. I

Elizabeth Blackadder *Still-Life with Indian Parrot* 1978 Watercolour 63·1x94cm (25x37in) Artist's Collection

Elizabeth Blackadder *Mirror and Tortoiseshell Box* 1976 Oil on canvas 106x127cm (40x50in) Artist's Collection

am less interested in the actual likeness of things than in setting up relationships between the objects and between them and the background.

The work falls into two main areas, landscape and still-life – occasionally figures. Still-life paintings are based on a very large collection of all kinds of objects – toys, boxes, ribbons, fans, pieces of paper, scraps of cloth, flowers, stones – anything at all that attracts my attention in some way or other, by shape, colour or by some association which to me is significant. I like to work on several paintings at the same time, but work slowly and each painting, watercolours included, may take months to complete. With landscapes I either paint them on the spot or work in the studio from detailed drawings and sketches.

Elizabeth Blackadder 1979

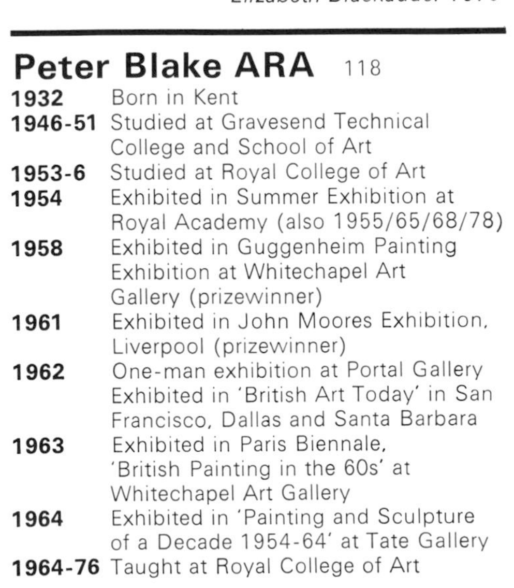

Peter Blake ARA 118

1932 Born in Kent
1946-51 Studied at Gravesend Technical College and School of Art
1953-6 Studied at Royal College of Art
1954 Exhibited in Summer Exhibition at Royal Academy (also 1955/65/68/78)
1958 Exhibited in Guggenheim Painting Exhibition at Whitechapel Art Gallery (prizewinner)
1961 Exhibited in John Moores Exhibition, Liverpool (prizewinner)
1962 One-man exhibition at Portal Gallery
Exhibited in 'British Art Today' in San Francisco, Dallas and Santa Barbara
1963 Exhibited in Paris Biennale, 'British Painting in the 60s' at Whitechapel Art Gallery
1964 Exhibited in 'Painting and Sculpture of a Decade 1954-64' at Tate Gallery
1964-76 Taught at Royal College of Art

Peter Blake *She had got rid of her tight trousers. Her shirt clung to her body* 1969 Drawing from *The Sun on The Water* by Roger Longrigg (Macmillan) 15.2x8.6cm (6x3$\frac{3}{8}$in)

1965 One-man exhibition at Robert Fraser Gallery (also 1969)
Exhibited in 'Pop Art – Nouveau Idealisme' at Palais des Beaux Arts, Brussels
1967 Exhibited in 'Jeunes peintres anglais' at Palais des Beaux Arts, Brussels
'English Drawings' at Museum of Modern Art, New York
1969 One-man exhibition at City Art Gallery, Bristol
Exhibited in 'Pop Art' at Hayward Gallery
1970 One-man exhibition at Waddington Galleries (also 1972)
1973 One-man exhibitions at Stedelijk Museum, Amsterdam, Kunstverein, Hamburg
1974 One-man exhibitions at Gemeente Museum, Arnhem, Palais des Beaux Arts, Brussels
Elected Associate of Royal Academy
1975 First Brotherhood of Ruralists meeting
1976 Exhibited in 'Arte inglese oggi' at Palazzo Reale, Milan
1977 One-man exhibition 'Souvenirs and Samples' at Waddington & Tooth Galleries

Dealer Waddington Galleries

Peter Blake *Ford Cottage, Coombe, Cornwall* 1976 Watercolour 41.9x26cm (16$\frac{1}{2}$x10$\frac{1}{4}$in) Private Collection

CP: There was a central issue about which I thought you might have particularly interesting views. Painting (or 'art') as an activity concerned with the expression and exploration of individual thought, experience and identity stands accused of being a socially unacceptable activity – at best designated as self-therapy. I imagine that you might have strong views on that.

PB: I don't quite know how to put the answer. I think that the accusation is wrong, but I'm not sure who you are suggesting is making it – other artists? the public? I went to art school at 14, and painting pictures is what I do. I have to believe that I am doing something that I think is valid. I am also a professional artist, I don't have any other income, it is the way I make my living. As I have said, I believe in making the kind of art which someone might buy to hang on their wall and enjoy.

Colin Painter and Peter Blake 1978
(*from* Aspects 3)

Norman Blamey RA 38

1914 Born in London
1931-7 Studied at Regent Street Polytechnic School of Art
1938-40 Taught at Regent Street Polytechnic School of Art
1941-5 War service in the Army
1946-63 Taught at Regent Street Polytechnic School of Art
1952 Elected Member of Royal Institute of Oil Painting
1956 Mural commission for St Luke's Church, Leagrave
1958 Exhibited in Royal Academy Summer Exhibition, since then exhibiting every year except 1964
1963- Senior Lecturer at Chelsea School of Art
1964 Mural commission for St Andrew's Church, Ruislip Manor
1970 Elected Associate of Royal Academy
1974 Elected honorary member of Royal Institute of Oil Painting
1975 Elected Royal Academician Commission for official portrait of Mrs Alison Munro, retiring High Mistress of St Paul's Girls' School
1975- Visiting Lecturer at Royal Academy Schools
1976 Exhibited in 'Body and Soul' at Walker Art Gallery, Liverpool
1977 Exhibited in 'British Painting 1952-1977' at Royal Academy
1978 Received Roy Miles Award Commission for official portrait of Dr Harry Pitt FRS, Vice Chancellor, University of Reading

Contact 39 Lyncroft Gardens, London NW6

Norman Blamey *Physiotherapy* 1961 Oil on panel 152x228cm (60x90in) Huntingdon Hartford Collection, New York

Right: Norman Blamey *Dr Harry Pitt FRS, Vice-Chancellor of Reading University* 1978 Oil on panel 121·9x121·9cm (48x48in) University of Reading

Throughout my painting life I have remained fully and exclusively committed to figurative painting, and that of the sort which depends for its initial stimulus upon things seen. My pictures, which are carried out in oil on gesso-primed panels, have the human figure as their principal theme, sometimes occurring singly, although more often in groups and usually in interiors. They have been of such a nature that I have rarely been able to paint direct from the subject, but have had to rely upon studied drawings made for the purpose of gathering information which has subsequently been assembled in pictorial form in the painting.

The interpretation of this information has varied as my interest and intentions have changed; there was a period, for instance, in the late 50s and 60s when I used a formal distortion, elongating figures, stressing verticals and seeking to bring horizontal surfaces as far as possible up to the picture surface so that the distinction between actual horizontal and vertical planes was dependent upon clues other than the normal perspectival ones. Later I abandoned this and reverted to the use of a more traditional perspective, but in this respect I have always been interested in the various choices open to the figurative painter, and the different kinds of projection he can achieve by varying the angle of his picture plane or by choosing some other sort of surface, such as a curved one, to intersect his visual cone.

The subject matter of my pictures has ranged from the ecclesiastical, concerned with various incidents in the Church's liturgy, to the domestic. In this respect they could be said to be largely autobiographical. I have also occasionally painted official portraits.

Norman Blamey 1979

Sandra Blow RA 61

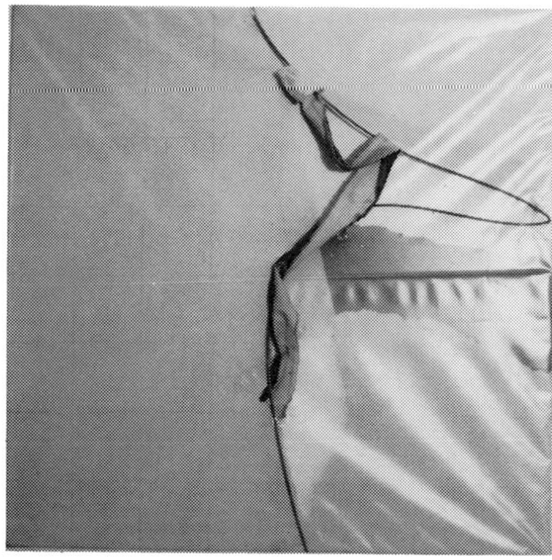

Sandra Blow *Untitled* 1978-9 Paper, polythene, willow cane on canvas 121·9x121·9cm (48x48in) Artist's Collection

1925 Born in London
1942-6 Studied at St Martin's School of Art
1947-8 Studied at Academy of Fine Arts, Rome
1951-60 Regular one-man exhibitions at Gimpel Fils Gallery
1957 One-man exhibition at Saidenberg Gallery, New York Exhibited in 'Young British Painters' at Arts Club, Chicago (toured USA for two years)
1958 Exhibited in 'Young British Painters' in Rotterdam, Zurich and Dusseldorf, International Guggenheim Award Exhibition, Venice Biennale
1959-60 Exhibited in 'Vitalità nel Arte' in Venice and travelling
1961 Exhibited in John Moores Exhibition, Liverpool (second prize; also 1965), Carnegie International Exhibition, Pittsburgh
1961- Teaching at Royal College of Art
1962 Exhibited in 'Painting in the 60s' at Tate Gallery
1964 Exhibited in 'Contemporary British Painting' at Albright-Knox Art Gallery, Buffalo, 'Young British Painters' at North Carolina Museum of Art, Raleigh
1965 Arts Council Purchase Award
1966 One-man exhibition at New Art Centre (also 1968/71/73)
1967 Exhibited in 'Aspects of New British Art', British Council travelling exhibition in Australia and New Zealand, 'Recent British Painting' at Tate Gallery (Peter Stuyvesant Foundation Collection)

1969 Exhibited in 'English Landscape in the 20th Century' at Camden Arts Centre
1971 Elected Associate of Royal Academy
1974 Exhibited in 'British Painting '74' at Hayward Gallery
1977 Exhibited in 'British Painting 1952-1977' at Royal Academy
1978 Elected Royal Academician
1979 Two-man exhibition with Peter Coker at Royal Academy

Dealer New Art Centre

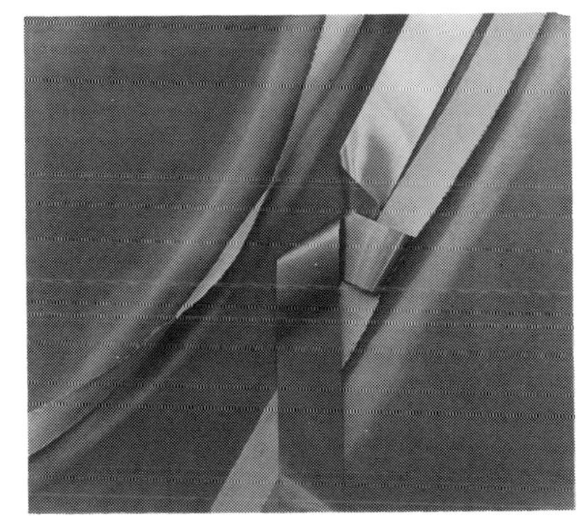

Sandra Blow *Canvas and Aluminium Relief* 1973 Canvas and acrylic 121.9x137.2cm (48x54in) Private Collection

Sandra Blow describes herself as an 'academic abstract painter' because she concerns herself primarily with the self-contained problems of 'pure' painting such as balance and proportion, tension and scale – 'issues that have been important since art began.' Although many critics doubt the continuing validity of abstract art, she is optimistic about its future. 'Something very good will happen in English abstract painting – there is such vigorous student work being done, especially by women: so far they are largely an untapped source who will make a powerful and fresh contribution.' But she misses 'that sense of being at the frontiers' felt back in the 50s suspecting that 'in a way abstract painting has been and gone' and that interesting new developments are likely to be located in other media. 'I have a sense of a changed situation. It's like moving house – I've enjoyed abstract painting but it is possibly time to move on.'

Sarah Kent 1978

At present I am using a new medium, PVC, which has exciting possibilities.

Sandra Blow 1979

Derek Boshier 194

1937 Born in Portsmouth
1953-62 Studied at Yeovil School of Art and Royal College of Art
1959 Exhibited in 'Young Contemporaries' (also 1960/61 prizewinner/1962)
1961 Exhibited in John Moores Exhibition, Liverpool
1962 First individual exhibition at Grabowski Gallery
1962-3 Received Indian Government Scholarship for travel in India
1963 Exhibited in Paris Biennale
1963- Teaching at Central School of Art and Design and Royal College of Art
1964 Exhibited in 'The New Generation' at Whitechapel Art Gallery
Received Peter Stuyvesant Foundation Travel Bursary to USA
1965 Individual exhibition at Robert Fraser Gallery (also 1968)
1967 Exhibited in 'New Shapes of Colour' at Stedelijk Museum, Amsterdam
1968 Exhibited in '6 Artists' at Victoria and Albert Museum and travelling
1970 Individual exhibition at Nigel Greenwood Inc
Exhibited in Tokyo Print Biennale (prizewinner)
Received Arts Council Grant to make film 'Link'
1971 Individual exhibition at Hayward Gallery
Exhibited in 'Multiples' at Philadelphia Museum of Art
Member of BFI Production Board's Advisory Committee
1973 Individual exhibition at Whitechapel Art Gallery
Exhibited in 'Henry Moore to Gilbert & George' at Palais des Beaux Arts, Brussels
1974 Individual exhibition at Angela Flowers Gallery (also 1976)
1975 Artist in Residence at University of Victoria, Vancouver Island
1979 Organized 'Lives' exhibition at Hayward Gallery and travelling
1979- Preparing papers on 'Directions in Art Education' for NUTFE Conference

Contact 25 Ladbroke Gardens, London W11

I passed through the art school system between 1953 and 1962, during which time I studied painting. I continued to paint and exhibit until 1966. I then began making sculpture and subsequently films, photography, design, drawing, prints, books and writing. I have recently begun oil-painting again.

Derek Boshier 1979

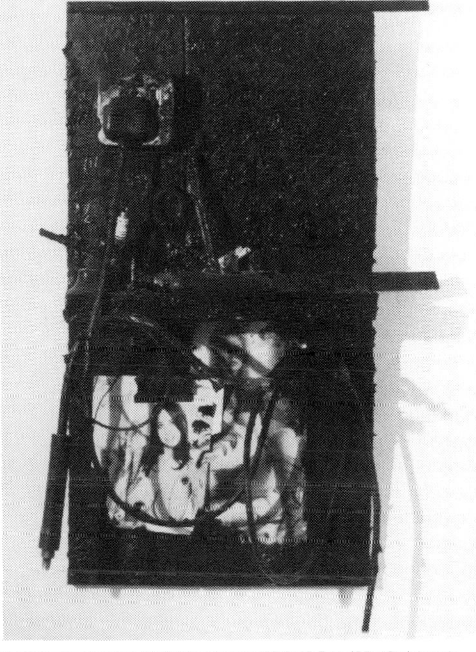

Derek Boshier *Garage* 1976 Mixed media 68.6x45.7cm (27x18in) Angela Flowers Collection

Boyd and Evans 179

1944 Fionnuala Boyd born in Welwyn Garden City
1945 Leslie Evans born in St Albans
1963-7 Fionnuala Boyd studied at Leeds University
1967-8 Leslie Evans studied at Leeds College of Art

Boyd and Evans *Point of View* 1972 Acrylic on canvas 76.2x91.4cm (30x36in) Private Collection

1968 Started working together
1971 First one-man exhibition at Angela Flowers Gallery (also 1972/74/77/79)
1971- Teaching at Wolverhampton Polytechnic
1972 One-man exhibition at Park Square Gallery, Leeds
Exhibited in Bradford Biennale (prizewinners; also 1974)
1973 Exhibited in 'Immagini come strumenta di realita' at Studio La Città, Verona
1974 Exhibited in John Moores Exhibition, Liverpool,
Tokyo Biennale
1975 Exhibited in Delhi Triennale, 'Body and Soul' Peter Moores Exhibition, Liverpool
1976 One-man exhibitions in Leigh, Sheffield, Glasgow, Wolverhampton and Sudbury
Exhibited in 'British Realist Show' at Ikon Gallery, Birmingham
'Aspects of Realism' organized by Rothmans in Canada
1977-8 Travelling in USA as Bicentennial Fellows
1978 One-man exhibition at Fendrick Gallery, Washington DC
Exhibited in 'Certain Traditions – Recent British and Canadian Art' travelling exhibition in Canada
1979 One-man exhibitions in Sheffield, Leicester and Wolverhampton

Dealer Angela Flowers Gallery

Boyd and Evans *Movement at a Station* 1977 Acrylic on canvas 182·9x91·4cm (6x3ft) Angela Flowers Gallery

In 1968 we first tried working together as an experiment to get ourselves working again after a year of inactivity. We soon started using photographs and sprayed paint to develop a technique in which our separate handwriting was not evident and to point the viewer's attention away from painterly concerns toward the subject matter. We use the camera as a sketch book, gathering events, people and places which could be of use some time or we take pictures expressly for a painting. The paintings are invented from parts of a number of slides which we project onto the canvas. We then make stencils, through which primary coloured acrylic paint is sprayed, the colours being mixed on the surface.

Photography (originally adopted as an expedient way of utilizing one-point perspective as a representational convention) has played an increasingly important part in our work. We are currently exhibiting photographs, and recent paintings include their source material.

We do not talk about the meaning of our work. Despite being representational and allegorical in character, its primary force is visual. Words about it limit the creative contribution of the viewer, not allowing the visual language to speak in its own vocabulary.

Boyd and Evans 1979

Mark Boyle

1934 Born in Glasgow
1955-6 Studied at Glasgow University
1963 First one-man exhibition at Woodstock Gallery
1969 One-man exhibition at Institute of Contemporary Arts (also 1970)
1970 One-man exhibition at Gemeentemuseum, The Hague
1971 One-man exhibition at Paul Maenz Gallery, Cologne (also 1972/74)
1975 One-man exhibition at Serpentine Gallery
1976 Exhibited in 'Arte inglese oggi' at Palazzo Reale, Milan

Dealer Felicity Samuel Gallery

John Bratby RA 46

1928 Born in London
1948-9 Studied at Kingston School of Art
1951-4 Studied at Royal College of Art
1954-9 One-man exhibitions annually at Beaux Arts Gallery
1955 Received Prize in Daily Express Young Artists Competition
1955- Exhibiting regularly in Summer Exhibition at Royal Academy
1956 Taught at Carlisle College of Art
Exhibited in Venice Biennale
Received Guggenheim Award for Great Britain (also 1958)
1956-9 One-man exhibitions annually at Zwemmer Gallery
1957 Exhibited in John Moores Exhibition, Liverpool (prizewinner)
1957-8 Taught at Royal College of Art
1958 Commissioned by Knightsbridge Films to produce paintings for use in film 'The Horse's Mouth'
1959 Elected Associate of Royal Academy
1960 Published first novel *Breakdown* (Hutchinson; further novels published 1961/62/63)
1970 One-man exhibition at Furneaux Gallery
1971 Elected Royal Academician
1971-7 One-man exhibitions at Thackeray Gallery
1977 Exhibited in 'British Painting 1952-1977' at Royal Academy
1979 One-man travelling exhibition in North of England

Contact Royal Academy

John Bratby *Dartmouth Row Studio* 1956 Drawing 163·9x315cm (5ft 6½inx11ft 4½in) Tate Gallery

John Bratby *Susan Ballam* 1956 Drawing 132x49.5cm (52x19½in) Tate Gallery

Ian Breakwell *The Walking Man Diary* (detail) 1975-8 Collage, photographs, pencil and typed text Artist's Collection

Ian Breakwell 174

1943 Born in Derby
1961-5 Studied at Derby College of Art
1967 Performance 'Restaurant Operations' at Exeter Festival and Bristol Arts Centre
1967-8 Visual Arts Director at Bristol Arts Centre
1969 Performance 'Unword 1' at Compendium Bookshop and 'Unword 2' at Institute of Contemporary Arts
1969-73 Taught at Somerset College of Art
1970 First one-man exhibition 'Evidence' at Greenwich Theatre Art Gallery
Two-man exhibition with John Hilliard at New Arts Lab
Made film 'Sheet' with Mike Leggett
Performances 'Unword 3' at Bristol Arts Centre and 'Unword 4' at University of Swansea
1971 One-man exhibition at Angela Flowers Gallery (also 1972/74)
1972 Exhibited in 'A Survey of the Avant-Garde in Britain' at Gallery House
1973 Exhibited in 'Photography into Art' at Camden Arts Centre (also Edinburgh and Glasgow)
Made film 'Repertory'
1974 One-man exhibition 'Le Journal et Travaux Annexes' at Galerie Bama, Paris
Exhibited in 'The Video Show' at Serpentine Gallery
1975 Made film 'The Journey'
1976- A PG Artist with Department of Health
1977 One-man exhibition 'Continuous Diary' at Arnolfini Gallery, Bristol, Institute of Contemporary Arts, Midland Group Gallery, Nottingham
BBC TV film on his work 'The Continuous Diary'
Published *Diary Extracts* (Midland Group, Nottingham)
1978 One-man exhibition 'Continuous Diary' at Scottish Arts Council Gallery, Edinburgh,
'Circus' at Third Eye Centre, Glasgow
Made film 'The Institution' with Kevin Coyne
Published *Continuous Diary* (Audio Arts, London) and *Fiction Texts 1966-78* (Third Eye Centre, Glasgow)
1979 One-man exhibition 'Continuous Diary and Circus' at Northern Ireland Arts Council Gallery,
Chapter Art Centre, Cardiff
Exhibited in 'Un certain art anglais' at Musée d'Art Moderne, Paris

Dealer Angela Flowers Gallery

My work over the last ten years has been in various media simultaneously: collages, visual texts, drawings, photo-collage, events, theatre performances, film, film performances, tapes, installations, environments, video, objects, photo-text sequences, film/slide projection sequences with sound, photo-assemblages, writing and reading of prose texts. I have used whatever medium or media seemed necessary for each statement I wished to make, and certain themes consistently recur.

The investigation of the relationship between word and image runs like a thread through all this work, as does the concept of personal time, the surreality of mundane 'reality' and the use of humour in various shades through to black.

Since 1965 much of my work as an artist has been in the form of Diaries which reflect my preoccupation with the relationship of word and image. The Diaries juxtapose hand-written and typed text with drawing, collage and photography. The Diaries record the side-events of daily life: by turns mundane, curious, bleak, erotic, tender, vicious, cunning, stupid, ambiguous, absurd, as observed by a personal witness.

Ian Breakwell 1976

Stuart Brisley 181

Stuart Brisley *Survival in Alien Circumstances* 1977 Performance in 'Documenta 6', Kassel

1933 Born in Haslemere
1949-54 Studied at Guildford School of Art
1956-9 Studied at Royal College of Art
1959 Received Abbey Minor Scholarship
1959-60 Received Bavarian State Scholarship and studied in Munich
1960-2 Studied at Florida State University
1960-4 Received Fulbright Travel Award
1970 One-man exhibition 'Guest of Honour' at Sigi Krauss Gallery
1970-1 Received Hille Fellowship

▶

1971 One-man exhibition in Buenos Aires
Exhibited in 'London Now' in Berlin,
'APG' at Hayward Gallery
1972 One-man exhibitions 'You know it makes sense' at Ikon Gallery, Birmingham,
'ZL656395C' and 'Artist as Whore' at Gallery House
Exhibited in group show at Serpentine Gallery,
'Survey of the avant-garde in Britain' at Gallery House
1973-4 Received DAAD Berlin Artists Programme Award
1975 'Moments of Decision/Indecision' performance at Teatr Studio, Palac Kultury i Nauki, Warsaw
1976 One-man exhibitions '1st Peterlee Report' at Northern Arts Gallery, Newcastle-upon-Tyne,
'Weather Work' at National Gallery of Art, Melbourne,
'26 Hours' at Experimental Art Foundation, Adelaide
Exhibited in Sydney Biennale,
'Arte inglese oggi' at Palazzo Reale, Milan

Stuart Brisley *Moments of Decision/Indecision* 1975 Performance at Teatra Studio, Palac Kultury i Nauki, Warsaw

1976-7 Town Artist at Peterlee, County Durham
1977 One-man exhibitions '2nd Peterlee Report' at Sunderland Arts Centre,
'3rd Peterlee Report' at Midland Art Gallery, Nottingham.
'Survival in Alien Circumstances' performed in 'Documenta 6', Kassel,
'Measurement and Division' performance at 'Hayward Annual'
1978 One-man exhibitions '180 Hours. Work for 2 people A & B' and '10 days' at Acme Gallery
'In Between and Outside' performance (with George Saxon) at Institute of Contemporary Arts
Exhibited in Vienna Performance Festival,
'A B & C' in Belfast and Londonderry
1979 Performance at De Appel Gallery, Amsterdam
Performance in 'Un certain art anglais' at Musée d'Art Moderne, Paris,
Artist Placement Group Exhibition at St Stephan Gallery, Vienna,
International Festival of Young Theatre of Brussels,
'Face to Face' performance at Theatre of Nations, Hamburg

Contact 54 Georgiana Street, London NW1

Stephen Buckley 150

1944 Born in Leicester
1962-7 Studied at University of Newcastle-upon-Tyne
1967-9 Studied at University of Reading
1969 Exhibited in 'Six at the Hayward' at Hayward Gallery
1969-71 Taught at Canterbury College of Art, Leeds College of Art and Chelsea School of Art
1970 One-man exhibition at Nigel Greenwood Inc
Exhibited in group show at Museum of Modern Art, New York
1972 One-man exhibitions at Hans Neuendorf, Cologne and Hamburg
Kasmin Gallery
1972-4 Artist in Residence at King's College, Cambridge
1973 One-man exhibition at Galleria dell'Arieta, Milan
Exhibited in 'La peinture anglaise aujourd'hui' at Musée d'Art Moderne, Paris

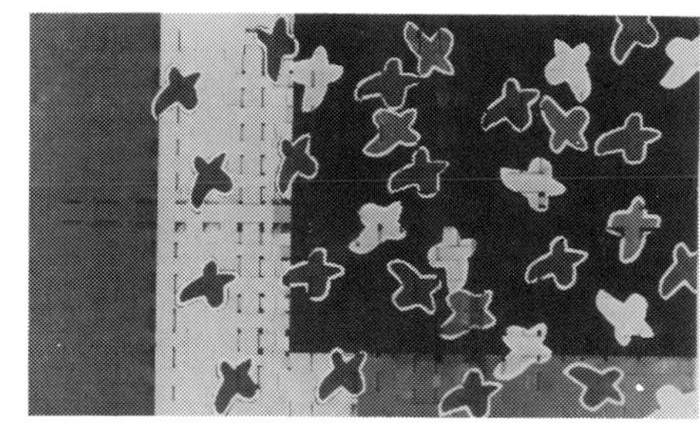

Stephen Buckley *Dancers* 1975 Oil on canvas 152x254x10cm (60x100x4in) Private Collection

1974 One-man exhibition at Kettle's Yard, Cambridge
Exhibited in John Moores Exhibition, Liverpool (prizewinner; also 1979)
'British Painting '74' at Hayward Gallery
1975 One-man exhibitions at Jacomo Santiveri Gallery, Paris,
Museum of Modern Art, Oxford
1976 One-man exhibition at Waddington Galleries (Kasmin Ltd)
Exhibited in 'The Human Clay' at Hayward Gallery and travelling
1977 One-man exhibition at Arnolfini Gallery, Bristol (also 1978)
Exhibited in Tolly Cobbold Eastern Arts National Exhibition (also 1979),
'Hayward Annual' at Hayward Gallery,
'British Painting 1952-1977' at Royal Academy
1978 One-man exhibitions at Robert Elkon Gallery, New York,
Knoedler Gallery
1979 Exhibited in 'Un certain art anglais' at Musée d'Art Moderne, Paris

Dealer Knoedler Gallery

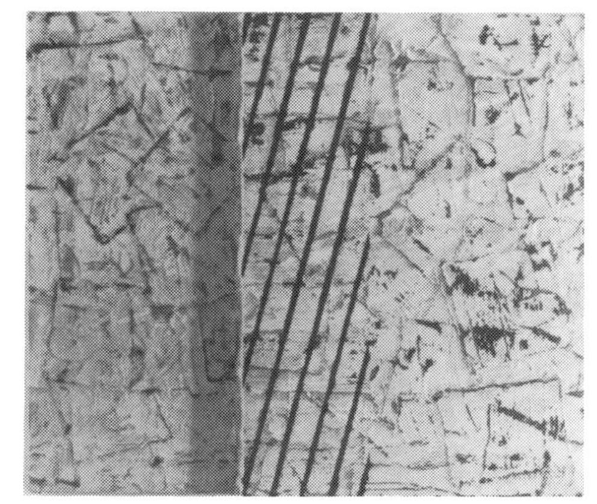

Stephen Buckley *Bridge* 1978 Oil on enamel on canvas 45.7x53.3cm (18x21in) Knoedler Gallery

Robert Buhler RA 15

Robert Buhler *Dame Edith Evans in Coriolanus* 1959 Oil 91.4x71.1cm (36x28in) Stratford upon Avon Museum

1916 Born in London
1933-5 Studied at St Martin's School of Art
1937-9 Taught at Wimbledon School of Art
1946 One-man exhibitions at Wildenstein Gallery,
Leger Galleries,
Redfern Gallery
1946-8 Taught at Chelsea School of Art and Central School of Art and Design
1947 Elected Associate of Royal Academy
1948-74 Taught at Royal College of Art
1956 Elected Royal Academician
1976- Trustee of Royal Academy
1978 Exhibited at Patricia Wells Gallery, Bristol

Dealer New Grafton Gallery

Landscape, portrait and still-life. Mainly oil, also pastel, gouache and watercolour. First influences: Impressionism and the Camden Town Group. As yet no major breakthrough or great innovation – but still working at it. Portraits painted of people from all walks of life, including Dame Edith Evans, Francis Bacon, Sir John Betjeman, Stephen Spender and many more from Auden to Zuckerman.

Robert Buhler 1979

Victor Burgin 184

Left and right: Victor Burgin *US77* 1977 (Two of 12 panels) Photographic prints 101.6x152.4cm (40x60in)

1941 Born in Sheffield
1962-5 Studied at Royal College of Art
1965-7 Studied at Yale University
1969 Exhibited in 'When Attitudes become Form at Institute of Contemporary Arts
1970-5 Annual one-man exhibitions at Daniel Templon Gallery, Paris,
Paul Maenz Gallery, Cologne
Exhibited in 'Information' at Museum of Modern Art, New York
1971 Exhibited in Guggenheim International Exhibition at Guggenheim Museum, New York
1972 One-man exhibition at Protech-Rivkin Gallery, Washington DC
Exhibited in 'The New Art' at Hayward Gallery,
'Documenta' in Kassel
1973 One-man exhibition at Lisson Gallery, Nigel Greenwood Inc
1973- Senior Lecturer in History and Theory of Visual Arts at Central London Polytechnic
1976 One-man exhibitions at Institute of Contemporary Arts,
Robert Self Gallery
1976- Lecturing at Yale, Princeton and UCLA
1976/7 Received US/UK Bicentennial Arts Exchange Fellowship
1977 One-man exhibitions at Van Abbe Museum, Eindhoven,
John Weber, New York (also 1979)
1978 One-man exhibitions at Museum of Modern Art, Oxford,
Durand-Dessert Gallery, Paris
1978/9 Received DAAD German Government Fellowship
1979 One-man exhibition at Max Hetzler Gallery, Stuttgart
Exhibited in 'Hayward Annual' at Hayward Gallery,
'Un certain art anglais' at Musée d'Art Moderne, Paris,
Sydney Biennale
1980 Picker Professor at Colgate University, New York

Dealer John Weber Gallery, New York
Liliane & Michel Durand-Dessert, Paris

Reg Butler 27

1913 Born in Buntingford
1920 First sculptures produced
1937 Elected Associate of Royal Institute of British Architects, having studied architecture
1949 First one-man exhibition at Hanover Gallery (also 1954/57/60/63)
1951 Exhibited in LCC Open Air Sculpture Exhibition (also 1954/57/60)
1951-3 Gregory Fellow in Sculpture at University of Leeds
1952 Exhibited in Venice Biennale (also 1954)
1952-67 Exhibited in Arts Council and British Council group shows
1953 Won International Sculpture Competition for 'A Monument to the Unknown Political Prisoner'
One-man exhibition at Curt Valentin Gallery, New York (also 1955)
Exhibited in Middelheim Biennale (also 1959/61)

▶

Reg Butler *Girl on Long Base* 1968-72 Painted bronze 142.2x160cm (58x63in) Pierre Matisse Gallery, New York

Reg Butler *Study for a Nude* 1977 Mixed media 74cm (29in) long Artist's Collection

1955 Exhibited in 'Documenta' in Kassel (also 1959)
1956 Exhibited in group show at Musée Rodin, Paris (also 1961)
1957 One-man exhibitions in Rotterdam and Berlin
Exhibited in Biennale Triventa, Padua (also 1961),
Sao Paulo Bienal
1958 One-man exhibition at Galerie Alex Vomel, Dusseldorf
Exhibited in Carnegie International Exhibition, Pittsburgh (also 1967/70)
1959- Regular one-man exhibitions at Pierre Matisse Gallery, New York
1960 One-man exhibitions in Goteborg and Stockholm
1961 One-man exhibition in Rome
1962 Published *Creative Development* (Routledge & Kegan Paul)
1963 Retrospective exhibition at J B Speed Art Museum, Louisville
1965 Exhibited in Brussels International Exhibition
Elected to Academie Royale des Sciences, des Lettres et des Beaux Arts de Belgique
1973 Exhibited in 'Erotic Art' at New School Arts Center, New York
1975 Exhibited in 'Figurative Sculpture' in Holland Park
1977 Exhibited in 'Contemporary British Sculpture' in Battersea Park,
'Real Life' at Walker Art Gallery, Liverpool,
'British Genius' in London
1979 Exhibited in 'Modern Realist Sculpture' in Bremen

Dealer Pierre Matisse Gallery, New York

Cameron and Miller 180

1944 Shirley Cameron born in Oxford
1959-62 Studied at Sutton School of Art
1962-6 Studied sculpture at St Martin's School of Art
1966-8 Exhibited in group shows at Grabowski Gallery, Camden Arts Centre and Whitechapel Art Gallery
1968-71 Taught at Swansea and Dyfed Colleges of Art

1938 Roland Miller born in London
1956-64 Studied at Wadham College, Oxford and Manchester University
1960-74 Worked as journalist
1964-7 Worked with Royal Shakespeare Theatre Company

Cameron and Miller and daughters *Celebration of Pre-metrication* 1979 Performance at Glynn Vivian Gallery, Swansea

1970- Cameron and Miller working together as performance artists
1970 Presented 'Railway Event' performance in Yorkshire
1971 Presented 'Cyclamen Cyclists' performance in England and Wales
1972 Presented 'Squares of Experience' performance at Serpentine Gallery
1973 Presented 'Naming our Vision' performance at Walker Art Gallery, Liverpool,
'In Air and Water' at Stedelijk Museum, Amsterdam
1973-8 Visited 11 different agricultural shows in Britain with 6 installations and 21 performances
1974 Presented 'Redman/Redwoman' performance in Antwerp
1975 Performed in 'Les six jours de la peinture' in Marseilles
1976 Presented 'Seed Drill' performance and banners in 'Arte inglese oggi' at Palazzo Reale, Milan

Cameron and Miller (and Miguel Yeco) *Children and Others* 1977 Performance at Caldas da Rainha, Portugal

1977 Presented 'The White Queen's Cakes' in food art exhibition on Midsummer Common, Cambridge,
'Pink and Green Icing' performance in 'Englische Kunst der Gegenwart' at Bregenz, Austria
1978 Presented 'Heads, Hands and Feet' performance travelling in Poland,
'Celebration of Pre-metrication' performance in 'Scale for Sculpture' at Serpentine Gallery and travelling
1979 Presented 'Noughts and Crosses – the History of Western Civilization' performance in Cardiff

Contact 25 Commercial Road, Grantham, Lincolnshire

My (our) work is in performance art. Many artists have moved into this field as a response to the present-day economic conditions and artistic climate. In terms of the materials used, it starts with the artist's own body as the basic source. Ideas can be expressed with this body alone and with any material extensions of hardware or software. Different locations are used, again, both as a response to economic conditions and to artistic decisions. It is an art form of possibilities, an opening up from the (necessary) narrowness of abstract art. Form and content can be worked on equally, any interest of the artist as a human person can be utilized as well as any formal or environmental interests, therefore it can encompass different art styles, ie surrealism, expressionism, formalism, concept art, multi-media art, political art and so on. My own interest is in sculptural formalism, acquired as a student in the sculpture department of St Martin's School of Art, and additionally a humanistic and autobiographical theme. My work has always been an expression of dualities, formal, physical and emotional. It is because of this, I believe, that I have been able to work with another person; a concretizing of the theme of self and other.

Shirley Cameron 1979

In my performance I use constructed objects, altered or coloured clothing; and occasional language for exposition or narrative: I try to re-establish the importance of our relationship as individuals with others, funny and sad. I try to project through my own body's actions our physical domination of one another, our postures of servitude, our ludicrousness, our physical presence in the world.

Roland Miller 1979

Jeffery Camp ARA 53

1923 Born in Suffolk
1941-4 Studied at Edinburgh College of Art
1945 Received Andrew Grant Travelling Scholarship
1946 Received David Murray Bursary for landscape painting
1950 Exhibited in group show at Edinburgh Festival
1955 Commission to paint altarpiece for St Alban's Church, Norwich
1958 First one-man exhibition at Galerie de Seine, Paris
Exhibited in group show at Aldeburgh Festival (also 1961/66)
1959 One-man exhibition at Beaux Arts Gallery (also 1961/63)
Exhibited in John Moores Exhibition, Liverpool (also 1961/63/74 [prizewinner]/78)
1961 Elected member of London Group
1961- Teaching at Slade School of Fine Art
1966 Exhibited in group show at Beaux Arts Gallery,
Group show at Marlborough Fine Art
1968 One-man exhibition at New Art Centre
1973 Retrospective exhibition at South London Art Gallery
1974 Elected Associate of Royal Academy
Exhibited in 'British Painting '74' at Hayward Gallery,
1975 Exhibited in Chichester National Art Exhibition (prizewinner),
'Drawings of People' at Serpentine Gallery,
Middlesbrough Drawing Biennale (prizewinner)
1977 Exhibited in 'British Painting 1952-1977' at Royal Academy
1978 One-man exhibitions at Serpentine Gallery and Bradford Art Gallery

Contact 12 The Croft, Hastings, Sussex

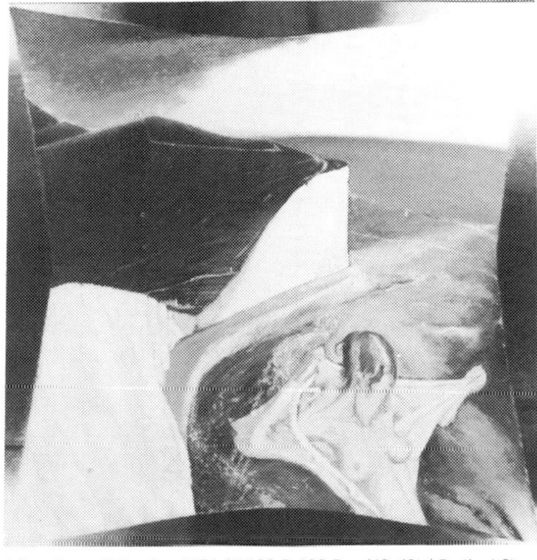

Jeffery Camp *Dirling Gap* 1974 Oil 106·7x106·7cm (42x42in) Bedford City Art Gallery

At some point in the five years since my 1973 retrospective exhibition I saw the first hang-gliders flying at Beachy Head.

In 1923 I began life in Lowestoft, a fishing port swept by cold winds. Conditioned by the flatness of East Anglia, to me fifty years later Beachy Head seems high, shocking and a dream come true.

William Gillies, who was part of the Edinburgh-Paris *bonne peinture* love affair, helped me to love oil paint. I spent a few years in a rich Suffolk landscape used by Cotman and Constable, and painted pictures filled with trees. Beachy Head is almost without trees, it is a high piece of chalk, and very still.

From 1950 onwards the quivering bodies of bathers in an open-air swimming pool at Oulton Broad and the scampering of figures across Lowestoft's beaches became my next difficult subjects. I was helped by Rubens' small oil panels. We depend on all the painters of the past (I looked at Watteau, Poussin, Boudin, Degas, Seurat, Piero della Francesca, Corot, Lautrec and Matisse). The concentrated Rubens sketches were done with tiny flowing marks – a living drama moving in a tiny compass. I tried to use these means for a different purpose, watching the passing show – out of doors, wherever people were together; at Beachy Head the gliders soar and float. The angels and cherubs of Rubens mark out the depths and extent of his open spaces, make exact the speed and rhythm of his design. The oceanic feelings inspired by Beachy Head, of flowing waters, flowing wind, soaring sails, pulsing hearts, flowing veins, moving gulls, whirring cine films, kicking flints, lurching jackdaws, powdering chalk, gleaming helmets, golden harness, shimmering fabrics of bright colours, the panting and the thrill, are presented to me in an aerial structure without attachment to the closed perspectives of the lowlands of my youth. The brush stroke is there as before, laying out the intangible, untouchable depths of the immeasurable action. The transparency of the idea and degree of presence and there can be no apology for the true sensation, only for the inadequacy of the painter if the figure fails and falls, to become a dead wraith or pale figment.

Jeffery Camp 1978

Jeffery Camp *Beachy Head Chasm* 1974 Oil 182x152cm (6x5ft) Artist's Collection

Anthony Caro 82

1924 Born in London
1942-5 Studied engineering at Christ's College, Cambridge
1946 Studied sculpture at Regent Street Polytechnic
1947-52 Studied at Royal Academy Schools
1951-3 Worked as part-time asistant to Henry Moore
1952-79 Taught at St Martin's School of Art
1958 Exhibited in Venice Biennale (also 1966/68/72),
Carnegie International Exhibition, Pittsburgh (also 1967)
1959 Exhibited in Paris Biennale
1960 Exhibited in Sculpture Exhibition in Battersea Park (also 1963/66)
1963 One-man exhibition at Whitechapel Art Gallery
1963-5 Taught at Bennington College, Vermont
1964 First one-man exhibition at André Emmerich Gallery, New York (also 1966/68/70/72/73/74/77/78)

▶

Anthony Caro *Orangerie* 1969 Painted Steel 224·8x162x231cm (7ft 4½inx5ft 4inx7ft 7in) Kenneth Noland Collection

1965 One-man exhibitions at Washington Gallery of Modern Art, Kasmin Gallery (also 1967/71/72)
Exhibited in 'British Sculpture out of the 60s' at Tate Gallery

1967 One-man exhibition at Rijksmuseum Kröller-Müller, Otterlo
Exhibited in International Sculpture Exhibition at Guggenheim Museum, New York

1968 Exhibited in 'New British Sculpture and Painting' at Berkeley and travelling in USA and Canada

1969 Exhibited in Sao Paulo Bienal (prizewinner)
Received CBE

1970 Exhibited in 'British Painting and Sculpture 1960-70' at National Gallery of Art, Washington DC, 'Contemporary British Art' at Museum of Modern Art, Tokyo

1972 Exhibited in '6 English Sculptors' at Museum of Fine Arts, Boston

1974 One-man exhibition at André Emmerich Gallery, Zurich (also 1978)
Exhibited in 'The Great Decade of American Abstract Art' at Museum of Fine Arts, Houston

1975 Retrospective exhibition at Museum of Modern Art, New York and travelling in USA
One-man exhibition at Galerie Wenzel, Hanover (also 1978)

1976 Presented with keys of New York

1977 One-man exhibitions at Galerie Piltzer-Rheims, Paris, Waddington & Tooth Galleries
Commission for new East Building, National Gallery of Art, Washington DC

Anthony Caro *Midnight Gap* 1976-8 Steel, rubbed with paint and slightly rusted and varnished 180·5x361x279cm (6x12x9ft) Ace Gallery, Vancouver

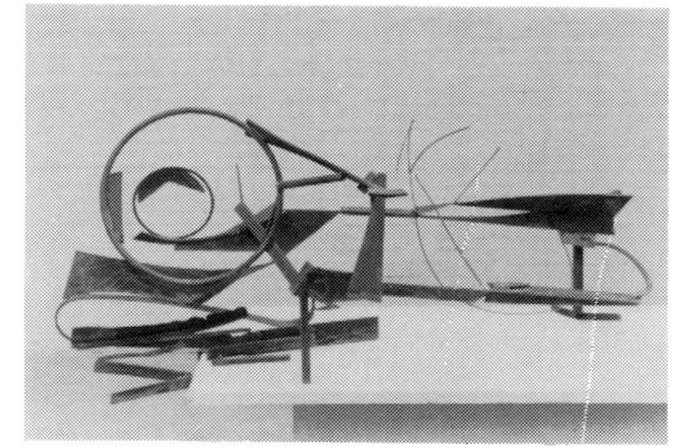

Anthony Caro *Z7* 1978-9 Steel rusted and varnished 99·1x198x111cm (39x78x44in) Artist's Collection

1978 One-man British Council exhibition travelling in Australia
One-man exhibition at Knoedler Gallery

1979 One-man exhibition at Gallery Kasahara, Osaka

Dealer Knoedler Gallery
André Emmerich Gallery, New York
Acquavella Contemporary Art, New York

My job is making sculpture; and by that I mean using visual means to say what I, a man living now, in 1978, feel like. And that can incorporate, as well as my emotional life, my living in London, and visiting the USA and any other experiences that have gone to enrich or delete from the sum total of being a human person. Add to that the practical logic of my trade. My tools, the steel I work with sometimes too heavy to manhandle, the need for triangulation to make things stand up; also my knowledge of the history of and my experience of sculpture. In the same way Matisse's art was to do with his women, flowers, colour, paint: all of these things, and to do with when and where he lived. People have asked me, 'What does your sculpture mean?' It is an expression of my feeling. The meaning in art is implicit, not explicit; and to require explanations suggests a real discomfort with the visual.

Anthony Caro 1978
(Interviewed by Peter Fuller, *Art Monthly 23*)

Patrick Caulfield 108

1936 Born in London

1956-9 Studied at Chelsea School of Art

1959-63 Studied at Royal College of Art

1961 Exhibited in 'Young Contemporaries' (also 1962/63)

1963 Taught at Chelsea School of Art

1964 Exhibited in 'The New Generation' at Whitechapel Art Gallery

1965 First one-man exhibition at Robert Fraser Gallery (also 1967)
Exhibited in 4th Paris Biennale (also 1967)
Awarded Prix des Jeunes Artistes for Graphics
Two-man exhibition with Derek Boshier at Galerie Aujourd'hui, Brussels (part of Saison de la Nouvelle Peinture Anglaise)

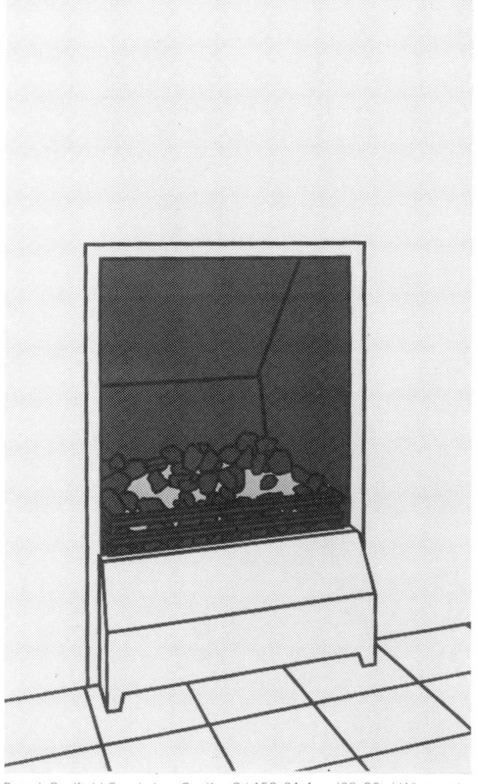

Patrick Caulfield *Smokeless Coalfire* Oil 152x91·4cm (60x36in) Whitworth Collection

Patrick Caulfield *Bistro* 1970 Oil on canvas 365x152cm (12ftx5ft) Private Collection

1966 One-man exhibition at Robert Elkon Gallery, New York (also 1968)
1967 One-man exhibition at Studio Marconi, Milan
Exhibited in Paris Biennale (des Jeunes),
'Jeunes peintres anglais' at Palais des Beaux Arts, Brussels,
Sao Paulo Bienal,
'Recent British Painting' at Tate Gallery (Peter Stuyvesant Foundation Collection)
1969 One-man exhibition at Waddington Galleries (also 1971/73/75)
Exhibited in 'Marks on a Canvas' at Museum am Ostwall, Dortmund,
'Pop Art' at Hayward Gallery
1971 Exhibited in 'Junge Engländer' at Kunststudio, Westfalen, Bielefeld
Patrick Caulfield by Christopher Finch published (Baltimore)
1973 One-man exhibition at Europalia, Brussels
1974 One-man exhibition at OK Harris, New York
Exhibited in 'British Painting '74' at Hayward Gallery
1976 Exhibited in 'Arte inglese oggi' at Palazzo Reale, Milan
1977 Print retrospective touring California
Exhibited in 'Recent British Art' British Council touring exhibition,
'New Prints' at Waddington & Tooth Graphics

Dealer Waddington Galleries

Lynn Chadwick 18

1914 Born in London
1950 One-man exhibition at Gimpel Fils Gallery (also 1952)
1952 Exhibited in Venice Biennale (also 1956 prizewinner)
1953 Exhibited in 'A Monument to the Unknown Political Prisoner' Sculpture Competition (prizewinner),
Middelheim Biennale (also 1959/61)
1954 Exhibited in 'British Painting and Sculpture' at Whitechapel Art Gallery,
Sculpture Exhibition in Holland Park (also 1957/75)
1955 Exhibited in 'The New Decade' at Museum of Modern Art, New York
1956 One-man exhibition at Wiener Secession, Vienna
Exhibited in group show at Musée Rodin, Paris (also 1961/71)
1957 One-man exhibitions at Saidenberg Gallery, New York,
Musée d'Art Moderne, Paris,
Stedelijk Museum, Amsterdam,
Exhibited in Sao Paulo Bienal (also 1962 prizewinner)
1958 One-man exhibition at Daniel Cordier Gallery, Paris
Exhibited in '50 ans d'art moderne' at Palais des Beaux Arts, Brussels
1959 One-man exhibitions in Zurich and Frankfurt
1961 One-man exhibitions at Knoedler & Co, New York (also 1965),
Marlborough Fine Art (also 1966/74/78)
1963 One-man exhibition at Carborundum Co, New York
1964 Received CBE
1965 Elected member of Accademia Nazionale di San Luca, Rome
1966 One-man exhibitions in Munich and Dusseldorf
1968 One-man exhibitions at Galerie Gerald Cramer, Geneva,
Waddington Gallery, Montreal,
Galerie d'Eendt, Amsterdam (also 1970/76/78)
1969 One-man exhibition at Dorsky Gallery, New York
1970 One-man exhibitions in Copenhagen and Stockholm
1972 One-man exhibitions in Toronto and Geneva
1974 One-man exhibitions at Galerie Farber, Brussels,
Marlborough Gallery, Zurich (also 1978) and Rome
1975 One-man exhibitions in Italy, South America, Canada, USA, Scandinavia
1976 One-man exhibition at Galerie Farber, Brussels

Lynn Chadwick *Teddy Boy and Girl 2* 1957 Bronze 208cm (82in) high Wichita University, USA

Lynn Chadwick *Pair of Walking Figures – Jubilee* 1977 Bronze 198cm (6ft 4in) high Private Collection, Belgium

1977 Exhibited in Silver Jubilee Contemporary British Sculpture Exhibition in Battersea Park
1979 One-man exhibition at Gallery 99, Miami,
Arts Council, Belfast

Dealer Marlborough Fine Art

▶

Lynn Chadwick *The Inner Eye* 1952 Iron and glass 228.6cm (7ft 6in) Museum of Modern Art, New York

Chadwick was searching for a technique which would combine solidity with the vitality of his metal structures and he found it in the combination of a metal armature and a plastic composition which allows full expressive value to the tendons of his fingers, while at the same time giving them a 'body' with complete tactile value. It will be observed that the underlying metal structure is not rough armature, such as is normally used in modelling, but an exactly articulated form carefully constructed in every detail. Having discovered an appropriate means of expression, the sculptor was free to develop what I have called his 'style'. By this ambiguous word I mean more than the formal characteristics of his work; I mean his peculiar 'ethos' or spiritual significance. Every great artist is a metaphysician. That is to say, the images he creates have a symbolic value: they are expressive of a state of mind or a feeling for which no other adequate signs or symbols exist. The artist is driven to create new signs and symbols because the degree of consciousness which they represent has not existed before, either in the evolution of human consciousness or in the history of art.

Herbert Read 1960
(from *Artists of Our Time*)

Marc Camille Chaimowicz

1947 Born in Paris
1964-8 Studied at Camberwell School of Art
1968-70 Studied at Slade School of Fine Art
1971 One-man exhibition at Sigi Krauss Gallery
1972 One-man exhibitions at Gallery House, Serpentine Gallery
1974 Presented 'Table Tableau' performance
1975 Presented 'Sur les marches du palais' performance
1976 Presented 'Fade' performance
1976-7 Wrote performance column in *Studio International*
1977 One-man exhibition at Galleria dell Cavallino, Venice
Exhibited in Paris Biennale
Presented 'Doubts . . . A sketch for video-camera and audience' performance in Geneva, Paris, Milan and London,
'Shift' performance in Vienna
Published *Dream, an anecdote* (Nigel Greenwood Inc)
1978 One-man exhibition at Galleria Cannaviello, Rome and Milan
Exhibited in International Performance Festival in Vienna,
'Hayward Annual' (Here and There) at Hayward Gallery
Presented 'Menage à trois' performance in Brussels
1979 Exhibited in 'Un certain art anglais' at Musée d'Art Moderne, Paris,
'Installationen – Raumkonzepte' at Galerie St Stephan, Vienna,
Tolly Cobbold Eastern Arts National Exhibition (prizewinner)

Dealer Nigel Greenwood Inc

Marc Camille Chaimowicz *Hier und Dort . . .* 1979 Installation (40 colour slides, changing, 40 black and white slides changing, automatic pendulum and text, Josef Hoffman furniture of *c.*1905) Galerie St Stephen, Vienna

HERE AND THERE . . .

'. . . As at the terrace of any anonymous provincial cafe, so here he could sit alone for hours, day-dreaming and wandering, dwelling on ills and pleasures . . .'

He thought of the Hayward Gallery, of the odd rooms with no windows or doors, neutral spaces with no identity, not really rooms at all . . .

Sitting in his lounge, this temporary truce between the ideal and the real, he dwelt on change . . .

How it is not possible to transfer his reality to another without this act of transference affecting that reality . . . How the transference of an experience qualifies that experience . . . How an idea, once subjected to change, is no longer that idea, how its purity is violated, modified . . .

He thought of black and white, . . . critically, and in this instance preferred greys and silvers, sometimes hazy as a Venetian dawn and sometimes crystalline . . . Greys that seem to annex a depth of nuances and colours, in a sense not really greys at all but greys that in their handling have become more than a mix of two extremes, rather, a new breed . . .

. . . and so with many false polarities . . . He thought of here and there, of this and that . . . (the fact that he was doing precious little, passively . . .)

He read Samuel Beckett on Marcel Proust '. . . He deplores his lack of will until he understands that will, being utilitarian, a servant of intelligence and habit is not a condition of the artistic experience . . .'

Hints of past cultural battles perhaps, between the German and the French . . .

Within this space, alien in its correctness, distant in its estrangement . . . He recalled it . . .

As sometimes reproachful, with a quality of abandonment . . . at times deliciously formal as with traditional hotel rooms . . . Sometimes sullen as adolescence, moody as delinquency . . .

The fountain screened out external noise establishing a particular silence . . . as with a well-matched duel, so the light from the mantelshelf lamp countered the daylight filtering in through the pale green curtains . . . As if natural light needed the qualification of electricity . . .

. . . within this intimacy he felt complete . . .

I realized that this space seemingly so singular, was infinitely composed . . . Still as to appear timeless, was fluid and prone to change . . .

And here, where possibilities of action seemed inappropriate, a multitude of activities were possible . . .

Marc Camille Chaimowicz 1978
(*Notes towards a Preface*, 'Hayward Annual')

Colin Cina 143

1943 Born in Glasgow
1961-3 Studied at Glasgow School of Art
1963-6 Studied at Central School of Art and Design
1966 Awarded Peter Stuyvesant Foundation travel bursary to USA
Exhibited in 'New Generation' at Whitechapel Art Gallery
1967 First one-man exhibition at Arnolfini Gallery, Bristol (also 1969/73)
Exhibited in John Moores Exhibition, Liverpool (also 1974/78),
'British Painting' Arts Council travelling exhibition

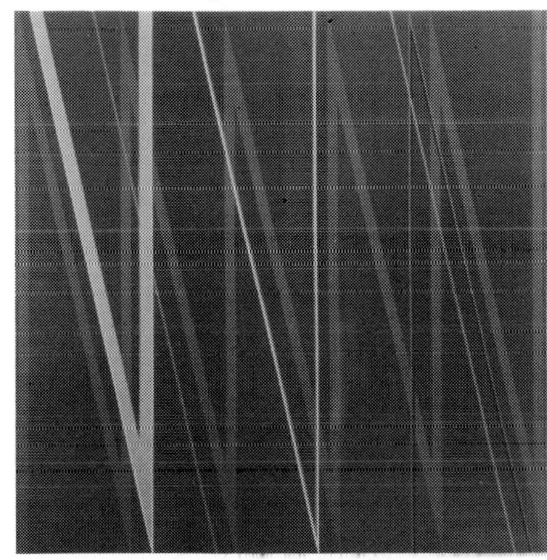

Colin Cina *MH/27* 1972 Acrylic on canvas 213x213cm (7x7ft) Konsthallen, Goteberg

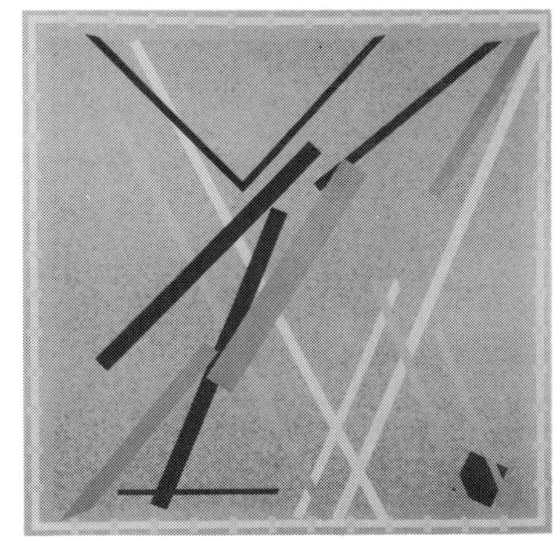

Colin Cina *Pineapple Day* 1976 Acrylic paint on canvas 274x274cm (9x9ft) Artist's Collection

1967- Part-time teaching at several London and provincial art schools
1972 One-man exhibition at Angela Flowers Gallery (also 1974)
Exhibited in 'British Drawings 1952-1972' at Wolverhampton City Art Gallery
1973 One-man exhibition at Galerie Wellmann, Dusseldorf
Exhibited in 'Ung Engelsk Konst' at Konsthallen, Goteborg,
'Summer Studio' at Institute of Contemporary Arts
1975 Appointed Principal Lecturer in Painting at Wimbledon School of Art
Exhibited in '20th Century Scottish Drawings' Scottish Arts Council exhibition
1977 Exhibited in 'Twelve British Artists' at Kjarvalsstadir, Reykjavik
1978 Exhibited in '20th century Scottish Painting' at Edinburgh Festival
1980 One-man exhibition at Serpentine Gallery

Dealer Galerie Wellmann, Dusseldorf
or
Contact 11B Elizabeth Mews, London NW3

Gillian Wise Ciobotaru 102

1936 Born in London
1954-7 Studied at Wimbledon School of Art
1959 Studied at Central School of Art
1961 Met and started to exhibit with British Constructivist Group
Exhibited in 'Construction: England: 1950-60' at Drian Galleries
Commission for constructed screen for International Union of Architects Congress
1963 Two-man exhibition 'Relief Structures' with Anthony Hill at Institute of Contemporary Arts
1965 Exhibited in 8th Tokyo Biennale, 'British Sculpture in the 60s' at Tate Gallery
1967 One-man exhibition at Axiom Gallery
1968 Exhibited in 'Relief-Construction-Relief' at Museum of Contemporary Art, Chicago,
'Four Artists' at Victoria and Albert Museum
UNESCO Fellowship, Prague
Commission for wall screen, with Anthony Hill, for Cunard liner Queen Elizabeth 2
Founder member of Arts Research Syndicate
1969 Exhibited in 1st Nuremberg Biennale, 'System, Syntactic Art from Britain' at Amos Anderson Museum, Helsinki

Gillian Wise Ciobotaru *Reduce X and Expand Green* 1977-8 Cellulose spray on acrylic sheet 121.9x91.4cm (48x36in) Artist's Collection

1969-70 British Council Postgraduate Award to Leningrad Academy of Art
1970-1 Taught at University of Illinois, Chicago
1971-8 Taught at Chelsea School of Art
1972 Exhibited in 'Systems' at Whitechapel Art Gallery
1973-5 Commission for wall relief for Nottingham University Hospital
1974 Exhibited in 'British Painting '74' at Hayward Gallery
1976 One-man exhibition 'Drawn from Structures' at Polytechnic of Central London
1977 Exhibited in 'British Painting 1952-1977' at Royal Academy
1978 Exhibited in 'Hayward Annual' (selector and co-ordinator of Constructivist section)
1978- Teaching at Royal College of Art

Contact Textum-Ars, 63 Hanger Lane, London W5

Since 1960 I have exhibited with the British Constructive movement, formed around Kenneth Martin, Victor Pasmore and Anthony Hill. Our works were made following certain tenets of form, material and composition that were still regarded as unacceptable in the English artistic climate of the time, although by the 60s this had improved to the point where, at my ▶

first major showing (with Anthony Hill) at the Institute of Contemporary Art, 1963, I had a work purchased by the Tate Gallery.

A central form-idea runs through my work: to build from the simplest elements, whether it be with a mystical or functional end in view. But within this spectrum I am aware of what might be called, roughly, a three-tier break-down in the perception of scale – the intimate, small scale relating to the size of the human body, that can be enveloped by the hand and eye, the middle, already less personal scale that is associated with the Bauhaus and Concrete Art, and lastly the heroic/universal/utopian scale, well demonstrated by Suprematism, in both pure and applied forms and by de Stijl.

I have an idea that a resolution – not necessarily simple – of this multi-scale proposal within 'Constructive Art' is of vital concern. In my own work there are no claims to a solution, rather an acceptance of the variables as they exist and still have meaning for me. There are traces of all three orientations in the objects I have made, and that is why I try to investigate and observe the 'artificial phenomena' of certain art objects. This is the reason why I like to make several versions of one piece, often varying in size and technique – it allows me to analyze, compare and reconstruct the idea into another 'reality'.

Gillian Wise Ciobotaru 1979

Gillian Wise Ciobotaru *Interlocking Reflex* 1978 Stainless steel, wood base, aluminium reflectors and cellulose paint 305x426cm (10x14ft) Artist's Collection

Robert Clatworthy RA 57

Robert Clatworthy *Standing Figure* 1965 Plaster for bronze 182 9cm (6ft) high No longer in existence

Robert Clatworthy *Untitled* 1979 Plaster for bronze 138.4cm (54½in) high Artist's Collection

1928 Born in Somerset
1945-6 Studied at West of England College of Art
1948-9 Studied at Chelsea School of Art
1950-2 Studied at Slade School of Fine Art
1954 One-man exhibition at Hanover Gallery (also 1956)
1957 Exhibited in Open Air Sculpture Exhibition in Holland Park
1960 Exhibited in Open Air Sculpture Exhibition in Battersea Park (also 1963)
1960-72 Taught at Royal College of Art
1961-72 Member of Fine Art Panel of National Council for Diploma in Art and Design
1965 One-man exhibition at Waddington Gallery
Exhibited in 'British Sculpture in the 60s' at Tate Gallery
1967-71 Taught at West of England College of Art
1968 Elected Associate of Royal Academy
1970-1 Governor of St Martin's School of Art
1971-5 Head of Department of Fine Art at Central School of Art and Design
1972 One-man exhibition at Basil Jacobs Fine Art
Exhibited in 'British Sculpture' at Royal Academy
1973 Elected Royal Academician
1977 One-man exhibition in Diploma Galleries, Royal Academy

Contact 15 Park Street, London SE1

Prunella Clough

1919 Born in London
1938-9 Studied at Chelsea School of Art
1947 First one-man exhibition at Leger Gallery
1949 One-man exhibition at Roland, Browse & Delbanco (also 1950)
1953 One-man exhibition at Leicester Galleries (also 1957)
1960 Retrospective exhibition at Whitechapel Gallery of Art
1964 One-man exhibition at Grosvenor Gallery (also 1967)
1972 Retrospective exhibition at Graves Art Gallery, Sheffield
1973 One-man exhibition at New Art Centre (also 1975/76/79)
1976 One-man exhibitions at National Gallery of Modern Art, Edinburgh, Serpentine Gallery

Dealer New Art Centre

Bernard Cohen 81

1933 Born in London
1949-50 Studied at South West Essex Technical College and School of Art
1950-1 Studied at St Martin's School of Art
1951-4 Studied at Slade School of Fine Art
1953 Exhibited in 'Young Contemporaries' (also 1954), 'Six Young Contemporaries' at Gimpel Fils Gallery
1958 One-man exhibition at Gimpel Fils Gallery (also 1960)
1961 Commission for mural for Congress of International Union of Architects Headquarters
Exhibited in 'New London Situation' at Marlborough New London Gallery, Paris Biennale

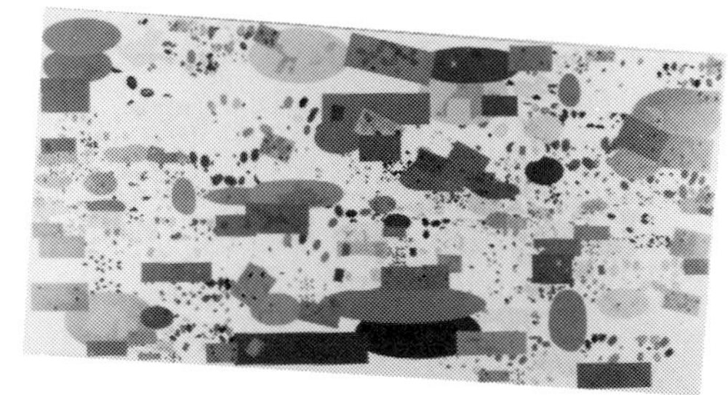

Bernard Cohen *Somewhere Between* 1975 Acrylic on linen 152x305cm (60x120in) Waddington Galleries

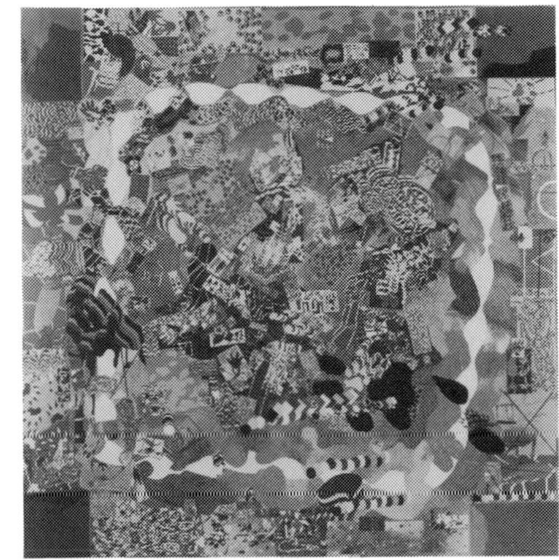

Bernard Cohen *Painting on a Domestic Theme* 1977-8 Acrylic on linen 182.9x182.9cm (6x6ft) Waddington Galleries

1962 One-man exhibition at Molton Gallery
1963 One-man exhibition at Kasmin Gallery (also 1964/67)
1964 Exhibited in 'London: The New Scene' at Minneapolis Art Center and travelling in USA
1965 Painted safety curtain for 'Stage 60' at Theatre Royal, Stratford (East London)
1966 Exhibited in Venice Biennale
1966-8 Taught at Chelsea School of Art
1967 One-man exhibitions at Betty Parsons Gallery, New York, Arnolfini Gallery, Bristol
1967-73 Taught at Slade School of Fine Art (also 1977-)
1969 Exhibited in 'Marks on a Canvas' travelling exhibition in Europe
1969-70 Visiting Professor at University of New Mexico
1972 Retrospective exhibition at Hayward Gallery, Arnolfini Gallery, Bristol
One-man exhibition at Waddington Galleries (also 1974/77)
1973 One-man exhibition at Annunciata Gallery, Milan
Exhibited in 'British Painting' at Musée d'Art Moderne, Paris
1976 Exhibited in 'Arte inglese oggi' at Palazzo Reale, Milan
1977 Exhibited in 'British Painting 1952-1977' at Royal Academy

Dealer Waddington Galleries

Peter Coker RA 30

1926 Born in London
1947-50 Studied at St Martin's School of Art
1950-4 Studied at Royal College of Art
1951 Awarded Royal Scholarship
1954 Elected Associate of Royal College of Art
Awarded British Institution Scholarship
1954-73 Taught at St Martin's School of Art
1956 First one-man exhibition at Zwemmer Gallery (also 1957/59/64/67)
1958 Exhibited in 'The Religious Theme' at Tate Gallery, 'English Artists' at Jordan Galleries, Toronto
1960 Exhibited in 'Das junge England' at Europaisches Forum, Alpbach, Group show at Neue Galerie der Stadt, Linz
1962 Exhibited in 'British Painting 1950-7' Arts Council travelling exhibition
1965 Elected Associate of Royal Academy
1966 Exhibited in 'Painters in East Anglia' Arts Council exhibition
1968 One-man exhibition at Magdalene Street Gallery, Cambridge
Exhibited in Bicentenary Exhibition at Royal Academy

▶

Peter Coker *Forest 8* 1959 Oil 225.4x129cm (6ft 4¾inx4ft 3in) Private Collection

Peter Coker *Yellow Diving Board, Etretat* 1978 Oil 101.6x152.4cm (40x60in) Artist's Collection

1969 One-man exhibition at Stone Gallery, Newcastle
1970 One-man exhibition at Thackeray Gallery (also 1972/74/75/76/78)
1972 Elected Royal Academician
Retrospective exhibition at The Minories, Colchester
1973 Retrospective exhibition at Victoria Gallery, Bath and travelling
1973- Teaching at City and Guilds London Art School
1975 Exhibited in 'British Painting 1900-1960' at Sheffield and Aberdeen Art Galleries
1976 Published *Etching Techniques* (Batsford, London)
Received Arts Council Award
1977 Exhibited in 'British Painting 1952-1977' at Royal Academy
1978 Retrospective exhibition at Chelmsford and Essex Museum
1979 Retrospective exhibition 'Paintings and Drawings of the Butcher's Shop' in Liverpool and travelling

Dealer Thackeray Gallery

He has moved from exceptionally thickly painted views of butchers' shops, dead hares on tables, stylized still lifes of great power and originality, and tender, touching and truthful portraits, to his later fascinations with landscape, and often the wilder the better, storm, forest and seascape.

In his paintings, whatever the subject, he seems to me more concerned with getting at, visually, the very structure, movement and life of what he is looking at so intensely. Texture is varied and vivid, although the unusually thick impasto of his earlier work has been somewhat refined down; colour is more tonal, blacks, whites, greys but there is often a surprisingly vivid and subtle spectrum of beautifully modulated and variegated tones, unexpected shafts of blues and reds which punctuate with a controlled exuberance the deeply expressive qualities of his views of landscape. The exhilarating quality of the variegated surface of the paintings ensure that they are very tactile, almost as though the spectator in a curious manner were nearly brushing up against the gorse and bracken, feeling the splendidly harsh wood of the trees; but this is in no way affected. It is simply that the surface of the painting is a kind of analogue for the surfaces of natural things, of sea, beach and stone, of wood and vegetation, of window and balcony overlooking the coast. He is particularly good too at catching the nuance of the moving, changing lights of the sky, skimming clouds and gathering storm, dusk and the inevitable movement of the tide.

His drawings, typically in charcoal and conté, exhibit with felicity his careful yet profound attention to the structure of landscape.

Marina Vaizey 1973

William Coldstream 17

William Coldstream *Central Hall, Westminster* 1975-6 Oil on canvas 50.8x61cm (20x24in) Private Collection

1908 Born in Northumberland
1926-9 Studied at Slade School of Fine Art
1929 Exhibited with New English Art Club and London Group
1933 Two-man exhibition at London Artists Association Gallery
1934 Elected member of London Group
Worked in GPO Film Unit under John Grierson, and with Cavalcanti
1935 Directed film 'The King's Stamp' and worked on film 'Coal Face' with W H Auden
1937 Left Film Unit to paint full-time
1938 With Claude Rogers and Victor Pasmore founded Euston Road School of Drawing and Painting
1939 Exhibited in 'British Art since Whistler' at National Gallery
1943-5 Official War Artist in Middle East and Italy
1946 Exhibited in United Nations International Exhibition in Paris
1948-55 Trustee of National Gallery (also 1956-63)
1949-55 Trustee of Tate Gallery (also 1956-63)
1949-75 Slade Professor of Fine Art at University College
1953-62 Chairman of Art Panel of Arts Council of Great Britain
1958-71 Chairman of National Advisory Council on Art Education
1962 Retrospective exhibition at South London Art Gallery and travelling
1962-70 Vice-chairman of Arts Council of Great Britain
1964 Exhibited in 'Painting and Sculpture of a Decade 1954-64' at Tate Gallery
1964-71 Chairman of British Film Institute
1976 One-man exhibition at Anthony d'Offay Gallery
1977 Exhibited in 'British Painting 1952-1977' at Royal Academy

Contact Slade School of Fine Art

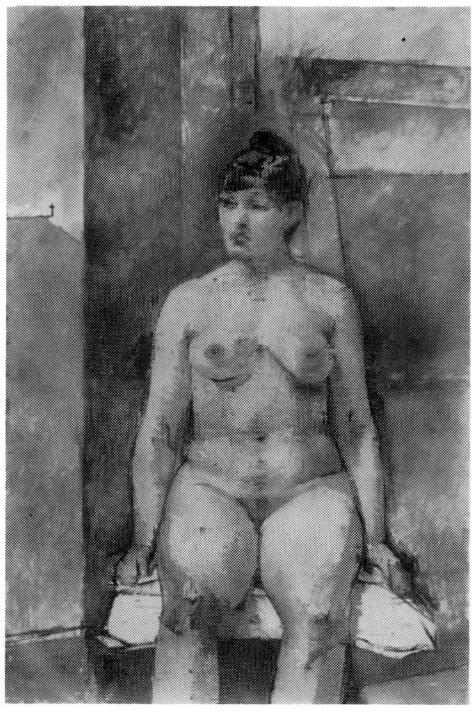
William Coldstream *Seated Nude* 1960 Oil on canvas 106.7x71.1cm (42x28in) Private Collection

All painting balances passivity with action, in different amounts differently distributed. The energy of some recent painting, for instance, is concentrated on the material of painting, on making itself big, puffing itself up into the enormous, irrefutable likeness of a real action, as if to balance an underlying mood of quiescence. The balance that Coldstream strikes is at the opposite extreme, but its extremity, its oddness and originality are equally marked; he is painting in the same world and his balance turns on an equally vital issue. His detachment, his very reticence, are designed to probe a vital question – the question of whether a pictorial action with respect to what is seen is any longer credible or possible. With an infinite delicacy he stalks the reality of vision; he catches it. He disdains to drop the cloak; he does not explain himself. But if we get the point the possibilities of painting in the 20th century never look the same again.

Lawrence Gowing 1962

Cecil Collins 25

Cecil Collins *Portrait of the Artist and his Wife* 1939 Oil on canvas 91.4x119.4cm (36x47in) Private Collection

1908 Born in Plymouth
1923-7 Studied at Plymouth School of Art
1927-31 Studied at Royal College of Art
1935 First one-man exhibition at Bloomsbury Gallery
1936 Exhibited in International Surrealist Exhibition
1937 Moved to Devon
1938 Important meeting with Mark Tobey, who encouraged him in his work
1939-43 Taught at Dartington Hall, Devon
1940 Began first series of paintings and drawings on theme of 'The Vision of the Fool'
1942 Exhibited in 'New Movements in Art' at London Museum, 'Contemporary British Art' British Council exhibition touring USA
1943 Returned to live in London
Began writing *The Vision of the Fool*, a meditation on the series of works of the same name
1944 One-man exhibition at Lefevre Gallery (also 1945/48)
1946 Lived in Yorkshire
Publication of *Cecil Collins: Paintings and Drawings 1935-1945* (Counterpoint Publications, Oxford)
1947 Lived in Cambridge
Published *The Vision of the Fool* (Grey Walls Press)
1949 Designed first tapestry for Edinburgh Tapestry Company (exhibited in 'Modern English Tapestries' Arts Council 1950)
1951 One-man exhibition at Leicester Galleries (also 1956)
1951- Teaching at Central School of Art
1953 Retrospective exhibition at Ashmolean Museum, Oxford
1959 Commissioned to design 'The Shakespeare Curtain' for British Embassy, Washington DC
Major retrospective exhibition at Whitechapel Art Gallery
1965-71 One-man exhibition at Arthur Tooth & Sons
1972 Retrospective exhibition at Hamet Gallery
1973 Commissioned to paint altarpiece *The Icon of Divine Light* for Chichester Cathedral
1975 Gave two major lectures at Tate Gallery on 'The Vision of the Angel and the Fool'
1976 One-man exhibition (of new drawings) at Anthony d'Offay Gallery
1978 Arts Council film directed by Stephen Cross 'The Eye of the Heart' made on his work

Dealer Anthony d'Offay

I am concerned with art as a metaphysical experience and in my painting with exploring the mystery of consciousness. A picture lives on many different levels at once, it is an interpenetration of planes of reality – it cannot be analyzed or anatomized into single levels, because one level can only be understood in the light of other levels. The reality or interior life of the picture can only be realized as a total experience. Partial experience – aestheticism, for example – is superficial.

The terms 'pure painting' and 'pure art' seem to me to be meaningless. For me, colours and forms are instruments, and I hold the 'instrumental' view that pictures are stations of transmission, and that painting is a metaphysical activity, whose function is to serve the contemplative life.

Cecil Collins 1979

Cecil Collins *The Quest* 1938 Oil on wood 109.2x144.8cm (43x57in) Private Collection

Jean Cooke RA 42

1927 Born in London
1943-5 Studied at Central School of Art and Design
1945-9 Studied at Camberwell School of Art, Goldsmiths College
1950-3 Set up Pottery Workshop in Sussex
1953-5 Studied at Royal College of Art
1964 One-man exhibition at Leicester Galleries
1964-74 Lecturer in Painting at Royal College of Art
1965 Elected Associate of Royal Academy
One-man exhibition at Bear Lane Gallery, Oxford
1966 One-man exhibition at Moyan Gallery, Manchester
1967 One-man exhibition at Lane Gallery, Bradford
1968 Exhibited in group shows at Furneaux Gallery,
Upper Grosvenor Gallery
1971 One-man exhibition at New Grafton Gallery
1972 Elected Royal Academician
1974 One-man exhibition at Ansdell Gallery
Exhibited in group show at Thomas Agnew & Sons

▶

Jean Cooke *Portrait of John Bratby* c 1965 Oil 152.4x76.2cm (5x2½ft) Royal College of Art

1976 One-man exhibition at J K Taylor Gallery, Cambridge
Exhibited in group show at Dulwich College Picture Gallery
1977 Exhibited in 'British Painting 1952-1977' at Royal Academy
1978 One-man Open Studio exhibition (also 1979)
1979 One-man exhibition at Norwich Gallery

Contact 7 Hardy Road, London SE3

As time passes I find myself less inclined to make a statement about my work; analysis and tight thinking make it less easy to plunge to the depths of one's being and potter about 'at the bottom of the treacle jar'. It is the surprise that is constantly stimulating. I do not know how a painting will finish when I start a new one. There is always a new idea to be found as one lives in the painting. I like to 'die' every night and start the day with nothing in my mind so that even if I am in the middle of a painting, I am open to a fresh view each day that I work on it. I never seem to finish a painting however long I work on it . . .

I have a very tactile approach to painting and need the feeling of space. I am very dependent on nature and the things around me. Each winter I hibernate and then with the first sun, like an old tortoise, I amble out with bleary eyes and start to see again . . . Mostly I use oil paint in my work, but I have also done water colours. These I do in a very keyed-up way like walking a tightrope – it is very exciting.

Jean Cooke 1979

Jean Cooke *Self-portrait with Tortoise through the Looking-glass* 1961 Oil 21.9x91.4cm (48x36in) Carel Weight Collection

John Copnall 73

1928 Born in Slinford, Sussex
1945-6 Studied at Architectural Association
1949-54 Studied at Royal Academy Schools
1955 First one-man exhibition at Piccadilly Gallery (also 1956/58/61)
1955-68 Lived in isolation in Spain
1956 One-man exhibition at Sala Veyreda, Barcelona
1957 One-man exhibitions in Munich, Cologne and Nuremburg
Exhibited in Internationale Kunstanstellung at Bayreuth
1958 One-man exhibition at Institut für Auslands-beziehungen, Stuttgart
Exhibited in group exhibition at Wildenstein Gallery
1960 One-man exhibition at Stone Gallery, Newcastle
Exhibited in group exhibition at Hamilton Gallery
1969 One-man exhibition at Bear Lane Gallery, Oxford
Exhibited in group exhibition at Annely Juda Fine Art (also 1973)
1970 E.A. Abbey Scholarship
1971 Exhibited in 'Art Spectrum' at Alexandra Palace
1972 One-man exhibition at Institute of Contemporary Arts
Exhibited in John Moores Exhibition, Liverpool (also 1974)
1973 One-man exhibition at Ikon Gallery, Birmingham,
Richard Demarco Gallery, Edinburgh
1973- Teaching painting at Central School of Art
1974 One-man exhibition at Aberdeen Art Gallery and Museum,
Prudhoe Gallery
Exhibited in 'British Painting '74' at Hayward Gallery
1975 Exhibited in 'From Britain '75' in Helsinki
1979 One-man exhibition at Galleri Mörner, Stockholm

Contact 4 Cumberland Gardens, London WC1

John Copnall *Landscape with Blue Jeans* 1967 Mixed media 101.6x152.4cm (40x60in) Bruckman Collection

From art school until 1958 I made figurative painting in oils. Over the next two years, influenced by de Stael, I slowly changed to abstract painting. During the 60s I constructed surfaces in earth colours and textures, using collaged found-objects, building materials and PVA in order to make an organic expression of the landscape I lived in.

When I returned to London in 1968 I saw American painting for the first time. I looked long at Morris Louis but I looked even more at Mondrian. Gradually I shed texture and took on colour and space, and my paintings became much larger, simpler, and more urban. By 1970 I

John Copnall *Diagonal Ebb and Flow* 1979 Acrylic 237.5x345cm (7ft 9½inx11ft 4in) Artist's Collection

was making totally abstract autonomous colour paintings. By pouring pure acrylic paint into large imprimed canvases in a vertical plane, I made stripes of varying widths which activated the real white fields to create a dynamic tension of interacting colour chords.

Some time in 1975 I started to find the flatness of the picture plane and the geometry of Post-Constructivist painting too constricting, and so after much experiment, I began to run the paint more freely, to superimpose semi-transparent colours, to create again the illusion of penetrating the picture surface. I am now absorbed with this process of pouring the colour down a more horizontal canvas to cover up preceding streams of thinned down acrylic paint. Trying to achieve a balance between control and chance, discovering unpredictable shapes and colour relationships while channelling the gravitational flow of the paint. The whole structure gets a rhythmic cohesion from the organic method of opening up the space.

John Copnall 1979

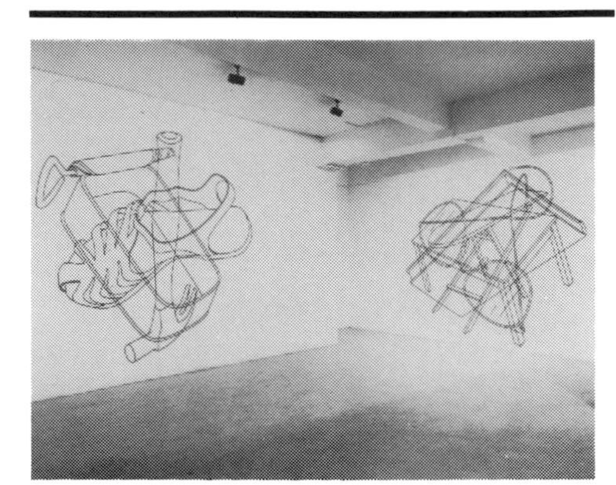

Michael Craig-Martin *Installation* 1978 Rowan Gallery

Michael Craig-Martin 175

1941 Born in Dublin
1961-6 Studied at Yale University
1966-70 Taught at Bath Academy and Canterbury College of Art
1969 First one-man exhibition at Rowan Gallery (and annually since then)
1970-72 Artist in Residence, King's College, Cambridge
1971 One-man exhibition at Arnolfini Gallery, Bristol
1972 Exhibited in 'Seven Exhibitions' at Tate Gallery,
'The New Art' at Hayward Gallery
1973 Exhibited in 'Henry Moore to Gilbert & George' at Palais des Beaux Arts, Brussels
1973- Teaching at Goldsmiths College
1974 One-man exhibition at Galerie December, Munster
Exhibited in 'Idea and Image in Recent Art' at Art Institute of Chicago.
'Art as thought process' at Serpentine Gallery
1975 Exhibited in Paris Biennale,
Sao Paulo Bienal
1976 One-man exhibition 'Michael Craig-Martin: Selected Works 1966-75' at Turnpike Gallery, Leigh and travelling
Exhibited in Sydney Biennale
1977 One-man exhibition at Oliver Dowling Gallery, Dublin
Exhibited in 'Hayward Annual' at Hayward Gallery,
'Reflected Images' at Kettles Yard Gallery, Cambridge
1978 One-man exhibition at Galerie December, Dusseldorf,
'Michael Craig-Martin, 10 works 1970-77' at Institute of Modern Art, Brisbane,
Coventry Gallery, Sydney (and 3 other Australian locations)
Exhibited in John Moores Exhibition, Liverpool
1979 Exhibited in 'Un certain art anglais' at Musée d'Art Moderne, Paris
'Books for Artists' at Felicity Samuel Gallery

Dealer Rowan Gallery

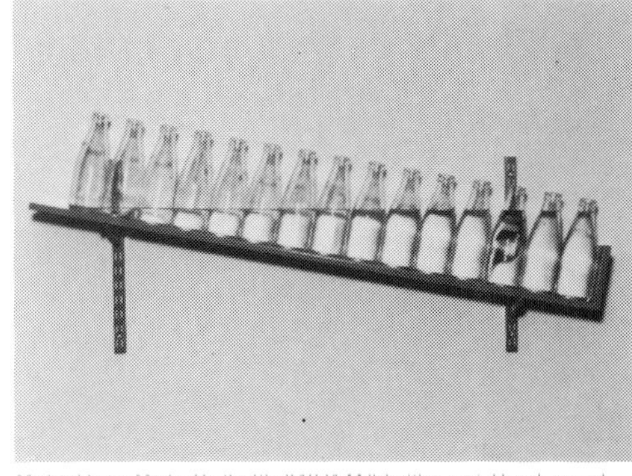

Michael Craig-Martin *On the Shelf* 1971 Milk bottles, metal brackets and water 61x15·2x121cm (24x6x48in) Private Collection

Dennis Creffield 45

1931 Born in London
1948-51 Studied at Borough Polytechnic with David Bomberg
1957-61 Studied at Slade School of Fine Art
1960 Exhibited in 'Seven Figurative Painters' at AIA Gallery

Dennis Creffield *The Blind Man* 1961 Charcoal on paper 55.9x78.7cm (22x31in) Artist's Collection

1961 Exhibited in 'Six Young Painters' Arts Council touring exhibition,
John Moores Exhibition, Liverpool (prizewinner)
1962 Elected member of London Group
1964-7 Gregory Fellowship in Painting, University of Leeds
1966 One-man exhibition at Leeds City Art Gallery
Exhibited in 'Survey 66: Figurative Painters' at Camden Art Centre

▶

Dennis Creffield *The Resource of Loneliness* (study) 1977 Charcoal on paper 50·8x76·2cm (20x30in) Artist's Collection

1967 One-man exhibition at Queen Square Gallery, Leeds
1968 Exhibited in 'The Nude' at Grosvenor Gallery
1971 One-man exhibition at Gardner Art Centre, University of Sussex
Exhibited in 'Art Spectrum South' Arts Council travelling exhibition
1974 One-man exhibition at Morley Gallery
1977 One-man exhibition at Brighton Polytechnic Gallery
Exhibited in 'British Painting 1952-1977' at Royal Academy
Major Arts Council Award

Contact 3/45 Marine Parade, Brighton

I learned the principles of good draughtsmanship from David Bomberg. This understanding, rooted in the physical apprehension of mass through painting and drawing, continues to be the substance of my work, of my approach to nature. I also try to learn from everything that is 'living' in life and art.

Dennis Creffield 1979

William Crozier 160

1930 Born in Yoker
1949-53 Studied at Glasgow School of Art
1953-78 Lived and worked in Dublin, Paris, Malaga and London
1957 One-man exhibitions at Institute of Contemporary Arts,
Drian Gallery (also 1958/60/61/62/65/69/70)
1958 One-man exhibition at Galleria Blu, Milan
1959 One-man exhibition at Arthur Tooth & Sons (also 1962/63/64)
1960 One-man exhibition at Galerie Madeleine, Paris
1960-3 Taught at Bath Academy of Art
1961 Exhibited in John Moores Exhibition, Liverpool (also 1963)
1962 Exhibited in Carnegie International Exhibition, Pittsburgh
1963 Exhibited in group shows at Arnolfini Gallery, Bristol,
San Francisco, Dallas, Santa Barbara
'British Painting in the 60s' at Whitechapel Art Gallery
1963-8 Taught at Central School of Art and Design
1968 One-man exhibition at Demarco Gallery, Edinburgh
1969 One-man exhibition at Compass Gallery, Glasgow (also 1975)
1969- Teaching at Winchester School of Art
1975 Exhibited in 'Body and Soul' Peter Moores Exhibition, Liverpool
1976 One-man exhibition at Stern Gallery, Cologne
1977 Exhibited in 'Expressionism' Scottish Arts Council exhibition
1978 Exhibited in group shows at Southampton University,
Serpentine Gallery,
'Painters in Parallel' Scottish Arts Council exhibition

Contact 2 Conway Road, London N14

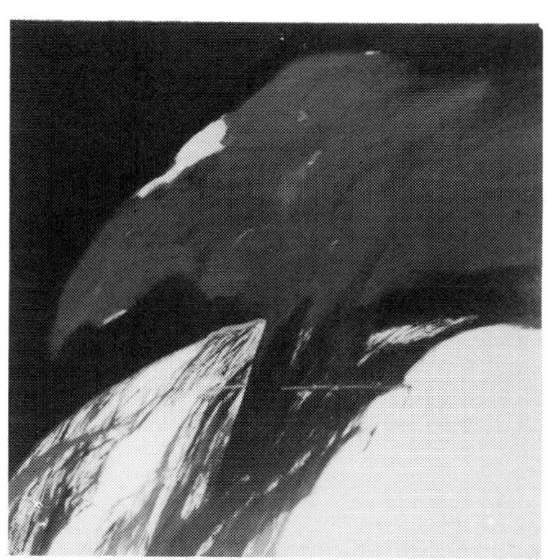

William Crozier *Islington* 1966 Oil on canvas 121·9x121·9cm (48x48in) Private Collection

Apart from acting upon the demands of necessity, I have tried to add something to my inheritance – to leave another stone on the mountain. I am deeply indebted to Masaccio and Bellini, to Giotto, Dürer, Munch, Malevich, Monet and Grünewald – to Van Gogh, Lippi, Kirchner, Mantegna and to Friedrich. Usually I refer to them by their Christian names – we are on those terms.

I have painted the landscape with or without the human figure, but never without a human presence and my world has existed between Galway and Vienna, Oslo and Malaga. Within and about that cross, all civilization exists. My work has always been the result of a direct response to observed nature and I try to imbue each work with something between Munch's 'I hear the scream of nature' and Yeats's 'monuments of unageing intellect'.

William Crozier 1979

Alan Davie 75

Alan Davie *Basket for Cats and Cabbage* 1965 Oil on canvas 122x152cm (48x60in) Artist's Collection

1920 Born in Grangemouth, Scotland
1937-40 Studied at Edinburgh College of Art
1947 Became professional jazz musician
1949-53 Worked as jeweller
1950 First one-man exhibition at Gimpel Fils Gallery (also 1951/52/54/55/56/60/61/63/65/66/67/69/70/71/73/74/75/77)
1956 One-man exhibition at Viviano Gallery, New York (also 1957)
Received Critic's Choice Award (also 1958/60) and Guggenheim Prize
1956-9 Gregory Fellow at Leeds University
1958 First retrospective exhibition at Whitechapel Art Gallery
Exhibited in Venice Biennale
1960 One-man exhibition at Galerie Charles Leinhard, Zurich
1961 One-man exhibitions at Galerie Rive Droite, Paris,
Martha Jackson, New York (also 1965)
Exhibited in Carnegie International Exhibition, Pittsburgh (also 1964)
1962 Retrospective exhibition at Stedelijk Museum, Amsterdam and travelling in Europe
1963 Exhibited in Sao Paulo Biennal (1st Prize)
1964 One-man exhibition at Gimpel Hanover Gallery, Zurich (also 1967/71/74)
1965 One-man exhibition at Galerie Rudolf Zwirner, Cologne

Alan Davie *Image of the Fish God No 1* 1956 Oil on canvas 152x122cm (60x48in) Gimpel Fils Collection

1966 One-man exhibition at Kunstring, Rotterdam (also 1967)
Exhibited in Cracow International Graphics Exhibition (prizewinner)
1967 One-man exhibitions at Galerie de France, Paris (also 1975), Arts Club of Chicago and Minnesota
1968 One-man exhibitions at Kunstverein, Dusseldorf
1969 One-man exhibition at Gimpel & Weitzenhoffer, New York (also 1972/74/75)
1970 Retrospective exhibition travelling in USA and Canada
Exhibited in 'British Painting and Sculpture 1960-70' at National Gallery of Art, Washington DC
1971 Gave first public recital of music at Gimpel Fils and Tate Gallery; Alan Davie Music Workshop first record produced

Alan Davie *Haussa Spirit No 2* 1974 Oil on canvas 173x213cm (68x84in) Private Collection, Houston, Texas

1972 Retrospective exhibition at Royal Scottish Academy
Received CBE
1973 One-man exhibition at Galleria d'Arte Rotta, Genoa
1974 Began to design tapestries
1975 One-man exhibition at Comsby Gallery, Los Angeles, Galerie de France, Paris
1976 One-man exhibitions at Galerie Farber, Brussels (also 1977), Hokin Gallery, Chicago
1977 One-man exhibition at Carone Gallery, Fort Lauderdale
Elected Honorary member of Royal Scottish Academy

Dealer Gimpel Fils Gallery, London
Gimpel & Weitzenhoffer, New York
Gimpel Hanover & André Emmerich Galleries, Zurich

For me, painting is a continuous process, which really has no beginning or ending. There never really is any point, when painting is *not*, and my work does not entail starting a new picture and finishing when it is done. In fact, in my condition of total involvement, I am simultaneously beginning new pictures, worrying about old ones, continuing with things which were begun yesterday, and making new pots of colour when necessary . . .

Alan Davie 1967

Robyn Denny 79

1930 Born in Surrey
1951-7 Studied at St Martin's School of Art and Royal College of Art
1953 Exhibited in 'Young Contemporaries'
1957-9 Taught at Hammersmith College of Art
1958 One-man exhibitions at Gallery One, Gimpel Fils
1959 Exhibited in Paris Biennale
1959-65 Taught at Bath Academy of Art
1960 Received Gulbenkian Foundation Purchase Award
1961 One-man exhibition at Molton Gallery
1961-3 Critic for *Das Kunstwerk* (Baden)
1962 One-man exhibitions at Galleria Scacchi Gracco, Milan, Galerie Muller, Stuttgart (also 1970 and in Cologne)
1963 Exhibited in Tokyo Biennale
1963-4 Critic for *Art International* (Lugano)
1964 One-man exhibition at Kasmin Gallery also 1967/69/71)
1965 One-man exhibition at Robert Elkon Gallery, New York (also 1967/71)
Exhibited in John Moores Exhibition, Liverpool (prizewinner)
1965-72 Taught at Slade School of Fine Art
1966 Exhibited in Venice Biennale ▶

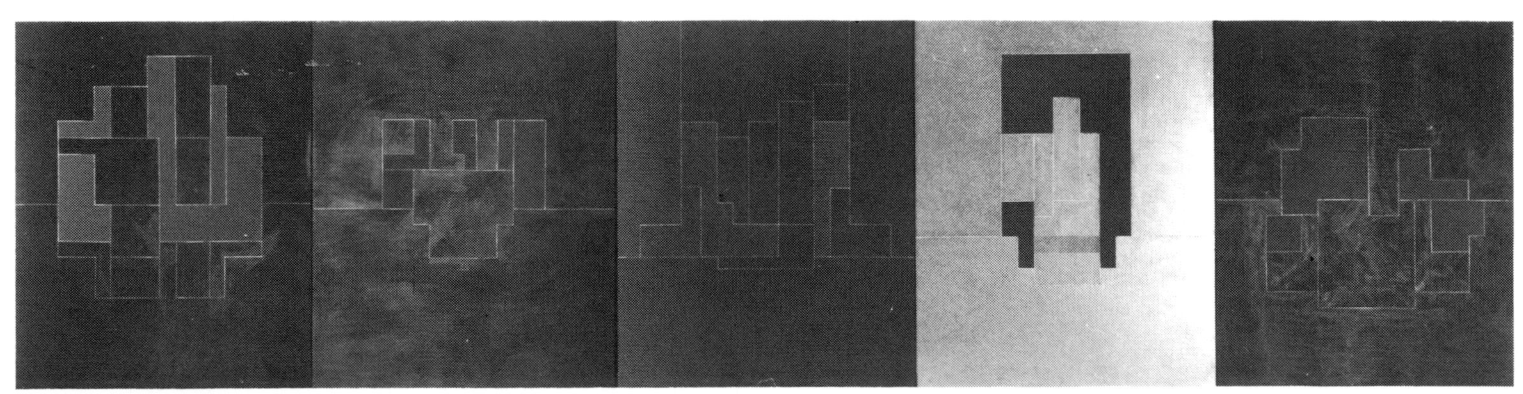

Robyn Denny *Graffiti Series 1-5* 1975-6 Oil on canvas Each panel 118x92cm (46x37in) Waddington Galleries

1967 Visiting Professor at Minneapolis School of Art
Exhibited in Carnegie International Exhibition at Pittsburgh
1968 One-man exhibitions at Renée Ziegler, Zurich,
Forum Stadtpart, Graz
Exhibited in International Print Exhibition, Ljubljana, Yugoslavia (prizewinner),
New Delhi Triennale
1969 One-man exhibition at Waddington Galleries
1970 Exhibited in 'British Painting and Sculpture 1960-70' at National Gallery of Art, Washington DC
1973 Retrospective exhibitions at Tate Gallery and in Stuttgart and Leverkusen
One-man exhibition at Studio La Citta, Verona
Exhibited in 'La peinture anglaise d'aujourd'hui' at Musée d'Art Moderne, Paris

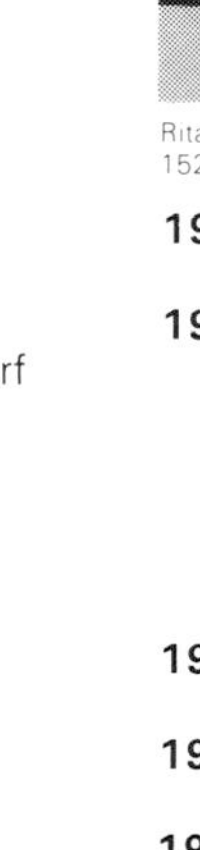

1974 One-man exhibitions in Rome, Venice, Turin, Hamburg, Dusseldorf and Paris
1975 One-man exhibition at Galleria La Polena, Genoa
Exhibited in 'Peintres anglais contemporains' at Musée de Grenoble
1976 One-man exhibition at Galleria Morone, Milan
Exhibited in 'Arte inglese oggi' at Palazzo Reale, Milan
1977 One-man exhibition at Waddington & Tooth Galleries
Exhibited in 'Hayward Annual' at Hayward Gallery
1978 One-man exhibition at Festival Gallery, Bath

Dealer Waddington Galleries
Bernard Jacobson, New York

Rita Donagh 111

1939 Born in Wednesbury, Staffordshire
1956-62 Studied Fine Art at Durham University
1964-72 Taught at School of Fine Art, Reading University
1972 Exhibited in John Moores Exhibition, Liverpool
Individual exhibition at Nigel Greenwood Inc
1973 Exhibited in 'Drawing' at Museum of Modern Art, Oxford,
'11 English Artists' in Baden Baden and Bremen
1973- Teaching part-time at Slade School of Fine Art

Rita Donagh *Bystander* 1977 Oil, pencil and collage on canvas 152.5x152.5cm (60x60in) Artist's Collection

1974 Exhibited in 'British Painting '74' at Hayward Gallery
1975 Display in collaboration with The Gallery
Exhibited in 7th International Festival of Painting at Cagnes-sur-Mer,
Sao Paulo Bienal,
'Body and Soul' Peter Moores Project 3, Liverpool
1976 Exhibited in 'Arte inglese oggi' at Palazzo Reale, Milan
1976-8 Taught part-time at Goldsmiths College
1977 Retrospective exhibition at Whitworth Art Gallery, Manchester and travelling
1978 Individual exhibition 'Working drawings and Studies for Ulster Subject' at Nigel Greenwood Inc
Exhibited in 'Hayward Annual' at Hayward Annual
1979 Exhibited in Sydney Biennale,
'British Drawings since 1945' at Whitworth Art Gallery, Manchester

Dealer Nigel Greenwood Inc

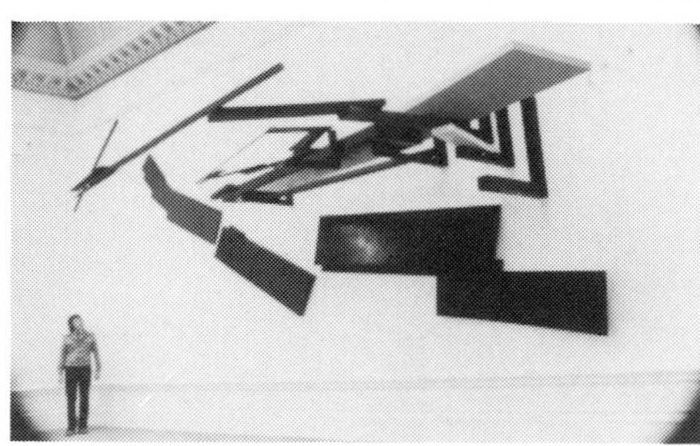

Ken Draper *'Sounds' Overhang V* 1971-2 Wood and steel 366x853x487cm (12x28x16ft) Artist's Collection

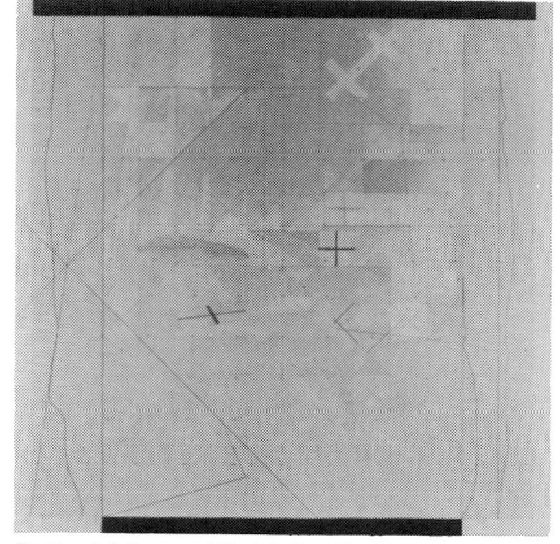

Rita Donagh *Reflection on 3 Weeks in May 1970* 1970-1 Oil and pencil on canvas 152.4x152.4cm (60x60in) Tate Gallery

Ken Draper 134

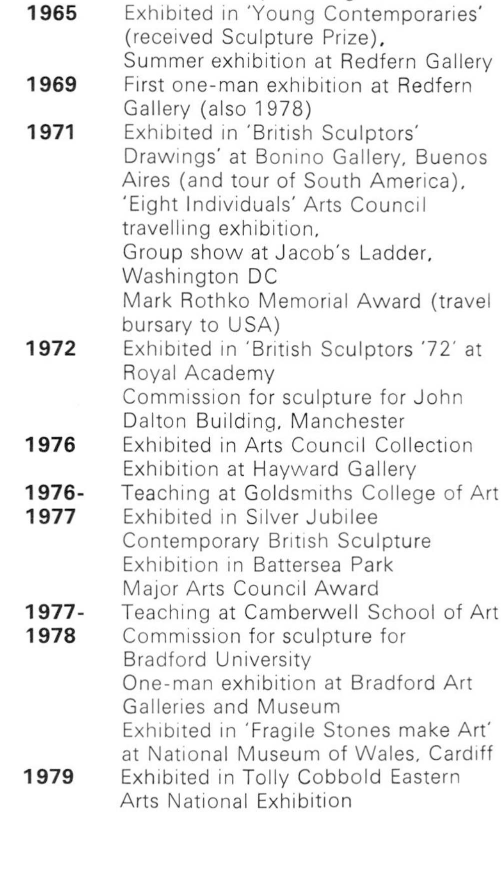

1944 Born in Sheffield
1959-62 Studied at Chesterfield College of Art
1962-5 Studied at Kingston School of Art
1965-8 Studied at Royal College of Art
1965 Exhibited in 'Young Contemporaries' (received Sculpture Prize),
Summer exhibition at Redfern Gallery
1969 First one-man exhibition at Redfern Gallery (also 1978)
1971 Exhibited in 'British Sculptors' Drawings' at Bonino Gallery, Buenos Aires (and tour of South America),
'Eight Individuals' Arts Council travelling exhibition,
Group show at Jacob's Ladder, Washington DC
Mark Rothko Memorial Award (travel bursary to USA)
1972 Exhibited in 'British Sculptors '72' at Royal Academy
Commission for sculpture for John Dalton Building, Manchester
1976 Exhibited in Arts Council Collection Exhibition at Hayward Gallery
1976- Teaching at Goldsmiths College of Art
1977 Exhibited in Silver Jubilee Contemporary British Sculpture Exhibition in Battersea Park
Major Arts Council Award
1977- Teaching at Camberwell School of Art
1978 Commission for sculpture for Bradford University
One-man exhibition at Bradford Art Galleries and Museum
Exhibited in 'Fragile Stones make Art' at National Museum of Wales, Cardiff
1979 Exhibited in Tolly Cobbold Eastern Arts National Exhibition

Ken Draper *Reflections on a Transient Meeting Place* 1977-78 Wood, steel and coloured resins 61x50·8x45·7cm (24x20x18in) Leicestershire Education Authorities

Contact Hall Farm, East Bilney, Dereham, Norfolk

Ken Draper has now reassimilated the large cantilevered wood/steel/aluminium structure of such works as *Overhang V 'Sounds'* into smaller more concentrated ceramic-like pieces that glow with intense idiosyncratic colour. Formalism has given way to a more personalized language that incorporates the gravity-defying lightness of the earlier work and a new quasi-metaphorical language that alludes to what he saw and experienced whilst travelling in India and Pakistan some years ago.

Sternly constructional elements have been transposed into a surreality where inexplicable shapes float or hover over apocalyptic landscapes, whose ruins have crosses, dashes and encrustations of colour organically growing from their main supports. The components function in an ambiguous area between formal and non-formal reading. Hence, the overall cross structure in *Reflections on a Transient Meeting Place* is a depiction of how the centre is not there but is suggested by the elements that lead internally, such as the inverted ziggurat shape. Conversely, this piece is also a visual suggestion of exactly what the title describes, at any moment the elements could slide into an as yet unrecognizable shape.

Draper is developing his *métier* into a sculptural language outside the parameters of formal categorization, yet continuing the dialogue of abstract-illusionism by illustrating his real concern for the outcome of the post-60s. In drawings he now uses the flatness that mark-making on paper allows to rediscover his prime concerns for shape and, above all, colour in sculpture.

Peter Rippon 1979

Bernard Dunstan RA 36

1920 Born in Teddington
1939 Studied at Byam Shaw School of Art
1939-41 Studied at Slade School of Art
1946 Elected member of New English Art Club
1946-9 Taught at West of England School of Art, Bristol
1949 Elected member of Royal West of England Academy (1979 President)
1950-64 Taught at Camberwell School of Art
1952-72 One-man exhibitions biennially at Roland Browse & Delbanco
1953-74 Taught at Byam Shaw School of Art
1959 Elected Associate of Royal Academy
1959-64 Taught at Ravensbourne Art College
1964-9 Taught at City and Guilds London Art School
1968 Elected Royal Academician
1970 Published *Learning to Paint* (Watson-Guptill, New York)
1973 One-man exhibition at Thomas Agnew & Sons (also 1975/79)
1975 Exhibited in 'British Painting 1900-75' at Thomas Agnew & Sons
1976 Published *Pictures in Progress* (Pitman) and *Painting Methods of the Impressionists* (Watson-Guptill, New York)
1977 Exhibited in 'British Painting 1952-1977' at Royal Academy

Dealer Thomas Agnew & Sons
Stremmel Galleries, Reno, Nevada

Bernard Dunstan *The Rehearsal* 1976 Oil 30.5x22.9cm (12x9in) Michael Laurie Collection

The greater part of my work is in oil paint and on a small scale, with the occasional large figure painting and excursions into other mediums such as pastel, distemper, etching and lithography. It is mostly to do with figures in interiors: nudes particularly, but also musical subjects, scenes in galleries and so on; a few portraits; also townscapes, mostly Italian, and the odd landscape.

I have always loved the French-English tradition of the 19th/20th century (pre-Cubist), was brought up in it (at the Slade and so on) and have never felt a need to do anything different. The combination of everyday charm and solid painting – finding the pattern and the colour by observation – seems to me inexhaustible. I work from drawings a lot. I suppose obvious influences are Degas, Bonnard, Sickert, Vuillard, but there are countless others in the museums.

Bernard Dunstan 1979

Bernard Dunstan *The Shuttered Room* 1975 Oil 27.9x27.9cm (11x11in) Michael Goldhill Collection

Jennifer Durrant 157

1942 Born in Brighton
1959-63 Studied at Brighton College of Art
1963-6 Studied at Slade School of Fine Art
1964 Received Abbey Minor Scholarship
1966 Exhibited in 'Young Contemporaries' (prizewinner)
1967 Exhibited in group show at Kasmin Gallery
1969 Exhibited in Arts Council Collection 1967/68 travelling exhibition
1970 Exhibited in John Moores Exhibition, Liverpool
1974 One-man exhibition at Serpentine Gallery
1974- Teaching at St Martin's School of Art ▶

Jennifer Durrant *Other Cloud Painting* 1978 Acrylic on cotton duck 314x243x228cm (10x8x7½ft) Artist's Collection

1975 One-man exhibition at University of Surrey
1976 Exhibited in 'Previous Exhibitors' at Serpentine Gallery, Arts Council Collection 1975/76 Exhibition at Hayward Gallery Received Arts Council Award
1977 Exhibited in 'Recent Acquisitions' at Museum of Fine Arts, Boston, 'British Painting 1952-1977' at Royal Academy
1978 Exhibited in 'Certain Traditions: British and Canadian Art' at Edmonton Art Gallery and travelling Received Arts Council Major Award
1979 One-man exhibition at Arnolfini Gallery, Bristol Exhibited in 'Hayward Annual' at Hayward Gallery
1979- Visiting Lecturer at Royal College of Art

Contact Stockwell Depot, Combermere Road, London SW9

I paint my pictures with the canvas stretched flat on the floor, viewing them from the top of my steps. I see the painting frontally, only when it feels whole or if I cannot choose what to do. I suppose I enjoy the surprise I get when the picture 'goes up', (as I have not changed this procedure for several years) – and I then feel either relieved or disappointed. I often experience difficulty in making choices within the painting. What the painting needs as opposed to what I want to put in the painting – be it a particular image/shape or colour, pitch/weight or texture. I work on several canvases at a time, intermittently, and I view them as a group although I feel each painting is separate and complete in itself. The sensation of 'place' in painting is very important to me. How close up and how far away you place yourself. How much you are enveloped, or brought in, or feel up against the painted surface. I rarely have a friend or visitor to the studio, I dislike the feeling of intrusion, and like to be alone in my space. I am aware of ways in which I use my experience of the visible world as starting-points for my painting. A starting-point can be my wish to create a visual equivalent for a particular experience in purely painterly terms within a tradition of painting – and in so doing, discover (for) myself. I believe the asking of visual questions *is* the practice of painting and both making pictures and looking at them takes much time and love.

Jennifer Durrant 1979

David Dye 177

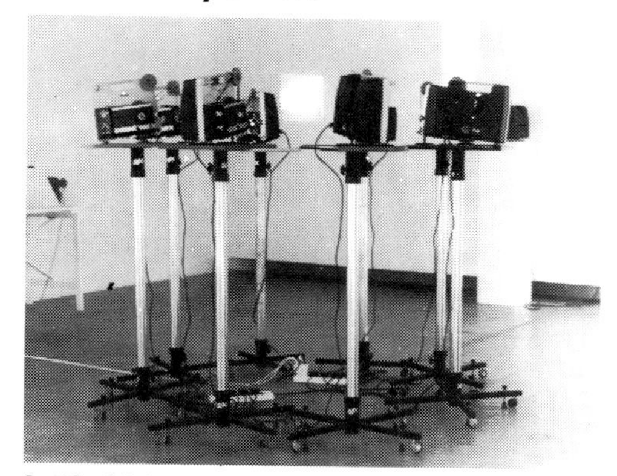

David Dye *8 Projector Piece* 1972 Installation in 'The New Art' at Hayward Gallery

1945 Born in Isle of Wight
1967-71 Studied sculpture at St Martin's School of Art
1970 Exhibited in 'Young Contemporaries'
1971 Exhibited in 'English avant-garde' at New York Cultural Centre, 'Art Systems' at Museum of Modern Art, Buenos Aires
1972 First one-man exhibition at Institute of Contemporary Arts Exhibited in 'The New Art' at Hayward Gallery
1972-6 Taught at Brighton Polytechnic
1973 Exhibited in 'Critic's Choice' at Arthur Tooth & Sons, 'Beyond Painting and Sculpture' Arts Council travelling exhibition
1974 Exhibited in 'Project 74' in Cologne, Independent Film Festival at Institute of Contemporary Arts
1975 One-man exhibition at Lisson Gallery Exhibited in Paris Biennale

David Dye *Mirror Film* 1971 Super 8 colour film, 5 minutes Arts Council Collection

1976 One-man exhibition at Robert Self Gallery, London and Newcastle Exhibited in 'Arte inglese oggi' at Palazzo Reale, Milan
1977 Exhibited in 'Time, Words and the Camera' in Graz and travelling in Austria and Germany, Festival of Avant-garde Film-making at Hayward Gallery Installation at Arnolfini Gallery, Bristol
1978 Received Eastern Arts Grant
1978/9 Exhibited in 'Scale for Sculpture' at Serpentine Gallery and travelling
1979- Teaching part-time at Newcastle Polytechnic

Contact 3A Market Hill, Saffron Walden, Essex

In reply to the question 'What is your work about?' I am tempted to say 'Nothing in particular'. Shorthand explanations of what is supposed to be behind the surface of a work of art lie in the realm of metaphor. I favour a more materialistic viewpoint, I seek to demystify, this, does not stand for that. To me a work is a production, not expression, or a reflection.

That is not to say that I don't have intentions, and also wish to elicit certain responses. But experience has taught me that what an artist has to say about his work, and what the work is, may be worlds apart. However, a list of some of my greatest influences may throw some light on the matter: Roland Barthes, Samuel Beckett, David Bowie, Jorge Luis Borges, Lewis Carrol, Marcel Duchamp, Jean-Luc Godard, Jacques Lacan, RD Laing, Marcel Proust, Jacques Rivette, Velasquez.

To be more specific my work is a form of hybrid; I studied sculpture, yet now I use film. Sculpture and film-making make uneasy bedfellows, but create an ambiguous play between 'real' and 'unreal'. I consider my best work to be installations done for specific gallery spaces. Elements I have used constantly are: mirrors, film-loops, two-way mirrors, tape cassettes and film projectors. Graft onto these material elements my ideas concerning my experiences of going to the cinema, my ideas about mirrors, identification, identity, voyeurism, means of production, and ideology, and you have a broad outline of a complex way of working.

David Dye 1979

John Edwards 158

1938 Born in London
1953-6 Studied at Hornsey College of Art (also 1958-60)
1961 Taught at Brighton College of Art
1962-3 Studied at Leeds University Institute
1963-4 British Council Scholarship to Belgium
1964- Teaching at St Martin's School of Art, Chelsea School of Art and Brighton School of Art
1967 First one-man exhibition at Rowan Gallery (also 1968/70/71/72/73/75/77/79)
1968 Exhibited in 'Britische Kunst Heute' at Kunstverein, Hamburg, Summer Exhibition at Museum of Modern Art, Oxford
1969 Exhibited in 'Contemporary Paintings', Sebastian de Ferranti Collection, at Whitworth Art Gallery, Manchester
1972 Exhibited in John Moores Exhibition, Liverpool (also 1974)
1973 One-man exhibition at Park Square Gallery, Leeds Appointed Senior Lecturer in Painting, St Martin's School of Art
1975 Lectured at Tyler School of Art, Philadelphia and Skidmore College of Art, Saratoga Springs, New York
1976 Exhibited in 'Contemporary British Art' at Cleveland Institute of Art Appointed Artist in Residence, University of Syracuse, New York
1977 Exhibited in 'British Painting 1952-1977' at Royal Academy
1977-8 Advisor to Visual Arts Advisory Panel, Greater London Arts Association
1977-9 Exhibited in Middlesbrough Biennale
1979 One-man exhibition travelling to Newcastle-upon-Tyne, Cambridge, Sheffield, Brighton and London Exhibited in 'British Art Now' at Guggenheim Museum, New York and travelling

Dealer Rowan Gallery

John Edwards *Green Shimmer* 1976 Acrylic on canvas 152·4x228cm (60x90in) Rowan Gallery

I want my paintings to be something nobody has ever seen before, not in other painting, nor derived from phenomena in the world. Maybe this is an impossible ambition, but it's a useful means of ridding myself of habits, nostalgia, academic decorum and distracting anecdotes. The truly new is always unfamiliar. I try to surprise myself.

I want my paintings to be direct, immediate, accessible. They're spontaneous in the way they're painted – I like to keep the handling frank, the colour fresh, the syntax flexible and the forms open. They are large, not because they conform to any fashion for large pictures, nor through a desire for monumentality, but because I want them to be intimate, to relate directly to the full span of the spectator's visual field. I want them to be as involving sensually, physically, imaginatively, for the viewers as they are for me.

My experience of the great art of the past has taught me that its greatness lies in the quality of attention it can attract and sustain. The 'look', the technique, the subject matter, even the medium are of secondary relevance compared with the art's capacity to engage a viewer. The end is what counts. The means are only the means.

'Finding myself' as an artist really entailed finding a pictorial space I could call my own, one that was broad and flexible enough to accommodate the possibilities of conflict and allow for the likelihood of unexpected events occurring in the process of painting. The space is a kind of constraint, but malleable and elastic enough to accommodate sensibility and yield to change. I can feel free within it.

The paint is primary. Expression and thought evolve out of it rather than being consciously imposed. I attempt to work without any preconceived idea of what the paint is going to do, what the picture will look like and ultimately express. I stop painting when I recognize an effect that is expressive, characterful. In a way, painting for me is a sublimation of self to the medium and its potentials.

John Edwards 1979

John Edwards *Eclipse* 1978 Acrylic on canvas 167.6x254cm (66x100in) Rowan Gallery

Richard Eurich RA 24

1903 Born in Bradford
1920-4 Studied at Bradford School of Arts and Crafts
1924-6 Studied at Slade School of Fine Art
1929 One-man exhibition (drawings) at Goupil Gallery
1932-60 Sixteen one-man exhibitions at Redfern Gallery
1939 Elected member of New English Art Club
1941 Elected Associate of Royal Academy
1941-6 War Artist to Admiralty
1949-68 Part-time teaching at Camberwell School of Art
1951 Retrospective exhibition at Bradford City Art Gallery
1952 Elected Royal Academician

▶

Richard Eurich *Gay Lane* 1952 Oil 76·2x63·5cm (30x25in) Private Collection

Richard Eurich *Reservoir, Yorkshire* 1974 Oil 40.6x61cm (16x24in) Private Collection

1968 One-man exhibition at Arthur Tooth & Sons (also 1971/74)
1969-71 Taught at Royal Academy Schools
1970 Elected honorary member of New English Art Club
1974 Elected member of Society of Marine Artists
1976 One-man exhibition at Ash Barn, Petersfield
1977 One-man exhibition at Fine Art Society

Dealer Fine Art Society

My painting is mainly in the oil medium, but drawings have been exhibited. I work from drawings, sometimes very slight but evocative. These are my very private property and are only understood by myself. I consider my painting to be self-taught, studying only drawing at the schools of art.

From the age of five or six the sea has always dominated my work. Why? I really do not know! Turner has always been my hero, even when I found he was under a shadow when I came to London in 1925.

My figure work is usually based on childhood memories of the northern scene, though of late, living near the Solent, figures on beaches have given me much to think about as compositions.

Richard Eurich 1979

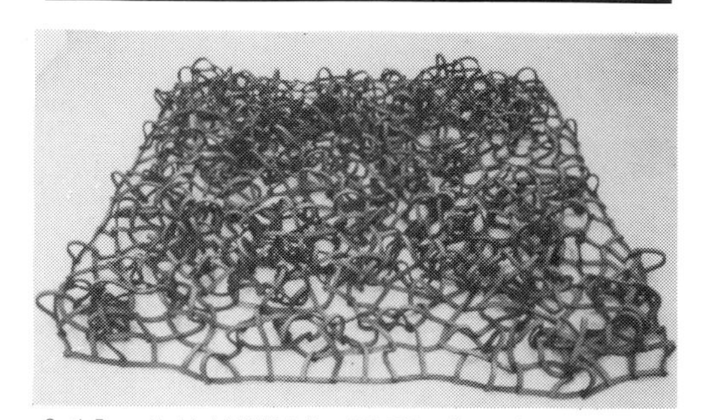

Garth Evans *Untitled 4* 1975 Rubber 305x305cm (10x10ft) Artist's Collection

Garth Evans 124

1934 Born in Cheshire
1955-60 Studied at Manchester and Slade School of Fine Art
1960 Exhibited in John Moores Exhibition, Liverpool (also 1965)
1962 First one-man exhibition at Rowan Gallery, London (also 1964/66/68/69/72/74/76/78)
1964 Gulbenkian Purchase Award
1966 Arts Council Sabbatical Award
1966- Visiting Lecturer at St Martin's School of Art
1967 Exhibited in 'Reliefs, Collages and Gouaches' Victoria and Albert Museum travelling exhibition, 'British Drawing, the New Generation' at Museum of Modern Art, New York
1968 Exhibited in 'New British Sculpture', Bristol
1969 British Steel Corporation Fellowship Exhibited drawings at Museum of Modern Art, New York Exhibited in Middelheim Biennale
1970- Visiting Lecturer at Slade School of Art
1971 One-man exhibitions at Faculty of Art and Design Gallery, Leeds Polytechnic, Ferens Art Gallery, Hull, and School of Art and Design Gallery, Sheffield

Garth Evans *Painting* 1977-8 Wood, plywood and PVA 233x127x30.5cm (7ft 8inx4ft2$\frac{1}{4}$inx1ft) Artist's Collection

1972 Exhibited in 'British Sculpture '72' at Royal Academy, London, Peter Stuyvesant City Sculpture Project, Cardiff
1973 Visiting Professor at Minneapolis College of Art and Design
1975 Exhibited in 'The Condition of Sculpture' at Hayward Gallery
1977 Exhibited in Silver Jubilee Contemporary British Sculpture Exhibition in Battersea Park
1978 Exhibited in 'The Square and the Circle' at House Gallery, 'Scale for Sculpture' at Serpentine Gallery and travelling

Dealer Rowan Gallery

Anthony Eyton ARA 70

1923 Born in London
1947-50 Studied at Camberwell School of Art
1951-2 Received Abbey Major Scholarship to work in Italy
1955 First one-man exhibition at St George's Gallery
1957 One-man exhibition at Galerie de Scène
1957- Teaching at Camberwell School of Art
1959 One-man exhibition at New Art Centre (also 1961/68)
1965- Teaching at Royal Academy Schools
1966 Exhibited in 'Survey '66' at Hampstead Art Centre

Anthony Eyton *Urbino* 1974 Oil 118.1x94cm (46$\frac{1}{2}$x37) Chantry Bequest

1967 Exhibited in 'Figurative Painters' at Hampstead Art Centre
1969 Head of Painting Department at St Lawrence College, Kingston, Ontario
1972 Exhibited in John Moores Exhibition, Liverpool (prizewinner)
1973 One-man exhibition at New Grafton Gallery
1974 Awarded Grocers Company Fellowship to work in Italy for six months
1975 One-man exhibition at Darby Gallery
Exhibited in 2nd British International Drawing Biennale (1st Prize)
'Drawings of People' at Serpentine Gallery
1976 Elected Associate of Royal Academy
1977 Exhibited in 'British Painting 1952-1977' at Royal Academy
1978 One-man exhibition at Browse & Darby

Dealer Browse & Darby

I started painting landscapes when I was fifteen which gave me a bias towards painting directly from nature. This interest was further emphasized by the teaching just after the war at Camberwell School of Art, where William Coldstream, Victor Pasmore and Claude Rogers were amongst the staff. Then followed two years of painting in Italy where I was greatly influenced by Piero della Francesca. I have always found the light and atmosphere abroad particularly stimulating – Italy, Greece, and recently India, have been places where I could absorb myself in my work completely. My main concern is with light, both for its own sake and also for the way in which it reveals objects. Perhaps the work of Turner and the Impressionists has helped me to form a spontaneous way of dealing with it. I am however also interested in the authenticity and order of the picture.

Painting from drawings, photographs and from memory, as opposed to nature, is my other interest. The subject could be people on beaches or in the streets, but the emphasis is on the figures in space and in their environment. The combining of different sources in one work interests me a lot, but with the memory of a certain place and time in mind.

I try to get that careful balance between abstraction and the purely factual through the process of working, and I strongly believe that art comes out of a regard for nature.

Anthony Eyton 1979

Sheila Fell RA 67

1931 Born in Cumbria
1947-9 Studied at Carlisle School of Art
1949-51 Studied at St Martin's School of Art
1955 One-man exhibition at Beaux Arts Gallery (also 1958/60/62/64)
1957 Exhibited in John Moores Exhibition, Liverpool (prizewinner)
1958 Received Boise Travelling Scholarship to France, Italy and Greece
1958- Teaching at Chelsea School of Art
1961 One-man exhibition at Derwent Centre, Cumbria
1962 One-man exhibition at Middlesbrough Art Gallery
1965 One-man exhibitions at Abbot Hall Gallery, Kendal,
Queen Square Gallery, Leeds
1967 One-man exhibition at Stone Gallery, Newcastle-upon-Tyne (also 1969)
Received Arts Council Purchase Award
1970 Received Austin Abbey Award for research into mural painting
1974 One-man exhibition at Ashgate Gallery, Farnham
Elected Royal Academician
1976 Received Arts Council Award
1977 Exhibited in 'British Painting 1952-77' at Royal Academy

Contact Royal Academy

I do not think my work falls into very strongly marked phases but the paintings have tended to become lighter in key and perhaps more fluid. My main concern is landscape (although I have painted several portraits) and I have mostly drawn and painted in Cumbria, Yorkshire and Wales. The chief influence has therefore been that of the country and the different activities which take place on the land, the presence of the mountains, moors, sea, and the effect of the changing light in relation to the earth.

Sheila Fell 1979

Anthony Eyton *Beach* 1976 Triptych in Oil 366x182.9cm (12ftx6ft) Arts Council

Sheila Fell *Potato Harvest, Cumbria* 1977 Oil 91.4x71.1cm (36x28in) Private Collection

Sheila Fell *Cottage on the Yorkshire Moors* 1975-6 Oil 50.8x61cm (20x24in) Private Collection

Brian Fielding 159

1933 Born in Sheffield
1950-4 Studied at Sheffield College of Art
1954-7 Studied at Royal College of Art
1958 Received Abbey Minor Travelling Scholarship
1960 Exhibited in group show at AIA Gallery (also 1963)
1962 One-man exhibition at Rowan Gallery (also 1964)
1962- Teaching at Ravensbourne College of Art and Design
1966 Exhibited in group show at Galerie Heide Hildebrand, Klagenfurt
1967 Exhibited in 'Survey of Abstract Painters' at Camden Arts Centre
1969 One-man exhibition at Sheffield University
1974 One-man exhibition at Consort Gallery
1975 One-man exhibition at Hoya Gallery
1977 One-man exhibition at Newcastle-upon-Tyne Polytechnic

Contact 22 Longstone Road, London SW17 ▶

Over a number of years Brian Fielding has constructed his paintings by carefully preparing variously coloured grounds on which to implant a quickly executed and incorrigible gestural mark. The prepared ground and gestural mark are not symbols of preparation leading up to action; they are instances of it.

What makes a Fielding painting a work of art is not that it is merely an instance of preparation and action, but that it exposes the relationship between the two. What makes it a painting rather than an illustration is that it

Brian Fielding *Oyster* 1962 Emulsion paint on canvas 127x76·2cm (50x30in) Artist's Collection

achieves this exposure by the inherent characteristics of the marks, not by using the marks as symbolic references to events taking place inside the artist's head.

The final painting is not merely a finished product but is evidence of the process of making – it would be inconceivable that the gestural mark was made first and the ground was filled in later. Further, the preparation for the gestural act is made clear on the picture surface and does not reside in the context of making the picture. Thirdly, the gestural act is determined by his apprehension of the painted marks already made. It is not the result of a causal process in which the act of preparing the ground induces a state of mind which forces him to make the mark. Neither is it governed by the inevitable logic of conclusion following from a series of premises. The gestural mark is in the nature of a committed and deliberate response to what has already been placed on the canvas.

Philip Hughes 1979

Brian Fielding *Drift* 1977 Dry colour on canvas 203·2x175cm (80x69in) Artist's Collection

Ian Hamilton Finlay 35

1925 Born in Nassau
1963 Wrote first concrete poems
1966 Received Scottish Arts Council Bursary (also 1967/68)
1967 Began to create Stonypath Garden at Dunsyre
First worked with graphic images
1968 One-man exhibition at Axiom Gallery
Received Atlantic-Richfield Award
1971 One-man exhibition at Winchester College of Art
Published *Poems to Hear and See* (Macmillan)

Ian Hamilton Finlay (with John Andrew) *The Last Cruise of the Emden* 1976 Stone with planting, Stonypath, Dunsyre, Scotland

1972 One-man exhibition at Scottish National Gallery of Modern Art
Published *Honey by the Water* (Black Sparrow Press, Los Angeles)
1974 One-man exhibition at National Maritime Museum
Founded Society for the Protection of the Arts against the Arts Council
1975 Environmental works commissioned for Max Planck Institute, Stuttgart
1976 One-man exhibitions at Graeme Murray Gallery, Edinburgh, Southampton Art Gallery
1977 One-man exhibitions at Kettle's Yard, Cambridge, Serpentine Gallery
Published *Selected Ponds* (West Coast Poetry Review, USA)
1978 One-man exhibition at Scottish Arts Council Gallery (withdrawn at moment of opening)
Co-founded Free Arts Society
Published *Heroic Emblems* (Z Press, Vermont)
1979 Commission for sundial and approach to British Embassy, Bonn

Dealer Ivy Sky Rutzky, New York

Contact Little Sparta, Stonypath, Dunsyre, Scotland

Ian Hamilton Finlay *Unda (Wave)* 1974 Cast concrete and stainless steel Max Planck Institute, Stuttgart

The subject of my work is culture, without any undemocratic distinction between past and present. I consider myself to be a poet rather than an 'artist' in the accepted narrow sense. I collaborate, as a poet, with artists and craftsmen, and have worked (with others) in glass, stone, in neon, on paper, card, metal . . . With Sue Finlay I have built a garden which exemplifies what my writings propose, a *truly* environmental art and that conception of the *noble* which Nietzsche associated with gardens.

As one who was described as 'the father of British concrete poetry' (oh dear) I state, categorically, that concrete poetry has not yet been understood – least of all by concrete poets.

Initially, I pursued the ironic disguised as the domestic. I was obliged to abandon these modes when the ironic was submerged in the satire-mire. I would now WISH to actualize the Epic. Any fool can see that the Epic is limited but Being (life) itself is a limitation of Anaximander's infinite.

Empedokles (the vegetarian) resolved the problem by sacrificing the equivalent of a nut cutlet (made from barley and honey, in the shape of a bull).

The motto of the TRUE poet is:
What is, is; what isn't, is not.

Ian Hamilton Finlay 1979

James Fitton RA 21

James Fitton *The Fire Bird* 1966 Oil 147.3x63.5cm (46x25in) Artist's Collection

1899 Born in Oldham
Studied at Central School of Art and Design
1932-52 Member of London Group
1933 First one-man exhibition at Arthur Tooth & Sons
1939 Exhibited in 'British Art since Whistler' at National Gallery
Published *The First Six Months are the Worst* (Peter Davies)
1940-65 Chief Assessor to Ministry of Education National Diploma of Design
1944 Elected Associate of Royal Academy
1954 Elected Royal Academician
1964 Exhibited in London Group Jubilee Exhibition at Tate Gallery
1968-75 Trustee of British Museum
1970- Honorary Surveyor of Dulwich College Picture Gallery
1977 Exhibited in 'British Painting 1952-1977' at Royal Academy

Contact Royal Academy

Barry Flanagan 167

1941 Born in Prestatyn
1964-6 Studied at St Martin's School of Art
1965 Received Institute of Contemporary Arts Dover Street Materials Award
1966 First one-man exhibition at Rowan Gallery (also 1968/70/71/72/73/74)
Exhibited in 'Young Contemporaries'
1967 Exhibited in Paris Biennale (also 1975/77/78),
Tokyo Biennale (also 1970)
1968 One-man exhibition at Galleria dell'Arieta, Milan
Exhibited in 'Young British Artists' at Museum of Modern Art, New York
1969 One-man exhibition at Museum Hans Lange, Krefeld,
Fishbach Gallery, New York
Exhibited in 'Nine Young Artists' at Guggenheim Museum (Theodoran Foundation), New York,
'Six Artists' at Hayward Gallery,
'Rope and String' at Sidney Janis Gallery, New York,
John Moores Exhibition, Liverpool
1970 Exhibited in 'British Sculpture out of the 60s' at Institute of Contemporary Arts,
'Contemporary British Art' at Museum of Modern Art, Tokyo

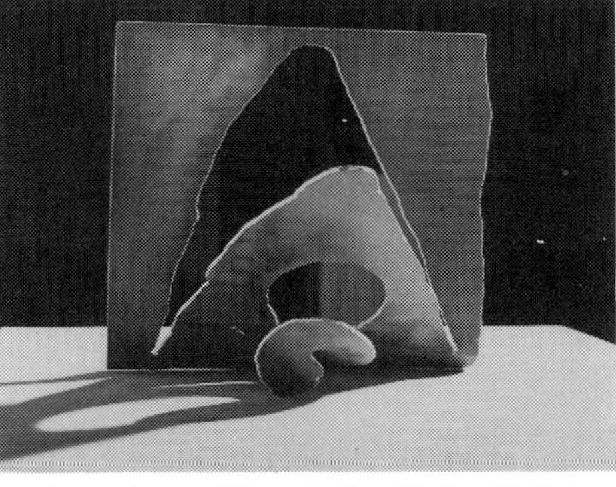

Barry Flanagan *As Night* 1978 Painted mild steel 25x25cm (10x10in) Waddington Galleries

1971 One-man exhibition at Galleria del Leone, Venice
Exhibited in 'British Avant-Garde' at New York Cultural Centre
1972 Received Gulbenkian Award for Dance
Exhibited in 'The New Art' at Hayward Gallery
1973 Exhibited in 'Henry Moore to Gilbert & George' at Palais des Beaux Arts, Brussels
1974 One-man exhibition at Museum of Modern Art, New York,
Museum of Modern Art, Oxford
Exhibited in 'Within the Decade' at Guggenheim Museum, New York
1975 One-man exhibition at Hogarth Galleries, Sydney,
Art & Project, Amsterdam (also 1977)
Received Arts Council Award (to work with a kiln)

▶

Barry Flanagan *Oh Mind How You Cross* 1976 Rope and Hornton stone 100x700x400cm (39⅜x273x157in) Art & Project, Amsterdam

1976 One-man exhibition at Hester van Royen Gallery
Exhibited in 'Arte inglese oggi' at Palazzo Reale, Milan
1977 One-man exhibitions at Van Abbemuseum, Eindhoven, Appeldorn Museum, Holland, Arnolfini Gallery, Bristol
Exhibited in Hayward Annual at Hayward Gallery, Silver Jubilee Contemporary British Sculpture Exhibition in Battersea Park
1978 One-man exhibition at Serpentine Gallery

Dealer Art & Project, Amsterdam
Waddington Galleries

My practice in sculpture is now twenty-one years old and I can safely say that it has been an application of the science of imaginary solutions.

Barry Flanagan 1979

Noel Forster 94

Noel Forster *Untitled* 1978 Acrylic on linen 142·2x121·9cm (54x48in) Artist's Collection

1932 Born in Seaton Delaval, Northumberland
1950-3 Studied at University of Newcastle-upon-Tyne
1955-7 Studied at University of Newcastle-upon-Tyne
1962-9 One-man exhibitions at Ikon Gallery, Birmingham, University of Sussex
Exhibited in group show at Kasmin Gallery, 'Big Pictures' at Royal Academy
1968 Exhibited in John Moores Exhibition, Liverpool
1970-1 Visiting Professor in Painting at Minneapolis College of Art and Design
1971 One-man exhibition at Camden Arts Centre
1971- Teaching part-time at Slade School of Fine Art
1972 Received 3rd Prize in John Moores Exhibition, Liverpool
1973 Exhibited in '7 aus London' at Kunsthalle, Bern, 'Three Painters' at Hayward Gallery
1974 Exhibited in 'British Painting '74' at Hayward Gallery
1975-6 Arts Council Major Bursary
Artist-in-Residence at Balliol College, Oxford, where elected to Supernumerary Fellowship
One-man exhibition at Kunsthalle, Basle, Museum of Modern Art, Oxford
Exhibited in Rijeka (Yugoslavia) Drawings Biennale
1976-8 Received Gulbenkian Award
1977 Exhibited in 'British Painting 1952-1977' at Royal Academy
1978 Exhibited in Summer Exhibition at Royal Academy
Received 1st Prize in John Moores Exhibition, Liverpool
1979 Artist-in-Residence at Musée Ste Croix, Les Sables d'Olonne for three months

Contact BCM3, London WC1

Noel Forster *Fast and Slow Marks* 1978 Acrylic on silk, linen and paper 182·9x182·9cm (6x6ft) Artist's Collection

Peter de Francia 22

1921 Born at Beaulieu, France
1938-40 Studied at Academy of Brussels
Studied at Slade School of Fine Art
1949-50 Worked in Canada
1951 Worked at American Museum in New York

Peter de Francia *Carnet d'un Retour au Pays Natal* (by Aimé Césaire) 1977 Charcoal on paper 62·2x48·3cm (24½x19in) Museum of Modern Art, New York

1951-3 Worked in BBC Television, producing and planning art programmes
1954-61 Taught at Morley College and St Martin's School of Art
1958 One-man exhibition at Colonna Gallery, Milan
1959 One-man exhibition at Waddington Galleries
1961 One-man exhibition at Galerie d'Eendt, Amsterdam
1961-9 Taught at Royal College of Art in General Studies department
1962 One-man exhibition at Forum Gallery, New York
1964 Exhibited in Carnegie International Exhibition, Pittsburgh
1969 Published *Fernand Leger – the Great Parade* (Cassell)
1970-2 Principal of Fine Art Department at Goldsmiths College
1972- Professor of Painting at Royal College of Art
1976 One-man exhibitions at New 57 Gallery, Edinburgh (also 1977), New Art Centre
Exhibited in 'Body and Soul' Peter Moores Exhibition, Liverpool, 'The Human Clay' at Hayward Gallery
1977 Retrospective exhibition at Camden Arts Centre
Exhibited in 'British Painting 1952-1977' at Royal Academy
1978 One-man exhibition at Institute for Cultural Relations Gallery, Budapest
1979 Preparing major study of art of Fernand Léger for publication in 1980 (Frasers)

Contact Royal College of Art

Peter de Francia *Disparates (Love Triumphs over All)* 1974 Charcoal on paper 77·5x55·9cm (30½x22in) Private Collection

Since the 20th century is overloaded with 'statements' I am reluctant to add to the number.

I have always worked as a figurative artist and I draw more than I paint. I frequently work in series, and the set of *Disparates*, charcoal drawings done over the last ten years, number over 250. These are mainly concerned with social comment, satire, metaphor and so on.

I admire relatively very few contemporary living artists. Amongst those whose work I do deeply admire are Philip Guston, R B Kitaj, Ipoustéguy, Torsten Renqvist.

Peter de Francia 1979

Donald Hamilton Fraser ARA 32

1929 Born in London
1949-52 Studied at St Martin's School of Art
1953 First one-man exhibition at Gimpel Fils (also 1956/59/61/63/65/69/71)
Exhibited in 'British Romantic Painting in the 20th century' Arts Council exhibition
1953-4 Studied in Paris
1954 Exhibited in 'British Painting' at Whitechapel Art Gallery
1957 One-man exhibition at Galerie Craven, Paris
1958 One-man exhibition at Paul Rosenberg & Co, New York (also 1960/63/64/66/68/70/72/73/75/76/78)
Exhibited in 'Contemporary Painting' at Albright-Knox Gallery, Buffalo (also 1964),
'Six British Painters' at Arts Club, Chicago
1958- Teaching at Royal College of Art
1963 Exhibited in 'British Painting Today' in San Francisco, Dallas and Santa Barbara
1964 Exhibited in 'Englische Kunst' at Stadtische Kunstgalerie, Bochum, 'Six Painters' at North Carolina Museum of Art
1967 One-man exhibition at Gimpel Hanover Galerie, Zurich
Exhibited in Carnegie International Exhibition, Pittsburgh
1968 Published *Gauguin's 'Vision after the Sermon'* (Cassell)
1972 Exhibited in Salon des Realités Nouvelles, Paris (also 1975)
1974 Exhibited in '100 years of Scottish Painting' at Fine Art Society, Edinburgh
1975 Elected Associate of Royal Academy
1975- Honorary Secretary of the Artists General Benevolent Institution
1977 Exhibited in 'British Painting 1952-1977' at Royal Academy

Dealer Paul Rosenberg & Co, New York

Contact Royal Academy

With the exception of a handful of paintings executed in acrylic during the 60s all the work is oil on canvas and on paper. It does not fall into any clearly defined periods except for two or three years in the mid-60s which were entirely devoted to a number of non-figurative paintings based upon torn paper collage. Otherwise the work has been generally figurative, and derived from landscape and still-life. Development was greatly influenced by contact with the Ecole de Paris in the late 1940s and early 50s.

Donald Hamilton Fraser 1979

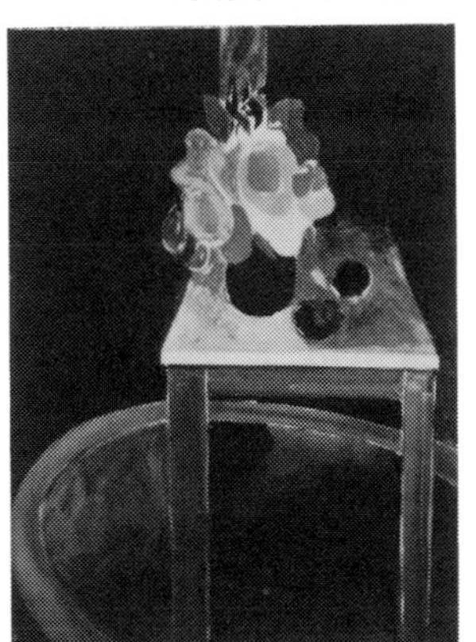

Donald Hamilton Fraser *Table with Flowers and Red Mat* 1958 Oil on canvas 121x91cm (48x36in) Hirshhorn Museum, Smithsonian Institute, Washington DC

Donald Hamilton Fraser *Lilies* 1978 Oil on canvas 121x91cm (48x36in) Paul Rosenberg & Co, New York

Lucian Freud

Lucian Freud *Girl with Leaves* 1948 Conté and pastel on grey paper 48x42cm (18⅞x16½in) Museum of Modern Art, New York

1922 Born in Berlin
1931 Came to live in Britain
1939-40 Studied at Central School of Art and Design (also 1942) and East Anglian School of Painting and Drawing

▶

1942-3 Studied at Goldsmiths College
1944 First one-man exhibition at Lefevre Gallery (also 1946)
1946-8 Visited France and Greece
1948 One-man exhibition at London Gallery (also 1951)
1948-58 Taught at Slade School of Fine Art
1951 Exhibited in '21 Modern British Painters' at Vancouver Art Gallery, '60 Paintings for '51' Arts Council Festival of Britain Exhibition
Received Arts Council Award
1954 One-man exhibition at Hanover Gallery (also 1956)
Exhibited in Venice Biennale
Received Daily Express Young Painters Exhibition Prize
1958 One-man exhibition at Marlborough Fine Art (also 1963/8)
1964-5 Taught at Norwich School of Art
1972 One-man exhibition at Anthony d'Offay Gallery (also 1974/78)
1974 Retrospective exhibition at Hayward Gallery and travelling to Bristol, Birmingham and Leeds
1978 One-man exhibition at Davis & Long Company, New York

Dealer Anthony d'Offay

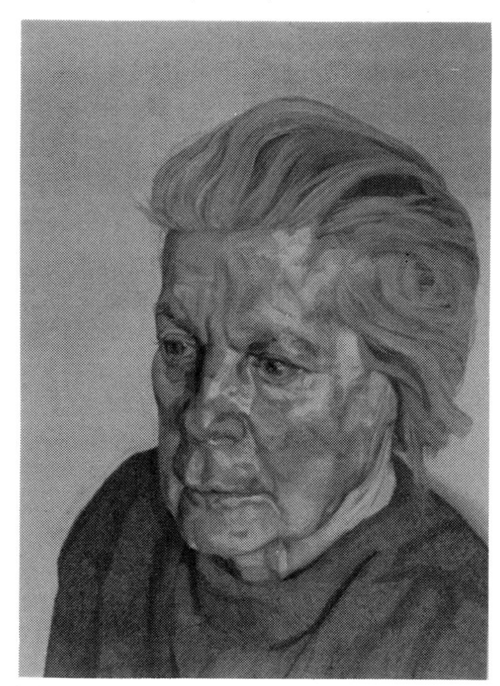

Lucian Freud *The Artist's Mother 3* 1972 Oil on canvas 32.4x23.5cm ($12\frac{3}{4}$x$9\frac{1}{4}$in) Private Collection

Lucian Freud *Buttercups* 1968 Oil on canvas 61x61cm (24x24in) Private Collection

Elisabeth Frink RA 49

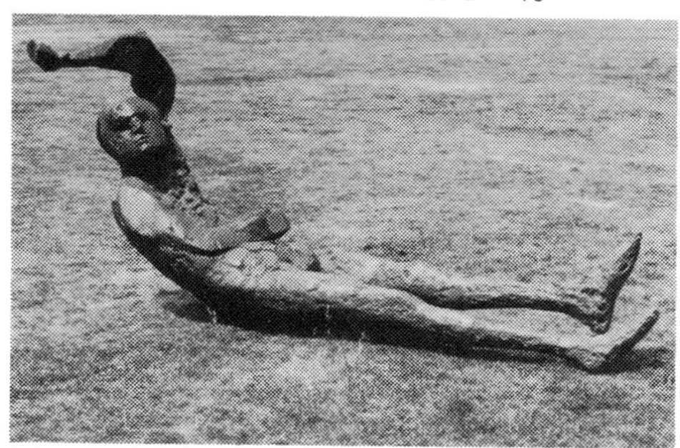

Elisabeth Frink *Dying King* 1961 Bronze (edition of 3) 85x175.3cm ($33\frac{1}{2}$x69in) Artist's Collection

1930 Born in Suffolk
1947-8 Studied at Guildford Art School
1948-51 Studied at Chelsea School of Art
1951 Exhibited with London Group
1951-61 Taught at Chelsea School of Art
1954-62 Taught at St Martin's School of Art
1955 One-man exhibition at St George's Gallery
1957 *Blind Beggar and Dog* commission for Bethnal Green
Exhibited in John Moores Exhibition, Liverpool (also 1959)
1959 One-man exhibitions at Waddington Galleries (also 1961/63/67/68/69/71/72/76),
Bertha Schaefer Gallery, New York (also 1961)
Exhibited in Middelheim Biennale
1960 Commission for façade of Carlton Towers Hotel
1961 One-man exhibition at Felix Landau Gallery, Los Angeles
1963 Commission for Alcock and Brown Memorial at Manchester Airport
1964 Commission for Kennedy Memorial in Dallas, Texas
1965-7 Visiting Instructor at Royal College of Art
1966 Commission for Altar Cross in Liverpool Cathedral
1967-73 Lived in France
1968 Received CBE
1971 Elected Associate of Royal Academy
1972 Illustrated *Canterbury Tales* (Waddington)
1975 Illustrated *The Iliad and the Odyssey* (Folio Society)
1976 Commission for *Horse and Rider* in Dover Street
Appointed Trustee of British Museum
1977 One-man exhibitions at Waddington Fine Arts, Montreal,
Galerie d'Eendt, Amsterdam
Exhibited in Silver Jubilee Contemporary British Sculpture Exhibition in Battersea Park
Elected Royal Academician
Appointed to Royal Fine Art Commission
1978 Exhibited in 'Hayward Annual' at Hayward Gallery
1979 One-man exhibition at Terry Dintenfass Gallery, New York

Dealer Waddington Galleries

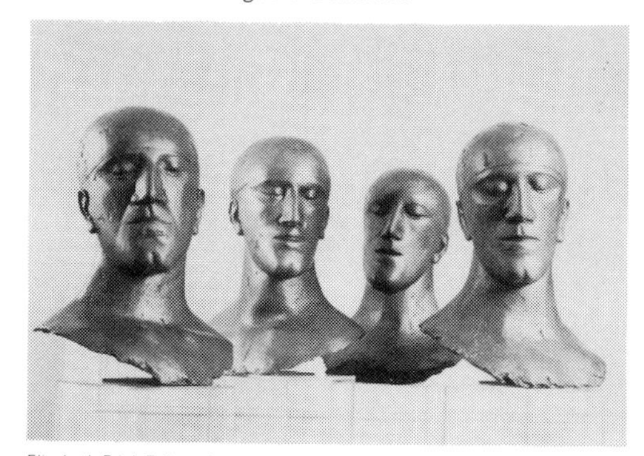

Elisabeth Frink *Tribute Group* 1975 Bronze (edition of 6) 73.7cm (29in) high Bernstein Collection, Philadelphia

The artist first showed when she was only twenty-one and quickly became known in the early 50s for the craggy rhetoric of her predatory birds and warrior figures. The roughness of the early sculpture can be seen in *Dying King* of 1961. The surface texture comes from working rapidly with wet plaster on to an armature – slapping on the plaster, smoothing the surface, letting it dry, attacking it again, breaking it up, and so on in a very physical interaction with the materials and their tactile qualities. This is heavy work which the artist

Elisabeth Frink *Rolling Horse* 1975 Bronze (edition of 6) 36x49cm (14½x19½in) Stanley Picker Trust Collection)

nevertheless enjoys, especially as the immediacy of the plaster is appropriate for the speed of her developing ideas – her ambitions to carve, for example, have never materialized because the process is too slow. Once the work in plaster is finished, the sculpture is then cast in bronze, a process which makes it permanent while at the same time preserving all the surface markings made by the artist's hand and tools. The more recent work is, however, smoother and less expressionist, since the surface is filed down in a much slower and less energetic action, that requires a more contemplative involvement. The sense of alert tension of the earlier work has also mellowed into an almost stiff restraint at the same time as the human, bird or animal aggressors have given way as subjects to male nudes and horses.

Sarah Kent 1978

Terry Frost 50

1915 Born in Leamington Spa
1947-9 Studied at Camberwell School of Art
1950-1 Studied at Penzance School of Art
1951 Worked as assistant to Barbara Hepworth
1952 One-man exhibition at Leicester Galleries (also 1956/58)
1952-4 Taught at Bath Academy of Art
1954-6 Gregory Fellowship in painting at Leeds University
1955 Exhibited at Carnegie International Exhibition, Pittsburgh (also 1958/59/61)
1957 Exhibited in 'New Trends in British Art' at New York Art Foundation, John Moores Exhibition, Liverpool (also 1959/61/63/65 prizewinner /67/69/72)
1958 Exhibited in Guggenheim World Prize Exhibition in New York (also 1959)
1960 One-man exhibition at Bertha Schaefer Gallery, New York (also 1962)
1961 One-man exhibition at Waddington Galleries (also 1969/71/74)
1962/3 Exhibited in 'British Art Today' at San Francisco, Dallas and Santa Barbara
1963 Exhibited in 'British Painting in the 60s' at Whitechapel Art Gallery and Tate Gallery
1964 Retrospective exhibition at Laing Gallery, Newcastle and travelling
One-man exhibitions in San Francisco, Santa Barbara and San José
Exhibited in 'Painting and Sculpture of a Decade 1954-64' at Tate Gallery
1965 One-man exhibition at Arnolfini Gallery, Bristol (also 1972)
1965- Teaching full-time in Department of Fine Art at Reading University
1967 Exhibited in 'Recent British Painting' at Tate Gallery (Peter Stuyvesant Foundation Collection)
1968 One-man exhibition at Bear Lane Gallery, Oxford (also 1970)
1969 One-man exhibition at Museum of Modern Art, Oxford
1970/1 Exhibited in 'British Painting 1960-70' at National Gallery of Art, Washington
1971 One-man exhibition at Institute of Contemporary Arts
1974 Exhibited in 'British Painting '74' at Hayward Gallery
1977 Retrospective exhibition at Serpentine Gallery and travelling
One-man exhibition at Le Balcon des Arts, Paris
Exhibited in 'British Painting 1952-1977' at Royal Academy
BBC Omnibus film on his work

Dealer Waddington Galleries

Terry Frost *Through Yellows* 1975 Collage and acrylic on canvas 193x259cm (78x102in) Artist's Collection

If you look you can't see for looking. Looking for something to inspire you to work is an escape from taking action. The decision to take action is the only way of seeing.

The imagination will throw up all possibilities. It's taking one of the ideas that makes the balloon go up. The image can so destroy what you saw.

If you look and look the tree becomes a tree and not a particular tree moment, the sun becomes the sun – any old sun, it's the contact via the imagination that touches the unknown and reveals possibilities.

Turn your back on looking and see.

If you must look stand on your head to do it.

Terry Frost 1973

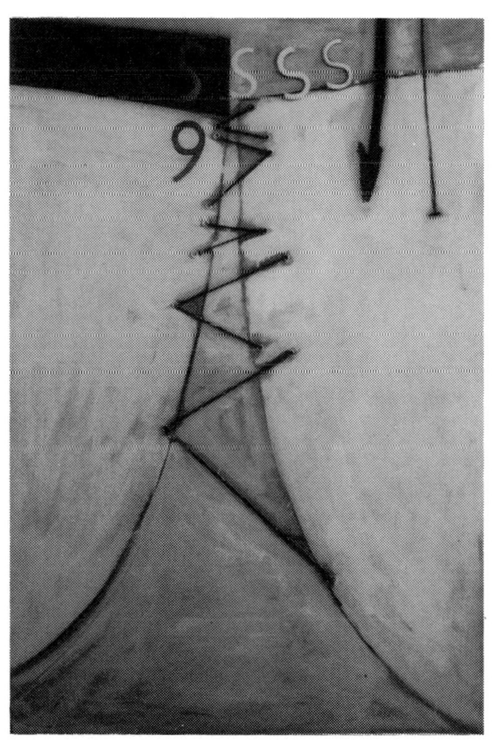

Terry Frost *SSSS9* 1962-3 Oil on canvas laced 152.4x101.6cm (60x40in) Artist's Collection

Patrick George 66

1923 Born in Manchester
Studied at Edinburgh College of Art and Camberwell School of Art
1974- Reader at Slade School of Fine Art
1975 One-man exhibition at Gainsborough's House, Sudbury

Contact 33 Moreton Terrace, London SW1

▶

Patrick George *Boutell's Farm, Lamarsh* 1972-3 Oil on canvas 68.6x142.2cm (27x54in) Knowland Collection

I try to paint a likeness of what I see. To this end I observe the apparent proportions and for the same reason try to make an order of colours similar to the order I see. In London I paint pictures of people, of things lying around my room and the view out of the window. In the country I go outside and paint the landscape. There seems to me all the difference between being in a field and looking at a field from a window. The pictures take a long time to paint, sometimes several years.

Patrick George 1979

Patrick George *Susan Engledow posing* 1966-71 Oil on canvas 160x106.7cm (63x42in) Artist's Collection

Gilbert and George 178

Gilbert and George *Bent* 1977 Photo-piece 203.2x243.8cm (6ft8inx8ft2in) Private Collection, Amsterdam

1942 George born in England
1943 Gilbert born in the Dolomites
1967 Met while studying at St Martin's School of Art
1968- Working together as living sculptures
1970 One-man exhibitions at Art and Project Gallery, Amsterdam (also 1971/74/77), Konrad Fischer Gallery, Dusseldorf (also 1972/74/77), Nigel Greenwood Inc (also 1972/74) Published *Side by Side* (Konig Brothers)
1971 One-man exhibitions at Sperone Gallery, Turin (also 1972/73/74), Sonnabend Gallery, New York (also 1971/76/78) Tour of 'The Paintings' sculpture at Whitechapel Art Gallery; Stedelijk Museum, Amsterdam; Kunstmuseum, Lucerne; Kunstverein, Dusseldorf
1973 One-man exhibition at Sonnabend Gallery, Paris
1974 Published *Dark Shadow* (Nigel Greenwood)
1975 One-man exhibitions at Lucio Amelio Gallery, Naples, Art Agency, Tokyo (also 1978)
1976 One-man exhibition at Robert Self Gallery

Contact Art for All, 12 Fournier Street, London E1

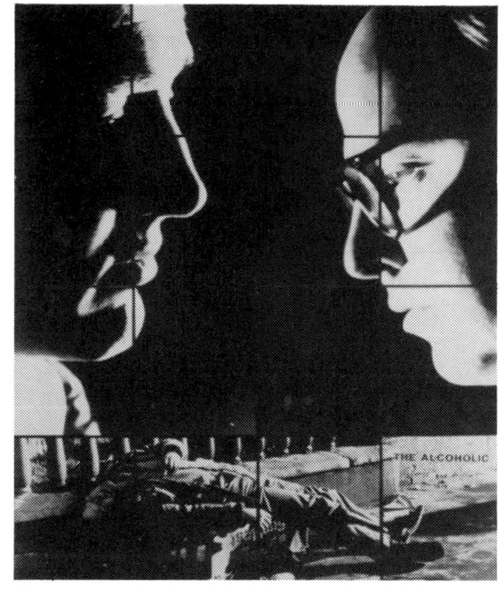

Gilbert and George *The Alcoholic* 1978 Photo-piece 203.2x243.8cm (6ft8inx8ft2in) Institute of Contemporary Art, Chacago

Being living sculptures is our life blood, our destiny, our romance, our disaster, our light and life. As day breaks over us, we rise into our vacuum and the cold morning light filters dustily through the window. We step into the responsibility-suits of our art. We put on our shoes for the coming walk. Our limbs begin to stir and form actions of looseness, as though without gravity. They bound about for the new day. The head afloat on top levels on the horizon of our thought. Our hearts pound with fresh blood and emotion and again we find ourselves standing there all nerved up in body and mind. Often we will glide across the room, drawn by the window's void. Our eyes are glued to this frame of light. Our mind points ever to our decay. The big happening outside the window floods our vision like a passing film. It leaves us without impressions, giving up only silence and repetitive relaxation. Nothing can touch us or take us out of ourselves. It is a continuous sculpture. Our minds float off into time, visiting fragments of words heard, faces seen, feelings felt, faces loved. We take occasional sips from our water glasses. Consciousness comes along and goes away, slipping from dreaming space into concrete awareness. The whole room is filled with the mass and weight of our own history . . .

Gilbert and George 1971

Katherine Gili 132

1948	Born in Oxford
1966-70	Studied at Bath Academy of Art
1971-3	Studied at St Martin's School of Art
1972-	Teaching at Norwich School of Art
1973	Exhibited in 'Platform 73' at Museum of Modern Art, Oxford
1974	Exhibited in 'Six Sculptors' at Chelsea Gallery, Sculpture Exhibition at Norwich Cathedral and University of Manchester
1974-	Annual studio exhibitions at Stockwell Depot
1975	Exhibited in 'The Condition of Sculpture' at Hayward Gallery
1975-	Teaching at St Martin's School of Art
1976	Exhibited in group show at Artists' Market
1977	Exhibited in Summer Exhibition at Serpentine Gallery, Silver Jubilee Contemporary British Sculpture Exhibition in Battersea Park
1978	Exhibited in 'Twelve Sculptors' at Farnham College of Art
1979	Exhibited in 'Hayward Annual' at Hayward Gallery Co-organizer of 'Summer Show 2' at Serpentine Gallery

Contact Old LEB Depot, 52 Crooms Hill, London SW10

Katherine Gili *Roundelay* 1977 Mild steel, varnished 125x114x154cm (49x45x60⅝in) Lugano

John Golding 91

John Golding *F(BS)II* 1977 Acrylic on cotton duck 160x243.8cm (63x96in) Rowan Gallery

1929	Born in England Educated in Mexico and Canada
1951-7	Post-graduate work at Courtauld Institute, University of London
1959	Published *Cubism 1907-14* (New York and London) Began teaching at Courtauld Institute
1962	First one-man exhibition at Gallery One
1970	Organized (with Christopher Green) 'Leger and Purist Paris' exhibition at Tate Gallery One-man exhibition at Nigel Greenwood Inc
1971	Began teaching at Royal College of Art Exhibited in group show at Museum of Modern Art, Oxford
1972	Exhibited in 'Large Paintings' at Hayward Gallery
1973	Published *Duchamp: The Bride Stripped Bare by her Bachelors, Even*
1974	One-man exhibitions at Rowan Gallery (also 1975, 1977), Holdsworth Gallery, Sydney Hayward Gallery Exhibited in 'British Painting '74' at Hayward Gallery Lecture tour in Australia
1975	One-man exhibition at Kettles Yard Gallery, Cambridge
1976	Selected 'Summer Show 2', exhibition at Serpentine Gallery Exhibited in John Moores Exhibition, Liverpool (also 1978)
1977	One-man exhibition at National Gallery of Modern Art, Edinburgh Exhibited in 'British Painting 1952-1977' at Royal Academy
1978	One-man exhibition at Ibis Gallery, Leamington Spa Appointed Slade Professor of Fine Art, Cambridge University

Dealer Rowan Gallery

Golding sees his own paintings as being 'basically reflective or contemplative'. They are on a scale to which the observer can respond physically, in particular to the large vertical rectangles of glowing colour which began to appear in his work about six years ago, balanced by squares of paler, softer colour. The architectural structure supporting these areas was then tighter and more controlled. Gradually the boundaries were loosened and pushed to the edges of the canvas itself, so that total involvement with the large colour areas became possible. The next stages was a blurring of the confines between the two rectangles and between them and the limits of the canvas: in a certain place the margin or band would fade out altogether, re-emerging again at another point along its course. This ambiguity was increased when Golding began to activate the large slabs by means of streaks and flashes of hot colour at their edges, which both divide and unite them, causing the whole to quiver and flicker gently in front of our eyes. Golding respects the flatness of the picture's surface (the pale squares in his paintings are like blank windows or mirrors) and yet a sensation of infinite space is subtly evoked – infinite but at the same time bounded. In the most recent work it seems that, while keeping mainly to the immensely satisfying format of the earlier, Golding has allowed the strips to assume a life of their own and their role, previously subsidiary, is now dominant; stronger and more intact than before, they break up the canvas horizontally as well as vertically, becoming almost the sole agents of that essential juxtaposition of two areas of different shape and different intensity. There is an inevitability about these works which is exciting to eye, mind and body; their colours, predominantly radiant yellows, cannot fail to warm and cheer us.

Richard Calvocoressi 1977

John Golding *CI* 1972-3 Acrylic on cotton duck 197.5x213.4cm (6ft5¾inx7ft) Rowan Gallery

Frederick Gore RA 39

1913 Born in Richmond, Surrey
1932-4 Studied at Trinity College and Ruskin School of Art, Oxford
1934-37 Studied at Westminster School of Art and Slade School of Fine Art
1937 First one-man exhibition at Redfern Gallery (also 1949/50/53/56/62)
1938 Travelled and painted in Greece
One-man exhibition of paintings of Greece at Galerie Borghese, Paris
1939 One-man exhibition of paintings of Greece at Stafford Gallery
1946-79 Taught at St Martin's School of Art
1951-79 Head of Painting Department at St Martin's School of Art
1954 Exhibited in Contemporary Art Society Exhibition at Tate Gallery (also 1956/58)
1956 Published *Abstract Art* (Methuen)
1958 One-man exhibition at Mayor Gallery (also 1960)
1963 One-man exhibition at Juster Gallery, New York
1964 Elected Associate of Royal Academy
1965 Published *Painting: Some Basic Principles* (Vista/Reinhold)
1969 Published *Piero della Francesca's 'The Baptism'* (Cassell)
1973 Elected Royal Academician
1977 Exhibited in 'British Painting 1952-1977' at Royal Academy (also Chairman of organizing committee and author of catalogue introduction)
1979 Retrospective exhibitions at Gainsborough's House, Sudbury, Bury St Edmunds Art Gallery

Dealer Redfern Gallery

Frederick Gore *Ariadne* 1945 Oil 116.8x152.4cm (46x60in) Artist's Collection

Frederick Gore *Piccadilly Circus* 1975 Oil 91.4x106.7cm (36x42in) Private Collection

A painter of landscapes directly from nature, Frederick Gore has worked largely in London, Kent, Paris, Provence, Majorca and Greece. He has also painted but exhibited rarely a variety of subjects with figures. His work derives from French painting but has an Englishman's interest in faithful characterization of the subject. Aware of contemporary developments, but perhaps because of strong intellectual interests outside painting, he is sceptical of the theoretical premises on which the movements in modern painting are said to be based. So although influenced, in common with others of his generation of English painters, at different stages by Impressionist, Cubist and Abstract Expressionist movements or revivals, he has remained profoundly interested in and continually returned to the interpretation of immediate visual experience. Much of his work is characterized by strong colour, but with a fuller development of form and sometimes of detail than earlier Fauve painters. Because of this positive and experimental attitude to colour and to the structural relationships set up in a painting, he has paradoxically been led to feel more affinity with abstract painters than with other figurative painters with whom his work is sometimes grouped.

Frederick Gore 1979

Lawrence Gowing ARA 19

1918 Born in Stamford Hill
1929 Introduced to painting at school in Herefordshire by Maurice Feild
1936 Pupil of William Coldstream
1937 Contributed to 'Pictures of London' exhibition, bought by CAS
1939 Conscientious objector
Painted in Wiltshire
1942- One-man exhibitions at Leicester Galleries and later at Marlborough Fine Art
1948-58 Professor of Fine Art at King's College, Newcastle
1952 Published *Vermeer* (Faber & Faber)
Received CBE
1953-8 Member of Art Panel of Arts Council (also 1959-65/1969-72/1976-); Member of Council 1970-2 and 1977-
1953-60 Trustee of Tate Gallery (also 1961-4)
1954 Organized Cezanne exhibition at Tate Gallery, and wrote catalogue
1958-65 Principal of Chelsea School of Art
1960- Trustee of National Portrait Gallery
1964 Co-organizer of Gulbenkian exhibition 'Art of a Decade'
1965-7 Keeper of British Collection and Deputy Director of Tate Gallery
1966 Organized Turner exhibition at Museum of Modern Art and wrote catalogue
1967-75 Professor of Fine Art at Leeds University
1971 Organized Hogarth exhibition at Tate Gallery, and wrote catalogue
1975- Slade Professor of Fine Art at University College
1977- Adjunct Professor of History of Art at University of Pennsylvania

Contact Slade School of Fine Art

Lawrence Gowing *Path Through Giffords Copse, Lambourne* 1960 Oil on canvas 61x71.1cm (24x28in) Department of Environment Collection

As a boy I formed the habit of painting in oil colour on strawboard outdoors and in the fifty years since I have gone on doing this fairly regularly in more or less the same way, except that in place of the easel and 15 x 11 in. boards used then I now prefer boards of 14 x 9.9 in. and a sketching box that hangs round my neck. In most years these sketches have led to larger landscapes, usually in the West of England, occasionally in France. After painting heads of people I knew I received my first portrait commission (from Balliol) in 1945 and I have gone on painting commissioned portraits. In the 40s I painted a succession of still-lifes with

Lawrence Gowing *Julia Asleep* 1947 Oil on canvas 76.2x63cm (30x25in) Private Collection

green cooking-apples, perhaps half in memory of Graham Bell, whose last figure pictures discovered apple-green half-tones in flesh. In the 40s I wrote from a painter's standpoint a periodical notebook about art, published anonymously, and came to think that I understood Vermeer, on whom I eventually produced a book. Since then I have written fairly frequently, and I have given much time to the enjoyable trade of running an art school. As a painter my work and my understanding remains limited by the attempt truthfully to reflect outward experience. I should be happy to make images less contingent on the chances of observation, but do not know if I shall manage to do so.

Lawrence Gowing 1979

Derrick Greaves 37

Derrick Greaves *Sheffield* 1953 Oil on canvas 114.3x205.7cm (45x81in) Balliol College, Oxford

1927 Born in Sheffield
1943-8 Worked as signwriter
1948-52 Studied at Royal College of Art
1952-4 Studied and exhibited in Italy
1953 First one-man exhibition at Beaux Arts Gallery (also 1955)
1956 Exhibited in Contemporary Arts Society Exhibition, Venice Biennale
1957 Visited USSR
Exhibited in group show at Pushkin Museum, Moscow,
John Moores Exhibition, Liverpool (Prizewinner; also 1959/61/63/69)
1958 One-man exhibition at Zwemmer Gallery (also 1960/62/63)
1960 Exhibited in Guggenheim Selection
1962 Received Purchase Prize in Belfast Open Painting Exhibition
1963 Exhibited in 'The Graven Image' at Royal Watercolourists Society, 'British Painting in the 60s' at Whitechapel Art Gallery
1964 Exhibited in Carnegie International Exhibition, Pittsburgh
1969 One-man exhibition at Institute of Contemporary Arts (also 1971)
1970 One-man exhibitions at Bear Lane Gallery, Oxford (also 1973), Verona and Padua
1972 One man exhibitions in Belfast and Dublin
1973 One-man exhibition at Whitechapel Art Gallery
1973- Annual one-man exhibitions at Monika Kinley (Open House Shows)
1974 Exhibited in 'British Painting '74' at Hayward Gallery
1975- Annual one-man exhibitions at City Gallery, Milton Keynes
1977 Exhibited in 'British Painting 1952-1977' at Royal Academy
1978 One-man exhibition at Cranfield Institute of Technology
Exhibited in 'Exposicion internacional de la plastica' in Chile

Dealer Monika Kinley

Some years ago in a large and cold studio I had a big cast iron coke stove. I think this type of stove was called 'slow but sure'. It was temperamental but when it was going well it gave out a constant throbbing hum, regular and satisfying. At these times it also generated its greatest heat. Standing by it and basking in its warmth, I thought how ideal it would be to have a similar efficient, even, firm, progressive productivity when working on the paintings, when suddenly without any warning the stove fell to pieces.

Derrick Greaves 1979

Derrick Greaves *Seated Woman* 1978 Drawing/Collage 144.8x96.5cm (57x38in) Collection of the artist's wife

Alan Green 140

Alan Green *Blocking Out* 1972 Acrylic on canvas 152.4x152.4cm (60x60in) Annely Juda Collection

1932 Born in London
1949-53 Studied at Beckenham School of Art
1955-8 Studied at Royal College of Art

▶

Alan Green *Drawing No 153* 1977 Mixed media on paper 106.6x110.4cm (42x43½in) Private Collection, Germany

1958-9 Royal College of Art Major Travelling Scholarship to France and Italy
1959-74 Taught at Hornsey College of Art
1963 One-man exhibition at AIA Gallery
1970 One-man exhibition at Annely Juda Fine Art (also 1973/75/78)
1971 Exhibited in 'Art Spectrum' at Alexandra Palace
1973 One-man exhibition at Galerie Liatowitsch, Basle
Exhibited in 'La peinture anglaise aujourd'hui' at Musée d'Art Moderne, Paris,
Sao Paulo Bienal
1974 One-man exhibition at Galerie Hervé Alexandre, Brussels
Exhibited in 'British Painting '74' at Hayward Gallery
Received Intaglio Print Prize at Bradford Print Biennale
1975 One-man exhibitions in Verona, Hamburg and Milan
1976 One-man exhibition 'Etchings '73-76' at Annely Juda Fine Art, Tate Gallery, Mappin Art Gallery, Sheffield and Newcastle-upon-Tyne University, Painting Box Gallery, Zurich
Received Giles Bequest Prize for a British Printmaker, Bradford Biennale
1977 One-man exhibitions at Galerie Art in Progress in Munich and Dusseldorf
Exhibited in 'Five British Painters' at Young Hoffman Gallery, Chicago, 'British Painting 1952-1977' at Royal Academy,
'Series' at Tate Gallery
1978 One-man exhibitions at Oliver Dowling Gallery, Dublin,
Susan Caldwell Inc, New York,
Clark Gallery, Boston,
Galerie Palluel, Paris
Received Grand Prix at Norwegian International Print Biennale
1978/9 Exhibited in 'Mechanised Image' Arts Council travelling exhibition
1979 One-man exhibition at Kunsthalle, Bielefeld
Exhibited in 'British Art Now' at Guggenheim Museum, New York

Dealer Annely Juda Fine Art

As opposed to other means of visual expression, painting has well-defined physical limitations. Today we live in a limited situation; all increases in knowledge only serve to make this more apparent. Painters should have the capability to make this explicit by employing limitations and through the work transcending them.

To this end I want to make ordinary paintings that can be looked at over and over again. This necessitates the carrying out of self evident truths to the point of being pedantic – of putting paint on canvas, of taking it off again, of time spent, of time not spent, of thick and thin, fixed and free, of meanness and generosity, of slow and fast, of smooth and rough, of decision and indecision – all this and much more should be made visible.

I am not interested in a 'social' art but in an art that can be seen to survive without recall to anything more than the matter of its own formation.

Alan Green 1979

Anthony Green *1958/Hall of Mirrors* 1977 Oil on board 228.6x208.3cm (7ft6inx6ft10in) Private Collection

Anthony Green RA

1939 Born in London
1956 Exhibited in 'Young Contemporaries (also 1958/59)
1956-60 Studied at the Slade School of Art
1959 Exhibited with London Group (also 1962/64/67/70/71)
1960 French Government Scholarship to Paris
1962 First one-man exhibition at Rowan Gallery (also 1964/66/67/69/71/72/74/76/78)
1963 Gulbenkian Purchase Award
1964 Elected member of London Group
Taught at Slade School of Fine Art
1967 Exhibited in John Moores Exhibition, Liverpool
Harkness Fellowship to USA
1967-9 Lived in USA
1968 One-man exhibition at Galerie Muller, Stuttgart
Exhibited in 'Britische Kunst Heute' at Kunstverein, Hamburg,
'From Kitaj to Balek, Non-abstract Artists in Britain' at Bear Lane Gallery, Oxford,
The Articulate Subconscious' at American Federation of Arts and touring USA
1970 Exhibited in 'Narrative Painting in the 20th Century' at Camden Arts Centre
1971 Elected Associate of Royal Academy
One-man exhibition at Frans Halsmuseum, Haarlem, Holland
1972 One-man exhibition at Galerie Leger, Malmo, Sweden
1973 One-man exhibition at Galerie Brusberg, Hanover (also 1976)
Exhibited in 'La peinture anglaise aujourd'hui' at Musée d'Art Moderne, Paris
1974 Exhibited in John Moores Exhibition, Liverpool (prizewinner),
'British Painting '74' at Hayward Gallery
1975 One-man exhibitions at Nishimura Gallery, Tokyo (also 1977),
Staempfli Gallery, New York (also 1979)
1976 One-man exhibition at Pyramid Gallery, Washington, DC
1977 Elected Royal Academician
Exhibited in 'British Painting 1952-1977' at Royal Academy
1978 One-man exhibitions at Rochdale, Sheffield, Southampton, Birmingham, Belfast and Diploma Galleries, Royal Academy

Dealer Rowan Gallery

Anthony Green *Noces d'Or/Lissac* 1976 Oil on board 152.4x228.6cm (60x90in) Private Collection, New York

. . . Slowly during the 60s quite a number of the works increased in scale – and on occasion in visual complexity. In the more 'empty' pictures the space between the objects or people became more adventurous and the switch in the relative scale of them very important. ('USA II': 'Love me').

With my growing confidence in the organization of the 'picture plane' I produced a number of large very full paintings ('Mr. and Mrs. Stanley Joscelyne/The second marriage') their sense of space expressed by the shift in scale of objects and the apparent flattening of the perspective.

Large scale and a wealth of detail were and are of continuing concern to me, together they produce a very concentrated image – in fact a total little world. When you stand close up to the picture plane, to inspect smaller details, your peripheral vision is confused and my reality becomes the spectator's? Perhaps when I paint my people over lifesize they are real from a distance and alive close to?

I am interested in the way spectators' memories influence how they see and what they usually remember.

I do not remember people, rooms, tents, incidents from a fixed view point – I just remember. I remember joy, sadness, colours, patterns, scale. I remember the personality of objects, radiators are hard and shiny, my wife's lips are red and soft and lip-like, my mother's hair is up and French and never down. I remember my father – big, fat, spectacled, pink and naked, dressed and eccentric, seated, standing, talking, suffering fools not at all, in bed with my mother, alone, sad and buried – all this I want in one image. It is who I am *now*.

Currently my subject matter includes my wife, both my children, the artist, my mother, my late father, my late step-father, aunts, in-laws and close friends – and the various environments that I live in or visit frequently.

Knowing what to paint, I am continuing to stretch the formal and abstract qualities of my pictures as far as possible. I am aware that they rest on a knife edge of total failure or qualified success – only infrequently am I completely satisfied with a finished work. My imagination is so filled with visions that the physical labour of making them tangible is only partially resolved. I complete about 10 pictures a year, working six days a week, 11 months of the year. I consider this a small output.

The 300-odd paintings by me, still in existence, are a beginning . . .

Anthony Green 1977

Roger de Grey RA 14

1918 Born in Buckinghamshire
1937-9 Studied at Chelsea School of Art (also 1946-47)
1947-51 Taught in Fine Art Department at University of Newcastle-upon-Tyne
1951-3 Master of Painting at King's College, University of Newcastle-upon-Tyne

Roger de Grey *Orchard* 1975 Oil on canvas 101.6x101.6cm (40x40in) Private Collection

Roger de Grey *Interior* 1969 Oil on canvas 91.4x91.4cm (36x 36in) Private Collection

1953-73 Senior Tutor (and later Reader) in Painting at Royal College of Art
1959 Elected Honorary Associate of Royal College of Art
1964 Elected Associate of Royal Academy
1967 One-man exhibition at Leicester Galleries
1969 Elected Royal Academician
1973- Principal of City and Guilds of London Art School
1976 Treasurer of Royal Academy
1979 Prizewinner in Summer Exhibition at Royal Academy

Contact City and Guilds of London Art School ▶

An obsession for working out of doors has been the motivation and limitation of my painting. The need to be present in the space I am trying to recall and retain has defined the intention and conditioned the method of its execution. It is only partly true, however, that it is a direct response to visual evidence, and that the forms are generated by imitation of nature. I have always been fascinated by the self-energizing paintmarks in certain of Soutine's landscapes and in particular the prophecy in them of self-expressive painting. In consequence the forms I deduce are only as true to nature as a photograph of the land surface to a geological section. My more recent concern with texture is, I suppose, a more imitative one involving the granulation of landscape itself.

Roger de Grey 1979

Anthony Gross ARA 7

Anthony Gross *Valley of Segos with Wild Orchids and Marguerites* 1978 Oil on canvas 89x130cm (33x51¼in) Artist's Collection

1905 Born in London
1922-6 Studied at Slade School of Fine Art, Central School of Art and Design, Academie Julian, Paris, Ecole des Beaux Arts, Paris and Escuela Real de San Fernando, Madrid
1926 Settled in Paris
1930 Exhibited in Salons d'Automne and des Tuileries
1934 One-man exhibition at Leicester Galleries (also 1940/47/54/57/59/62)
1934-40 Produced experimental cartoon films with Hector Hoppin
1937 Illustrated Cocteau's *Les Enfants Terribles* (limited edition by Les Cents Unes)
1940-5 Official War Artist in North Africa, India, Burma, France and Germany
1948 Taught at Central School of Art and Design
Illustrated *The Forsyte Saga* (Heinemann) and *Wuthering Heights* (Paul Elek)
1948-71 Member of London Group
1955-71 Taught etching and engraving at Slade School of Fine Art
1956 Published *Heures du Boulvé* (St George's Gallery)
1957 Received 1st prize at Philadelphia Print Club
1968 Retrospective exhibition of graphic work at Victoria and Albert Museum
1971 Illustrated *Sixe Idyllia Theocritus* (Clover Hill Editions)
1974 Retrospective exhibition of etching at Graphotek, Berlin
1976 Retrospective exhibition at New Art Centre (also one-mans 1977/79)
1978 Retrospective exhibition of prints at Sidney Mickelson, Washington DC
1979 Elected Associate of Royal Academy and Honorary Fellow of Royal Society of Painters and Etchers

Dealer New Art Centre
Associated American Artists, New York
Sidney Mickelson, Washington DC

Anthony Gross *Poet's House* 1936 Etching 18.5x24.5cm (7½x9⅝in)

It was in 1924 while in Algeria that I met Kay Scott, an American painter. He explained to me the theory of colour as invented by Cezanne and taught to him by de Segonzac and this has had a profound influence on my paintings. I also met in 1929 Picabia who explained and enthused me with Surrealist thinking. The engravers Hecht and Hayter became great personal friends and we benefited from each other in our development. Courneault, Alix and not forgetting Lotiron all also helped to broaden my mind in the early 1930s, while another painter who became a personal friend and who helped me to understand painting and drawing was Fernand Léger.

I have always held an unfashionable view that drawing is the prime factor in pictorial art – the understanding of how things are constructed, the shape of everything, be it flower or factory girl, landscape or insect. The composition of a picture is drawing. Of course it depends on each artist's own temperament – for me, as I understand drawing, it is of prime importance. For an artist who sees in areas of colour, it is colour that comes first! It is drawing and proportion for me, and I have always felt this and have never changed from it.

I have been through several periods of development. The illustrations of my work show the extremes of my abstract and realistic boundaries. Above all, however, I am interested in life and things and people alive and in painting, etching or engraving all of *this*.

Anthony Gross 1979

Nigel Hall 126

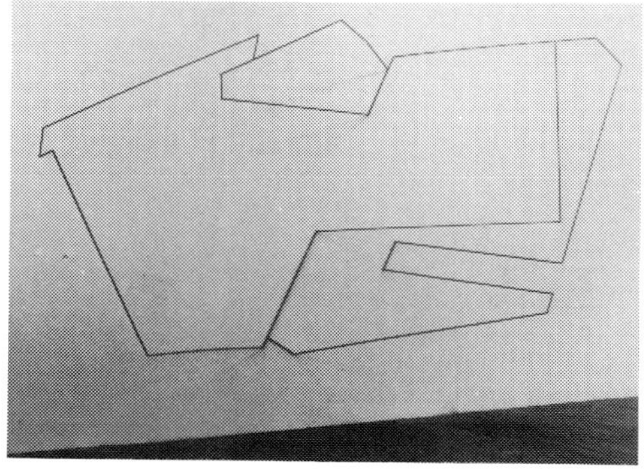

Nigel Hall *Threshold* 1977 Painted aluminium 233.7x137.2cm (7ft8inx12ft10inx4ft6in) Artist's Collection

1943 Born in Bristol
1960-4 Studied at West of England College of Art
1964-7 Studied at Royal College of Art
1967 First one-man exhibition at Galerie Givaudon, Paris
Exhibited in group show at Salon de Mai, Paris
1967-9 Received Harkness Fellowship for travel in USA, Canada and Mexico
1968 One-man exhibition at Nicholas Wilder Gallery, Los Angeles (also 1972)
1969 Exhibited in 'Young and Fantastic' at Institute of Contemporary Arts and travelling in USA and Canada
1970 One-man exhibitions at Galerie Neuendorf, Hamburg and Cologne, Serpentine Gallery
1972 One-man exhibition at Felicity Samuel Gallery (also 1974/76)
1972-4 Taught at Royal College of Art
1974 One-man exhibition at Primo Piano Gallery, Rome (also 1979), Robert Elkon Gallery, New York (also 1977/79)
1974- Principal Lecturer at Chelsea School of Art
1975 One-man exhibition at Galerie Jacomo Santiveri, Paris
1976 One-man exhibition at Arnolfini Gallery, Bristol
1977 Exhibited in 'Documenta 6' in Kassel

1978 One-man exhibitions at Melbourne, Brisbane and Sydney, Annely Juda Fine Art, Roundhouse Gallery, Aberdeen Art Gallery, Southampton University Gallery

Dealer Annely Juda Fine Art
Robert Elkon Gallery, New York

Maggi Hambling 154

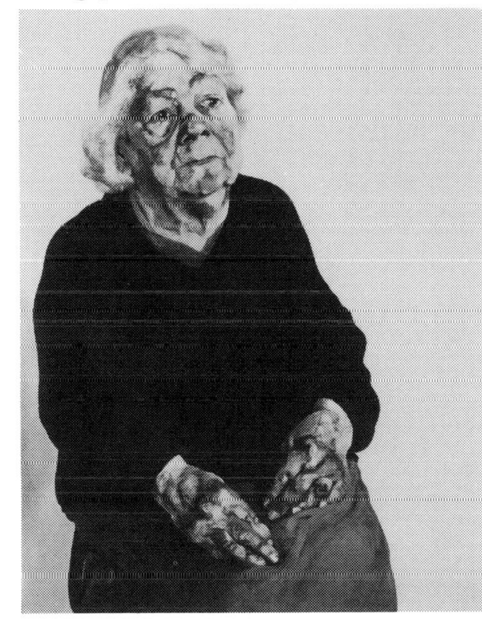

Maggi Hambling *Frances Rose (2)* 1973 Oil on canvas 119.4x91.4cm (47x36in) Artist's Collection

1945 Born in Suffolk
1960 Studied with Lett Haines and Cedric Morris
1962-4 Studied at Ipswich School of Art
1964-7 Studied at Camberwell School of Art
1967 First one-man exhibition at Hadleigh Gallery, Suffolk
1967-9 Studied at Slade School of Fine Art
1969 Received Boise Travel Award to New York
1970 Exhibited in 'A space of 5 Times' at Grabowski Gallery, John Player Biennale, Nottingham
1971 Exhibited in 'Art Spectrum' at Alexandra Palace
1973 One-man exhibition at Morley Gallery
1974 Exhibited in 'Critic's Choice' at Arthur Tooth & Sons, John Moores Exhibition, Liverpool (also 1978), 'British Painting '74' at Hayward Gallery
1975 Exhibited in 'The Nude' at Morley Gallery, Middlesbrough Biennale
1976 Exhibited in 'The Human Clay' at Hayward Gallery
1977 One-man exhibition at Warehouse Gallery
Exhibited in 'Sculpture Banners and Flags' at Warehouse Gallery, Summer Exhibition at Royal Academy
Received Arts Council Award

Contact 45 Tennyson Street, London SW8

I returned to painting in 1972 following a period of experiment with more 'avant-garde' means of expression. I committed myself then to trying to paint people and I believe that this work will continue for the rest of my life. In Walia's photograph I am sitting beside the portrait *Lett Laughing* (1975-6). Lett Haines was and still is my 'master' – despite his death last year I continue to paint him.

Maggi Hambling 1979

Richard Hamilton 104

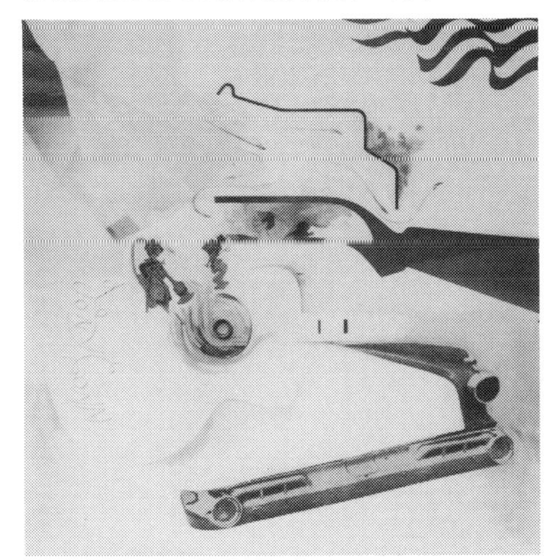

Richard Hamilton *Glorious Techniculture* 1961-4 Mixed media on panel 122x122cm (48x48in) Private Collection

1922 Born in London
1936 Studied at Westminster Technical College and St Martin's School of Art (evening classes)
1937 Worked at Reimann Studios
1938 Studied at Royal Academy Schools (also 1946)
1940 Studied to be engineering draughtsman
1941-5 Worked as engineering draughtsman at EMI
1948-51 Studied at Slade School of Fine Art
1950 First one-man exhibition at Gimpel Fils Gallery
1952-3 Taught at Central School of Art and Design
Member of Independent Group
1953-66 Lecturer at King's College, University of Durham
1955 One-man exhibition at Hanover Gallery (also 1964)
1956 Exhibited in 'This is Tomorrow' at Whitechapel Art Gallery
1957 Two-man exhibition (with Victor Pasmore) 'An Exhibit' at Hatton Gallery, Newcastle-upon-Tyne (also 'Exhibit 2' in 1958)
1957-61 Taught interior design at Royal College of Art

Richard Hamilton *Lux 50 (maquette)* 1977 Mixed media 100x100cm ($39\frac{3}{8}$x$39\frac{3}{8}$in) Artist's Collection

1960 Received William and Noma Copley Foundation Award
1963 First visit to USA
1964 Exhibited in Carnegie International Exhibition, Pittsburgh
1965 Began reconstruction of Marcel Duchamp's *Large Glass*
1966 One-man exhibition at Robert Fraser Gallery (also 1967/69)
Exhibited in 'European Drawings' at Guggenheim Museum, New York
Organized exhibition 'The Almost Complete Works of Marcel Duchamp' at Tate Gallery
1967 One-man exhibitions at Galerie Ricke, Kassel, Alexandre Iolas Gallery, New York

▶

1968 One-man exhibition at Studio Marconi, Milan (also 1969/71/72/74)
Exhibited in 'Documenta 4' in Kassel
1969 Exhibited in John Moores Exhibition, Liverpool (prizewinner)
1970 Retrospective exhibition at Tate Gallery and travelling in Europe
One-man exhibitions at Galerie René Block, Berlin (also 1971/73), National Gallery of Canada, Ottawa and travelling
Exhibited in 'Contemporary British Art' at Museum of Modern Art, Tokyo, 'British Painting and Sculpture' at National Gallery of Art, Washington DC
Received Talens Prize International
1971 One-man exhibitions at Stedelijk Museum, Amsterdam, Castelli Graphics, New York
1972 One-man exhibitions at Whitworth Art Gallery, Manchester, Institute of Contemporary Arts
1973 Retrospective exhibition at Guggenheim Museum, New York and travelling in USA and Germany
1974 Retrospective exhibitions in Cincinnati, Munich, Tubingen and Berlin
1975 One-man exhibitions at Kaiser Wilhelm Museum, Krefeld, Serpentine Gallery
1976 One-man exhibition at Stedelijk Museum, Amsterdam and travelling in Europe
1977 One-man exhibition at Musée Grenoble
Two-man exhibition 'Collaborations' (with Dieter Roth) at Institute of Contemporary Arts and travelling in Europe and USA
1978 Retrospective exhibitions 'Studies' at Kunsthalle, Bielefeld, Tubingen and Gottingen, 'Graphics' at Vancouver Art Gallery
Two-man exhibition 'Interfaces' (with Dieter Roth) at Waddington Galleries and travelling in Europe

Contact Tate Gallery

Although some of my pre-Pop pictures may seem to the casual observer to be 'abstract' I believe it is true to say that I have never made a painting which does not show an intense awareness of the human figure. In the case of earlier work it was the human configuration (two eyes situated at a certain distance from two mobile feet) confronting the picture that determined its composition. Assumptions about the human figure were fundamental to the location of elements within the painting and the painting's relationship to the viewer was

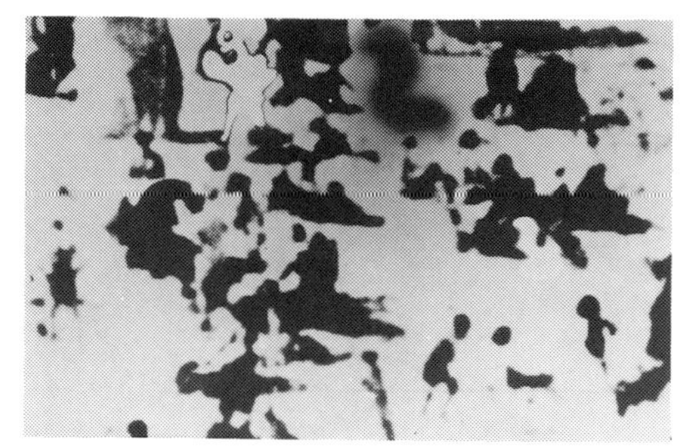

Richard Hamilton *People* 1965-6 Oil and cellulose on photograph 81x122cm (31¾x47¾in) Artist's Collection

prescribed. That is to say, one justification for the picture was its value as a contribution to the total perspective of the spectator: a candid demonstration of the platitudinous concept that a work of art does not exist without its audience.

Later pictures of mine have absorbed into this external concern a recognition of the potency that representation of the human figure adds to this dialogue between image and witness. A fellow creature in the viewer's environment, either artificial (a semblance) or real, must be the strongest, most emotive, factor in it; he will command attention for no other reason than his figurative identification with the ego. The force with which this *dramatis persona* can provide displeasure is no less great than its capacity to provide companionship or to alter the construct of our lives. It, another self, real or semblance, revealed or implied, will always be a major factor in my art.

(Statement in response to question 'What kind of significance and/or importance does the image of the human figure have in your works?' put by Yoshiaki Toni from Tokyo 1971)

Tim Head 166

Tim Head *Interference* 1976 Installation at Rowan Gallery

1946 Born in London
1965-9 Studied at Department of Fine Art, University of Newcastle-upon-Tyne
1968 Worked as assistant to Claes Oldenburg in New York
1969-70 Studied sculpture at St Martin's School of Art
1971 Worked as assistant to Robert Morris at Tate Gallery
1971- Teaching at Goldsmiths College and Slade School of Fine Art
1972 First one-man exhibition at Museum of Modern Art, Oxford
1973 One-man exhibition at Gallery House
Published *Reconstruction* (Idea Books)
1974 One-man exhibition at Whitechapel Art Gallery, Garage Gallery
1975 One-man exhibition at Arnolfini Gallery, Bristol, Rowan Gallery (also 1976/78)
Received Gulbenkian Foundation Visual Arts Award
1976 Exhibited in 'Arte inglese oggi' at Palazzo Reale, Milan, 'Time, Words and the Camera' at Kunstlerhaus, Graz
1977 One-man exhibition at Anthony Stokes Gallery
Exhibited in 'Documenta 6' at Kassel, Paris Biennale, 'On Site' at Arnolfini Gallery, Bristol, 'Reflected Images' at Kettle's Yard, Cambridge
1977-8 Artist in Residence at Clare Hall and Kettle's Yard, Cambridge
1978 One-man exhibition at Kettle's Yard, Cambridge

Contact 17 Belsize Park Gardens, London NW3

Tim Head *Present* 1977 Installation at Rowan Gallery

Up until quite recently artists who observed the world around them wound up offering their audience an unique 'interpretation'. Tim Head does not do this, although his work is perfectly consistent with the traditional aim of provoking the viewer into entering a different world. But unlike traditional artists, Head does not in any sense fabricate his alternative reality. We accept his world as real because we can see it has been recorded by a camera, and, in almost all his work we are given the opportunity to check it out against the original. He uses the camera for its own sake, because it conveys information, but then goes on to enlist that information in the service of age-old artistic concerns. In his hands it becomes a painterly means of expression, capable of provoking powerful flights of imagination, but it also, at all times, is a tool far more precise than the laborious devices invented by Renaissance artists, who believed that once they had mastered perspective they would have full control of their art.

Fenella Crichton 1978

Adrian Heath 65

1920 Born in Burma
1938 Studied painting in Newlyn under Stanhope Forbes RA
1939-40 Studied at Slade School of Fine Art (also 1945-7)
1947-8 Lived in South of France
First one-man exhibition at Musée de Carcassonne
1953 One-man exhibition at Redfern Gallery (also 1966/73/75/78)
Published *Abstract Art, The Origins and Meaning* (Alec Tiranti)
1954-64 Chairman of Artists International Association
1956-77 Principal Visiting Lecturer at Bath Academy of Art
1959 One-man exhibition at Hanover Gallery (also 1961/63)
1961 One-man exhibition at Museum am Ostwall, Dortmund
1962 Elected member of London Group
1962-3 Exhibited in 'British Art Today' in San Francisco, Dallas and Santa Barbara, 'British Painting in the 60s' at Tate Gallery
1964 Exhibited in 'Painting and Sculpture of a Decade 1954-1964' at Tate Gallery (Gulbenkian Foundation)
1967 One-man exhibition at Mickery Gallery, Amsterdam
Exhibited in 'Recent British Painting' at Tate Gallery (Peter Stuyvesant Foundation Collection)
1971 Retrospective exhibition at Bristol City Art Gallery
1972 One-man exhibition at Graves City Art Gallery, Sheffield
1974 Exhibited in 'British Painting '74' at Hayward Gallery
1975 One-man exhibition at Camden Arts Centre
1977 Exhibited in 'British Painting 1952-1977' at Royal Academy

Dealer Redfern Gallery

My earliest works were conventional portraits and landscapes – the result of the traditional academic training that I had received at the Slade just before and immediately after the war. I was able to escape from this tradition by the study of Cubism and in particular the paintings of Jacques Villon and Juan Gris. I did not like their work as much as that of Picasso and Braque but their use of geometry seemed to offer a more rational and impersonal means of development. My own early work was based on proportional divisions and subdivisions of the format of the canvas. This early work of 1950-58 was entirely non-objective and the direct perception of nature was severely excluded. Paradoxically, I did not think of geometry as a means of creating static structures of ideal proportions but rather as a tool to enable me to create and control movement. I thought of my paintings in organic terms; their forms had to evolve and grow. During the 60s my work became more sensuous and painterly, more spontaneous and casual in appearance. My methods of work had changed. I made a great many drawings from the figure and landscape and then drew again from these drawings, usually in another medium and on a different scale. The paintings were based not on a single drawing but on a series and they soon lost touch with their point of departure. I feel that the successful paintings gained their own identity and lost any direct reference to figure or landscape.

Adrian Heath *Curved Forms: Yellow and Black* 1954 Oil on Canvas 91.4x61cm (36x24in) Artist's Collection

Adrian Heath *Heaval* 1974 Oil 182.9x172.7cm (6ftx5ft8in) Artist's Collection

During the present decade my pictures have become tightly painted and considered in their composition. The speed, accident and gesture of direct painting is left behind in the studies (of which I make a great many) and on the canvas I strive for something both monumental and mysterious.

Adrian Heath 1979

David Hepher 193

1935 Born in Surrey
1955-61 Studied at Camberwell School of Art and Slade School of Fine Art
1960 Exhibited in 'Young Contemporaries' (also 1961)
1962 Exhibited with London Group
1965 Exhibited in Summer Exhibition at Piccadilly Gallery
1971 First one-man exhibition at Serpentine Gallery
1972 One-man exhibition at Angela Flowers Gallery (also 1974)
Exhibited in 'Realists' at Galerie Thelen, Cologne,
'Hyper-realism' at Galerie des 4 Mouvements, Paris
1973 One-man exhibition at Galerie Thelen, Cologne
Exhibited in 'La peinture anglaise aujourd'hui' at Musée d'Art Moderne, Paris,
'Immagini come strumento di realità' at Studio La Città, Verona

▶

1974 Retrospective exhibitions at Mappin Art Gallery, Sheffield, Whitechapel Art Gallery
Exhibited in Tokyo Biennale (First Prize),
'British Painting '74' at Hayward Gallery

1975 One-man exhibition 'New Work 1' at Hayward Gallery
Exhibited in 'From Britain '75' AIR exhibition in Helsinki

1976 Exhibited in 'Ausblick, Einblick' at Ruhr Festspiele, Recklinghausen

1977 Exhibited in 'Works on Paper' at Royal Academy,
'Real Life' Peter Moores Exhibition, Liverpool

Dealer Angela Flowers Gallery

David Hepher *Stockwell Flats* 1974-5 Oil on canvas 274.3x193cm (9ftx6ft4in) Private Collection

Although my work may seem very 'realist' I don't feel that it is. I don't work from photographs but from drawings, notes and a lot of looking. I would like to *re-create* a world in its own terms, which is both contemplative and approachable.

David Hepher 1979

David Hepher *No 19, Townley Road* 1973 Oil on canvas 188x243.8cm (6ft2inx8ft) Artist's Collection

Josef Herman 48

1911 Born in Warsaw

1929-31 Studied at School of Art and Decoration, Warsaw

1932-7 Worked as graphic artist and designer in Warsaw

1940 Came to live in England

1943 One-man exhibition at Lefevre Gallery

1944-55 Lived and worked in Welsh mining village of Ystradgynlais

1946 First one-man exhibition at Roland, Browse & Delbanco (also 1948/52/53/57/60/62/65/68/71/73)

1952 Exhibited in Carnegie International Exhibition, Pittsburgh

1953 Exhibited in International Watercolours Exhibition at Brooklyn Museum, New York

1956 Retrospective exhibition at Whitechapel Art Gallery
One-man exhibition at National Gallery of Victoria, Melbourne
Exhibited in John Moores Exhibition, Liverpool (prizewinner)
Published *A Welsh Mining Village* (Arnolfini Press)

1957 One-man exhibition at Galerie B Thommen, Basle

1958 One-man exhibitions at Scottish Art Gallery, Edinburgh, Kunstkabinett, Frankfurt

1960 Exhibited in 'British Art 1720-1960' in Moscow and Leningrad
BBC film 'The Artist Speaks – Josef Herman' produced by John Read

1961 One-man exhibitions in Bristol, Manchester and Dublin

1962 Received Gold Medal at Royal National Eisteddfod of Wales

1963 Retrospective exhibition at Glynn Vivian Gallery, Swansea
One-man exhibitions at Helene Seiferheld Gallery, New York, Benjamin Galleries, Chicago
Exhibited in 'British Painting in the 60s' at Tate Gallery

1964 One-man exhibitions at Galerie Dresdnere, Toronto and Montreal

1965 One-man exhibition at Ben Uri Gallery

1969 One-man exhibition at Scottish National Gallery of Art, Edinburgh
Illustrated *Persons, Places and Things* by Allen Freer (CUP)

1971 One-man exhibition at Sands Gallery, Harrogate (also 1972/73)

1972 One-man exhibition at University of Sussex

1974 Exhibited in 'Anglo-French Contemporary Portraiture' at Wildenstein Gallery

1975 Retrospective exhibitions at Kelvingrove, Glasgow, National Museum of Wales, Cardiff
Published autobiography *Related Twilights* (Robson Books)

Contact 120 Edith Road, London W14

Josef Herman *Two Miners* 1959 Lithograph 66x55.9cm (26x22in)

Josef Herman *Pembrokeshire Scene* 1972 Oil on canvas 66x55.9cm (26x22in) Philip Solomon Collection

Painting must be about something. It cannot be about nothing. This is why I find the subject matter so important for my work. It conditions the activity of the imagination but also the final mood and spiritual atmosphere. The materiality of things interests me very little. Form and colour, in this order. Form directs the idea content, colour follows naturally. When I set out on a new picture I have only a vague idea about its scheme of colours; in the process of work it may change several times till I get the right intensity and the right expression. The form is often clear to me from the start though it too may get new accents according to the strength and stability it will require. Form must be decisive, it cannot be vague or merely suggestive; its solidity and its stability is to establish the emotional energies at work in each picture. But finally it is the overall feeling content which matters most; to rediscover it in each picture is yet another mysterious journey. The eye may be the compass but feeling is the map. Years of work and experience makes this feeling familiar to us but how to bring it on to the surface of a picture remains as mysterious as ever – in this sense each picture is a new beginning and we painters are eternal beginners.

Josef Herman 1979

Patrick Heron 55

1920 Born in Leeds
1947 First one-man exhibition at Redfern Gallery (also 1948/50/51/54/56/58)
1947-50 Art critic to *New Statesman and Nation*
1952 Retrospective exhibition at Wakefield City Art Gallery and travelling
1953 Exhibited in Sao Paulo Bienal (also 1965 prizewinner)
1955 Published *The Changing Forms of Art* (Routledge & Kegan Paul/Noonday Press, New York) and *Ivon Hitchens* (Penguin)
1955-8 London correspondent to *Arts* (New York)
1958 Published *Braque* (Faber & Faber)
1959 One-man exhibition at Waddington Galleries (also 1960/63/64/65/67/68/70/73/75/77/79)
Exhibited in John Moores Exhibition, Liverpool (Grand Prize)
1960 One-man exhibition at Bertha Schaefer Gallery, New York (also 1962/65)
1961 Exhibited in Carnegie International Exhibition, Pittsburgh
1962 Exhibited in 'British Art Today' in San Francisco, Dallas and Santa Barbara
1963 One-man exhibition at Galerie Charles Leinhard, Zurich
1964 Exhibited in 'Painting and Sculpture of a Decade 1954-64' at Tate Gallery
1967 Retrospective exhibition at Demarco Gallery, Edinburgh
Exhibited in 'Recent British Painting' at Tate Gallery (Peter Stuyvesant Foundation Collection)
1968 Retrospective exhibition at Museum of Modern Art, Oxford
1970 One-man exhibitions in Canada and Australia
Exhibited in 'British Painting and Sculpture 1960-70' at National Gallery of Art, Washington DC
1972 One-man exhibition at Whitechapel Art Gallery
1973 One-man exhibition at Bonython Art Gallery, Sydney
Exhibited in Sydney Biennale
Delivered Power Lecture in Contemporary Art for 1973 'The Shape of Colour' in six Australian cities
1974 Exhibited in 'British Painting '74' at Hayward Gallery
1977 One-man exhibition at Galerie le Balcon des Arts, Paris
Exhibited in 'British Painting 1952-1977' at Royal Academy
Received CBE
1978 One-man exhibition at University of Texas at Austin Art Museum
Delivered Doty Lectures 'The Colour of Colour' at University of Texas
1979 Designed two carpets for foyer of Cavendish Hotel

Dealer Waddington Galleries

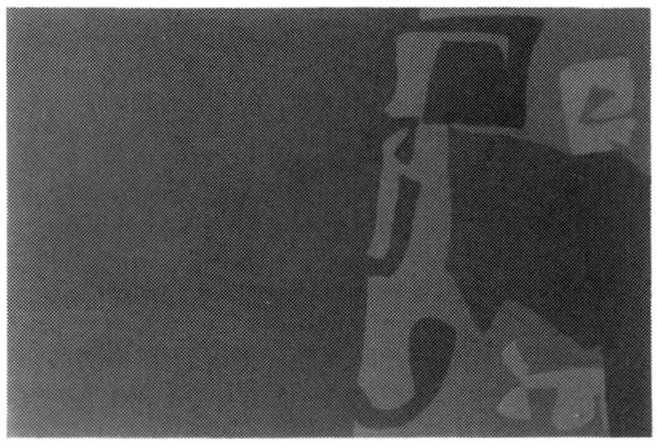

Patrick Heron *Emerald Penetrating Reds on Right: April - July, 1977* Oil on canvas 101.6x152.4cm (40x60in) Waddington Galleries

For a very long time, now, I have realized that my over-riding interest is *colour*. Colour is both the subject and the means; the form and the content; the image and the meaning, in my painting today . . . It is obvious that colour is now the *only* direction in which painting can travel. Painting has still a continent left to explore, in the direction of colour (and in no other direction) . . . It seems obvious to me that we are still only at the beginning of our discovery and enjoyment of the superbly exciting facts of the world of colour. One reels at the colour possibilities now: the varied and contrasting intensities, opacities, transparencies; the seeming density and weight, warmth, coolness, vibrancy; or the superbly inert 'dull' colours – such as the marvellously uneventful expanses of the surface of an old green door in the sunlight. Or the terrific zing of a violet vibration . . . a violent violet flower, with five petals, suspended against the receptive furry green of leaves in a greenhouse!

Patrick Heron 1962
(From *A Note on My Painting*)

Patrick Heron *Big Cobalt Violet: May 1972* Oil on canvas 208.3x457cm (6ft10inx15ft) Waddington Galleries

Anthony Hill 101

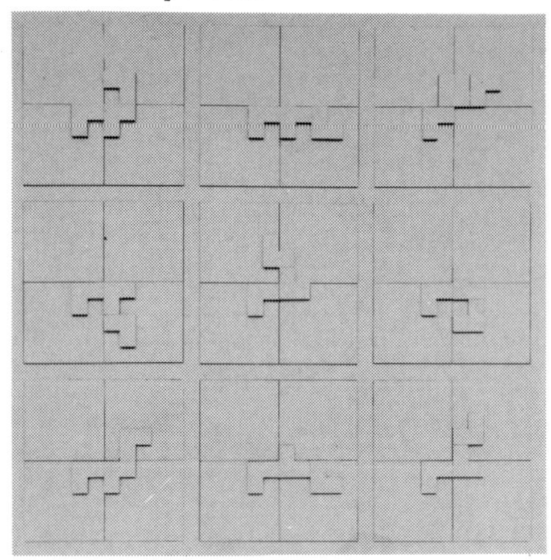

Anthony Hill *The Nine — Hommage à Khlebnikov (No 1)* 1975 White vinyl laminate 86.4x86.4cm (34x34in) Lipschultz Collection, Chicago

1930 Born in London
1947-9 Studied at St Martin's School of Art
1950 Exhibited in 'Aspects of British Art' at Institute of Contemporary Arts
1956 Exhibited in 'This Is Tomorrow' at Whitechapel Art Gallery
1958 One-man exhibition at Institute of Contemporary Arts (also 1963)
1960 Exhibited in 'Konkrete Kunst' at Helmhaus, Zurich
1961 Exhibited in Paris Biennale
1962 Exhibited in 'Experiment in Construction' at Stedelijk Museum, Amsterdam
1965 Exhibited in Tokyo Biennale, 'Art and Movement' at Tel Aviv Museum
1966 One-man exhibition at Kasmin Gallery (also 1969)
1968 Exhibited in 'Relief-Construction-Relief' at Museum of Contemporary Art, Chicago, 'Documenta 4' at Kassel
1969 Exhibited in Middelheim Sculpture Biennale
1971 Exhibited in '4 Artists' at Victoria and Albert Museum and travelling
1974 Exhibited in 'British Art from the Tate Gallery' at Palais des Beaux Arts, Brussels, 'British Painting '74' at Hayward Gallery
1975 Exhibited in 'British Art '75' at Basle, 'Recent British Painting' Peter Stuyvesant Foundation Collection travelling exhibition, 'New Work 1' at Hayward Gallery
1976 Exhibited in John Moores Exhibition, Liverpool, 'Arte inglese oggi' at Palazzo Reale, Milan
Commenced work on film '66 Canonical Variations'
1977 Exhibited in 'Hayward Annual' at Hayward Gallery, 'Aspects of Geometric Art' at Musée d'Art Moderne, Paris, 'British Painting 1952-1977' at Royal Academy
1978 Exhibited in 'Constructive Context' at Warehouse Gallery

Contact 24 Charlotte Street, London W1

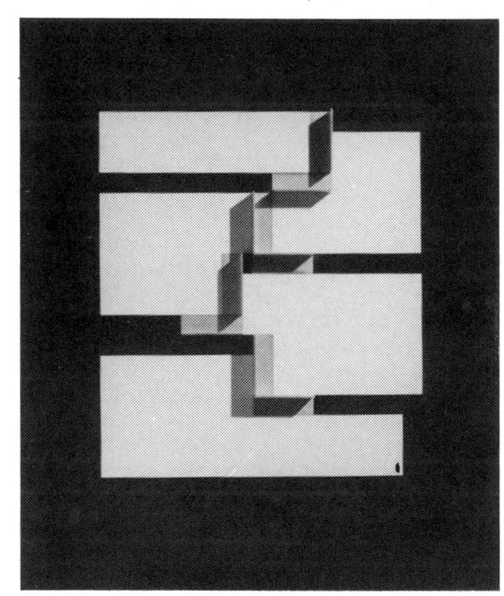

Anthony Hill *Relief Construction* 1963 Vinyl laminate and aluminium 91.4x108.6x48cm (36x$42\frac{3}{4}$x$1\frac{7}{8}$in) Tate Gallery

Susan Hiller 190

1940 Born in USA
1957-65 Studied at Smith College, Massachusetts and Tulane University, Louisiana
1967- Resident in Great Britain
1967/8 Individual USIS touring exhibition
1968 Received Karolyi Foundation Award
1969 Group investigation piece 'Pray/Prayer'
1972 Exhibited in 'Photography into Art' at Camden Arts Centre (and touring)
1973 Individual exhibition at Gallery House
Group investigation pieces 'Street Ceremonies' and 'The Dream Seminar'
Received GLAA Award
1974 Individual exhibition at Garage Art
Group investigation piece 'Dream Mapping'
1975 Artist-in-Residence at University of Sussex
1976 Individual exhibitions at Serpentine Gallery, Gardner Centre Gallery, University of Sussex
Exhibited in 'American Artists in Britain' Winsor & Newton Bicentennial travelling exhibition
Received Gulbenkian Foundation Visual Artists' Award (also 1977)
1977 Individual exhibition at Hester van Royen Gallery (also 1978)
Exhibited in 'Kunstlerinnen International 1877-1977' in Berlin, 'Reflected Images' at Kettles Yard, Cambridge, 'On Site' at Arnolfini Gallery, Bristol
1978 Individual exhibitions at Museum of Modern Art, Oxford, Kettles Yard, Cambridge, and Peterloo Gallery, Manchester
Exhibited in 'Hayward Annual' at Hayward Gallery

Contact 25 Artesian Road, London W2

After my first show of paintings and drawings in 1967, I concentrated for several years on work that can perhaps be classified as 'performance', if that word is considered in its sense of *enactment* and not taken to imply any hierarchical distinction between the roles of spectator and participant. My work in this area was always deliberately non-theatrical, conducted in the spirit of a collective investigation. I did not exhibit canvas or paper works again until 1973.

My most recent pieces extend the interest in examining signs of the communal origins of our images and ideas that began with my earlier group investigations: *Dedicated to the Unknown Artists* is based on my discovery and analysis of the 'Rough Sea' set of postcards, *Fragments* on broken bits of handpainted Pueblo Indian pottery, *Enquiries/Inquiries* on excerpts from two popular encyclopedias of 'facts', and *The Photomat Portrait Series* on pictures taken in automatic photo booths. All these recent works are contained within the classic framework of an art exhibition, as were my paintings.

I think it is fair to say that my work mostly proposes a 'paraconceptual' notion of culture – that is, I aim to reveal the extent to which existing cultural models are inadequate because they exclude or deny some perceivable part of reality. I cherish the exclusions which I find perplexing, beautiful, complex or disturbing.

If I could simply *say* what my work was 'about', I would not need to or want to do it . . .

Susan Hiller 1979

two dragonflies calling the rain	clouds with eyes and feathers with eyes	cloud stripe	red triangle	cloud circle	striped steps
square within heart	deer in the house of flowers	deer house	a prayer in rain	feathers	milky way with hook
wavy hooks with triangles along the edge	hook circles	striped clouds with milky way	two birds	hooks with feathers	red triangle with eyes
black steps	squares	wavy striped clouds	hanging feathers	wavy square	striped triangles hanging down
wavy checks	butterfly calling the rain	star inside stripes	rain blanket	snow blanket	spider web
flowers everywhere	striped feathers, red feather and square	striped square	red steps	checked square	cloud triangle
flowers	feathers meeting face to face				

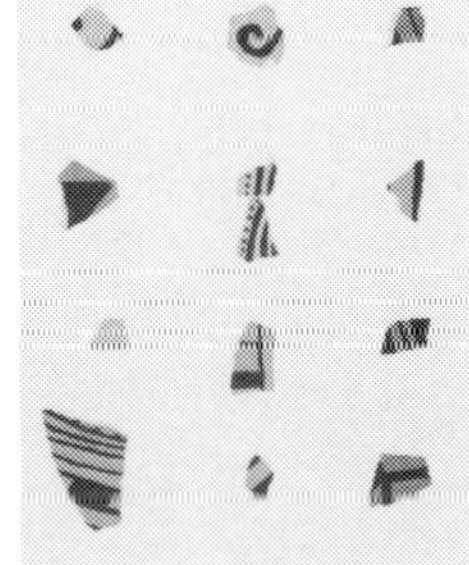

Susan Hiller Detail from *Fragments* 1978 Gounache drawing, potsherds and chart

John Hilliard 176

1945 Born in Lancaster
1964-7 Studied at St Martin's School of Art
1965 Travel Scholarship to USA
1971 First one-man exhibition at Lisson Gallery (also 1973/75/78)
Exhibited in Sao Paulo Bienal, 'Prospect '71' at Kunsthalle, Dusseldorf
1972 Exhibited in 'The New Art' at Hayward Gallery
1973 Exhibited in 'From Henry Moore to Gilbert & George' at Palais des Beaux Arts, Brussels
1974 One-man exhibition at Museum of Modern Art, Oxford,
Galleria Toselli, Milan
Published *Elemental Conditioning* (Museum of Modern Art, Oxford)

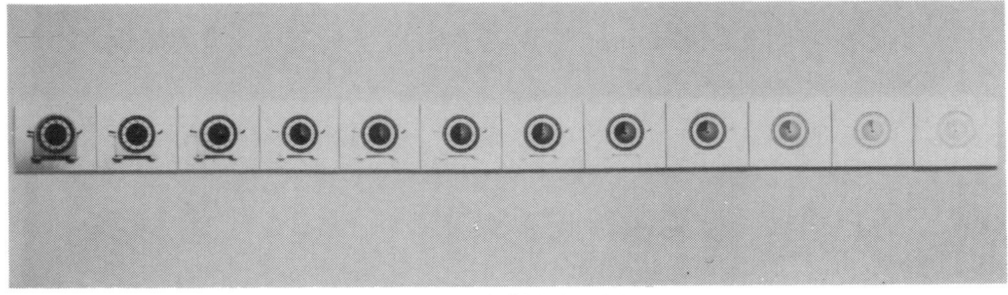

John Hilliard *Sixty Seconds of Light* 1970 Mounted photographs 40x600cm (15¾x218in) Tate Gallery

1975 One-man exhibition at Galleria Banco, Brescia
1976 One-man exhibition at Galerie Hetzler & Keller, Stuttgart (also 1979), Galerie Durand-Dessert, Paris (also 1977/79)
Exhibited in 'Arte inglese oggi' at Palazzo Reale, Milan
Published *Black Depths, White Expanse, Grey Extent* (Robert Self)
1977 One-man exhibition at Badischer Kunstverein, Karlsruhe,
Paul Maenz Gallery, Cologne
Exhibited in 'Documenta 6' in Kassel,
'Hayward Annual' at Hayward Gallery,
Paris Biennale
Published *Analytical Photography* (Badischer Kunstverein, Karlsruhe)
1978 One-man exhibition at John Gibson Gallery, New York
Published *From the Northern Counties* (Lisson Gallery)
1979 One-man exhibition at Ikon Gallery, Birmingham
Exhibited in 'Un certain art anglais' at Musée d'Art Moderne, Paris

Dealer Lisson Gallery
John Gibson Gallery, New York

LV: Why are you so concerned with photography as a medium?

JH: My use of photography originally comes out of making sculpture and needing documentary evidence, and out of a subsequent recognition that those documents were almost always employed as the sole representatives of the work – thereby attaining first-order status, albeit by default. I began first deliberately to extend and improve the use of photographs as viable substitutes (for whatever they represented), and then to examine the problems inherent in that use of photography (as employed both by myself and by others).

LV: Is there a main issue throughout your work?

JH: You could say that since 1969 I've been investigating the reliability of photographs as representatives of their objects – although that statement wouldn't tell you everything about the work. But my attitude to the use of photographs is ambivalent. Even though I'm totally suspicious of their adequacy to that end, I like using them as access to work I would never see at first-hand – and also to supplement my experience of work I have seen. I value the peculiar properties of photographs, where space and time are frozen in an unreal stasis which invites an abnormally objective scrutiny, and I like their discreet form (initially, expanding the use of documentation was for me one way of eliminating a material excess that I found intrusive, depressing and wasteful).

Extract from interview with Luca Venturi 1974

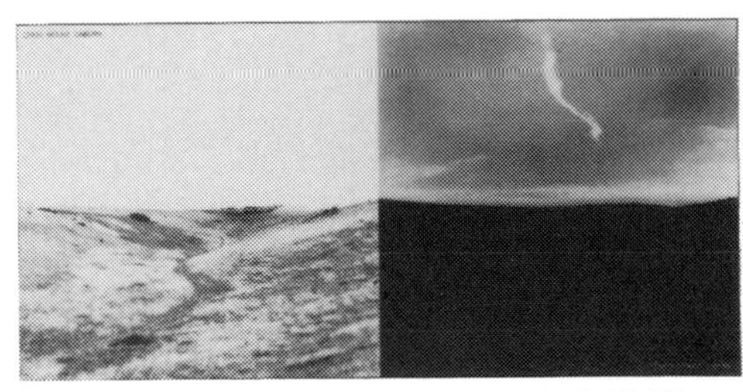

John Hilliard *Over Mount Caburn* 1978 Mounted photographs 85x130cm (33½x51in) Artist's Collection

Tristram Hillier RA 11

1905 Born in Peking
1922-3 Lived in Peking studying Chinese
1924-5 Studied at Christ's College, Cambridge
1926-7 Studied at Slade School of Fine Art
1926-40 Lived and worked in France
1927-8 Studied under André Lhote in Paris ▶

1929 One-man exhibition at Galerie Barreiro, Paris
1930 Exhibited as member of Unit One in group show at Mayor Gallery
1931 One-man exhibition at Lefevre Gallery (also 1933)
1940-5 Served with Free French Naval Forces
1945- Settled in Somerset, but spending much of his time in Spain and Portugal
1946 One-man exhibition at Arthur Tooth & Sons.(also 1948/50/54/60/68/73)
1954 Published autobiography *Leda and the Goose* (Longmans)
1957 Elected Associate of Royal Academy
1960 Retrospective exhibition at Worthing Museum and Art Gallery
1967 Elected Royal Academician
1973 One-man exhibition at Langton Gallery
1975 One-man exhibition at Pieter Wenning Gallery, Johannesburg

Dealer Alex Reid & Lefevre

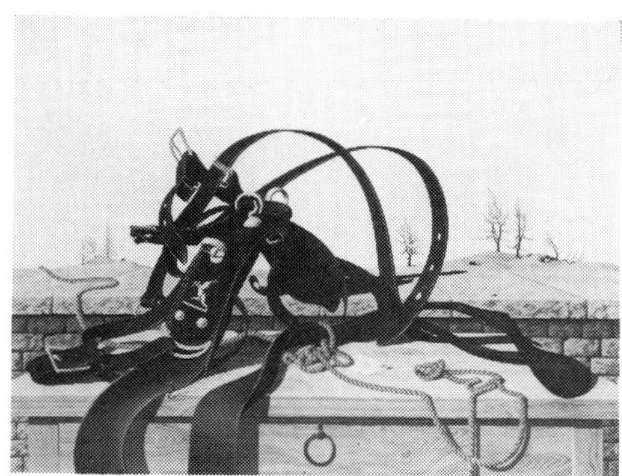
Tristram Hillier *Harness* 1944 Tempera on canvas 59.1x81.3cm (23¼x32in) Tate Gallery

Probably the strongest contemporary influence on my work was Surrealism. During the late 1920s and early 1930s I knew most of the Surrealist painters in Paris and from Max Ernst, Lurçat, and the early de Chirico I received influences so powerful that they have, I think, remained with me – in a muted form – until the present time. As a young man in Paris I started to paint abstract pictures, then followed a long period of Surrealist paintings, and it was not until 1938 that I discarded the more obvious forms of Surrealism to paint – for lack of a better word – in a representational manner which I have followed ever since. But I have never been a representational painter in the Academic sense of the term. My landscapes are painted in the studio from notes and drawings done on the spot in the manner of the Dutch and Flemish Masters who have really always been the underlying influence in all my work. All my pictures have been painted in oil on canvas, or sometimes on wood. I have seldom painted portraits and my work consists of landscape, still-life and architectural compositions.

Tristram Hillier 1979

Derek Hirst 148

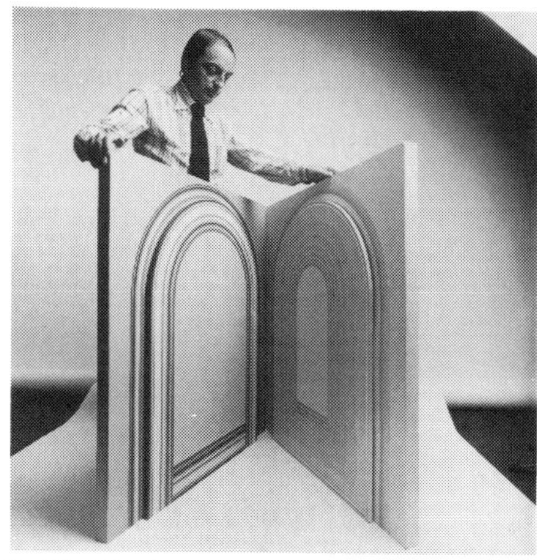
Derek Hirst *Odeon: Yellow/Purple* 1970-3 and *Montserrat* (2nd version) 1970 Cryla on relief panel 111.8x101.6cm (44x40in) Artist's Collection

1930 Born in Doncaster
1946-8 Studied at Doncaster School of Art
1948-51 Studied at Royal College of Art
1951-76 Visiting Lecturer at art schools and colleges in London
1960-79 Exhibited in group shows in Europe, Australia, Brazil, Canada and USA
1961 One-man exhibition at Drian Galleries
1962 One-man exhibition at Arthur Tooth & Sons (also 1963)
1963 One-man exhibition at Stone Galleries, Newcastle-upon-Tyne
1966 First Artist in Residence at University of Sussex
One-man exhibitions at University of Sussex,
Towner Art Gallery, Eastbourne
1970 One-man exhibition at Angela Flowers Gallery (also 1971/73/75)
1971-2 Visiting Lecturer at Philadelphia College of Art
1971-3 Visiting Professor of Painting at York University, Toronto
1976- Principal Lecturer in Painting at School of Fine Art, Kingston Polytechnic
1979 Retrospective exhibition at Angela Flowers Gallery

Dealer Angela Flowers Gallery

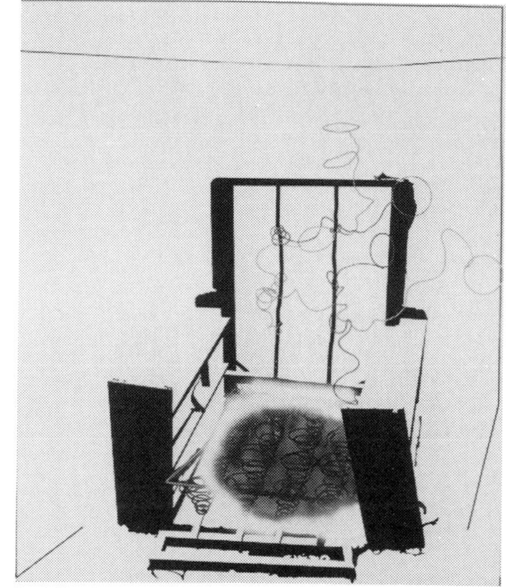
Derek Hirst *Second Visit* 1966/7 Acrylic on canvas 182.9x152.4cm (6x5ft) Artist's Collection

Over the years there have been times when the appearance of my work has seemingly changed quite radically but the preoccupation and obsessions have remained the same. Hopefully they are self-evident in the work itself.

My attitude to Art is most eloquently expressed by a hero of mine, the marvellous American poet, William Carlos Williams, in a fragment from his great book: *Paterson* (New Directions, USA, 1963):

'To make a start
out of particulars
and make them general, rolling
up the sum, by defective means –
Sniffing the trees
just another dog
amongst a lot of dogs. What
else is there? And to do?
The rest have run out –
after the rabbits.
Only the lame stands – on
three legs. Scratch front and back.
Deceive and eat. Dig
a musty bone.'

Derek Hirst 1979

Ivon Hitchens 4

1893 Born in London
1911-14 Studied at St John's Wood School of Art and Royal Academy Schools (also 1918-19)
1925 First one-man exhibition at Mayor Gallery
1931 Elected member of London Group
1933 One-man exhibition at Lefevre Galleries (also 1935/37)
1937 Elected member of Society of Mural Painters
1939 Exhibited in British Exhibition at World's Fair, New York
1940 One-man exhibition at Leicester Galleries (also 1942/44/47/50/52/54/57/59)
1945 First retrospective exhibition at Temple Newsam, Leeds (with Henry Moore)
1946 Exhibited in UNESCO International Exhibition of Modern Painting in Paris
1948 Retrospective exhibition at Graves Art Gallery, Sheffield
1950 Exhibited in Carnegie International Exhibition, Pittsburgh, 'From Gainsborough to Hitchens' Howard Bliss Collection at Leicester Galleries
1951 Exhibited in '60 Paintings for '51' Arts Council exhibition at Festival of Britain (prizewinner)
1955 Publication of *Ivon Hitchens* by Patrick Heron (Penguin Modern Painters)
1956 Exhibited in 'Masters of British Painting 1800-1950' at Museum of Modern Art, New York, Venice Biennale
1957 Retrospective exhibitions at Musée d'Art Moderne, Paris, Stedelijk Museum, Amsterdam Received CBE

Ivon Hitchens *Lone Fishing* 1975 Oil on canvas 53.3x132.1cm (21x52in) Artist's Collection

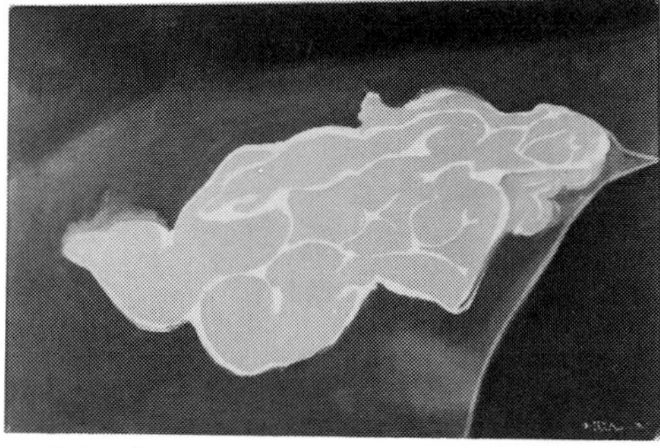
Ivon Hitchens *Figure on Dark Shore* 1967 Oil 50.3x76.2cm (20x30in) Artist's Collection

1958 Exhibited in '50 ans d'art moderne' at Palais des Beaux Arts, Brussels
1960 One-man exhibition at Waddington Galleries (also 1962/64/66/68/69/71/73/76)
Exhibited in 'British Painting 1720-1960' in Moscow and Leningrad
1961 Retrospective (with Stanley Spencer and Graham Sutherland) Arts Council travelling exhibition
1962 Exhibited in 'British Art Today' in San Francisco, Dallas and Santa Barbara
1963 Installation of commissioned mural painting *Day's Rest, Day's Work* at University of Sussex
1973 Publication of *Ivon Hitchens* by Alan Bowness
1974 Exhibited in 'British Painting '74' at Hayward Gallery
1977 Exhibited in 'British Painting 1952-1977' at Royal Academy
1979 Retrospective exhibition at Royal Academy

Dealer Waddington Galleries

David Hockney 105

1937 Born in Bradford
1953-7 Studied at Bradford College of Art
1959-61 Studied at Royal College of Art
1960 Exhibited in 'Young Contemporaries' (also 1962)
1961 Exhibited in John Moores Exhibition, Liverpool (prizewinner/also 1973/67 prizewinner), Paris Biennale (also 1963 prizewinner/78)
Received Guinness Award
1962 Exhibited in Tokyo Biennale
1963 First one-man exhibition at Kasmin Gallery (also 1965/66/68/69/70/72)
Exhibited in 'British Painting in the 60s' at Whitechapel Art Gallery
1964 One-man exhibitions at Alan Gallery, New York, Museum of Modern Art, New York (also 1968)
Exhibited in 'British Artists of Today' at Kunsthalle, Dusseldorf and travelling in Germany, 'Painting and Sculpture of a Decade 1954-64' at Tate Gallery, 'Contemporary Painters, Sculptors and Printmakers' at Museum of Modern Art, New York
1965 Exhibited in 'London: The New Scene' at Walker Art Centre, Minneapolis and travelling in USA and Canada, 'Pop Art – Nouveau Realisme' at Palais des Beaux Arts, Brussels
1966 One-man exhibition at Stedelijk Museum, Amsterdam
Taught at University of California (also 1967)
1967 Exhibited in Carnegie International Exhibition, Pittsburgh, Sao Paulo Bienal, 'British Art Today' in Hamburg, 'European Painters of Today' at Musée des Arts Décoratifs, Paris and travelling in USA
1968 One-man exhibition at Galerie Mikro, Berlin
Exhibited in Venice Biennale
1968-71 Travelled in USA, Europe, Japan, Indonesia, Burma and Hawaii
1969 One-man exhibition at André Emmerich Gallery, New York (also 1970/72/77)
1970 Retrospective exhibition at Whitechapel Art Gallery and travelling in Europe
Exhibited in 'Contemporary British Art' at Museum of Modern Art, Tokyo, 'British Painting and Sculpture 1960-1970' at National Gallery of Art, Washington DC

David Hockney *Two Boys in a Pool, Hollywood* 1965 Acrylic on canvas 153x153cm (60x60in) Private Collection

1971 One-man exhibition at Kunsthalle, Bielefeld
1972 Exhibited in 'La peinture anglaise aujourd'hui' at Musée d'Art Moderne, Paris
1973 Exhibited in 'Henry Moore to Gilbert & George' at Palais des Beaux Arts,
1974 One-man exhibition at Musée des Arts Décoratifs, Paris
Film made by Jack Hazan on Hockney 'A Bigger Splash'
1975 One-man exhibition at Galerie Claude Bernard, Paris
Exhibited in 'European Painting in the 70s' at Los Angeles County Museum of Art and travelling in USA
Designed sets and costumes for Stravinsky's 'The Rake's Progress' at Glyndebourne
1976 One-man exhibition at Nicholas Wilder Gallery, Los Angeles
Exhibited in 'Arte inglese oggi' at Palazzo Reale, Milan,
'Pop Art in England' at Kunstverein, Hamburg and travelling
Published *David Hockney by David Hockney* (Thames & Hudson)
1977 One-man exhibitions at Stadtliche Graphische Sammlung, Munich, Gulbenkian Foundation, Lisbon
Exhibited in 'Hayward Annual' at Hayward Gallery,
'British Painting 1952-1977' at Royal Academy
Designed sets for Mozart's 'The Magic Flute' at Glyndebourne
1978 Exhibited in '20th-century Portraits' at National Portrait Gallery
Travelled to India
1978-80 One-man International Exhibitions Foundation travelling exhibition in USA and Canada
1979 One-man exhibition 'Paper Pools' at André Emmerich Gallery, New York, Warehouse Gallery, Knoedler Gallery

Dealer Knoedler Gallery

David Hockney *Celia in Black Slip (with Platform Shoes)* 1973 Crayon drawing 50.2x64.8cm (19¾x25½in) Private Collection

Water in swimming pools changes its look more than in any other form. The colour of a river is related to the sky it reflects, and the sea always seems to me to be the same colour and have the same dancing patterns. But the look of swimming-pool water is controllable – even its colour can be man-made – and its dancing rhythms reflect not only the sky but, because of its transparency, the depth of the water as well. So I had to use techniques to represent this (in the later swimming-pool pictures of 1971 I became more aware of the wetness of the surface). If the water surface is almost still and there is strong sun, then dancing lines with the colours of the spectrum appear everywhere. If the pool hasn't been used for a few minutes and there's no breeze, the look is of a simple gradation of colour that follows the incline of the floor of the pool. Added to all this is the infinite variety of patterns of material that the pool can be made from. I once saw a pool in France where the floor had been painted with loose blue brush strokes, which gave a marvellous contrast between artistically rendered water and the natural. As yet I've not been tempted to do anything with that.

David Hockney 1976
(from *David Hockney by David Hockney*)

David Hockney *Still-Life, Taj Hotel, Bombay* 1977 Crayon drawing 43.2x35.6cm (17x14in) Private Collection

Howard Hodgkin

1932 Born in London
1949-50 Studied at Camberwell School of Art
1950-4 Studied at Bath Academy of Art
1956-66 Taught at Bath Academy of Art
1959 Exhibited with London Group (also 1960/61)
1962 First one-man exhibition at Arthur Tooth & Sons (also 1964/67)
1963 Exhibited in 'British Painting in the 60s' at Whitechapel Art Gallery
1964 Exhibited in 'British Malerei der Gegenwart' at Kunsthalle, Dusseldorf and travelling
1965 Exhibited in 'London, the New Scene' travelling in USA
'Pop Art – Nouveau Realisme' at Palais des Beaux Arts, Brussels
1966-72 Taught at Chelsea School of Art
1967 Exhibited in 'Recent British Painting' at Tate Gallery (Peter Stuyvesant Foundation Collection),
Paris Biennale
1969 One-man exhibition at Kasmin Gallery (also 1971)
1970 One-man exhibition at Arnolfini Gallery, Bristol (also 1975)
Exhibited in 'Contemporary British Art' at Museum of Modern Art, Tokyo
1971 One-man exhibition at Galerie Muller, Cologne
1972 Exhibited in John Moores Exhibition, Liverpool (also 1974/76 prizewinner/ 1978)

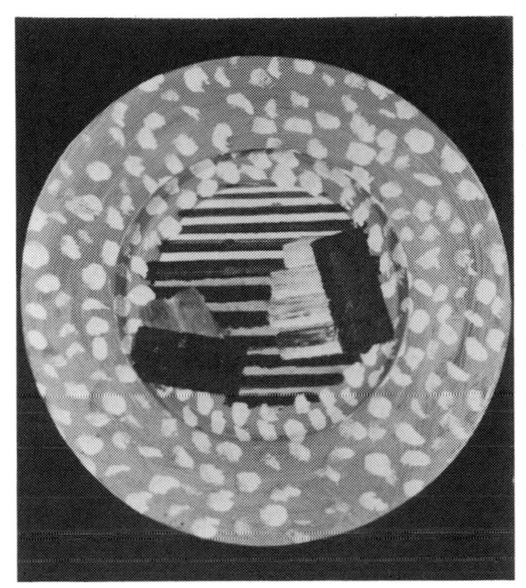

Howard Hodgkin *Small Simon Digby* 1977 Oil on wood 31.8 (12½in) diameter Private Collection

1973 One-man exhibition at Kornblee Gallery, New York
Exhibited in 'La peinture anglaise aujourd'hui' at Musée d'Art Moderne, Paris,
'Henry Moore to Gilbert & George' at Palais des Beaux Arts, Brussels

1974 Exhibited in Tokyo Biennale,
'British Painting '74' at Hayward Gallery

1976 One-man exhibitions at Museum of Modern Art, Oxford (also 1977),
Serpentine Gallery and travelling,
Waddington Galleries
Exhibited in 'The Human Clay' at Hayward Gallery

1976-7 Artist in Residence at Brasenose College, Oxford

1977 One-man exhibitions at André Emmerich Gallery, New York and Zurich
Exhibited in 'Hayward Annual' at Hayward Gallery,
'British Painting 1952-1977' at Royal Academy
Received CBE

1978 Exhibited in group show at Knoedler Gallery (also 1979)

Dealer Knoedler Gallery
André Emmerich Galleries, New York

. . . He starts from a particular visual subject and gradually transforms it. The manner of this transformation is conditioned by various factors: by the aesthetic demands of the picture itself (composition, colour relationships, and so on), by stylistic influences (Matisse has always been important to him . . .), and of course by his personality. None of these contributes separately and what they offer always seems to pass through a filter of wit and irony.

The result is a curious intensity. Hodgkin's titles restate the original subject: a portrait, often. The pictures hover just on nature's side of complete abstractness, so we can't let ourselves off his notional hook by opting for a non-representational reading. We stand there perplexed, but also engaged by their vividness and quite unusual images. Hodgkin's long involvement with Indian miniatures seems to have taught him how to join a convincing sense of life to abstraction and flatness. And time seems to bring a memorable, memory-like succinctness.

Norbert Lynton 1969

Howard Hodgkin *Robyn Denny and Katherine Reid* 1975 Oil on wood 91.4x121.9cm (36x48in) Private Collection

Knighton Hosking *Three Views Revisited* 1977 Acrylic on canvas 274.3x243.8cm (9x8ft) Artist's Collection

Knighton Hosking

1944 Born in Sidmouth

1959-63 Studied at Exeter College of Art

1963-6 Studied at Central School of Art and Design

1964 Exhibited in 'Young Britons' at Altman Gallery, New York

1966 Peter Stuyvesant Foundation Bursary for travel in USA
Exhibited in 'The New Generation' at Whitechapel Art Gallery, and touring

1967 Exhibited in 'Interim' at Whitechapel Art Gallery

1968- Teaching at Wolverhampton Polytechnic

1970 First one-man exhibition at Wolverhampton Polytechnic (also 1974)

1973 Exhibited in group show at Warehouse Gallery (also 1977/78)

1974 One-man exhibition at Serpentine Gallery
Exhibited in 'British Painting '74' at Hayward Gallery,
Industrial Sponsors Exhibition at Finance for Industry Building

1975 One-man exhibition at Sunderland Arts Centre

1976 Exhibited in 'Recent Arts Council Acquisitions' at Hayward Gallery

1977 Exhibited in 'British Painting 1952-1977' at Royal Academy,
'Works on Paper' Contemporary Art Society exhibition at Royal Academy
Received Arts Council Major Award

1977/8 Exhibited in 'Working Process' at Sunderland Arts Centre
Exhibited with Alan Davie and Michael Major in 'Three Painters' South West Arts travelling exhibition

1978 Exhibited in John Moores Exhibition, Liverpool

1979 One-man exhibitions at Plymouth Arts Centre,
Ikon Gallery, Birmingham

Contact 2 The Tower House, 56 Sedgley Road, Penn Common, Wolverhampton

From late 1966 to mid-1974 all my work was concerned with self-representational ideas and imagery. My primary aim at that time was to examine the nature of surface space, pictorial structure, and the painted mark. Much of this work evolved out of itself and was entirely studio based.

During 1974 I became increasingly unhappy with what seemed to me to have become a narrow creative activity, not only intellectually but spiritually. I reached the point where I actually stopped painting altogether for ▶

Knighton Hosking *One Year On* 1978-9 Oil on canvas 274.3x243.8cm (9x8ft) Artist's Collection

six months in an attempt to assess my previous eight years' work.

At this time I moved into the country to live. Although I had spent the first eighteen years of my life in Devon, landscape had never interested me as source material. However now living in the country again I began to see things that related very strongly to many of my early paintings. To be able to look and draw was such a liberating experience after eight years of studio painting.

I now gather visual information by drawing on sight and by taking photographs. I then re-examine the work in the studio through drawing. This provides a basic structure for the painting. I also draw throughout the growth of the painting. The drawings never provide solutions but help to define the problems.

Although all my recent work has used landscape figuration, I am not interested in painting landscape. I still feel the need to pull the landscape space back to the canvas surface. Figuration and surface space and the balance between them are important issues in my current work.

Knighton Hosking 1979

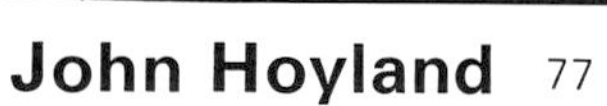

John Hoyland 77

1934 Born in Sheffield
1951-6 Studied at Sheffield College of Art
1956-60 Studied at Royal Academy Schools
1959 Exhibited in 'Young Contemporaries'
1962 Exhibited in 'British Art Today' in San Francisco, Dallas and Santa Barbara
1964 First one-man exhibition at Marlborough New London Gallery
Exhibited in 'The New Generation' at Whitechapel Art Gallery
Received Peter Stuyvesant Bursary and International Young Artists Award, Tokyo

John Hoyland *Trickster* 1977 Acrylic on canvas 228.6x213.4 (7ft6inx7ft) Wayne Anderson Collection USA

John Hoyland *Untitled* 1973 Acrylic on cotton duck 254x228.6cm (8ft 4in x 7ft 6in) Artist's Collection

1965 Exhibited in John Moores Exhibition, Liverpool (prizewinner; also 1976/78), Paris Biennàle
Principal Lecturer at Chelsea School of Art
1967 One-man exhibitions at Whitechapel Art Gallery,
Robert Elkon Gallery, New York (also 1969),
Waddington Fine Art, Montreal (also 1971/78 and in Toronto),
Nicholas Wilder Gallery, Los Angeles (also 1974),
Waddington Galleries (also 1969/70/72/73/74/76/78)
1968 Exhibited in 'New British Painting and Sculpture' in Los Angeles and travelling in USA
1969 One-man exhibition at André Emmerich Gallery, New York (also 1970/71/79)
Exhibited in Sao Paulo Bienal
1969-70 Travelled in South America and USA
1972 One-man exhibitions in Boston and New York
Professor of Fine Arts at Colgate University, Hamilton, New York
1973 Exhibited in 'La peinture anglaise aujourd'hui' at Musée d'Art Moderne, Paris
1974 One-man exhibition at Studio La Città, Verona (also 1976)
1975 One-man exhibitions in Pittsburgh and Detroit
1976 One-man exhibitions in Lisbon, Milan, Genoa and Turin
1979 One-man exhibition at Bernard Jacobsen, New York

Dealer Waddington Galleries
André Emmerich Gallery, New York

The shapes and colours I paint and the significance I attach to them I cannot explain in any coherent way. The exploration of colour, mass, shape is, I believe, a self-exploration constantly varied and changing in nature: a reality made tangible on the painted surface.

John Hoyland 1964

Malcolm Hughes 99

Malcolm Hughes *Three Dimensional Maquette* 1975 Wood and PVA 61x61x61cm (24x24x24in) Artist's Collection

1920 Born in Manchester
1938-9 Studied at Manchester College of Art
1946-50 Studied at Royal College of Art

Malcolm Hughes *Thematic Drawing No 4* 1977 Gouache on paper 36x36cm (14¼x14¼in) Artist's Collection

1960-70 Taught at Bath Academy of Art
1965 One-man exhibition at Institute of Contemporary Arts
1967 One-man exhibition at Axiom Gallery
1968- Teaching at Chelsea School of Art and Slade School of Fine Art
1969 Co-founded Systems Group
1971 Exhibited in 'Four Artists: Reliefs, Constructions and Drawings' at Victoria and Albert Museum
1972 One-man exhibition at Lucy Milton Gallery
Exhibited in 'Systems' at Whitechapel Art Gallery (travelling exhibition)
1973 Exhibited in 'Engelse Systemstische Kunst' at Galerie Swart, Amsterdam
1974 Exhibited in 'Basically White' at Institute of Contemporary Arts, 'Art as Thought Process' at Serpentine Gallery
1975 Exhibited in 'New Work 2' at Hayward Gallery
1976 Exhibited in 'Arte inglese oggi' at Palazzo Reale, Milan, 'Sculpture for the Blind' at Tate Gallery
1977 Exhibited in 'British Artists of the 60s' at Tate Gallery, 'British Painting 1952-1977' at Royal Academy, Second Symposium, IFGK in Varese
1978 Exhibited in 'Constructive Context' Arts Council exhibition, 'Circular' IFGK exhibition in Bonn, 'Arte Britanica de Hoje' at Gulbenkian Foundation, Lisbon

Contact 37 Haldon Road, London SW18

The conceptual basis of the systems I work with are either banal or trivial. They are no more (or less) conceptually original than Morandi's still life objects (or Cézanne's cherished motif 'Sainte Victorie') are perceptually original.

Number systems in general and the prime numbers in particular have been around for quite some time (!) and a variety of artists have worked with them and investigated their potential. What interests me in this conceptual area is that which can be realized and constructed with them – what new unities between and beyond the conceptual/perceptual orderings can emerge. As a constant these logical systems are semantically neutral, therefore, what can emerge from their usage is a limited, but nevertheless personal, contribution to the syntactic structure of art . . .

Malcolm Hughes 1975

Patrick Hughes 114

Patrick Hughes *Endless Snake* 1969 Gloss painted ceramic 61cm (24in) square Artist's Collection

1939 Born in Birmingham
1959-61 Studied at James Graham Teachers Training College, Leeds
1961 First one-man exhibition at Portal Gallery (also 1963)
Exhibited in John Moores Exhibition, Liverpool (also 1963/69/72/78)
1961-4 Taught in state schools in Leeds
1962 Exhibited in 'Critic's Choice' at Arthur Tooth & Sons
1964-9 Senior Lecturer in Painting and Drawing at Leeds College of Art
1965 One-man exhibition at Hanover Gallery
1968 Exhibited in Lignano Biennale
1969-70 Studied Art Education at London University
1970 One-man exhibition at Angela Flowers Gallery (also 1971/73/76/78)
Exhibited in '10 Sitting Rooms' at Institute of Contemporary Arts
1970-4 Taught at Chelsea School of Art and Wolverhampton School of Art
1971 Exhibited in group show at Angela Flowers Gallery (also 1974/75/76)
1973 Exhibited in Middlesbrough Drawing Biennale (also 1975/77)
Received equal First Prize in Transatlantic Review Erotic Drawing Competition
Joint holder of world record for unsupported sitting circle
1974 Exhibited in Bradford Print Biennale (also 1976), 'British Painting '74' at Hayward Gallery
1976 Exhibited in '8 from Angela Flowers' at Gulbenkian Gallery, Newcastle
1977 Exhibited in Tolly Cobbold Eastern Arts Exhibition, Cambridge (also 1979), 'South West Artists' at Artists Market
1978 One-man exhibitions at Tom Caldwell Gallery, Belfast and Dublin, Gallery 39, Manchester
Published *Vicious Circles and Infinity* (with George Brecht; Penguin Books, Harmondsworth) and *Upon the Pun, Dual Meaning in Words and Pictures* (with Paul Hammond; W H Allen)

Dealer Angela Flowers Gallery

Visual paradoxes. Serious humour. Formal figuration. Solid space. Perspective inside-out. Black and white rainbows. Oxymoron and pun. Substantial shadows. Real reflections. Vicious circles.

Patrick Hughes 1978

Patrick Hughes *Fear Itself* 1975 Screenprint 27.9x38.1cm (11x15in)

Paul Huxley 92

Paul Huxley *Untitled No 150* 1974 Acrylic on canvas 213.4x213.4cm (7x7ft) Rowan Gallery

1938 Born in London
1953-6 Studied at Harrow School of Art
1956-60 Studied at Royal Academy Schools
1959 Exhibited in 'Young Contemporaries' (also 1960)
1963 First one-man exhibition at Rowan Gallery (also 1965/68/69/71/74/78)
1964 Exhibited in 'The New Generation' at Whitechapel Art Gallery (prizewinner), Tokyo Biennale (also 1966), 'Contemporary British Painting and Sculpture' at Albright-Knox Art Gallery, Buffalo
1965 Exhibited in Paris Biennale (prizewinner), 'The English Eye' at Marlborough-Gerson Gallery, New York, John Moores Exhibition, Liverpool
Received Harkness Fellowship to USA
1965-7 Lived in New York
1967 One-man exhibition at Kornblee Gallery, New York (also 1970)
Exhibited in Carnegie International Exhibition, Pittsburgh, 'Recent British Painting' at Tate Gallery (Peter Stuyvesant Foundation Collection)
1968 Exhibited in 'New British Sculpture and Painting' at UCLA Art Galleries, Los Angeles and travelling in USA, 'British Artists: 6 Painters, 6 Sculptors' at Museum of Modern Art, New York and travelling in USA

1973 Exhibited in 'Magic and Strong Medicine' at Walker Art Gallery, Liverpool
1974 One-man exhibition at Galeria da Emenda, Lisbon
Exhibited in 'British Painting '74' at Hayward Gallery
1975 One-man exhibition at Forum Kunst, Rotweil
Exhibited in Sao Paulo Bienal
1976 Exhibited in 'Arte inglese oggi' at Palazzo Reale, Milan
1977 Exhibited in 'British Painting 1952-1977' at Royal Academy
Received Linbury Trust Award

Dealer Rowan Gallery

Huxley is an outstanding example of a painter totally as is possible for any human being to be anything – intent on exploring his pictorial language. Language? The tongue has little to do with it, but it is reasonable to read Huxley's forms as phrases or statements which he uses again and again, always in different ways which become more importantly different as we study his paintings one after the other. One can also experience them as events: his canvases as arenas on which colour forms meet or pass by, come into conflict or stand together convivially.

His particular quality, in these paintings, is a kind of nakedness. Without imposing on himself a specific vocabulary of forms, as Mondrian did, he is using simple shapes that we recognise easily and holding them in a fine balance between geometrical exactness and individual life. His colours are not at all self-evident or habitual; it is striking that he always keeps a substantial degree of contrast between the field colour of his picture surface and the colours of the shapes that he establishes on it. The shapes exist on and in this field colour.

Norbert Lynton 1973
(from 'Magic and Strong Medicine' catalogue)

Paul Huxley *The Studio* 1978 Acylic on canvas 203.2x203.2cm (6ft8inx-6ft8in) Power Institute of Art, Sydney

David Inshaw 117

1943 Born in Staffordshire
1959-63 Studied at Beckenham School of Art
1963-6 Studied at Royal Academy Schools
1964 Received French Government scholarship to work in Paris
1966 Organized 'Young Contemporaries' exhibition
1966-75 Taught at West of England College of Art, Bristol
1967 Left London to live in Bristol
1968 Exhibited in Bicentenary Exhibition at Royal Academy
1969 Individual exhibitions at Arnolfini Gallery, Bristol (also 1972), Dartington Hall, Devon
1970 Exhibited in group show at Serpentine Gallery
1971 Exhibited in 'Art Spectrum South' Arts Council travelling exhibition
1972 Formed Broad Heath Brotherhood with Graham and Ann Arnold
1973 Exhibited in 'Bristol in Common' at Arnolfini Gallery, Bristol, Summer Studio Exhibition at Institute of Contemporary Arts
First meeting with Peter Blake
1974 Exhibited in John Moores Exhibition, Liverpool, 'Peter Blake's Choice' at Festival Gallery, Bath
BBC film 'Private Landscapes' on his work
1975 First meeting of Brotherhood of Ruralists held
Individual exhibition at Waddington Galleries
Exhibited in Bath Festival Exhibition
1975-7 Fellow Commoner in Creative Art at Trinity College, Cambridge
1976 Exhibited with Brotherhood of Ruralists in Summer Exhibition at Royal Academy
1977 BBC TV film 'Summer with the Brotherhood' made
Individual exhibition at Wren Library, Trinity College, Cambridge
Exhibited with Brotherhood of Ruralists at Bath Festival, Fine Arts Society, Edinburgh Festival, Doncaster and Southampton University
1978 Individual exhibition at Brighton Festival

Dealer Waddington Galleries

David Inshaw *The Cricket Game* 1976 Oil on Canvas 94x139cm (37x55in) Private Collection

David Inshaw *She Did Not Turn* 1974 Oil on canvas 137.2x182.9cm (54x72in) Private Collection

Albert Irvin 145

1922 Born in London
1940-1 Studied at Northampton School of Art
1941-6 Served in RAF
1946-50 Studied at Goldsmiths College
1960 First one-man exhibition at 57 Gallery, Edinburgh
1960-4 Part-time teaching at various colleges and Wandsworth Prison
1961 One-man exhibition at New Art Centre (also 1963/65/67/71/73/75)
1962-3 Visiting Lecturer at Hornsey College of Art

Albert Irvin *Across* 1974 Acrylic on canvas 248x426cm (8x14ft) Aberdeen Art Gallery and Museum

1962- Senior Lecturer in Painting at Goldsmiths College of Art
1964 One-man exhibition at Edinburgh University
1968 Received Arts Council Travel Award to USA
1970 Exhibited with London Group (also 1978)
1971 Exhibited in 'London Now in Berlin' at Messehalle, Berlin
1972 One-man exhibitions in Berlin and Frankfurt
Exhibited in group shows at Arts Council Galleries, Glasgow and Edinburgh,
'15 Years of the 57 Gallery' at Edinburgh Festival
1974 One-man exhibitions in Ludwigshafen and Stuttgart
Exhibited in 'British Painting '74' at Hayward Gallery
1975 One man exhibition at Berlin Opera House
Received Arts Council Major Award
1976 One-man exhibition at New 57 Gallery, Edinburgh,
Aberdeen Art Gallery and Museum
1977 Exhibited in 'Whitechapel Open' at Whitechapel Art Gallery,
'British Painting 1952-1977' at Royal Academy
1978 One-man exhibition at Newcastle Polytechnic Gallery
Exhibited in 'Maler der Farbe' at Galerie Folker Skulima, Berlin

Dealer Galerie Folker Skulima, Berlin
Contact 19 Gorst Road, London SW11

I'm in love with painting.

And I can say how I do it. I put the paint on the canvas with brushes and a variety of tools of my own devising, or in any way that seems appropriate. I work with the canvas on the wall or on the floor or propped up in between if it suits me better. And I struggle. Towards what? Impossible to say, but I can recognize it when I see it. An activity within the space of the painting that enables me to reach the world of my experience. If I could say what it was, it wouldn't be worth painting. Statements about painting are impossible. The statement *is* the painting.

I rejoice in the manipulation of the paint. It's joyous, but it can be a bastard. I want the painting to happen as inevitably as tomorrow will happen; to be a natural occurrence.

Over the years the emphasis has shifted, the rhythm altered. But the quest continues.

Albert Irvin 1979

Albert Irvin *Flodden* 1978 Acrylic on canvas 213.4x305cm (7x10ft) Artist's Collection

Gwyther Irwin 135

1931 Born in Cornwall
1951-4 Studied at Central School of Art and Design
1957 One-man exhibition at Gallery One
1958 One-man exhibition at Institute of Contemporary Arts
1959 One-man exhibition at Gimpel Fils (also 1960/62/67/70)
1960 Exhibited in Paris Biennale,
'Situation' at RBA Gallery
1961 Exhibited in Carnegie International Exhibition, Pittsburgh (also 1967/70),
'New London Situation' at Marlborough Fine Art,
Group show at Museum of Modern Art, New York
1963 Exhibited in John Moores Exhibition, Liverpool (also 1978),
'British Painting in the 60s' at Whitechapel Art Gallery
1964 Exhibited in Venice Biennale,
'New Painting' Arts Council travelling exhibition (also 1972),
'Painting and Sculpture of a Decade' at Tate Gallery
1965 Commission for bas relief in Portland stone for British Petroleum
1966-8 Taught at Hornsey College of Art
1967 Exhibited in 'Recent Painting' at Tate Gallery (Peter Stuyvesant Foundation Collection)
1967-9 Taught at Chelsea School of Art
1969- Head of Fine Art at Brighton Polytechnic
1973 One-man exhibition at New Art Centre (also 1975/77)
1975 Exhibited in 'Recent British Painting' at Fondation Maeght, St Paul de Vence
1978 Two-man exhibition at Newcastle-upon-Tyne Polytechnic Gallery

Dealer New Art Centre

►

Gwyther Irwin *No 21* 1979 Oil on canvas 124 6x172 7cm (49x68in) Artist's Collection

In the past I have made collage, assemblage, constructions and paintings, using the backs of old posters, string, wood-shavings, cardboard, matches, nails, wood, cloth, paint and so on, but I am currently working with oil paint on canvas.

My method is invariable, and always has been. I write the pictures. Starting in the top left-hand corner I work along, adding individual ribbon-like unit to individual unit, until I reach the right-hand edge. I then return to the left-hand edge and repeat the process – until the bottom right-hand corner is reached, some 400 hours after beginning. I make no changes or corrections of any sort, nor indeed do I use any mechanical or physical aids of any sort, or make any preparatory drawings or guide marks on the canvas.

I am engaged in a sort of gestural slow-motion, a 'stopping down', *right down*, of a painterly process that normally functions at a bodily speed somewhere between the arm actions of dog patting and benediction. I am making, infinitely slowly, those types of marks sometimes produced inadvertently by the gestures of expressive painters.

In terms of attitude however, I feel myself not only to be writing the paintings but also to be weaving them. Given some basic iconographic differences I might really be making the equivalent of Persian carpets. It is, though, the iconography itself which carries the meaning of the work.

I believe that the subtle interplay between perception and recognition is most likely to occur in alluding to much intuitively and little specifically. The marks I make clearly have reference to the natural world but they are not descriptive marks. They are about implication and innuendo, structurally taut but implicitly free. I watch with wonder and excitement as the colours and marks, falling from my hand as if propelled by a source of guidance other than myself, slowly spread across the surface.

Gwyther Irwin 1979

Gwyther Irwin *Midnight Hour* 1963 Cardboard on blockboard 121 9x76 2cm (48x30in) British Council Collection

Bill Jacklin 196

Bill Jacklin *Tabletop 11am* 1977-8 Oil on canvas 61x40 6cm (24x16in) Private Collection

1943 Born in London
1960-1 Studied graphics at Walthamstow School of Art
1961-2 Worked as graphic designer
1962-4 Returned to Walthamstow School of Art to study painting
1964-7 Studied at Royal College of Art
1967-75 Taught at various art colleges, including Hornsey, Maidstone, Kingston, Chelsea and Royal College of Art
1970 One-man exhibition at Nigel Greenwood Inc (also 1971/75)
Exhibited in group show at Museum of Modern Art, New York (also 1971/72).
'Recent Acquisitions' at Victoria and Albert Museum
1972 Exhibited in group show at Museum of Modern Art, Oxford
1973 One-man exhibition at Hester van Royen Gallery (also 1977)
Exhibited in 'English Painting Today' at Musée d'Art Moderne, Paris
1974 Exhibited in Menton Biennale
1975 Exhibited in 'The Mezzotint Rediscovered' at Colnaghi & Co
Received Arts Council Bursary
1977 Exhibited in 'Artists at Curwen' at Tate Gallery,
'British Painting 1952-1977' at Royal Academy,
Drawings exhibition at Waddington Galleries
1978 Exhibited in group shows at Marlborough Fine Art, London and New York
1979 One-man exhibition at Marlborough Fine Art

Dealer Marlborough Fine Art

Bill Jacklin *Double Buddha* 1975-6 Oil on canvas and wood 81 3x111 8cm (32x44in) Arts Council Collection

Throughout my career I have had two main preoccupations: studying the changing nature of light and an interest in geometry. From 1968 until 1974 I attempted to channel these concerns into non-representational work, developing systems in painting that paralleled structures I had observed in nature. Here the scale was so varied that I could find units of the strictest symmetry and yet at the other extreme units that as a group appeared to manifest themselves in asymmetry. I moved back and forth across this scale and produced numerous pen and ink drawings, some precise and formalized, others soft and atmospheric. It was not until 1975 that I became directly involved with describing the effects of light representationally, beginning a series of watercolours of objects on tables using the subject matter as a vehicle to create light and pattern.

I now find myself continuing this duality of purpose – wishing to convey as simply as possible my observation of something as it is, and the need to experiment with paint. The question is how to find a link between an interest in systems of painting and what I am looking at. Lately the paintings have become more complicated now including people and places all relating to specific situations I have experienced, and in this sense I paint what I know.

Bill Jacklin 1979

Tess Jaray 89

Tess Jaray *Minuet* 1967 Oil on canvas 182.9x228.6cm (6ftx7ft6in) Graves City Art Gallery, Sheffield

1937 Born
1954-7 Studied at St Martin's School of Art
1957-60 Studied at Slade School of Fine Art
1960 Received Abbey Minor Travelling Scholarship
1961 Awarded French Government Scholarship
1963 Individual exhibition at Grabowski Gallery
1964-8 Taught at Hornsey College of Art
1965 Individual exhibition at Hamilton Gallery (also 1967)
1967 Individual exhibition at Richard Demarco Gallery, Edinburgh
Mural commission for British Pavilion at Expo 67, Montreal
1968- Teaching at Slade School of Fine Art
1969 Individual exhibition at Axiom Gallery
1972 Individual exhibitions at Graves Art Gallery, Sheffield,
City Art Gallery, Bristol
1973 Individual exhibition at Whitechapel Art Gallery
1976 Individual exhibition at Angela Flowers Gallery
1978 One of selectors of and exhibitor in 'Hayward Annual' at Hayward Gallery

Contact 29 Camden Square, London NW1

Tess Jaray's paintings are concerned not with static arrangements of colour and form on a flat surface, but with the suggestion of a complex interaction between these elements, locked in an endless succession of potential events through time. The titles, such as *Pass*, *Flight* and *Encounter* emphasize this aspect of movement and apparent change. The process of looking is equally an ongoing one, since the paintings are open to a multitude of interpretations and can never, therefore, be fully grasped.

Sarah Kent 1979

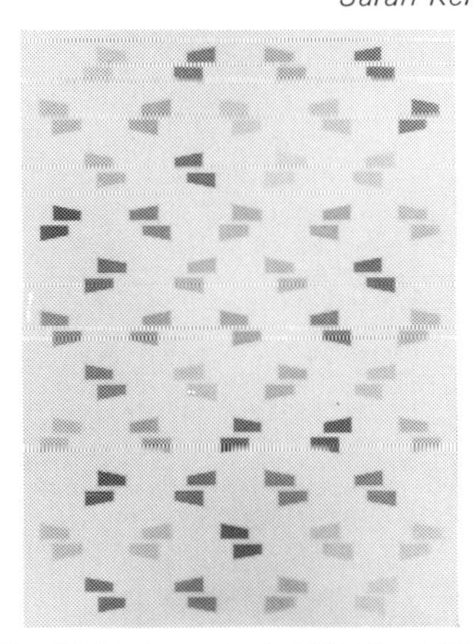

Tess Jaray *Nexus* 1977 Acylic on cotton duck 241x175cm (7ft11inx5ft9in) Artist's Collection

Allen Jones 109

1937 Born in Southampton
1955-9 Studied at Hornsey College of Art
1959-60 Studied at Royal College of Art
1961 Exhibited in Paris Biennale (also 1963 prizewinner/65/71/77),
John Moores Exhibition, Liverpool (also 1963/65/67/69/78)
1962 Exhibited in 'British Art Today' in San Francisco, Dallas and Santa Barbara
1963 First one-man exhibition at Arthur Tooth & Sons (also 1964/67/70)

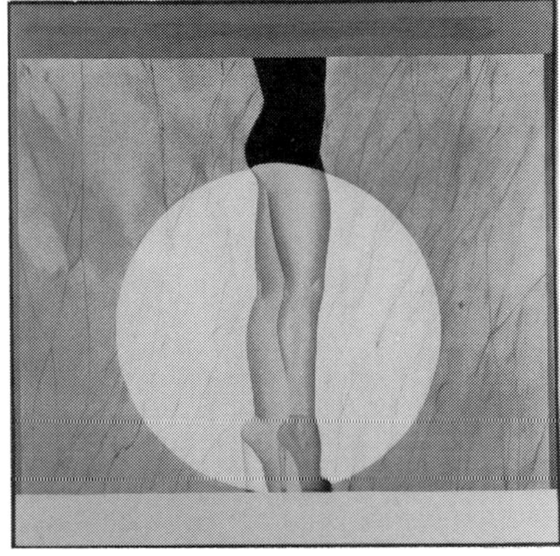

Allen Jones *Thigh High* 1975 Oil on canvas 152.4x152.4cm (60x60in) Private Collection

1964 One-man exhibition at Richard Feigen Gallery, New York (also 1965 and in Chicago/70)
Exhibited in 'Painting and Sculpture of a Decade 1954-64' at Tate Gallery,
'Documenta 3' in Kassel (also 4 in 1968),
Tokyo Biennale (also 1966/74)
1964-5 Lived in New York
1965 One-man exhibition at Feigen/Palmer Gallery, Los Angeles
1966 One-man exhibitions at Galerie Bischofsberger, Zurich,
'London – New York – Hollywood' at Museum of Modern Art, New York
1967 One-man exhibition at Galerie der Spiegel, Cologne (also 1971)
Exhibited in Carnegie International Exhibition, Pittsburgh,
Sao Paulo Bienal
1968 Exhibited in 'Britische Kunst heute' at Kunstverein, Hamburg,
'British Artists: 6 Painters, 6 Sculptors' at Museum of Modern Art, New York
1969 One-man exhibition at Galleria Milano, Milan (also 1970/72)
Exhibited in 'Pop Art Redefined' at Hayward Gallery
1970 One-man exhibition at Studio d'Arte Condotti, Rome (also 1972)
Exhibited in 'British Painting and Sculpture 1960-70' at National Gallery of Art, Washington DC
1972 One-man exhibition at Marlborough Fine Art
1973 One-man exhibitions in Melbourne and Sydney
1974 One-man exhibitions in Japan ▶

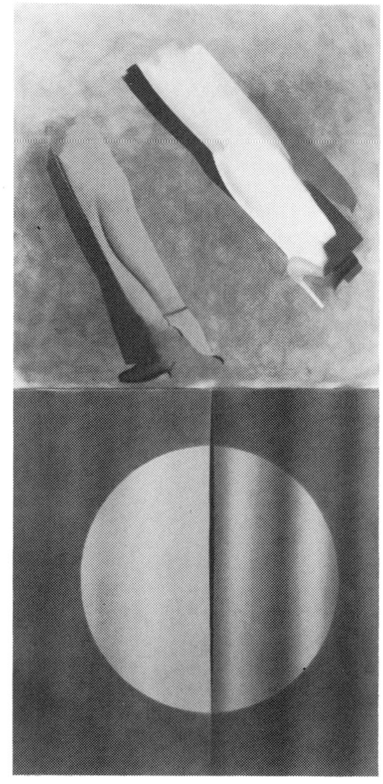

Allen Jones *Grand Opening* 1976 Oil on two canvases 243.8x121.9cm (8x4ft) Waddington Galleries

1975 One-man exhibitions at Fruit Market, Edinburgh,
Arnolfini Gallery, Bristol
1976 One-man exhibitions at Waddington Galleries, and in Hamburg and Dusseldorf
Exhibited in 'Pop Art in England 1947-63' at Kunsthalle, Nuremberg and travelling in Europe,
'Arte inglese oggi' at Palazzo Reale, Milan,
1977 One-man exhibition at James Corcoran Gallery, Los Angeles
Exhibited in 'Hayward Annual' at Hayward Gallery,
'British Painting 1952-1977' at Royal Academy
Guest teacher at University of California
1978 Retrospective graphics exhibition at Institute of Contemporary Arts and travelling
One-man exhibitions at Waddington Galleries, Montreal and Toronto
1979 Retrospective exhibition at Serpentine Gallery and travelling in England and Germany

Dealer Waddington Galleries

Jones's work is generally regarded as the embodiment of British Pop. The fundamental concerns of the artist, however, are the human figure and the fusion of representational content with 'abstract' form. The shaped canvas *Buses and Parachutes* of 1962-3 and the self-portraits and *Hermaphrodites* of the same period pay homage to pioneers of abstraction such as Delaunay and Kandinsky. Jones's attitude to style, however, remains self-consciously detached, with different language systems juxtaposed within a single painting to distinguish between the illusionism of the image and its substance as paint. It is this 'marriage of styles' which links Jones to other British artists associated with Pop.

Since the mid-1960s Jones has found inspiration in the dynamic treatment of the human figure in fetish and transvestite magazines, and has invested his own images of women with a provocative eroticism as a means of arousing the viewer's emotional response. The veristic fibreglass sculptures of the late 1960s, depicting women as furniture, provide the most extreme statement of this theme. In the wake of the women's movement these works have acquired social overtones not consciously intended, but which in retrospect the artist accepts may reflect the current upheaval in sexual roles.

Jones has also engaged his work with the popular arts by designing posters, costumes for stage and film, and even the Pirelli calendar, along with essays in video and photography. His influence has been felt on fashion, graphic design and photography. These are fruitful but incidental excursions. Jones remains dedicated above all to extending the traditions of painting and lithography through reference to modern urban experience.

Marco Livingstone 1979

Peter Joseph 142

1929 Born in London
1965 Exhibited in John Moores Exhibition, Liverpool (also 1972/79 Prizewinner)
1966 First one-man exhibition at Greenwich Theatre Gallery
Exhibited in group show (environmental work) at Signals Gallery
1967 Exhibited in 'Survey 1967, Abstract Painting' at Camden Arts Centre,
'Four English Artists' at Gelsenkirchen
1968 Exhibited in John Player Exhibition, Nottingham (First Prize)
1969 One-man exhibitions at Lisson Gallery (also 1971/76/78),
Kenwood House (environmental work)

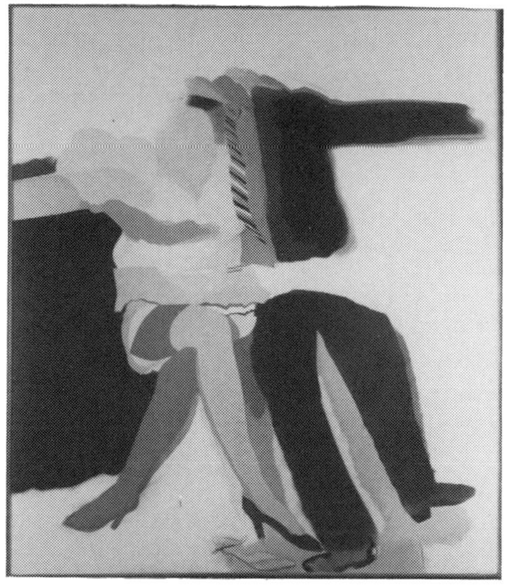

Allen Jones *Man Woman* 1963 Oil on canvas 213x189cm (7ft$\frac{1}{2}$inx6ft2$\frac{1}{4}$in) Tate Gallery

1970 One-man exhibition (environmental work) at Camden Arts Centre
1971 Exhibited in group show at Edinburgh Festival (environmental work)
1973 Exhibited in 'Three Painters' at Hayward Gallery
1974 Exhibited in 'Post-minimal Painting' at Edinburgh Festival,
'British Painting '74' at Hayward Gallery
1975 Exhibited in Sao Paulo Bienal
1977 One-man exhibition at Galerie Gillespie/De Laage, Paris
Exhibited in 'British Artists' at Fine Arts Building, New York,
Group show at Galerie Art in Progress, Munich,
'British Painting 1952-1977' at Royal Academy

Peter Joseph *Grey and Blue Painting* 1977 Acrylic 223.5x279.4cm (6ft4inx9ft2in) Biewirth Collection, Paris

Peter Joseph *Paintings* 1974 and 1975 Acrylic 167x266cm (66x105in) and 203.2x142cm (80x56in) Panza di Biumo Collection, Varese

1978 One-man exhibition at Orion Gallery, Newlyn
1979 Exhibited in 'British and Belgian Artists' at Palais des Beaux Arts, Brussels

Contact 22 Cleveden Mansions, Lissenden Gardens, London NW5

Thoughts about the process of painting

Doubt is a movement between light and dark. Certainty is an attitude, an isolation.

Doubt is a continuous unfolding of possibility. It is the space of hope between objects.
Its realization is in a flash of meaning. The meeting of light and dark in the minds infinity.

Peter Joseph 1979

Mary Kelly 191

1941 Born in USA
1959-63 Studied at College of St Teresa, Minnesota
1963-5 Studied at Pius 12th Institute, Florence
1965-8 Lecturer in Fine Art at American University, Beirut
1968- Living and working in London
1968-70 Postgraduate study at St Martin's School of Art
1973 Began the *Post-Partum Document*
Received Greater London Arts Association Fellowship
1974- Teaching at Camberwell School of Art
1975 Exhibited in 'Sexuality and Socialization' at Northern Arts Gallery, Newcastle-upon-Tyne,
'Women and Work: A Document on the Division of Labour in Industry' at South London Art Gallery
1976 Individual exhibition at Institute of Contemporary Arts
1977 Individual exhibition at Museum of Modern Art, Oxford
Published *Footnotes and Bibliography, Post-Partum Document* (Museum of Modern Art, Oxford)
Received Arts Council Award
1978 Exhibited in 'Art for Society' at Whitechapel Art Gallery,
'Hayward Annual' at Hayward Gallery
Received Lina Garnade Memorial Foundation Award
1978- Lecturer in Fine Art at Goldsmiths College of Art
1979 Individual exhibition at University Gallery, Leeds
Exhibited in 'Un certain art anglais' at Musée d'Art Moderne, Paris,
'Both Sides Now' at Artemesia Gallery, Chicago

Contact 97 Blurton Road, London E5

Mary Kelly *Post-Partum Document* Detail: Documentation 5 1977 Mixed media 3 units 17.8x12.7cm (7x5in) from a series of 33 Museum of Modern Art, Oxford

In the *Post-Partum Document* the art objects are used as fetish objects, explicitly to displace the potential fetishisation of the child, and implicitly to expose the fetishistic function of representation. The stained liners, folded vests, child's markings or insect specimens have a minimum sign value in relation to the commodity status of art, but they have a maximum affective value in relation to the economy of the unconscious. They are representations, in the psychoanalytic sense, of cathected memory traces. These traces, in combination with the diaries, speech events and feeding charts, construct the discourse of the mother's lived experience. At the same time, they are set up in an antagonistic relationship with the diagrams, algorithms and footnotes which construct the discourse of feminist analysis. In the context of an installation, this analysis is not meant to definitively theorize the postpartum moment, but rather, to describe a process of secondary revision. In a sense, this text is also included in that process.

Mary Kelly 1979

Michael Kenny ARA 127

Michael Kenny . . . *Also Wounded by Love* 1977-8 Steel, wood, resin, aluminium glass and porcelain 104x157x305cm (41x61x120in) Artist's Collection

1941 Born in Liverpool
1959-61 Studied at Liverpool College of Art
1961-4 Studied at Slade School of Fine Art
1963 Exhibited in 'Young Contemporaries' (also 1964)
1964 First one-man exhibition at Bear Lane Gallery, Oxford
Received John Moores Prize for Sculpture
1965 Film 'Cathedral' commissioned by Southampton University
1966 One-man exhibition at Hamilton Galleries
Exhibited in Open Air Sculpture Exhibition in Battersea Park
1967 Exhibited in 'British Sculpture 1960-1966' Arts Council travelling exhibition

▶

Michael Kenny *Crucifixx* 1976 Plaster, wood, metal, perspex and glass 201x252x203cm (6ft5inx8ft3inx6ft8in) Artist's Collection

1969 One-man exhibition at Hanover Gallery
1972 Exhibited in 'Hacia un Perfil del Art Latin Americano' in Buenos Aires (toured Latin America, Western and Eastern Europe)
1974 Received St Helens National Award for Water Sculpture
Exhibited in 'Art into Landscape' at Serpentine Gallery
1975 Received Arts Council Major Award (also 1977)
1976 Elected Associate of Royal Academy
Exhibited in 'Decade of the 70s' in Buenos Aires and touring Latin America
1977 One-man exhibition at Peterloo Gallery, Manchester
Two-man exhibition with Arshile Gorky at Serpentine Gallery
Exhibited in Silver Jubilee Contemporary British Sculpture Exhibition in Battersea Park, 'Documenta 6' in Kassel
1978 One-man exhibition at Annely Juda Fine Art
1979 One-man exhibition at Round House Gallery
Exhibited in Sydney Biennale
Publication of *Poetry and Drawings* by Harold Pinter and Michael Kenny (Greville Press, Warwick)

Dealer Annely Juda Fine Art

My sculpture has always had – more or less – a figurative basis. The figure is austerely pared down to an anonymous presence, without hands, feet, head or sexual parts – an alone, uncommunicative distant presence, an isolation of existence and a certainty of death. The works do not inhabit any specific point in time – things have happened in reality or by implication – and their physical state of 'finish' leaves open the possibility of what *might* happen; a 'halo' exists before and after. The first sculpture to involve these implications was . . . *Place* (1967-9), and the biggest, most enduring influence has been the work of Medardo Rosso whose sculptures involve similar ambiguities. The drawings that I make do not for the most part work towards the sculpture. They are independent, related but different – parallel.

Michael Kenny 1979

Michael Kidner 95

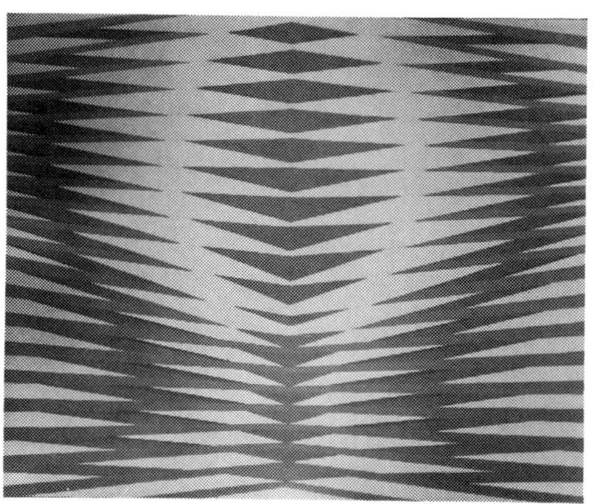

Michael Kidner *Orange, Blue and Green* 1964 Oil on canvas 124.6x152.4cm (49x60in) British Council Collection

1917 Born in Kettering
1936-9 Studied at University of Cambridge
1940-1 Studied at Ohio State University
1941-6 Military service in Canadian army
1960 One-man exhibition at AIA Gallery
1964 One-man exhibition at Grabowski Gallery
1964- Senior Lecturer at Bath Academy of Art
1965 Exhibited in 'The Responsive Eye' at Museum of Modern Art, New York, John Moores Exhibition, Liverpool (major prizewinner)
1967 One-man exhibition at Axiom Gallery, University of Sussex
Two-man exhibition with Malcolm Hughes at Arnolfini Gallery, Bristol
Exhibited in 'Recent British Painting' at Tate Gallery
Artist in Residence at University of Sussex
1968 Artist in Residence at American University of Washington DC
1969 Exhibited in Arts Council of Northern Ireland exhibition, Belfast (major prizewinner)
1972 Exhibited in 'Systems' at Whitechapel Art Gallery
1974 One-man exhibition at Lucy Milton Gallery
Exhibited in 'British Painting '74' at Hayward Gallery
1975 Exhibited in three-man show at Jacomo Santiveri Gallery, Paris
1975- Visiting Lecturer at Slade School of Fine Art
1976 Exhibited in 'Rational Concepts' travelling exhibition in Holland
1977 Exhibited in 'British Painting 1952-1977' at Royal Academy
1978 Exhibited in 'Constructive Context' Arts Council travelling exhibition, Norwegian Print Biennale (major prizewinner)

Contact 18 Hampstead Hill Gardens, London NW3

In the late 1950s and early 60s my painting was about colour, but since colour has to have shape I became increasingly concerned with shape as an ingredient for colour sensation. Expressionism, I decided, the abstract gesture, automatic writing, were, for me at least, too self-conscious and too arbitrary to be convincing. Colour on the other hand provided an objective with its own expressive requirements. The excitement of making the paintings lay in the energy which the colour generated and this emerged only as the painting was completed. The constructive process was urged on by suspense; will the proposition match its expectations?

As time went on the pattern of shapes began to dominate the colour intention. Colour became a distracting element or at best a code to help in deciphering the pattern. The sensation of a pattern intrigues the eye and at the same time it offers clues to understanding. In 1970 I built a column to express in concrete terms the intersection of two wavy surfaces and then interpreted the column, as it revolved, in a two dimensional pattern.

More recently my interest in wave forms and curved or warped planes has suggested the use of elastic fabric to generate drawings. I would like my paintings to be metaphors for systems and structures which operate in the real world. I want to link things which seem to be mysterious or not fully understood to things which are less mysterious. I want in Professor Zieman's words 'to reduce the arbitrariness of description'. I find the mystery of the moon's image no less mysterious since man's visit. The mystery exists in a new context. I would like my painting to shift the context in which mystery occurs towards a materialist interpretation.

Michael Kidner 1979

Phillip King ARA 84

1934 Born in Tunis
1954-7 Studied at Cambridge University
1957-8 Studied at St Martin's School of Art
1959-60 Worked as assistant to Henry Moore
1960 Received Boise Scholarship
1963 Exhibited in Paris Biennale
1964 First one-man exhibition at Rowan Gallery (also 1970/72/73/75/77/79)
1965 Exhibited in 'London: the New Scene' at Walker Art Center, Minneapolis and travelling in USA
Received Peter Stuyvesant Travel Bursary
1966 One-man exhibitions at Richard Feigen Gallery, New York and Chicago,
Isaac Delgado Museum of Art, New Orleans
1967 Exhibited in Carnegie International Exhibition, Pittsburgh,
Guggenheim International Exhibition, New York
1967- Teaching at St Martin's School of Art
1967-9 Trustee of Tate Gallery
1968 One-man exhibitions at Galerie Yvon Lambert, Paris,
Whitechapel Art Gallery,
Museum Boymans van Beuningen, Rotterdam
Exhibited in Venice Biennale
1969 Exhibited in Middelheim Biennale
1970 Exhibited in 'Contemporary British Art' at Museum of Modern Art, Tokyo

Phillip King *Open Place* 1977 Slate and steel 131x233.5x269cm (51x92x106in) Kroller - Muller Museum, Otterlo

1972 Exhibited in 'British Sculpture '72' at Royal Academy
1973 Exhibited in 'Henry Moore to Gilbert & George' at Palais des Beaux Arts, Brussels
1974 Received CBE
1974/5 One-man travelling exhibition to museums in Europe
1975 Exhibited in 'The Condition of Sculpture' at Hayward Gallery
1975/6 One-man Arts Council exhibition travelling in England
1976 Exhibited in 'Arte inglese oggi' at Palazzo Reale, Milan
1977 Exhibited in Silver Jubilee Contemporary British Sculpture Exhibition in Battersea Park
Elected Associate of Royal Academy

Dealer Rowan Gallery

Phillip King *Through* 1965 Plastic 226x335x29cm (7ft5inx11ftx9in) (Edition of 3) Tate Gallery, Galleria dell' Ariete, Milan and Ulster Museum, Belfast

When I begin a work I start with nothing in my mind. Total emptiness – no other work, past or present, seems important. It is as if I have to give the future work a chance to be anything it possibly might like to be, and that in its final revelation I will know that *it* came from nothing.

Very often, I begin with some kind of despair, perhaps less now. I know I intend to make a 'thing'. Here I am, my material is there. I am in my body with my height, my weight, my eyes looking out, I have the feel of looking out. The material has weight and certain rapidity – it can be built up from the ground – the same ground on which I stand. I know that in the future, it will stand in front of me like I stand – to allow it to stand up and be visible is the only goal I can allow myself. I am the onlooker, the agent for the material to build itself up. If I can make it visible it will occupy a position and when *it* finds a position *I* also will find a place.

I want to make things visible but not graspable, I make them so they cannot be possessed. They are there according to their own needs. They say something only to themselves – they do not speak to me nor do they send messages to others – they find a distance away from me and that also establishes a nearness to me. The sort of nearness that no other object can give me. I do not reflect on my role – I act and react – I make it like I might make a table or chair but there are no rules that I can follow, feelings are aroused in me about what I do – good and bad ones. From nothing something happens. I begin to feel better. When I look at 'it' I begin to breathe more easily, I feel lighter on my feet. I act so that this can happen more. It becomes visible to me, takes on a character – like dogginess is dog. I did not give it character, it became an identity when it became visible. I am the spectator of something revealing itself to me and as this process of identity takes place, I find my own position. The thing is there and I am here in my place.

Visibility and identity are one with the world and I am one with them too.

Phillip King 1976
(from Australian lecture series statement)

Peter Kinley 93

Peter Kinley *Two Geese* 1977 Oil on canvas 182.9x182.9cm (6x6ft) Artist's Collection

1926 Born in Vienna
1949-53 Studied at St Martin's School of Art
1951 Exhibited in 'Young Contemporaries' (also 1952/53)
1954 First one-man exhibition at Gimpel Fils (also 1957/61/64)
1955-64 Taught at St Martin's School of Art

▶

Peter Kinley *Interior with Figure* 1962 Oil on canvas 152x127cm (60x50in) Private Collection

1956 Exhibited in 'Critic's Choice' at Arthur Tooth & Sons, 'Statements' at Institute of Contemporary Arts
1958 Exhibited in 'Young British Painters' in Rotterdam, Zurich and Dusseldorf
1961 One-man exhibition at Paul Rosenberg & Co, New York (also 1962)
1961-2 Exhibited in 'Drawing towards Painting' Arts Council travelling exhibition
1962-3 Exhibited in 'British Art Today' in San Francisco, Dallas and Santa Barbara
1963 Exhibited in 'British Painting in the 60s' at Whitechapel Art Gallery
1965-70 Taught at Wimbledon School of Art
1968 One-man exhibition at Arthur Tooth & Sons (also 1970/73/75)
1969 Exhibited in John Moores Exhibition, Liverpool (prizewinner; also 1978)
1971- Teaching at Bath Academy of Art
1974 Exhibited in 'New Image in Painting' in Tokyo, 'British Painting '74' at Hayward Gallery
1977 Exhibited in 'British Painting 1952-1977' at Royal Academy
1978 One-man exhibition at Waddington & Tooth Galleries
1979 One-man exhibitions at Waddington Galleries, Montreal and Toronto

Dealer Waddington Galleries

R B Kitaj 110

1932 Born in Ohio
1950-2 Studied at Cooper Union, New York and Academy of Fine Art, Vienna
1958-9 Studied at Ruskin School of Drawing, Oxford
1959-61 Studied at Royal College of Art
1960- Living and working in London and Spain
1962-6 Taught at Camberwell School of Art
1963 One-man exhibition at Marlborough New London Gallery (also 1970)
1965 One-man exhibitions at Marlborough Gerson Gallery, New York (also 1974), Los Angeles County Museum of Art
1967 One-man exhibitions at Stedelijk Museum, Amsterdam, Museum of Art, Cleveland, Ohio, University of California, Berkeley
1967-8 Guest Professor of Art at University of California, Berkeley
1969 One-man exhibition at Galerie Mikro, Berlin and travelling in West Germany
1970 One-man exhibition at Kestner Gesellschaft, Hanover
Two-man exhibition (with Jim Dine) at Boymans van Beuningen Museum, Rotterdam (also 1973 at Cincinnati Museum of Art)

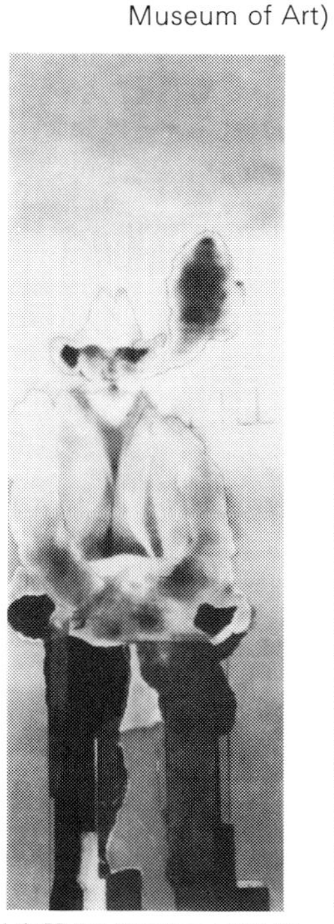

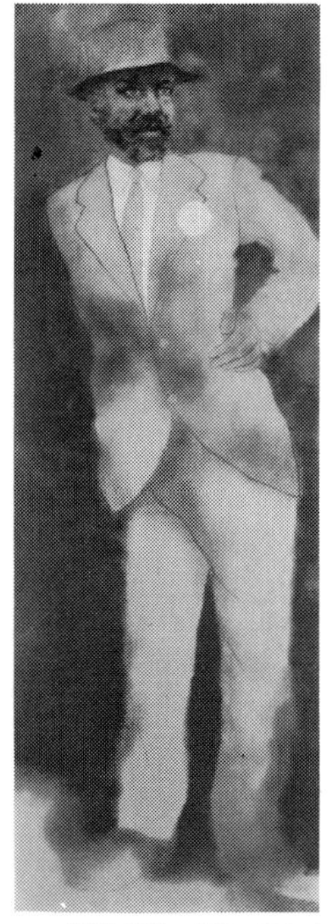

Left: RB Kitaj *Bill at Sunset* 1973 Oil on canvas 243.8x76.2cm (8ft2inx2ft6in) Private Collection

Right: RB Kitaj *Slav Soul* 1977 Oil on canvas 182.9x81cm (6x2ft) Private Collection

1976 Organized 'The Human Clay' exhibition at Hayward Gallery
Exhibited in 'Arte inglese oggi' at Palazzo Reale, Milan
1977 One-man exhibition at Marlborough Fine Art
1978 One-man exhibition at FIAC at Grand Palais, Paris
1979 One-man exhibition at Marlborough Gallery, New York

Dealer Marlborough Fine Art

RB Kitaj *Dismantling the Red Tent* 1963-4 Oil on canvas on collage 122x122cm (48x48in) Private Collection

Bryan Kneale RA 40

1930 Born in Isle of Man
1947 Studied at Douglas School of Art
1948-52 Studied at Royal Academy Schools
1949-51 Rome Scholar in Painting
1954 First one-man exhibition of paintings at Redfern Gallery (also 1956/58 [paintings]/60/62/64/67/70/73/74/76/78)
1959/60 Turned from painting to sculpture
1961 Exhibited in John Moores Exhibition, Liverpool, 6th Congress of International Union of Architects, South Bank
1962- Teaching at Royal College of Art
1963 Exhibited in 'Art d'aujourd'hui' at Grand Palais, Paris, International Sculpture Exhibition in Battersea Park
1965 Exhibited in 'British Sculpture in the 60s' at Tate Gallery, 'The English Eye' at Marlborough Gerson Gallery, New York
1966 Retrospective exhibition at Whitechapel Art Gallery

1966/7 Exhibited in 'Sculpture from the Arts Council Collection' travelling exhibition, 'New British Painting and Sculpture' at UCLA Galleries, Los Angeles
1968 Exhibited in 'City of London Open Air Sculpture' in Paternoster Square
1970 Elected Associate of Royal Academy
1972 Exhibited in 'British Sculptors '72' at Royal Academy
1972-3 Exhibited in Peter Stuyvesant Foundation City Sculpture Project, Southampton
1973 Elected Royal Academician
1975 Exhibited in 'New Work 2' at Hayward Gallery
1977 Exhibited in Silver Jubilee Contemporary British Sculpture Exhibition in Battersea Park
1978 One-man exhibition 'Work in Progress' at Serpentine Gallery

Dealer Redfern Gallery

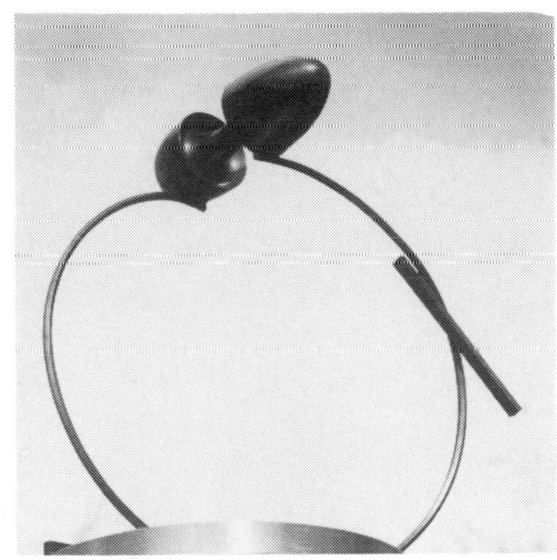

Bryan Kneale *Tarquinia* 1977 Steel 320cm (10ft 6in) high Manx Museum, Douglas, Isle of Man

Although I began my work as an artist by painting, I suppose it was inevitable that I should eventually become a sculptor. Form was always my paramount concern and when I made my first welded steel sculpture I found a freedom of expression which I had long sought after. I worked rapidly at first in light steel and then by forging heavy iron sections much as a blacksmith or armourer might do. Soon I began to combine other materials, wood, and then in 1962 slate, with the forged iron. From this, two sides of my work began to develop simultaneously, on the one hand the manipulation of metal through welding, cutting and bending, using pre-formed shapes in many instances, and on the other hand an increasing interest in how the various sections of a sculpture were in fact linked or joined together.

Towards the end of the 60s the latter concern had become the dominant factor in my work. Ceasing to weld entirely I began increasingly to use mechanical means of construction, and machined sections were linked precisely into place, forming sculptures concerned with what might be described as a mechanical anatomy. By the early 70s other concerns began to emerge, and I became involved in large outdoor pieces in which details of construction were less important than clarity of form and rightness of scale. In small works too I am now more interested in a kind of inevitability of form where the material of the sculpture takes a secondary place to the idea behind it.

Bryan Kneale 1979

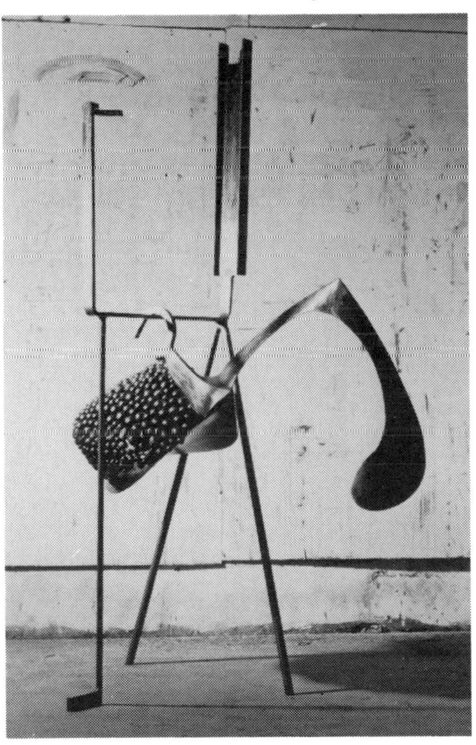

Bryan Kneale *Catalyst* 1964 Steel 208.3cm (6ft10in) high Anglo American Tobacco Collection

Leon Kossoff 74

1926 Born in London
1949-53 Studied at St Martin's School of Art
1950-2 Studied at Borough Polytechnic with David Bomberg (evenings)
1953-6 Studied at Royal College of Art
1957 First one-man exhibition at Beaux Arts Gallery (also 1959/61/63/64)

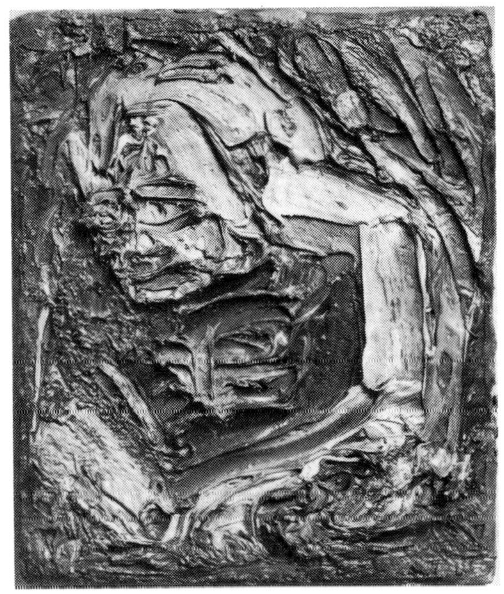

Leon Kossoff *Small Seated Figure* 1959 Oil 27.9x22.9cm (11x9in) Private Collection

Leon Kossoff *Small Portrait of Father No 1* 1978 79x63cm (31x24in) Artist's Collection

1959-64 Taught at Regent Street Polytechnic and Chelsea School of Art
1963 Exhibited in 'British Painting in the 60s' at Tate Gallery
1964 Exhibited in 'Painting and Sculpture of a Decade 1954-1964' at Tate Gallery
1966-9 Taught at St Martin's School of Art

1967 Exhibited in 'Recent British Painting' at Tate Gallery
1968 One-man exhibition at Marlborough Fine Art
1972 One-man exhibition at Whitechapel Art Gallery
1973 One-man exhibition at Fischer Fine Art (also 1979)
1974 Exhibited in 'British Painting '74' at Hayward Gallery
1977 Exhibited in 'British Painting 1952-1977' at Royal Academy

Dealer Fischer Fine Art

I work in oil paint, ground in linseed oil, and draw, mostly with charcoal or compressed charcoal. Looking back, it seems that I have been endlessly engaged in the self-imposed activity of trying to teach myself to draw from life. I think of painting as a form of drawing.

Leon Kossoff 1979

Bruce Lacey 182

Bruce Lacey *R.O.S.A. B.O.S.O.M.* (Radio operated simulated actress — Battery or stand-by operated mains) 1965 Mixed media including electrics and radio control Artist's Collection

1927 Born in London
1949-51 Studied at Hornsey School of Art
1951 Received Knapping Prize
1951-54 Studied at Royal College of Art
1954 Received Abbey Minor Travelling Scholarship
1963 One-man exhibition of assemblages at Gallery One
1965 One-man exhibition of assemblages at Marlborough New London Gallery
1968 Exhibited in 'Cybernetic Serendipity' at Institute of Contemporary Arts
1975 Retrospective exhibition at Whitechapel Art Gallery, Fruit Market Gallery, Edinburgh
1977 Elected member of British Astronomical Association
1978 Two-man exhibition (with Jill Bruce) 'Ancient Forces' at Acme Gallery

Contact Brentwood Farm, Silfield, Wymondham, Norfolk

Bruce Lacey *Elemental Ritual* 1978 Performance with Jill Bruce at Albion Fair, Brome, Suffolk

In retrospect, the significant thing about my work is that at all times it has been an expression of the particular fear, passion, hate, love or any other emotional feeling or psychological engrossment I was experiencing at the time. This expression has not limited itself to any particular medium. I have not restricted myself by saying: 'I am a painter' or 'I am a performer'. I am whatever I want to be or whatever by *necessity* I have to be. So, I have made films, environments, simulators, robots, sculpture, and music. I have danced, performed rituals and sung and I have even written poetry to express these obsessions. Of course, in England, this is frowned upon: 'Jack of all trades, master of none,' they hurl at you, but I believe that the human is a non-specialist individual. I believe an artist who classifies and labels himself as of only one kind is denying his imagination free reign of expression. He is in fact putting himself into creative prison.

I currently work in partnership with my wife, Jill Bruce, as a performance artist, performing in outdoor festivals and so on, and at ancient sites. Performing our own instinctively devised rituals in homage to the ancient elements of earth, air, fire, water, to fertility, to the sun and moon and all the mysterious forces of the earth and cosmos.

Bruce Lacey 1979

John Latham 187

John Latham *Government of the First and Thirteenth Chair* 1978 Performance at Riverside Studios

1921 Born in Africa
1946-50 Studied at Chelsea School of Art
1954 Wittgenstein's atomic proposition discovered as a graphic idiom
1959 Exhibited in 'Venti Quadri' at Galleria dell'Ariete, Milan
1960 One-man exhibitions at Institute of Contemporary Arts, Martha Jackson Gallery, New York
Formulation of concept of art as Structure in Events
1961 Work *Shem* bought by Museum of Modern Art, New York permanent collection
1962 One-man exhibition at Galerie Internationale d'Art Moderne, Paris
Exhibited in 'The New Realists' at Sidney Janis Gallery, New York
1963 One-man exhibitions at Kasmin Gallery, Alan Gallery, New York
1964 One-man exhibition 'Skoob Tower Ceremony' in Oxford and Edinburgh
1965 Formation of Artist Placement Group
1966 One-man exhibitions 'Tower Ceremony' and 'Wordless Play' at Mercury Theatre
1966-7 Taught at St Martin's School of Art
1969 Exhibited *Art and Culture* at Seattle World Fair
Convenor of APG artists
1970 Exhibited *Art and Culture* in 'Information' at Museum of Modern Art, New York (acquired for permanent collection)
1971 Exhibited in 'Art and Economics' APG exhibition at Hayward Gallery
1972 One-man exhibition at Gallery House
Development of Time-Base Theory exhibited at Gallery House
1975 One-man exhibition 'State of Mind' at Kunsthalle, Dusseldorf
1976 Exhibited in 'Arte inglese oggi' at Palazzo Reale, Milan

Contact 5 Boscombe Road, London W12

I am grateful for this opportunity to state some differences between what has appeared as critical opinion, and what I recognize as the sources of my own action.

John Latham *Film Star* 1960 Mixed relief 160x198x22.9cm (63x78x9in) Tate Gallery

In 1954, the preoccupations of artists included the following: (a) truth to the medium used, tachismus; (b) the function of action in static forms; (c) rejection of reference to appearances, literariness; (d) rejection of proportion and dimensionality, as no longer meaningful.

A related factor had to do with verbal language and the logic it carried. The search for the atomic, ultimate proposition from which one might systematize understanding was set going by Wittgenstein in 1918. This idea foundered for reasons never yet found expressible in words – leaving the world in a state of high energy fragmentation. The instrument which came to hand in 1954 held a singular resolution in each of these fields, since it proposed by enactment the first and only graphic representation of the atomic proposition. It is however not so easy to give a verbal account of the way the construct works.

First it is necessary to quote a distinction made by Hillier, Leaman and others in a paper, Space Syntax (UC Press, 1976), between ordinary (verbal) language and the *morphic language*. The former uses a restricted syntax and a maximized vocabulary. The latter *reduces the vocabulary* so that syntax, spatial ordering, carries the meaning. An example of a morphic language is the collection of shapes forming an alphabet.

The Idiom of 1954 *reduced the initial vocabulary to one*. It resolved preoccupations (a) to (c) to a conclusion, and to (d) it brought a novel and greatly augmented conception. Visually, and later by the visualizing capacity, it introduced dimension and proportion in two fields not otherwise spatially represented, namely 'time', with a new relationship *to atemporality*; and the *in-forming* process about which we are still, according to Chomsky, as ignorant as ever, 'within the framework of science'.

The 1954 works may have appeared to the casual onlooker as gesture, especially in the use of books. In practice they are steps in a formal representation of the world which the verbal medium is unable to handle . . .

John Latham 1979

Bob Law 96

Bob Law *Yellow Brown Blue Black* 1977 Acrylic on canvas 152.5x160cm (60x63in) Artist's Collection

Bob Law *Castle XXXII* 1976 Pentel and acrylic on canvas 152.5x160cm (60x63in) Artist's collection

1934 Born in Brentford

1949 Apprenticed as architectural designer

1960 Two-man exhibition (with Peter Hobbs) at Institute of Contemporary Arts

1961 Exhibited in 'New London Situation' at Marlborough Fine Art

1962 One-man exhibition at Grabowski Gallery (also 1967)

1963 One-man exhibition at Christchurch College, Oxford

1967 Received Arts Council Purchase Award

1969 Exhibited in John Moores Exhibition, Liverpool

1970 One-man exhibitions at Konrad Fischer Gallery, Dusseldorf, Galerie Onnasch, Berlin
Exhibited in 'Paperworks' at Museum of Modern Art, New York

1971 One-man exhibition at Lisson Gallery (also 1975/77)
Exhibited in 'Art Spectrum' at Alexandra Palace,
'Wall Show' at Lisson Gallery (also group shows in 1974/77/78)

1972 Exhibited in 'Seven Exhibitions' at Tate Gallery

1973 Exhibited in '7 aus London' at Kunsthalle, Berne,
'Critic's Choice' at Arthur Tooth & Sons

1974 One-man exhibition at Museum of Modern Art, Oxford

1976 Exhibited in 'Arte inglese oggi' at Palazzo Reale, Milan

1977 One-man exhibition at Rolf Preisig Gallery, Basle
Exhibited in 'Hayward Annual' at Hayward Gallery,
'British Artists of the 60s' at Tate Gallery,
'British Painting 1952-1977' at Royal Academy

1978 One-man exhibition at Whitechapel Art Gallery
Received Arts Council Award

1979 One-man exhibition at Galerie Gillespie-Laage, Paris
Exhibited in 'Art actuel en Belgique et Grande-Bretagne' at Palais des Beaux Arts, Brussels

Dealer Lisson Gallery

I have, or I think I have, my perfect work in my mind's eye. To bring that work into reality or existence is another matter – there is always some small flaw. Some improvements to be made. And it is this seeking after quality that most interests me. (After all you cannot examine the goods until they are delivered. Which is how one gets into the serial paintings.) The work becomes a very serious trial and examination process in which the artist is solely responsible himself for the quality and conviction of the work.

The justification of the work is in the endeavour of the artist to seek out the quality and skill within his own mind and correlate his inner spirit with the art he can touch and make.

Bob Law 1978

Edwina Leapman 195

1934 Born in Hampshire
1951-7 Studied at Slade School of Fine Art and Central School of Art and Design
1963-75 Taught part-time at various art schools
1974 One-man exhibition at New Art Centre
Exhibited in 'Post-Minimal Painting' Scottish Arts Council exhibition, John Moores Exhibition, Liverpool (also 1976 prizewinner)
1976 One-man exhibition at Annely Juda Fine Art
Received Arts Council Major Award
1977 Exhibited in group show at Galerie Loyse Oppenheim, Geneva
1978 Exhibited in 'A Free Hand' Arts Council travelling exhibition, 'Hayward Annual' at Hayward Gallery
1979 One-man exhibition at Galerie Loyse Oppenheim, Geneva

Dealer Annely Juda Fine Art

Edwina Leapman *Untitled* 1976 Acrylic on canvas 167.7x182cm (66x72in) Annely Juda Fine Art

Edwina Leapman *Untitled* 1978 Acrylic on canvas 167.7x152.4cm (66x60in) Annely Juda Fine Art

My work is concerned with intention and chance. I choose processes that are simple and repetitious so as to allow the interplay of formal and contingent elements. I use different densities of white paint over raw or sealed linen or stained cotton duck. White acrylic is chosen for its range from translucency to opaqueness. The formal elements are horizontal parallel lines or bands. The paintings show the process of working – the movement of the brush, the thickness of the paint and the texture of the canvas.

Edwina Leapman 1979

Michael Leonard 201

1933 Born in India
1954-7 Studied graphic design at St Martin's School of Art
1957-72 Worked as illustrator
1972 Exhibited in group show at Fischer Fine Art (also 1973/74/75/76/77/78)
1972- Working mainly as painter
1975 Exhibited in 'Realismus und Realität' at Kunsthalle, Darmstadt
1976 Exhibited in 'Aspects of Realism' Rothmans travelling exhibition in Canada, John Moores Exhibition, Liverpool (also 1978)
1977 One-man exhibitions at Harriet Griffin Gallery, New York, Fischer Fine Art
Exhibited in Summer Exhibition at Royal Academy
1977/8 Retrospective exhibition at Gemeente Museum, Arnhem

Dealer Fischer Fine Art

Michael Leonard *The Itinerants* 1976 Acrylic on canvas 74.9x116cm ($29\frac{1}{2}$x$33\frac{3}{4}$) Private Collection

I paint using acrylic paint on canvas or board, and I also produce drawings which on the whole tend to be ends in themselves rather than studies for paintings. In place of working drawings I use a camera because I find it the most efficient way of obtaining the kind of information that I need.

The subject matter is usually, but not exclusively, the human figure. Generally it is men rather than women, usually people I know well and almost always particular people rather than types. Either they occupy rooms or are seen engaged in various everyday activities in an urban setting.

Although I work at structuring the images, the pictures are arrived at as intuitively as possible. While often they may evoke the work of painters of the past that I admire, I would hope that they speak with my own individual voice. Possibly this is a voice more suited to conversation than to public speaking for I work quite small. This is partly because I like room-sized, fairly intimate pictures and partly because I want to preserve what might be called a surface tension over the whole area of the painting – also, I work rather slowly.

It is not my aim to make statements of a moral or socio-political nature or to man the barricades on the frontiers of art, nor do I wish to be an illustrator of stories in my paintings. Rather I seek to observe, enjoy, show what is, suggest what might be and generally celebrate the subjects of my choice in images that have as much formal rigour as I can muster.

Michael Leonard 1979

John Lessore 144

John Lessore *St James's Church, Peckham* 1970 Oil on board 37.5x62.2cm ($14\frac{3}{4}$x$24\frac{1}{2}$in) Private Collection

1939 Born in London
1957-61 Studied at Slade School of Fine Art
1961 Received Abbey Minor Travelling Scholarship to Italy
1965 One-man exhibition at Beaux Arts Gallery
1965- Exhibited in Summer Exhibitions at Royal Academy
Teaching at Royal Academy Schools

1968 Exhibiting in 'Helen Lessore and the Beaux Arts Gallery' at Marlborough Fine Art
1969 One-man exhibition at Ashgate Gallery, Farnham
1971 One-man exhibition at New Art Centre
1978- Teaching at Norwich School of Art

Contact 44 Elm Grove, London SE15

Ben Levene ARA 47

1938 Born in London
1956-61 Studied at Slade School of Fine Art
1959- Exhibited in group shows at Beaux Arts Gallery, Camden Art Centre, Royal Academy, Jasper Gallery, New York and with London Group
1961-2 Received Boise Scholarship
Lived and worked in Spain
1963- Teaching part-time at Camberwell School of Art
1969 Two-man exhibition (with Olwyn Bowey) at New Grafton Gallery
1973 One-man exhibition at Thackeray Gallery (also 1975/78)
1975 Exhibited in Chichester National Art Exhibition
Elected Associate of Royal Academy
1977 Exhibited in Tolly Cobbold Eastern Arts National Exhibition, 'British Painting 1952-1977' at Royal Academy

Dealer Thackeray Gallery

Ben Levene *Still-Life with Dead Chrysanthemums* 1974-5 Oil on board 101.6x101.6cm (40x40in) Private Collection

Ben Levene *A Cold Day, Herefordshire* 1974-5 Oil on board 91.4x99.1cm (36x39in) Private Collection

My paintings are in oil paint, although I make drawings and watercolours. I have always painted things around me. I paint mainly landscapes and still-life, and the occasional portrait. I do not know what stages my work falls into, it has not changed violently but has just evolved over the years.

During the 60s abstract art was all the rage, and so very little encouragement was given to figurative painters. Now the artistic climate has changed along with the views of the establishment. I am not well known, so people who buy my paintings do so because they like them.

Ben Levene 1979

David Leverett 200

1938 Born in Nottingham
1957-61 Studied at Nottingham College of Art
1962-5 Studied at Royal Academy Schools
1965 One-man exhibition at Redfern Gallery (also 1968/70/72)
Exhibited in 'Young Contemporaries'
1967 Exhibited in John Moores Exhibition, Liverpool
1968 Exhibited in 'British Painting and Sculpture' at Whitechapel Art Gallery, Bicentenary Exhibition at Royal Academy
1970 One-man exhibitions at Alecto Gallery (also 1972), Editions Alecto, New York
1971 One-man exhibition at Studio La Città, Verona (also 1972/74/75)
1972 One-man exhibitions at Bear Lane Gallery, Oxford, Galleria del Cavallino, Venice (also 1976/78), Galerie Britte Herberle, Frankfurt
1972- Teaching part-time at Slade School of Fine Art
1973 One-man exhibition at Ikon Gallery, Birmingham
1974 One-man exhibition at Institute of Contemporary Arts
Exhibited in 'British Painting '74' at Hayward Gallery
1975 One-man exhibitions at Galleria G7, Bologna, Galerie Skulima, Berlin (also 1977)
1976 One-man exhibition at Galleria Vinciana, Milan
1977 One-man exhibition at Oliver Dowling Gallery, Dublin
Exhibited in 'British Painting 1952-1977' at Royal Academy
1978 One-man exhibition at House Gallery
Exhibited in 'Recent Acquisitions' at Tate Gallery
1978-9 Taught at Reading University

Contact 132 Leighton Road, London NW5

David Leverett *Lost Messages*, from 'Janus Suite' 1977-8 Silkscreen print 71x105cm (28x41⅜in) Artist's Collection

There are certain associations and relationships that exist between Philosophy and Art that I find particularly interesting. On its most basic level these properties refer to a mutual curiosity and desire for creating procedures of enquiry and forms of expression that question the ways that we perceive our reality and intellectually quantify it. The pictographic evaluation and the ideographic characteristics of the written word are, I believe, relevant to its power and potency as its capacity to articulate thought and experiences. The co-existence of the word and image in my work depends on the particular concerns or theme I am dealing with at the time. However the word content is usually my own and generally takes the shape of poetry because as a means of expression I find it has the most effective form that is capable of reducing ideas or propositions to their most simplistic communicative structure. It also has a ▶

David Leverett Detail from *Proustian Series* 1978-9 Glass fibre resin 103x131cm (40½x51⅝in) Artist's Collection

rhythm that is needed to complement the dynamic of the image and as a consequence confirms the relationship between the two. The evocative nature of the word acts as a subliminal trigger device that sets up a series of word-image associations that rebound off each other like reciprocal metaphors.

David Leverett 1979

Garth Lewis 198

Garth Lewis *Calyx* 1978 Acrylic and sand on canvas 146.1x254cm (57½x100in) Artist's Collection

1945 Born in Coventry
1964-7 Studied at Hornsey College of Art
1967-9 Studied and taught at University of New Mexico
1969 One-man exhibition at Fine Arts Museum, University of New Mexico
1969-71 Studied and taught at Queens College, City University of New York
1971 One-man exhibition at The Art Gallery, Queens College, New York
1972 Taught at Hornsey College of Art and Liverpool Polytechnic School of Fine Art
1974 Designed abstract jigsaw puzzle published as educational aid (E J Arnold & Son, Leeds) and exhibited at Design Centre
1974- Teaching at Central School of Art and Design
1976 Exhibited in 'Summer Show 4' at Serpentine Gallery
1977 Exhibited in International Painting Festival at Cagnes-sur-Mer
1978 Taught at Slade School of Fine Art

Contact 88 Lenthall Road, London E8

Garth Lewis *Liane* 1978 Acrylic and sand on canvas 182.9x152.4cm (6ftx5ft) Artist's Collection

My formal art education was rather protracted. It started with a basic grounding in figuration but I made an early move into non-representational painting. I completed my training in America, studying painting and art history at the University of New Mexico and at Queens College at the City University of New York. In my last year there I worked as a research assistant in colour to the painter Herb Aach. I returned to London in 1971, set up a studio and began teaching in art schools.

My work represents my contribution to what has been termed 'colour thinking'. Historically this stems from Impressionism and the colour theories of Chevreul, while formally it is the use of colour as the primary pictorial language. I am specifically involved with the expressive and structural meanings of colour-space painting. Colour-space refers to a colour's capacity to create space, and for its spatiality and identity to change in relation to other formal elements. Within my work space is a continuously mobile, invented structure of energy and light; meaning is a certain drift, a movement from one state of affairs to another through changing visual relationships. My concern is not to imitate appearance or illustrate ideas but to develop a reality from pictorial practice itself.

Garth Lewis 1979

Liliane Lijn 172

1939 Born in New York
1958 Studied archaeology and art history in Paris
1961-2 Lived in New York
First worked with light, reflection and motion
1963 First individual exhibition at La Librairie Anglaise, Paris
1963-4 First kinetic poems shown in Paris
1964-6 Lived in Athens
1966 Settled in London
1967 Individual exhibition at Indica Gallery
Exhibited in 'Lumière et Mouvement' at Musée d'Art Moderne, Paris, Paris Biennale
1968 Exhibited in 'Prospect 68' in Dusseldorf,
'Art Vivant' at Fondation Maeght, St Paul de Vence
1970 Individual exhibition at Hanover Gallery
Exhibited in 'Kinetics' at Hayward Gallery
1972 Individual exhibition at Germain Gallery, Paris
Commission for City Sculpture Project (Peter Stuyvesant Foundation)
1973 Individual exhibition at Jordan Gallery
1975 Exhibited in 'The Video Show' at Serpentine Gallery
1976 Individual exhibition at Serpentine Gallery
Exhibited in 'Boîtes' at Musée d'Art Moderne, Paris,
'Art of the 60s' at Tate Gallery
1977 Individual Arts Council travelling exhibition
1978 Exhibited in 'Hayward Annual' at Hayward Gallery

Contact 28 Camden Square, London NW1

Liliane Lijn *Firespine* 1977 Cornish stone and optical glass prisms 38.1cm (15in) diameter Artist's Collection

D T Suzuki once said:
'Buddhists have conceived an object as an event and not as a thing or substance.'

I have been working with light since 1961 mainly exploring an area which could be called receptive: the receival of light, its reflection, refraction, and eventual re-emission. I have worked with many materials from paper to water, wood to stone, metals of all kinds, glass and plastics. I do not wish to create images nor do I wish to present optical illusions. I attempt an approach to life itself and the ambiguity of its objective reality.

One could call the objects I have made to receive light, sculptures. I have often thought of them as *transformers*. Transformers in that a transformation of some kind, whether real as in the refraction of light through prisms, or virtual as in the metaphorical code of the wire wound columns, occurs within my sculptures. This situation of *exchange*, which I like to think of as energy exchange, cannot take place if the object in question has not reached a state of *resonance*. There is a critical moment in the making of a piece at which one is aware of its own intrinsic life. It is as if the piece itself has reached a certain level of energy, or a frequency at which it begins to resonate. It is at this point that an object ceases to be an object, becoming a system of flow, a dynamic pattern, an event. And saying this I should add that this differentiation is a relative one, and that therefore the flow I speak of in an object which has reached what I call a state of resonance, is of a kind which can be perceived by human eyes, and often felt without absolute visual attention, i.e. subliminal. I would like to maintain that human *perception* is of crucial importance. To say therefore – here is a black box; it contains and emits energy on a high frequency – is totally irrelevant if that energy cannot be felt or perceived by the observer. A prerequisite of existence is our perception of it, although whole universes may exist unseen by us.

Liliane Lijn 1978

Liliane Lijn *Liquid Reflections* 1967-8 Perspex, water and light revolving at 8rpm 109.2cm (43in) diameter Tate Gallery

Kim Lim 87

Kim Lim *Day* 1966 Steel, shot blasted and painted 215cm (7ft) high Betty Parsons Collection, USA

1936 Born in Singapore
1954-6 Studied at St Martin's School of Art
1956-9 Studied at Slade School of Fine Art
1961 Exhibited in '26 Young Sculptors' at Institute of Contemporary Arts, Paris Print Biennale
1962 Exhibited in Tokyo Print Biennale (also 1979)
1966 Individual exhibition at Axiom Gallery (also 1968)
Exhibited in 'Sculpture in the Open Air' in Battersea Park
1967 Exhibited in Expo 67 in Montreal, Nagoaka Prize Exhibition in Nagoaka
1968 Exhibited in Summer Exhibition at Museum of Modern Art, Oxford, 'Prospect 68' in Dusseldorf
1969 Exhibited in 'Open Air Sculpture' at Middelheim
1970 Exhibited in group show at Musée Cantonal des Beaux Arts, Lausanne and Musée d'Art Moderne, Paris, 'British Sculpture out of the 60s' at Institute of Contemporary Arts
1973 Individual exhibition of prints at Waddington Galleries
1974 Individual exhibition at Alpha Gallery, Singapore
1975 Individual exhibitions of prints at Museum of Modern Art, Oxford, Felicity Samuel Gallery
1976 Exhibited in Inaugural Exhibition at National Museum of Art, Singapore
1977 Individual exhibition of prints at Tate Gallery
Exhibited in 'Hayward Annual' at Hayward Gallery
1979 Individual exhibition at Round House Gallery

Contact 40 Camden Square, London NW1

Kim Lim *Stone/Water Piece* 1979 York stone 97cm (38¼in) diameter Artist's Collection

Richard Lin (formerly Lin Show Yu) 97

1933 Born in Taiwan
1952 Came to England
1952-6 Studied art and architecture at Regent Street Polytechnic
1959 One-man exhibition at Gimpel Fils Gallery (also 1961/64)
1960 One-man exhibition at Stone Gallery Newcastle-upon-Tyne
1962 Exhibited in 'Kompas 2' at Stedelijk van Abbemuseum, Eindhoven
1963 One-man exhibitions at Royal Marks Gallery, New York, Architectural Association

▶

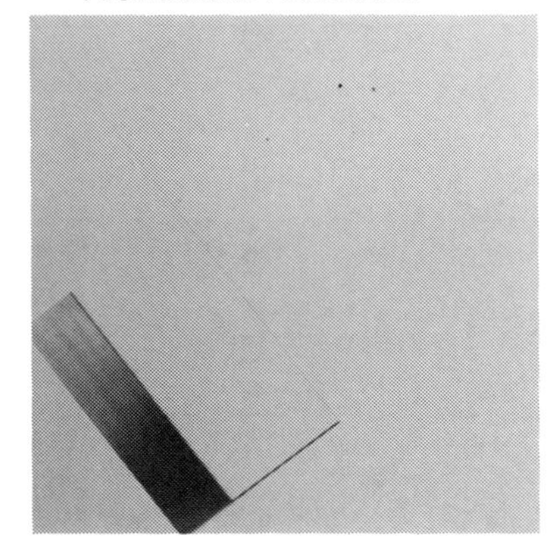

Richard Lin *Painting Relief* 1961 Aluminium and oil on canvas 127x127cm (50x50in) Damiano Collection

Richard Lin *Two, Three, Four* 1969 Aluminium and oil on canvas 102x102cm (40x40in) SF Lin Collection

1964 Exhibited in Carnegie International Exhibition, Pittsburgh (also 1967 prizewinner), 'Documenta 3' in Kassel, 'Britische Malerei der Gegenwart' at Kunstverein, Dusseldorf, 'Contemporary British Painting and Sculpture' at Albright-Knox Art Gallery, Buffalo
1966 One-man exhibition at Marlborough New London Gallery (also 1970) Exhibited in 'Weiss auf Weiss' at Kunsthalle, Berne
1968 One-man exhibition at Marlborough Galleria d'Arte, Rome
1969 One-man exhibition at Galerie Semiha Huber, Zurich Commission for two paintings for liner Queen Elizabeth 2
1970 One-man exhibition at Galerie Withofs, Brussels
1971 One-man exhibition at Galerie Teufel, Cologne and Koblenz
1972 One-man exhibition at Galerie Loehr, Frankfurt
1974 One-man exhibition at Marlborough Fine Art (also 1975)

Contact 9 New Street, Aberystwyth, Dyfed

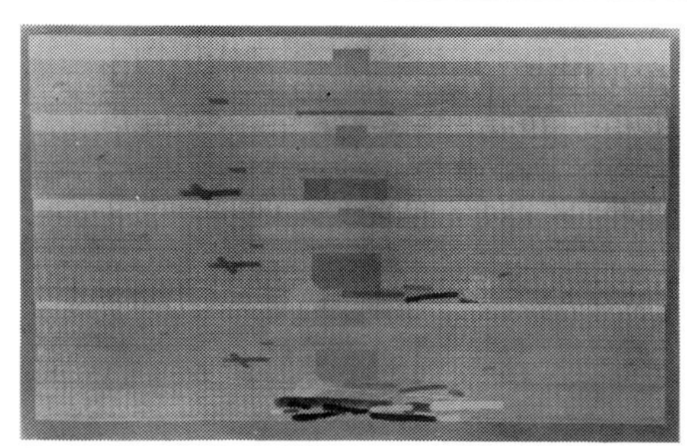

John Loker *Four Extracts IV* 1977 Acrylic on canvas 150x244cm (60x90in) Leeds City Art Gallery

John Loker 156

1938 Born in Leeds
1954-8 Studied graphic design at Bradford College of Art and Design
1960-3 Studied painting at Royal College of Art
1963 Received Abbey Minor Travelling Scholarship
1969 One-man studio exhibition (also 1975)
1970 One-man exhibition 'Horizontals and Drawings' at Angela Flowers Gallery and Institute of Contemporary Arts
1972 Exhibited in 'Art Spectrum' at Alexandra Palace, John Moores Exhibition, Liverpool (also 1974/78)
1973 One-man exhibition at Angela Flowers Gallery (also 1975/78) Exhibited in 'An Octet from Angela Flowers' at Scottish Arts Council Gallery, Edinburgh
1974 Exhibited in 'New British Prints' in New York and travelling in USA
1975 One-man exhibition at Park Square Gallery, Leeds (also 1978) Exhibited in 'British Art in the mid-70s' in Hoechst and Leverkusen, International Painting Festival at Cagnes-sur-Mer
1976 Exhibited in 'Arts Council Collection 1975-6' at Hayward Gallery
1977 Exhibited in 'Small Works' at Royal Academy, 'Aspect du paysage' British Council exhibition in Paris
1978 One-man exhibition at Wetering Galerie, Amsterdam Exhibited in 'Het Landschap' at Apeldoorn, Holland, 'Landscape to Land Art' in Norway

Dealer Angela Flowers Gallery

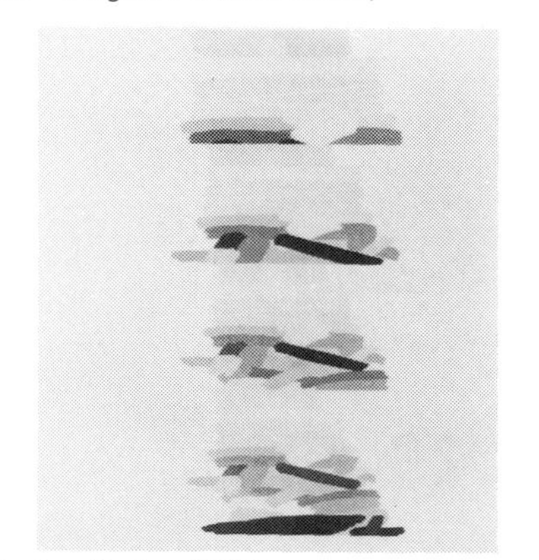

John Loker *Four shifts Centre I* 1978 Acrylic on canvas 213.4x182.9cm (7x6ft) Wetering Galerie, Amsterdam

During 1970 I had been making very large pieces consisting of horizontal panels of opaque and translucent resin. When asked to design a postcard it became obvious that the impact of the pieces would be entirely lost if reproduced on a small scale. So I took a photograph of a wide sweep of horizon. This step began a whole new phase of work leading directly to my present 'landscape' concerns. I became not only interested in the process of scanning, but also in the shifts of scale which occur when the viewer changes position.

These considerations were not altogether new; but the difference now was that the long horizontal strips of colour were based on landscape, and that real objects, such as a beach hut or figure, were used as points of reference and to indicate the scale of the whole.

With reference to the recent painting *Four Shifts Centre 1*, it is one of a series which has pursued the notion of 'landscape extracts', ie referring to parts of the landscape extracted from the whole, a parallel to the way we see the whole but select and perceive more fully, particular parts and incidents.

The grid is a means of increasing the content of the landscape section in stages, moving upwards through the work – hence the title *Shifts*, implying a shift in viewpoint, moving closer to the subject and becoming aware of its constituent parts and details rather than the overall view, which also establishes a parallel time sequence. The composition looks after itself, determined by the disposition of the original statement and the programme of the grids.

John Loker 1979

Richard Long

1945 Born in Bristol
1962-6 Studied at Bristol School of Art
1966-8 Studied at St Martin's School of Art
1971 One-man exhibition at Whitechapel Art Gallery (also 1977) Exhibited in Guggenheim International Exhibition at Guggenheim Museum, New York
1972 One-man exhibition at Museum of Modern Art, New York
1973 One-man exhibition at Stedelijk Museum, Amsterdam
1976 One-man exhibition at Museum of Modern Art, Oxford Exhibited in 'Arte inglese oggi' at Palazzo Reale, Milan
1979 One-man exhibition at Anthony d'Offay Gallery

Contact 121 York Road, Montpellier, Bristol

Peter Lowe 100

Peter Lowe *Grey Diagonal Relief* 1974 50.8x50.8x7cm (20x20x3in) Artist's Collection

1938 Born in London
1954-60 Studied at Goldsmiths College
1957 Exhibited in 'Young Contemporaries'
1960 Produced first systematic constructions
1963 Two-man exhibition (with Colin Jones) 'Plus and Minus Inventions' at AIA Gallery
Exhibited in 'Construction England' Arts Council travelling exhibition
1966 Exhibited in 'Relief Structures' at Institute of Contemporary Arts
1966- Teaching at Goldsmiths College
1967 Exhibited in 'Unit, Series, Progression' Arts Council travelling exhibition
1968 Exhibited in 'Cinetisme – Spectacle – Environment' at Maison de la Culture, Grenoble
1969 Exhibited in 'Systemi' at Amos Anderson Museum, Helsinki
1970 Exhibited in 'Space Dimensions' travelling exhibition in Holland
1971 Exhibited in 'Matrix' at Arnolfini Gallery, Bristol and travelling
1972 Exhibited in 'Systems – Drawings, Reliefs' at Lucy Milton Gallery, 'Systems' at Whitechapel Art Gallery and travelling
1973 Exhibited in 'Systems 2' at Central London Polytechnic
1973- Member of IAFKG, taking part in symposiums and exhibiting with group in many locations in Europe
Teaching at Slade School of Fine Art
1974 One-man exhibition at Lucy Milton Gallery
Exhibited in 'Basically White' at Institute of Contemporary Arts, 'British Painting '74' at Hayward Gallery
1975 One-man exhibition at Galerie Swart, Amsterdam
1976 Exhibited in 'Arte inglese oggi' at Palazzo Reale, Milan
1977 Exhibited in 'Dilworth, Hughes, Lowe and Steele' at Annely Juda Fine Art
1978 Exhibited in 'Constructive Context' at Artists Market

Contact 27 Lanercost Road, London SW2

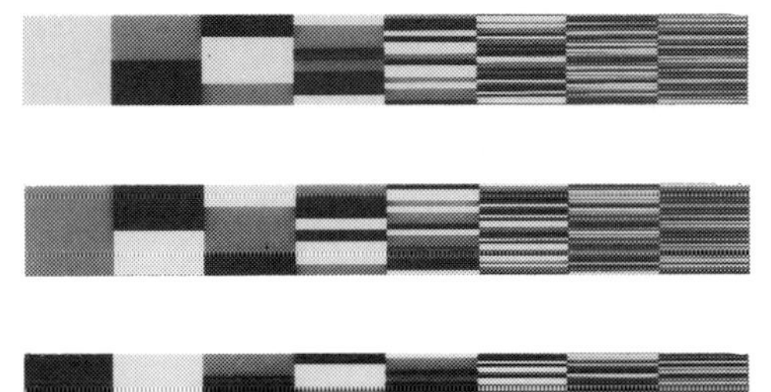

Peter Lowe *Triple Transformation* (Series 17.36.17) 1979 Computer generated microfilm version of serial collage based on transformational rules Artist's Collection

I regard art as a form of communication. For me art is not synonymous with beauty, taste, utility, propaganda or self-expression. I do not accept the hedonist view that it is to do with making pleasing shapes. If I thought that were so, I would turn away from art on the grounds that there are already plenty of shapes around that please me.

If art is a form of communication how does it differ from other forms of communication? I think that the answer to this question is that the difference between art and other rule-bearing activities (which is what communication is) is that art makes clear that it is a rule-bearing activity. (Here I am referring to rules that govern communication not conduct.) Rules of communication are more fundamental than rules of conduct since a rule of conduct needs to be expressed in language.

Having outlined the theoretical position there remains the problem of actual practice. As I make no direct reference in my work to conventional modes of communication like language or gesture, it is essential that the rules are self-evident and deducible from the artifact itself. In order to do this I construct serial works in which any member of a given series (other than the first member) is generated by a simple transformational rule from the previous member in the series. Understanding the meaning of my work is a matter of understanding the rules on which it is based. Although I make constructions, I do not see myself as a Constructivist.

As Kenneth Martin says: 'If I say I construct I am by that only stating here a method of thought and work, and not that I am a Constructivist, Constructionalist, Structuralist or Structurist, which also define adherence to particular schools and philosophies.' (*Studio International*, January 1970.) Construction has a larger and more distinguished history than the movements emanating from Russia sixty years ago even though these movements and their supporters have appropriated the term for their own purposes.

Peter Lowe 1979

Lucy MacKenzie 115

1952 Born in Sudan
1970-3 Studied at Bristol Polytechnic
1971 Exhibited in Westward Television Exhibition (prizewinner)
1973 Exhibited in 'Bristol in Common' at Arnolfini Gallery, Bristol
1973-6 Studied at Royal College of Art (Princess of Wales scholarship)
1974 Exhibited in 'Recollections' South West Arts travelling exhibition
1976 Exhibited in 'The Figurative Approach' at Fischer Fine Art (also in 'The Figurative Approach 2' in 1977)
1976-7 Fellowship at Gloucestershire College of Art
1977 Commissioned to paint 2 miniatures by Royal College of Art as Silver Jubilee gift for HM The Queen
Exhibited in 'British Painting 1952-1977' at Royal Academy

Lucy Mackenzie *The Cactus House, Tresco Gardens* 1978 Oil paint on gesso 12.7x10.2cm (5x4in) Fischer Fine Art

1977- Teaching part-time at Gloucestershire College of Art
1978 Exhibited in 'Flowers' Welsh Arts Council travelling exhibition

Dealer Fischer Fine Art

My work at present consists of oil paintings, assemblages, colour pencil drawings, embroideries and notebooks, all made on a small scale. The paintings are worked on gesso panels using fine sable brushes. This enables me to obtain a high degree of precision and realism while still enjoying the quality of the paint. The subject matter varies; I paint things I come across which appeal to me. Recently I have painted flowers, a hat, a sandcastle, a wicker chair, a greenhouse and some glass marbles. Often I use photographs as an aid, since it is usually a transient arrangement of light and shade that attracts me.

The time I spend at home in the Isles of Scilly has been a consistently important factor in my work. Several paintings refer to the sea, and the tideline provides a constant source of the sea-worn objects and shells I like to incorporate into my assemblages. The assemblages are generally glass-fronted boxes containing found and made objects, combined with fragments of painting and writing. The motivation could be a specific place, relationship or event. Alternatively it may be something less tangible, such as the poignancy of a few lines of poetry, or the dream of a Treasure Island with brightly coloured birds and palm trees.

Lucy MacKenzie 1979

Barry Martin *The King is Dead* 1977 Collage and paint 91.4x61cm (36x24in) Contemporary Art Society

Barry Martin 163

Barry Martin *High Edge* 1974 Acrylic on cotton duck 182.9x182.9cm (6x6ft) No longer in existence

1943 Born in Amersham
1961-6 Studied at Goldsmiths College
1966 Exhibited in 'Young Contemporaries' With London Group (also 1967/68/70/71/74)
1966-7 Studied sculpture at St Martin's School of Art
1968 One-man exhibition 'Pavilions in the Parks' in Chelsea
Exhibited in 'Poet's Choice' at AIA Gallery
1969 Two-man exhibition at Compass Gallery, Glasgow
1969/70 Exhibited in 'British Movements' in Berlin and Gelsenkirchen
1970 One-man exhibition at Serpentine Gallery
Exhibited in 'Manufactured Art' at Camden Arts Centre,
'Kinetics' at Hayward Gallery
1971 One-man exhibition at Richard Demarco Gallery, Edinburgh
Exhibited in 'Electric Theatre' at Institute of Contemporary Arts
1972 Exhibited in 'Art Spectrum' at Alexandra Palace
1975 One-man exhibition at Hoya Gallery
1976 Exhibited in group show at Artists Market (also 1977/78)
1977 One-man exhibitions at Studio International Gallery,
Newcastle Polytechnic Gallery
Exhibited in 'British Painting 1952-77' at Royal Academy,
'12 British Painters' in Iceland
1978 One-man exhibitions at Taranman Gallery,
Patrick Seale Gallery
1980 One-man exhibitions at Goya Gallery, Zaragosa and Barcelona

Contact 4 Ellington Road, Ramsgate, Kent

The phenomenon of painting is material evidence that forms a substantive part of subjective awareness. This awareness holds clues to the absolute. I place my concept of art, at its highest aspiration, in the realm of absolute judgement. Intuition is the sensing apparatus through which this absolute state is understood.

The creation of new forms in art is something akin to the old godlike pursuit of forming man from the dust of the earth and breathing life into him through his nostrils. Unlike the finality of this process however, the search for significant form for the artist is continuous. The relevance of form cannot be sidestepped. It is the basis on which all rests and I have through a slowly evolved consciousness become aware of its essential purpose. Form is like a portrait. The face of the child is both like and unlike the man but time changes the important features.

My recent work has in hindsight come closer to fulfilling some inner need than much that went before. I say 'some' inner need because aspects of it remain constantly hidden from the searching analysis of my consciousness. This hidden portion constitutes the intuitive basis on which appreciation depends. My work isn't explained by describing the methods, ideas and particular intentions meant at the time of making, but a partial explanation is reflected in the questions of *how* are they *remembered*? It is in this remembering that I gauge how close the work measures up to the form of my inner need.

Barry Martin 1979

Kenneth Martin 54

1905 Born in Sheffield
1921-3 Studied at Sheffield School of Art (also 1927-9)
1929-32 Studied at Royal College of Art
1946-67 Visiting Lecturer at Goldsmiths College
1951 Made first kinetic constructions
1956 Exhibited in 'This is Tomorrow' at Whitechapel Art Gallery
1960 Two-man exhibition (with Mary Martin) at Institute of Contemporary Arts
1961 Exhibited in 'British Constructivist Art' American Federation of Art travelling exhibition

1962 One-man exhibition at Lords Gallery
1963 Exhibited in 'Construction: England' Arts Council travelling exhibition
1964 Exhibited in 'Painting and Sculpture of a Decade' at Tate Gallery
1965 Exhibited in Tokyo Biennale, 'British Sculpture of the 60s' at Tate Gallery
Received Gold Medal at International Congress of Artists and Critics, Verucchio
1967 Exhibited in 'Recent British Painting' at Tate Gallery
1968 Exhibited in 'Documenta 4' in Kassel (also in 6 in 1977)
1969 Exhibited in John Moores Exhibition, Liverpool
1970 One-man exhibition at Waddington Galleries (also 1974/78)
Exhibited in 'Kinetics' at Hayward Gallery
1971 Received OBE
1973 Exhibited in 'Henry Moore to Gilbert & George' at Palais des Beaux Arts, Brussels
1974 One-man exhibition at Galerie Swart, Amsterdam (also 1979)
Exhibited in 'Basically White' at Institute of Contemporary Arts, 'British Painting '74' at Hayward Gallery
1975 Retrospective exhibition at Tate Gallery
One-man exhibition at Galerie m, Bochum (also 1976 in The Hague and Dusseldorf)
1976 Two-man exhibition (with Henry Moore) at Scottish National Gallery of Modern Art, Edinburgh
Exhibited in 'Arte inglese oggi' at Palazzo Reale, Milan
Received Midsummer Prize from City of London
1977 One-man Arts Council travelling exhibition
Exhibited in 'Hayward Annual' at Hayward Gallery, 'British Painting 1952-1977' at Royal Academy, Silver Jubilee Contemporary British Sculpture Exhibition in Battersea Park
1978 One-man exhibition at Galerie Lydia Megert, Berne
Exhibited in 'Numerals 1924-77' at Leo Castelli Gallery, New York and travelling
1979 Retrospective exhibition at Yale Center for British Art, New Haven

Dealer Waddington Galleries

Kenneth Martin *Rotary Rings* (2nd version) 1967 Brass 54.6cm (21½in) high McCrory Corporation Collection, New York

Kenneth Martin *Chance, Order, Change 3 (Black)* 1977 Oil on canvas 91.5x91.5cm (36x36in) Tehran Museum of Contemporary Art

Until after World War Two I was a naturalistic artist then, even in front of nature, my work became more and more composed and abstract until it was necessary for me to make a decision between representational and constructed art.

There were many examples of the abstract and constructed to learn from in the world of 20th-century art. I began to realize the developments which had been going on outside England. I studied mathematics and science relative to art and started to work in the third dimension. My wife, Mary, began making reliefs and I to make kinetic objects.

Our works were not like the old sculptors', a series of contours, but were drawn and built from a nucleus outwards. The idea, the nucleus, was a forming principle which was being developed.

For the past 10 years I have been making drawings and paintings based on 'Chance and Order'. The drawings are dynamic, the paintings related to them are contemplative.

The manner of working is the opposite of the way of drawing from nature. If one makes a portrait of a man or draws a tree one cannot draw every hair on the head or all the leaves on the tree. It is necessary to reduce and select what interests you. Every line that you put down has the property that it belongs to such and such a man or tree respectively.

In abstract constructed art the line has a character entirely of its own to be worked with. A straight line has size, scale, position, direction, thickness, length, two ends, two sides when drawn on the plane. These are the materials one uses. One can build an edifice out of natural forming laws, repetition, reflection and so on. The time sequence of making plays an important part. All these are the motivating subject of the work.

Kenneth Martin 1979

Robert Mason 197

1946 Born in Leeds
1963-5 Studied at Harrogate School of Art
1965-8 Studied at Hornsey College of Art
1968 Received Italian Government scholarship
1968-70 Worked at British School in Rome
1970 One-man exhibitions at Galleria d'Arte, Rovigo, Galerie Asinus, Hamburg (also 1973)
1970-1 Taught at University of Florida
1971 Exhibited in 'Artists of the South East and Texas' at Delgado Museum, New Orleans
1973 One-man exhibition at Galerie Beck, Erlangen
Exhibited in 'Serpentine Graphics' at Serpentine Gallery
1974 Exhibited in 'Critic's Choice' at Arthur Tooth & Sons
Received first prize in Bayer Herzlandschaften International

▶

1975 Exhibited in 'British Art in the mid-70s' in Leverkusen and Frankfurt, Middlesbrough Biennale (also 1977 2nd Prize)
'New Work 1' at Hayward Gallery
1976 Exhibited in 'Art into Landscape' Yorkshire Arts Association exhibition (prizewinner)
Received Arts Council Minor Award (also Major Award 1977)
1977 One-man exhibition at University of Sheffield
Exhibited in 'British Painting 1952-1977' at Royal Academy,
'Works on Paper' at Royal Academy and travelling
1977- Teaching part-time at Chelsea School of Art
1978 One-man exhibition at Institute of Contemporary Arts
Exhibited in Rijeka Biennale, Yugoslavia
1979 One-man exhibition at Hester van Royen Gallery
Exhibited in 'Drawing Today' at Kunsthalle, Nuremberg,
Tolly Cobbold Eastern Arts National Exhibition

Dealer Hester van Royen Gallery

Robert Mason *Chetma* 1977 Acrylic and paper on card 159x111cm (62½x43¾in) Artist's Collection

For the last 10 years my work has been involved with collage. Drawings are built up in layers of thin paper over card, so that images are embedded in each layer. The paper is then scraped off to reveal the drawing beneath. The process is repeated many times using pencil, acrylic and crayon as well as paper. The initial impetus for this work came from the peeling billboards and dereliction surrounding my studio in the East End of London. From this environment I developed an interest in the decayed surfaces and forms of antiquity, especially the shapes of broken monuments and half-buried remains.

The most recent work relates to the autobiographical writings of André Gide and his descriptive prose based on his travels in North Africa. I have used as a starting point objects from North Africa which I have photographed or drawn in various ethnographical collections. These images have acted as a catalyst within an assemblage of lines and details which are intended to be meaningful as a totality, particular to the individual work.

Robert Mason 1979

Robert Mason *Biskra Figure* 1978 Acrylic, pencil and paper on card 68x96cm (26⅞x37⅜in) Wakefield City Art Gallery

David McFall RA 10

1919 Born in Glasgow
1935-9 Studied at Birmingham College of Art
1940-1 Studied at Royal College of Art (Scholarship)
1943 Exhibited in Summer Exhibition at Royal Academy (and annually since)
1944-56 Worked with Jacob Epstein
1955 Elected Associate of Royal Academy
1956 Commission for figure of Pocahontas (Red Lion Square)
1956-75 Master of Sculpture at City and Guilds of London Art School
1957 Commission for bronze portrait bust of Ralph Vaughan Williams (Royal Festival Hall)
1959 Commission for bronze figure of Sir Winston Churchill (Woodford Green)
1962 Commission for stone figure of Lord Balfour (Palace of Westminster)
1963 Elected Royal Academician
1974 Commission for stone group of Oedipus and Jocasta (Norbury Library)
1974-5 Commission for bronze portrait of Prince of Wales (Buckingham Palace)

Contact 10 Fulham Park Gardens, London SW6

David McFall *Alexandra Dane Seated on a Sofa* 1973-8 Bronze 188cm (6ft2in) high Artist's Collection

My work falls into three distinct formats. I put first carving in stone (what the French call *pierre-direct*). This is my preference and I judge other sculptors by their ability to carve 'direct'.

Diametrically opposite to stone-carving, I learnt the *métier* of 'busting' from Jacob Epstein – hence *bustier* in French, and always in bronze. In contrast to the slow contemplative process of carving, the bust is modelled at white heat before the sitter has time to get bored so as to animate the portrait with the nervosity of life.

Thirdly, and as an intellectual recreation, I work on bas-relief compositions. The structure may be derived from mathematical or musical intervals, but the subject matter is most often the female form – observed as Degas remarked 'through the keyhole' – seen unawares.

I am sometimes asked if I ever do abstract work and from time to time I have toyed with this concept, but always to abandon it very soon, as I find it too easily arrived at, too arbitrary and I am unwilling to fool myself or anyone else. The female form and face remain for me as ever the most wondrous inspiration and I am not ashamed to be seduced by it every day of my life.

Of living sculptors, I admire Manzu most of all – the only woman sculptor I respect is Käthe Kollwitz, now deceased.

David McFall 1979

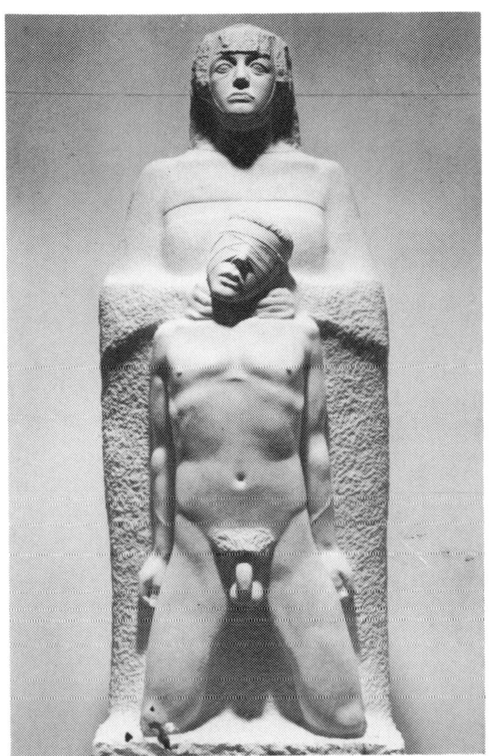

David McFall *Oedipus and Jocasta* 1972 Direct carving in Lary's roche 231cm (7ft7in) high Norbury Library Centre, Lambeth

John McLean 152

1939 Born in Liverpool
1957-62 Studied at St Andrews University
1963-6 Studied at Courtauld Institute
1966-74 Taught at Chelsea School of Art, Goldsmiths College and Canterbury School of Art
1971 Exhibited in group show at Museum of Modern Art, Oxford, 'Big Paintings for Public Places' at Whitworth Art Gallery, Manchester, Group show at Serpentine Gallery
1974 Exhibited in 'British Painting '74' at Hayward Gallery
1974-8 Taught at University College
1975 One-man exhibition at Talbot Rice Art Centre, Edinburgh
Exhibited in 'New Work 1' at Hayward Gallery
1977 Exhibited in 'British Painting 1952-1977' at Royal Academy, '4 Abstract Artists' at Fruit Market Gallery, Edinburgh
1978 One-man exhibition at House Gallery

Dealer House Gallery
William O'Reilly Inc, New York

John McLean *Chris's Choice* 1979 Acrylic on canvas 167x88.9cm (66x33in) Private Collection

FE McWilliam 29

1909 Born in Banbridge, County Down
1928-31 Studied at Slade School of Fine Art
1931-2 Studied in Paris
1939 One-man exhibition at London Gallery
1946-8 Taught at Slade School of Fine Art
1949 One-man exhibition at Hanover Gallery (also 1952/56)
1953 Exhibited in '20th-century Form' at Whitechapel Art Gallery
1956 Exhibited in '11 British Sculptors' at Galerie Chalette, New York, Open Air Sculpture Exhibition at Musée Rodin, Paris (also 1961)
1957 Exhibited in 'Sculpture in the Open Air' in Holland Park
1958 Retrospective exhibition at West of England Academy, Bristol
1959 Exhibited in Middelheim Biennale
1959-60 Exhibited in 'British Artist Craftsmen' at Smithsonian Institute, Washington DC
1961 One-man exhibition at Waddington Galleries (also 1963/66/68/71/73/76/79)
1962 Member of Arts Panel of Arts Council of Great Britain
1963 One-man exhibition at Felix Landau Gallery, Los Angeles
Exhibited in International Sculpture Exhibition in Japan
1964 Exhibited in 'Painting and Sculpture of a Decade' at Tate Gallery
1966 Received CBE

F E McWilliam *Girl Seated* 1971-3 Bronze 23cm (9in) high Private Collection

1970 One-man exhibition at Waddington Galleries, Montreal
1971 Exhibited in Surrealist Group Exhibition at Hamet Gallery
1973 One-man exhibitions at Dawson Gallery, Dublin, McClelland International Gallery, Belfast
1977 One-man exhibition at Bell Gallery, Belfast
1980 One-man exhibition at Taylor Gallery, Dublin

Dealer Waddington Galleries

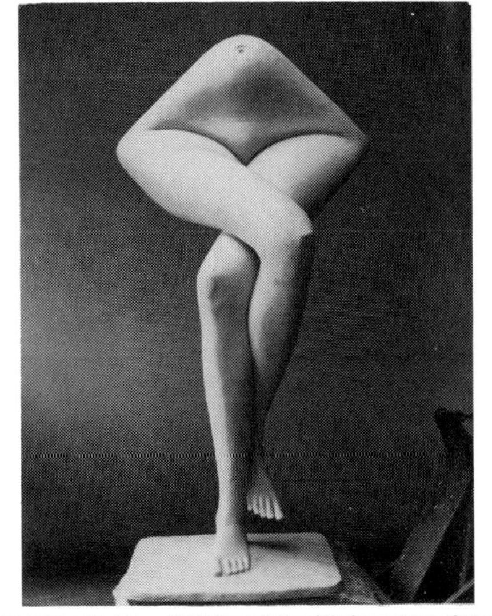

F E McWilliam *Umbilicus* 1978 Plaster 173cm (68in) high Private Collection

Bernard Meadows 59

Bernard Meadows *Help* (small version) 1966 Bronze 35.6cm (14in) long Private Collection

1915 Born in Norwich
1934-6 Studied at Norwich School of Art
1936-7 Studied at Chelsea School of Art
1938-40 Studied at Royal College of Art (also 1945-7)
1952 Exhibited in Venice Biennale (also 1964),
'Sculpture in the Open Air' in Battersea Park (also 1958)
1953 Exhibited in open air sculpture exhibition in Middelheim
1955/7 Exhibited in 'Young British Sculptors' exhibition travelling in Europe and USA
1957 One-man exhibitions at Gimpel Fils Gallery (also 1959/63/65/67),
Paul Rosenberg & Co (also 1962/66)
Exhibited in Sao Paulo Bienal
1958 Exhibited in Sculpture Biennale in Middelheim,
'Expo 58' in Brussels
1959 Exhibited in 'Documenta 2' in Kassel,
Carnegie International Exhibition, Pittsburgh (also 1962/64)
1960- Professor of Sculpture at Royal College of Art
1961 Exhibited in 'Recent British Sculpture' exhibition travelling in Canada, Australia and Japan
1964 Exhibited in 'Painting and Sculpture of a Decade 1954-64' at Tate Gallery
1965 One-man exhibition at Stedelijk Museum, Amsterdam and in Berlin, Recklinghausen and Brunswick
1966 Exhibited in International Contemporary Sculpture Exhibition at Musée Rodin, Paris
1972 Exhibited in 'British Sculptors '72' at Royal Academy
1975 One-man exhibition at Taranman Gallery (also 1978)
1977 One-man exhibition at Galerie Villand-Galanis, Paris
1978 One-man exhibitions in Angers and Rouen
1979 One-man exhibition in Tokyo

Dealer Gimpel Fils
Taranman Gallery

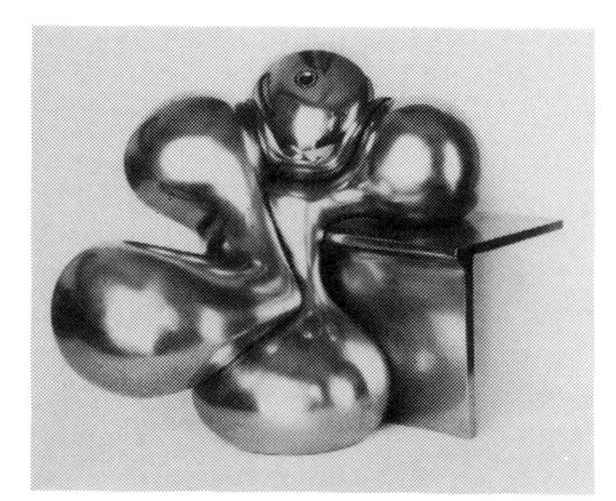

Bernard Meadows *Seated Figure* 1978 Bronze 22.9cm (9in) high Private Collection

Robert Medley 31

1905 Born in London
1923-6 Studied at Byam Shaw School of Art and Slade School of Fine Art
1926-7 Studied in Paris
1929-34 Assisted Duncan Grant and Vanessa Bell on various projects
1931 Elected to London Artists Association
1932 First one-man exhibition at London Artists Association Gallery
Started to work with Rupert Doone, director of the Group Theatre, designing plays by Auden, Isherwood and Eliot
1932-9 Taught at Chelsea School of Art (also 1946-50)
1932- Exhibited with London Group
1947 One-man exhibition at Reid & Lefevre
1950 One-man exhibition at Hanover Gallery
1950-8 Taught stage design and painting at Slade School of Fine Art
1952 One-man exhibition at Leicester Galleries (also 1956/58/65)
1958-64 Head of Fine Art Department at Camberwell School of Art
1960-3 Made BBC radio programmes on Matisse, Watteau and Poussin in 'Picture of the Month' series
1963 Retrospective exhibition at Whitechapel Art Gallery
1966 Published monograph on Rubens (Collins)
1967-77 Chairman of Faculty of Painting at British School of Rome
1971 One-man exhibition at Lisson Gallery
1978 Exhibited in 'Milton's Samson Agonistes' at Artists Market

Contact 10 Gledhow Gardens, London SW5

Early influences until 1939 were the Bloomsbury Group and the Ecole de Paris, though from 1932 surrealist and political pressures also exerted their influence. After the war my work was concerned with the movement of human figures in space (such as the *Cyclist* picture) and with industrial landscape.

In the 1950s a need for closer academic study of drawing (light and shade) produced the *Antique Room* series. By the 1960s the freedom of line and direct brushstroke disintegrated the 'representational' but the pictures remained metaphors for actual visual experiences. This was followed by an entirely non-figurative and geometric period – an academic discipline of drawing using enclosed shapes rather than freely running line. I now work in both conventions – non-figurative and figurative – as I feel inclined.

Robert Medley 1979

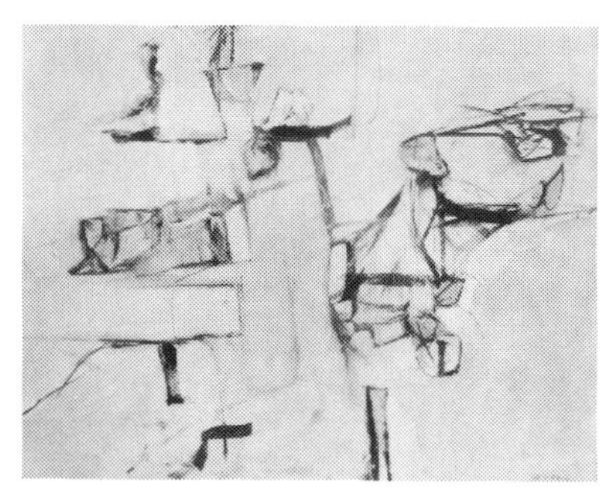

Robert Medley *Movement in Rock Landscape* 1962 Oil 114.3x99.1cm (45x39in) Artist's Collection

Edward Middleditch RA 12

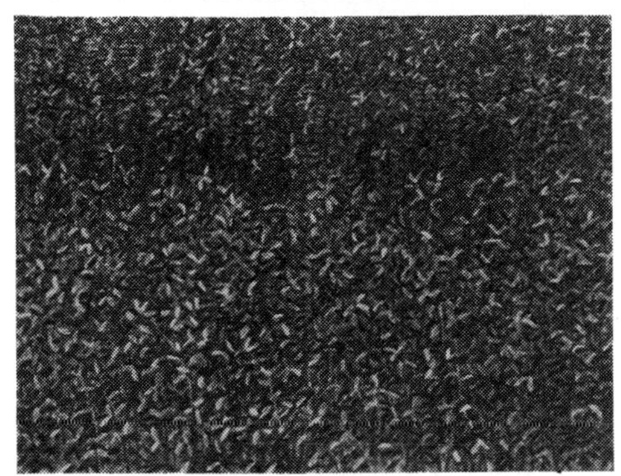

Edward Middleditch *Beanfield* 1978 Drawing 40.6x50.8cm (16x20in) Artist's Collection

1923 Born in Chelmsford
1948-52 Studied at Royal College of Art
1954 One-man exhibition at Beaux Arts Gallery (also 1956/58/60/62)
1956 Exhibited in Carnegie International Exhibition, Pittsburgh (also 1958), Venice Biennale
1957 Exhibited in '6 Young Painters' Arts Council exhibition
1959 Exhibited in 'The Graven Image' at Whitechapel Art Gallery
1960 Exhibited in 'Critic's Choice' at Arthur Tooth & Sons
1962 Received Gulbenkian Foundation Scholarship
1964 Received Arts Council Bursary (also 1968)

Edward Middleditch *Winter* 1960 Oil on canvas 260x209.6cm (8ft6½inx7ft10½in) Toledo Museum of Art, Ohio

1866 One-man exhibition at Roland, Browse & Delbanco
Exhibited in 'Painters in East Anglia' Arts Council travelling exhibition
1967 Exhibited in 'Drawing towards Painting' Arts Council travelling exhibition
1968 Exhibited in 'Helen Lessore and the Beaux Arts Gallery' at Marlborough Fine Art
1969 One-man exhibition at New Art Centre (also 1971/74/78)
Exhibited in 'The English Landscape Tradition in the 20th Century' at Camden Arts Centre
1973 Exhibited in 'Landscape' at Serpentine Gallery
1974 Exhibited in 'British Painting '74' at Hayward Gallery
1977 Exhibited in 'British Painting 1952-1977' at Royal Academy

Contact School House, Edwardstone, Boxford, Essex

Robert Medley *The Perambulator* 1953 Oil 152.4x127cm (60x50in) Birmingham City Art Gallery

Keith Milow *Just Crosses* 1978 Concrete, resin and fibreglass Exhibited at Round House Gallery

Keith Milow 169

1945 Born in London
1962-7 Studied at Camberwell School of Art
1967 Exhibited in 'Young Contemporaries'
1967-8 Studied at Royal College of Art
1968 Did experimental work at Royal Court Theatre
1968-70 Taught at Ealing School of Art
1969 Exhibited in '6 at the Hayward', Hayward Gallery
1970 Artist in Residence, Leeds University (Gregory Fellowship)
First one-man exhibition at Nigel Greenwood Inc (also 1972/73/74/76/78)
Exhibited in Tokyo Print Biennale, 'Works on Paper' at Museum of Modern Art, New York
1971 One-man exhibition at Institute of Contemporary Arts
1972 One-man exhibitions at Kings' College, Cambridge, Leeds City Art Gallery, Utrechtkring, Utrecht
Exhibited in 'The New Art' at Hayward Gallery,
John Moores Exhibition, Liverpool (also 1974/78)
1972-4 Harkness Fellowship to America
1973 One-man exhibition at J. Duffy & Sons, New York
Exhibited in 'Homers' at Museum of Modern Art, New York
1974 Exhibited in 'British Painting '74' at Hayward Gallery

Keith Milow *Ninety Second Cross* 1978 Concrete and fibreglass 101.6x76.2x19.1cm (40x30x7½in) Rowan Gallery

1975 One-man exhibition at Arnolfini Gallery, Bristol
Exhibited in 'Buckley, Milow & Hall' at Galerie Jacomo Santiveri, Paris
1975- Teaching at Chelsea School of Art
1976 One-man exhibition at Kettles Yard Gallery, Cambridge
Exhibited in 'Arte inglese oggi' at Palazzo Reale, Milan,
'Six English Artists' at Houston, Texas
Calouste Gulbenkian Foundation Visual Arts Award
1977 One-man exhibition at Galerie Albert Baronian, Brussels
Exhibited in 'Five British Artists' at Young Hoffman Gallery, Chicago,
'Hayward Annual' at Hayward Gallery,
'25 Years of British Painting' at Royal Academy
1978 One-man exhibition 'Just Crosses' at Roundhouse Gallery
1979 Exhibited in Tolly Cobbold Eastern Arts National Exhibition (First Prize)

Dealer Rowan Gallery

Nicholas Monro 112

Nicholas Monro *Morris Dancers* 1978 Fibreglass Life-size Galerie Bucholtz, Munich

1936 Born in London
1958-61 Studied at Chelsea School of Art
1963-8 Taught at Swindon School of Art
1968 One-man exhibitions at Robert Fraser Gallery,
Galerie Pribaut, Amsterdam
Exhibited in 'Salon des Jeunes Peintures' in Paris,
'Prospekt 69' in Dusseldorf
1969 One-man exhibition at Galerie Thelen, Essen
Exhibited in 'Pop Art' at Hayward Gallery
Received Arts Council Award
1970 Exhibited in 'Klischee und Antiklischee' at Neue Galerie, Aachen
1971 One-man exhibition at Waddington Galleries 2 and 3
1972 One-man exhibition at City Art Gallery, Bristol
1973 One-man exhibition at Central Art Gallery, Wolverhampton
1975 Exhibited in 'New Work' at Hayward Gallery
1976 Exhibited in group show at Montreal Olympics
1977 Exhibited in 'Hayward Annual' at Hayward Gallery,
'British Genius' in Battersea Park
1978 One-man exhibition at Felicity Samuel Gallery
Exhibited in 'Scale for Sculpture' at Serpentine Gallery
1979 Exhibited in group show at City Art Gallery, Nuremberg

Contact Potters Cottage, Shefford Woodlands, Newbury, Berkshire

I think one feels as great a sense of freedom in doing figurative art today as must have been felt by those artists who abandoned it in favour of abstraction.

To ignore the strictures of representation must have appeared to offer unlimited scope for exploration and revelation (which indeed it does), but finally non-figurative art has its boundaries and limitations and there are things it is unable to do.

One of the most important lessons to be learned from the great movements in art over the last hundred years is the significance of the idea; the idea is all, and this puts skill and ability in its proper place. There is nothing worse in figurative art than when skill becomes an end in itself, for then, like a good speaker with nothing to say, it appears fatuous and glib. On the other hand, a criticism more applicable to non-figurative work, is that so many artists seem to feel an overpowering need to educate, and we all know how dull and boring that can be. If one is presented with an image as potent as, say, *Concorde*, then it will only diminish one's pleasure if one is being fed statistics on wing stress and engine thrust at the same time. Of course without these irrefutable facts there would be no Concorde and without knowledge and education there would be no art, but the education is not the art, and should not purport to be so.

The only really important things in art are choice and style – a well chosen image transformed by style can best translate an idea. And the only idea I seriously think I hold is that, far from being any kind of virtue, abstinence is a sin, and that we all from time to time unwittingly abstain by creating our own barriers when adopting particular attitudes.

Nicholas Monro 1978

Nicholas Monro *Max Wall* 1978 Fibreglass Life-size Southampton Art Gallery

Michael Moon 153

1937 Born in Edinburgh
1958-62 Studied at Chelsea School of Art
1962-3 Studied at Royal College of Art
1963-73 Taught at Chelsea School of Art
1969 One-man exhibition at Waddington Galleries (also 1970/72/78)
1972 Exhibited in 'Caulfield, Hodgkin, Moon' at Galerie Stadler, Paris
1973 Exhibited in 'La peinture anglaise aujourd'hui' at Musée d'Art Moderne, Paris
Final colour strip painting done
1973- Teaching at Slade School of Fine Art
1974 Exhibited in 'British Painting '74' at Hayward Gallery
1976 One-man exhibition at Tate Gallery
1977 Exhibited in 'British Painting 1952-1977' at Royal Academy

Dealer Waddington Galleries

Michael Moon *Two-Fold* 1976 Acrylic on mixed materials 238x368cm (7ft10in x 12ft1in) Waddington Galleries

My work up until 1973 was concerned with colour. The paintings took the form of plastic strips some 10ft wide and 6in deep and set some ½in apart on which I gradated or 'measured' colour sequences. The medium used was acrylic. The main idea was to get as much colour into and onto the painting in as controlled a way as possible without losing sight of the surface as a whole. The gaps between the strips helped this by giving the eye a chance to 'fill in' between very disparate colour. The format was almost always the same so that I could concentrate on widely different colour ideas between each painting.

Feeling I had exhausted the possibilities inherent in these paintings my work changed radically between 1973 and 1976. It is now concerned mainly with a loosely based exploration of my own immediate surroundings, usually my studio. Surfaces such as walls, floors, windows and sometimes specific objects are cast in acrylic and calico and then reorganised in their soft form into assemblages which attempt some synthesis of studio activity or in a wider sense, painterly activity. The works' appearance, through the nature of the cast, is usually soft and I try to pay great attention to the qualities inherent in that softness, eg folds, wrinkles, to stress as rich a surface quality as possible. The wear and tear imposed on surfaces and objects are of great importance and I like the finished painting to have a 'lived-in' feel to it, where the previous history of the cast material forges an intimate link with those marks that I impose on it. The work probably fits into a loose collage tradition and would for me have its roots based firmly in Cubism, with a love of Braque's work informing some of its basic ideas and ideals.

Michael Moon 1979

Michael Moon *Double Glaze* 1976 Acrylic on canvas 226x243cm (7ft5inx8ft) Waddington Galleries

Henry Moore OM 1

Henry Moore *Three Piece Reclining Figure; Draped* 1975 Bronze 472cm (15ft6in) long (Edition of 7) Private Collections

1898 Born in Castleford, Yorkshire
1919 Studied at Leeds College of Art
1921-4 Studied at Royal College of Art
1922-32 Taught at Royal College of Art
1931 One-man exhibition at Leicester Galleries (also 1933/36/46/51/54/55)
1932 Established Sculpture Department at Chelsea School of Art
1936 Exhibited in 'Fantastic Art, Dada and Surrealism' at Metropolitan Museum of Art, New York
1940-5 Official War Artist
1941 One-man exhibition at Temple Newsam, Leeds
1941-54 Trustee of Tate Gallery
1945- Received Honorary Doctorates from many international universities
1946 One-man exhibition at Museum of Modern Art, New York
1947 One-man exhibitions at Art Institute of Chicago,
San Francisco Museum of Art,
National Gallery of New South Wales, Sydney and travelling in Australia
1947-71 Member of Royal Fine Art Commission
1948 Exhibited in Venice Biennale (prizewinner)
1949 One-man exhibition at Wakefield City Art Gallery and travelling in England and Europe (also 1963)
1951 One-man exhibition at Tate Gallery (also 1968)
1952 One-man exhibitions at National Gallery of South Africa, Cape Town, Kestner Gesellschaft, Hanover and travelling in Germany
1953 Exhibited in Sao Paulo Bienal (prizewinner)
1955 One-man exhibition at Museum of Fine Arts, Montreal and travelling in Canada and New Zealand
Exhibited in 'Documenta 1' in Kassel
Received CH
1955-74 Trustee of National Gallery
1958 One-man exhibition at Marlborough Fine Art (also 1959/62/63/64/65/66/67)
Exhibited in Carnegie International Exhibition, Pittsburgh (prizewinner)
1959 One-man exhibition at Metropolitan Art Gallery, Tokyo and travelling in Japan
1960 Retrospective exhibition at Kunsthalle, Hamburg and travelling in Germany
1963 One-man exhibition at La Jolla Art Center, California and travelling in USA
Received OM
1964 One-man exhibition at Palacio de Bellas Artes, Mexico and travelling in South America
1966 Retrospective exhibition at Philadelphia College of Art
One-man exhibition at Smithsonian Institute, Washington DC

▶

1968 One-man exhibition at Rijksmuseum Kroller-Müller, Otterlo and travelling in Germany and Holland
1969 One-man exhibition at Museum of Modern Art, Tokyo and travelling in Far East
1970 One-man exhibition at Galerie Cramer, Geneva and travelling in Europe and USA
1972 One-man exhibition at Forte di Belvedere, Florence
1973 Exhibited in 'Henry Moore to Gilbert & George' at Palais des Beaux Arts, Brussels
1974 One-man exhibition at County Museum of Art, Los Angeles
Opening of Henry Moore Sculpture Centre at Art Gallery of Ontario, Toronto
1976 One-man exhibition at Zurcher Forum, Zurich
1977 Formed Henry Moore Foundation
One-man exhibition at Orangerie des Tuileries, Paris
1978 One-man exhibition at Bradford City Art Gallery

Contact Hoglands, Much Hadham, Hertfordshire

I am a sculptor because the shape of things matters even more to me than the colour of them. It may be that a painter is excited as much by colour as by form. Some painters have been like this, though others have been as interested by form as sculptors are. For me, it is the three-dimensional reality and shape which one wants to understand, to grasp and to experience. This is, I think, what makes me a sculptor – I need these three dimensions, as a musician needs sound and notes of music, and a writer must be interested in words. The different arts call for a diferent sense – sight, touch, hearing, taste. The actual three dimensions of a form are what I like and need. I want to

Henry Moore *Reclining Figure: Holes* 1975-8 Elm wood 222cm (7ft3½in) long Henry E Foundation

Henry Moore *Two Piece Reclining Figure; Armless* 1977 Black granite 222cm (7ft3¼in) long Henry Moore Foundation

produce the complete thing, rather than a sketch or an illusion of it.

To understand real three dimensions is to train your mind to know when you see one view what it is like on the other side, to envelop it inside your head, as it were. This is not something that you are born with – a child has to learn how far away a toy is, hung up in its pram, by touching and feeling. We learn distances originally by walking them. We understand space through understanding form.

Henry Moore 1978
(from *With Henry Moore* published by Sidgwick & Jackson)

Rodrigo Moynihan 8

1910 Born in Canary Islands
1918 Came to England
1928 Began art studies in Florence and Rome
1928-31 Studied at Slade School of Fine Art
1933 Elected member of London Group
1934 Became a leader of Objective Abstraction Group
Exhibited in 'Objective Abstractions' at Zwemmer Gallery
1937 Associated with Euston Road School
1940 First one-man exhibition at Redfern Gallery (also 1944/47/58/61)
First exhibited in Summer Exhibition at Royal Academy (also annually 1944-56)
1941 Exhibited in 'Artists of Fame and Promise' at Leicester Galleries (also exhibited in group shows 1943/45-50)
1943 Official War Artist
1944 Elected Associate of Royal Academy
1946 One-man exhibition at Leicester Galleries (also 1955)
1948-57 Professor of Painting at Royal College of Art
1951 Exhibited in '60 Paintings for '51' Festival of Britain Exhibition

Rodrigo Moynihan *Self-portrait with a Round Canvas* 1977 Oil on canvas 52.1x45.7cm (21½x18in) Private Collection

1952 Received CBE
Commissioned to paint *After the Conference* by Penguin Books
1954 Elected Royal Academician (resigned in 1957)
1957 Exhibited in 'Statements' at Institute of Contemporary Arts, 'Peinture anglaise contemporaine' in Geneva and Liège
1958- Living and working in France, Canada and USA as well as Britain
1963 One-man exhibition at Hanover Gallery (also 1967)
Exhibited in 'British Painting in the 60s' at Whitechapel Art Gallery
1963-8 Co-editor of *Art and Literature* (Paris)
1966 One-man exhibition at Egan Gallery, New York
1968 One-man exhibition at Tibor de Nagy Gallery, New York
1970 One-man exhibition at Myers Gallery, New York
1973 One-man exhibition at Fischer Fine Art
1977 Exhibited in 'British Painting 1952-1977' at Royal Academy
1978 Retrospective exhibition at Royal Academy

Dealer Fischer Fine Art

I left the Slade in 1931. The next few years were spent exploring and experimenting in the various contemporary styles young painters were exposed to. In an effort to arrive at something different to the prevailing trends of Cubism and Surrealism we arrived at a lyrical neo-impressionist form of abstraction. The paintings resulting 'Objective Abstractions' were shown at the Zwemmer Gallery in 1934.

In 1937, together with many of my friends, I turned towards realism. Some part-time teaching at the Euston Road School brought me into association with Coldstream, Pasmore and Rogers and I started painting portraits and drawing from the model. On the winding-up of the school in 1938 I left for the country and my first show at the Redfern in 1940 contained a large proportion of landscapes. Later on as a War Artist I was given many portraits to paint. I also completed *Medical Inspection* planned during my time as a private in the Artillery.

After the war I continued to paint portraits. My life-long interest in still-life also dates from this period and I was, of course, very involved in teaching at the Royal College where I had been appointed Professor of Painting by Robin Darwin in 1948. The culminating point in the objective naturalism I was practising then was reached in the painting of the Penguin Editors *After the Conference*. This work followed the large Royal College staff group painting of 1951.

About 1956-7 I turned to new possibilities based on the 30s' 'Objective Abstractions' and I painted in Paris and the South. After my first New York show in 1966 the paintings became more defined as spatial areas with ruled lines and divisions of colour. In 1970 I began to introduce objects seen in the area of the studio. This development seemed easy and natural and not at all traumatic (as it had been in the 50s) – I have continued to paint in this way since then.

Rodrigo Moynihan *The Teaching Staff of the Painting School, Royal College of Art* 1949-50 Oil on canvas 426x305cm (14x10ft) Tate Gallery

Except for a few canvases in acrylic paint worked on in New York in 1970, all my paintings have been oil on canvas or panel. My drawings are in a variety of media: charcoal, pen and ink, chalk or pastel, water-colour and body colour – quite often all are used in the same drawing.

Rodrigo Moynihan 1979

Henry Mundy 56

Henry Mundy *Texture, Drop, Change* 1971 Acrylic on canvas 205x421.2cm (6ft9inx13ft9¾in) Artist's Collection

1919 Born in Birkenhead
1933-7 Studied at Laird School of Art, Birkenhead
1946-50 Studied at Camberwell School of Art
1957 One-man exhibitions at Gallery KB, Oslo, Gallery One
1958 Exhibited in Carnegie International Exhibition, Pittsburgh (also 1961 1st Prize)
1960 One-man exhibition at Hanover Gallery (also 1962/65/66)
1961 Exhibited in John Moores Exhibition, Liverpool
Received William Frew Prize
1962 Exhibited in 'British Art Today' in San Francisco, Dallas and Santa Barbara
1963 'British Painting in the 60s' at Tate Gallery
1964 Exhibited in Guggenheim International Exhibition, New York (also 1966), 'Painting and Sculpture of a Decade 1954-64' at Tate Gallery
1966- Teaching at St Martin's School of Art
1972 One-man exhibition at Kasmin Gallery
1974 Exhibited in 'British Painting '74' at Hayward Gallery
1975 Received Abbey Major Award
1977 Exhibited in 'British Painting 1952-1977' at Royal Academy

Contact 23 Wellesley Road, London W4

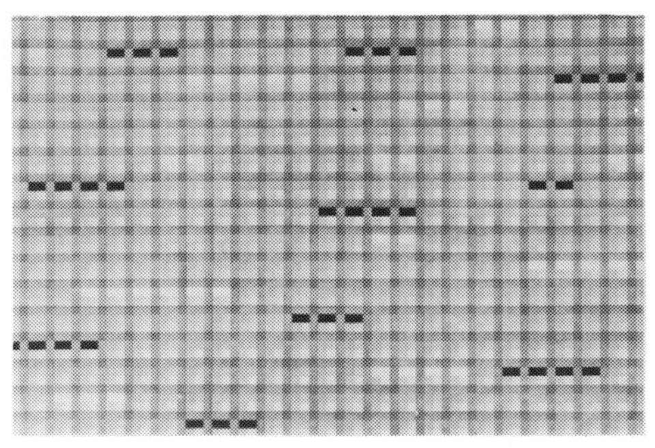

Henry Mundy *Untitled* 1978 Acrylic on canvas 182x274cm (6x9ft) Artist's Collection

Myles Murphy 71

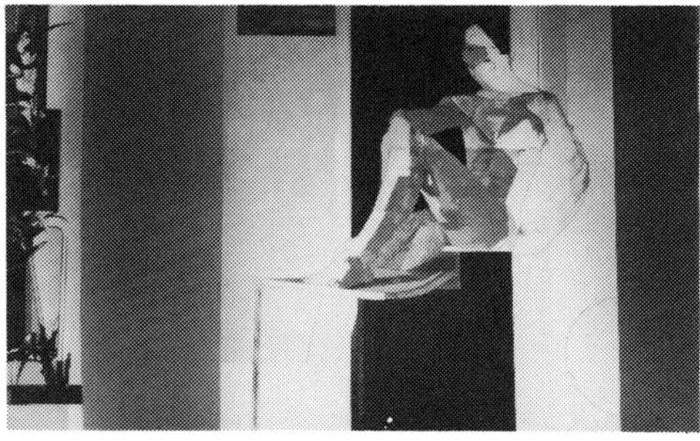

Myles Murphy *Figure against a Yellow Foreground* 1974 243.8x152.4cm (8x5ft) Artist's Collection

1927 Born in Bury, Lancashire
1951-4 Studied at Slade School of Fine Art
1952 Exhibited in 'Young Contemporaries' (also 1953)
1954-5 Studied at Slade School of Fine Art (post-graduate work)
1955 Received Abbey Travelling Scholarship
1958-9 Taught at Slade School of Fine Art
1960 Exhibited in 'Modern British Portraits' Arts Council travelling exhibition
1960- Teaching at Chelsea School of Art
1964 Exhibited in 'New Painting' Arts Council travelling exhibition, with London Group (also 1965/68)
1973 Received Lorne Award

Myles Murphy *David Hume at Clapham* 1957 142.2x106.7cm (56x42in) Artist's Collection

1974 Exhibited in John Moores Exhibition, Liverpool (1st Prize; also 1978 Hors Concours), 'British Painting '74' at Hayward Gallery

Contact 28 Gauden Road, London SW4

Martin Naylor 131

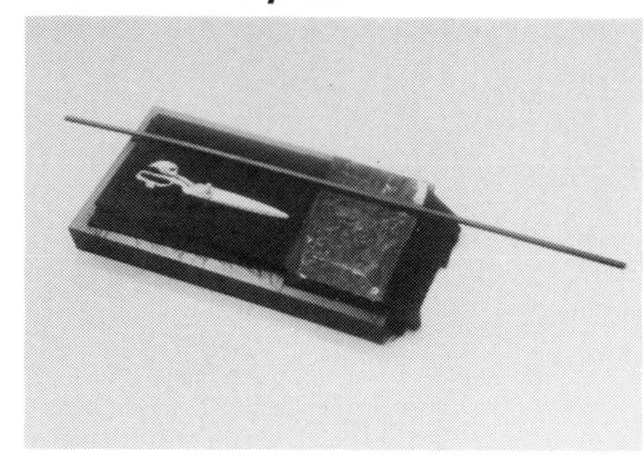

Martin Naylor *Rotten with Bogus Learning* 1977 Wood, worsted, scissors and varnished paper 11x124x36cm ($4\frac{3}{8}$inx49x$14\frac{1}{4}$in) Arts Council of Great Britain

1944 Born in Yorkshire
1961-5 Studied at Dewsbury & Batley Technical and Art School
1965-6 Studied at Leeds Art College
1967-70 Studied at Royal College of Art
1969 Exhibited in 'Young Contemporaries'
1971 Received Arts Council Award
1972 First one-man exhibition at Serpentine Gallery
Exhibited in 'British Sculptors 72' at Royal Academy
1972- Teaching at Royal College of Art and Hornsey College of Art
1973 One-man exhibition at Arnolfini Gallery, Bristol
1973-4 Gregory Fellowship at Leeds University
1974 One-man exhibitions at Rowan Gallery (also 1975/77/78), Park Square Gallery, Leeds
Exhibited in John Moores Exhibition, Liverpool (also 1978), Bradford Print Biennale, 'Art into Landscape' at Serpentine Gallery (1st Prize)
1975 One-man exhibition at Leeds City Art Gallery
Exhibited in 'British Art of the mid-70s' in Leverkusen and Frankfurt, Sao Paulo Bienal (also 1977)
Received Gulbenkian Foundation Visual Arts Award
1976 One-man exhibitions at Sunderland Arts Centre, Museum of Modern Art, Oxford
Visiting Professor at Ecole Nationale des Beaux Arts, Bourges
1977 Exhibited in Silver Jubilee Contemporary British Sculpture Exhibition in Battersea Park, Summer Exhibition at Royal Academy (also 1978), Sao Paulo Bienal
1979 One-man exhibition at Corroboree Gallery, Iowa University, Elise Meyer Inc, New York
Exhibited in Tolly Cobbold Eastern Arts National Exhibition, Cambridge and travelling

Dealer Rowan Gallery

Martin Naylor *Fortress 1* 1975 Blockboard, steel, paint and varnish 287.7x15.2x287.7cm (9ft $3\frac{1}{4}$inx6inx9ft5in) Loxley Hall, Warwickshire

Naylor does not see art as a quest for simplification, he wants it to express real life. Pictures can contain many disparate elements simultaneously, in ways denied the sequential forms of books and films and even music, and it is this that he exploits. If he finds he cannot say everything he wants to say pictorially, then he expresses it in words or objects. Eliot said that art should communicate before it is understood.

In its strident male and fragile female symbolisms, its half-memories and blurred reflections, its illusions and delusions, this 'picture' Naylor makes speaks a multiple language of unease in the relationship of men and women, a man and a woman.

John McEwen 1978

Paul Neagu 122

1938 Born in Bucharest
1959-65 Studied at Institute Grigoresco, Bucharest
1969 One-man exhibitions at Amphora Gallery, Bucharest, Demarco Gallery, Edinburgh
1969-76 Exhibited regularly in group shows at Demarco Gallery, Edinburgh
1970 One-man exhibition at Sigi Krauss Gallery
Exhibited in John Moores Exhibition, Liverpool (also 1974/76)
1971 One-man exhibition at Compass Gallery, Glasgow (also 1975)
Exhibited in Paris Biennale
1972 One-man exhibition at Rivolta Gallery, Lausanne
Exhibited with Foundation of Generative Arts Group
1972- Teaching at Hornsey College of Art
1973 Exhibited in 'Serpentine Sculpture' at Serpentine Gallery, 'Earth Images' at Scottish National Gallery of Modern Art, Edinburgh
Received Arts Council Award (also 1975/78)
1975 One-man exhibitions at Museum of Modern Art, Oxford, Sunderland Arts Centre
Exhibited in 'The Condition of Sculpture' at Hayward Gallery
1976 One-man exhibition at Leeds Polytechnic Gallery
Exhibited in 'Six Times' at Serpentine Gallery, Tolly Cobbold Eastern Arts National Exhibition (prizewinner)
1977 One-man exhibition at Cavallino Gallery, Venice
Exhibited in Silver Jubilee Contemporary British Sculpture Exhibition in Battersea Park
1977- Teaching at Chelsea School of Art
1978 One-man exhibition at Newcastle Polytechnic Gallery
1979 One-man exhibitions at Elise Meyer Inc, New York, Third Eye Centre, Glasgow

Dealer Elise Meyer Inc, New York
Contact 73a Highbury New Park, London N5

My work can be divided into 4 major themes: 'Palpable Art' (1965-76) describes mixed media works that are tactile and palpable, involving all five senses, performance, happenings and rituals.

'Anthropocosmos' (1968-78) is the conceptualization of philosophical and figurative elements through drawings on paper or canvas, paintings and three-dimensional objects.

Paul Neagu *Anthropocosmos* 1977 Drawing on gesso, canvas, 33x25.4cm (13x10in) Artist's Collection

'Generators/Hyphens' (1975-present day) involve sculptures of all sizes, from 1 foot to 25 feet, in wood and steel, as well as drawings, photographs, architectural situations, monumental concepts and charts. 'Hyphens' are variations on a principle of relations and connections. They exist between intuition and universal reason. They are epistemologic metaphors.

'Fusions' (1978-present day) describes the drawings, paintings and sculptures in radial forms which usually represent the fruition/fusion of previous experiences.

Paul Neagu *Fusion* 1978 Mahogany wood 35.6cm (14in) diameter Artist's Collection

In the late 60s I was looking closely at the work of Klee, Brancusi, Duchamp, Gaudi, Le Corbusier and Klein. A few years later I found myself interested in Picabia, Kupka, El Lissitsky, Kandinsky. And now in the late 70s I feel closer to Malevich, Mondrian and David Smith. These are cross-references that apply to and extend the art to which I am attached, the roots to which I belong, and at the same time their work is a spring-board into the untried.

Paul Neagu 1979

Brendan Neiland 192

1941 Born in Lichfield
1962-6 Studied at Birmingham College of Art
1966-9 Studied at Royal College of Art
1969 Received John Minton Scholarship
Exhibited in 'Young Contemporaries', 'Young and Fantastic' at Institute of Contemporary Arts and New York and Toronto,
'Big Pictures for Public Places' at Royal Academy
1970 Exhibited in Bradford Print Biennale (also 1972/74/76)
1971 One-man exhibition at Angela Flowers Gallery (also 1972/74/76)
1973 One-man exhibition at Victoria and Albert Museum and travelling
Exhibited in 'Immagini come strumento di realità' at Studio La Città, Verona
1974 Exhibited in 'Five Painters' at Manchester City Art Gallery,
'Contemporary British Prints' at Brooklyn Museum, New York and travelling in USA
1975 Exhibited in Basle International Art Fair,
'From Britain 75' in Helsinki
1976 One-man exhibition at Park Square Gallery, Leeds

Brendan Neiland *Pool Reflection* 1978 Acrylic on canvas 122x183cm (48x72in) Fischer Fine Art

1977 One-man exhibition at The Minories, Colchester and travelling
Exhibited in 'Real Life' Peter Moores Exhibition, Liverpool,
'Doors' at Camden Arts Centre
1978 Exhibited in 'The Figurative Approach 3' at Fischer Fine Art,
John Moores Exhibition, Liverpool (prizewinner)
1979 One-man exhibitions at Fischer Fine Art,
Newcastle Polytechnic Gallery
Exhibited in Tolly Cobbold Eastern Arts National Exhibition

Dealer Fischer Fine Art

Brendan Neiland *Exterior* 1978 Acrylic on canvas 182.9x128.3cm (6ftx4ft2½in) Fischer Fine Art

My painting is concerned with the contemporary city environment. There are various visual elements within the city that interest me, the reflections of buildings within the steel and concrete grid of other high rise buildings, the distortions that occur within these reflections, the contrast between the stable structural elements and these distortions. These visual elements are evocative of the activity and life in the city. Within the painted image itself there are three main concerns, the structure of the building that is reflecting, the suggestion of the interior behind the facade, and the reflected buildings. Whilst concerned with depicting the urban environment, the painting itself; its structure form and colour, are very important . . .

Brendan Neiland 1978

Victor Newsome 146

1935 Born in Leeds
1953-5 Studied painting at Leeds College of Art (also 1957-60)
1960-2 Received Prix de Rome and studied in Rome
1961 Began to make sculpture
1962 Exhibited in 'The Visual Adventure' at Drian Gallery
1963 Exhibited in 'Six Artists' at Leicester Museum
With London Group
1963-4 Taught at Nottingham School of Art
1964-70 Taught at Hull College of Art
1966 One-man exhibition at Grabowski Gallery
Exhibited in 'Structure 66' Welsh Arts Council exhibition (prizewinner), 'The New Generation' at Whitechapel Art Gallery
Received Peter Stuyvesant Travel Bursary to USA
1967 Exhibited in 'Open 100' at Edinburgh
1968 Exhibited in 'Interim' at Whitechapel Art Gallery
1969 Exhibited in 'Six at the Hayward' at Hayward Gallery
1973 Exhibited (painting) in group show at Warehouse Gallery (also 1976/78)
1974 Exhibited in 'British Painting '74' at Hayward Gallery
1975 Exhibited (painting) in 'New Work 2' at Hayward Gallery
1976 One-man exhibition at Anthony d'Offay Gallery
1977 Exhibited in 'British Painting 1952-1977' at Royal Academy
1979 One-man exhibitions at Hester van Royen Gallery, Ikon Gallery, Birmingham

Dealer Hester van Royen Gallery

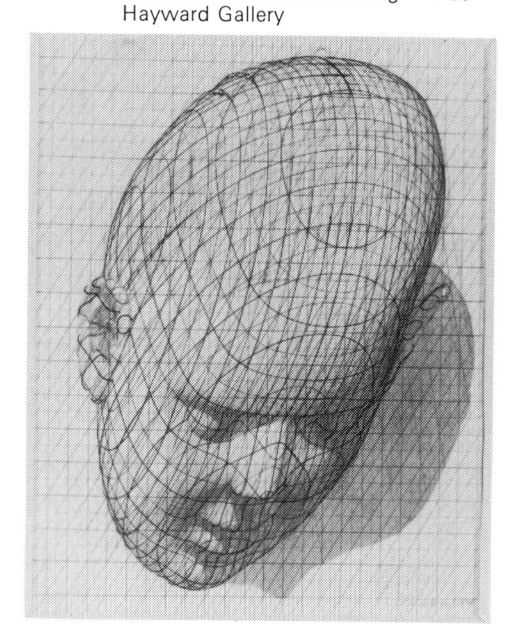

Victor Newsome *Head* 1978 Pencil and ink on paper 27.5x22cm ($10\frac{7}{8}$x$8\frac{3}{4}$in) Private Collection

Ben Nicholson OM

1894 Born in Buckinghamshire
1910-11 Studied at Slade School of Fine Art
1911-14 Studied in Europe
1924-36 Member of 7 & 5 Group
1929 One-man exhibition at Lefevre Gallery (also 1930/32/35/37/39/47/48/50/52/54)
1933-5 Member of Unit One
1934 Exhibited in Venice Biennale (also 1954 Ulisse prizewinner)
First visit to Mondrian's studio
1936 Exhibited in 'Cubism and Abstract Art' at Museum of Modern Art, New York

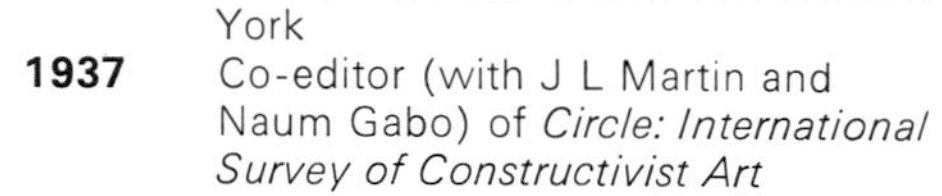

1937 Co-editor (with J L Martin and Naum Gabo) of *Circle: International Survey of Constructivist Art*

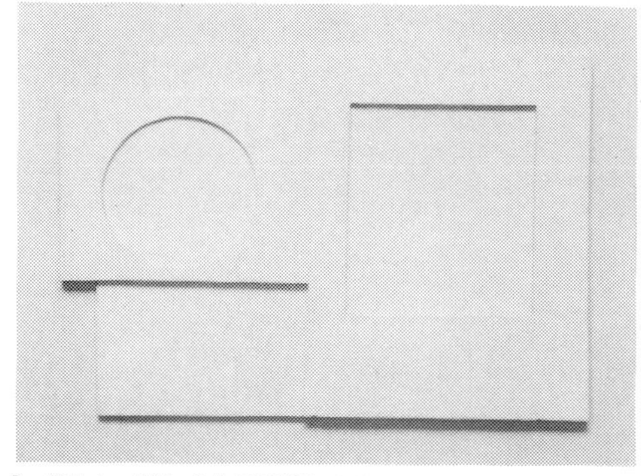

Ben Nicholson *White Relief* 1935 Oil, relief and water colour 101.6x166.4cm (40x$65\frac{1}{2}$in) Tate Gallery

1938 Exhibited in 'Abstract Art' at Stedelijk Museum, Amsterdam
1944 Retrospective exhibition at Leeds City Art Gallery
1946 Exhibited in UNESCO International Exhibition of Modern Art in Paris
1947-8 Exhibited in 'Masters of British Painting 1850-1950' at Museum of Modern Art, New York
1949 One-man exhibition at Durlacher Gallery, New York (also 1951/52/55/56)

Ben Nicholson *Dolphin* (Version 2) 1972 Relief 41.6x60cm ($16\frac{3}{8}$x$23\frac{5}{8}$in) Private Collection

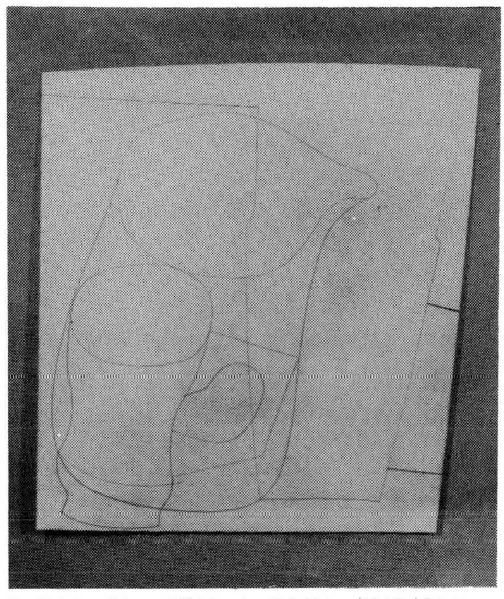

Ben Nicholson *Brissago* 1964 Drawing 40.6x39.1cm (16x15in) Private Collection

1952 Retrospective exhibitions at Detroit Institute of Arts, Dallas, Walker Art Center, Minneapolis
Exhibited in Carnegie International Exhibition, Pittsburgh (1st Prize), International Exhibition, Tokyo (1st Prize; also 1955 prizewinner)
1954 Retrospective exhibition at Stedelijk Museum, Amsterdam and travelling in Europe
1955 Retrospective exhibition at Tate Gallery (also 1956/69/70)
One-man exhibition at Gimpel Fils Gallery (also 1957/59/60/73)
1956 Received Guggenheim Foundation, New York Major Painting Prize, Grand Prix, Lugano
1957 Exhibited in Sao Paulo Bienal (International Prize)
1958-72 Lived in Switzerland
1959 One-man exhibitions at Kestner Gesellschaft, Hanover and travelling (also 1967), Galerie Leinhard, Zurich (also 1960/62)
1961 Retrospective exhibition at Kunsthalle, Berne
One-man exhibition at André Emmerich Gallery, New York (also 1965/74/75)
1963 One-man exhibition at Marlborough New London Gallery (also 1967/68)
1964 Retrospective exhibition at Dallas Museum of Fine Art
1966 Retrospective exhibition with Alfred Wallis and Christopher Wood at Crane Kalman Gallery
1968 One-man exhibitions at Galerie Beyeler, Basle (also 1973), Crane Kalman Gallery (also 1974)
Received OM
1971 One-man exhibition at Marlborough Fine Art
1973 Exhibited in 'Henry Moore to Gilbert & George' at Palais des Beaux Arts, Brussels
1974 Received Rembrandt Prize
1976 One-man exhibition at Waddington Galleries (also 1978)
1977 One-man exhibition at Kasahara Gallery, Osaka

Dealer Waddington Galleries
André Emmerich Gallery, New York

Bryan Organ 113

1935 Born in Leicester
1952-5 Studied at Leicester College of Art and Royal Academy Schools
1958 One-man exhibition at Leicester Museum and Art Gallery
1959-65 Taught at Loughborough College of Art
1965 One-man exhibition at Gadsby Gallery, Leicester (also 1968/73/76/79)
Commission for portrait of Sir Michael Tippett
1967 One-man exhibition at Redfern Gallery (also 1969/71/73/75/78)
1968 Exhibited in group show at Kunsthalle, Darmstadt

Bryan Organ *HRH Princess Margaret* 1969 Acrylic on canvas 152x152cm (60x60in) Lincoln's Inn Collection

1969 Exhibited in 'Mostra mercato d'arte contemporanea' in Florence
Commission for portrait of Princess Margaret
1970 Exhibited in International Drawings Exhibition at Darmstadt
Commission for portrait of Dr Roy Strong
1973 Commission for portrait of Elton John
1976 One-man exhibition at Harold Reed Gallery, New York
1977 One-man exhibition at Baukunst Gallery, Cologne

Dealer Redfern Gallery

Graham Ovenden 119

1943 Born in Alresford, Hampshire
1965-8 Studied at Royal College of Art
1969 One-man exhibition at Gallery 200, Amsterdam
1970 One-man exhibition at Piccadilly Gallery (also 1972/74/78)
Two-man exhibition (with Peter Blake) 'Alice' at Waddington Galleries
1971 Exhibited in 'Critic's Choice' at Arthur Tooth & Sons
Edited *Illustrators of Alice* (Academy Editions)
1972 Edited *Pre-Raphaelite Photography* (Academy Editions)
1973 One-man exhibition at Waddington Galleries
Edited *Victorian Erotic Photography* (Academy Editions)
1974 Edited *Alphonse Mucha Photographs* and *Hill and Adamson Photographs* (Academy Editions)
1975 One-man exhibition 'Lolita – Drawings and Prints' at Waddington Galleries
Co-founded Brotherhood of Ruralists ▶

Graham Ovenden *The Old Garden* 1978 oil on canvas 91.5x137cm (36x54in) Private Collection

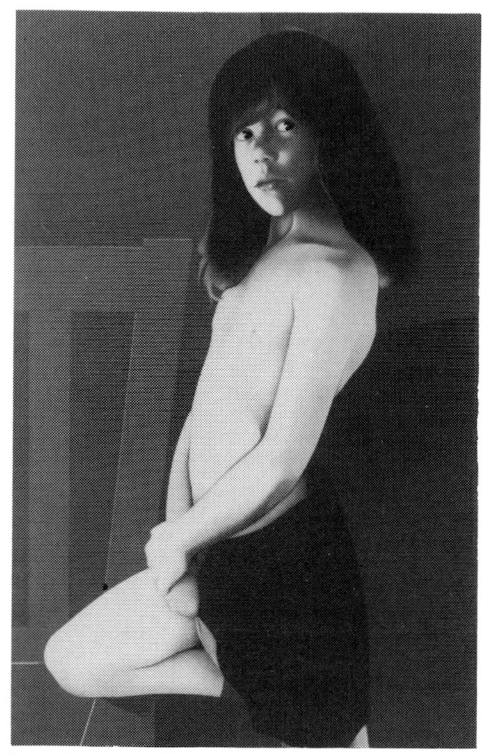

Graham Ovenden *Lea del Rivo* 1978 Oil on canvas 76.2x55.8cm (30x20in) Private Collection

1976 Exhibited with Brotherhood of Ruralists at Summer Exhibition at Royal Academy
Published *Aspects of Lolita* (Academy Editions)
Edited (with Lord David Cecil) *A Victorian Album* (Secker & Warburg)

1977 Exhibited with Brotherhood of Ruralists in Bath, Edinburgh, Doncaster and Bregenz
Published *Nymphets and Fairies* (Academy Editions)

1978 Exhibited with Brotherhood of Ruralists at Up Ottery Festival and Southampton Art Gallery

1979 Exhibited with Brotherhood of Ruralists at Charleston Festival, Sussex,
Gainsborough's House, Sudbury,
in 'Ophelia' at Trinity College, Cambridge and travelling

Dealer Piccadilly Gallery
Waddington Galleries

My work is the celebration of youth and spring – the fecundity of nature and our relationship to it. This is why the subject-matter of my work tends towards the girl child (more often than not at the point of budding forth) and the English landscape in all its richness and mystery. I also have great emotional affinities with the Celtic and Gothic idiom, not least so because of its structural and organic intensity. In other words I stand in wonder of life and its regeneration.

Believing that art (for me painting and drawing) is more than decoration I paint figuratively. I am interested as much in the minutiae of existence as in its monumental prospect. I feel that one should build aesthetic structure on to the emotional experience. Too often in the last few decades there seems to have been a poverty of humanity in art. This attitude seems to be synonymous with building the high tower on sandy soil – a great edifice of art theory lacking in any structural soundness. Simply the striving for innovation and originality in art has directed it towards sterility. It has in fact become the 'academic' art of our age !

By the way, I paint in watercolour and oil, and draw with pencils – all thoroughly ordinary, with no gimmicks.

Graham Ovenden 1979

Eduardo Paolozzi RA

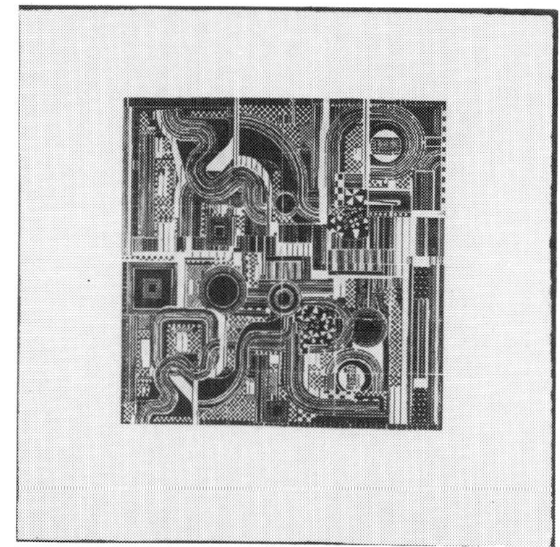

Edwardo Paolozzi *For the Four* from series *For Charles Rennie Mackintosh* 1975 Woodcut 64.9x65.4cm (25½x25¾in) Marlborough Fine Art

1924 Born in Leith, Scotland

1943 Studied at Edinburgh College of Art

1944-7 Studied at Slade School of Fine Art

1947-50 Worked in Paris

1947 First one-man exhibition at Mayor Gallery (also 1948/49)

1949-55 Taught textile design at Central School of Art and Design

1950-4 Worked on architectural projects

1952 Exhibited in Venice Biennale (also 1960 prizewinner)

Eduardo Paolozzi *Shattered Head* 1956 Bronze 28.6x24.1x19.1cm (11¼x9½x7½in) Tate Gallery

1955-8 Taught sculpture at St Martin's School of Art

1957 Exhibited in Sao Paulo Bienal (also 1963)

1958 Exhibited in Carnegie International Exhibition, Pittsburgh (also 1961/67 prizewinner)

1959 Exhibited in 'Documenta' at Kassel (also 1964/68)

1960 One-man exhibition at Betty Parsons Gallery, New York (also 1962)
Exhibited in International Print Biennale at Museum of Modern Art, New York

1960-2 Visiting professor at Staatliche Hochschule für Bildende Kunste, Hamburg

1961 Received prize in 64th Annual American Exhibition, Chicago

1962 Exhibited in Tokyo Biennale (also 1964),
'British Art Today' in San Francisco, Dallas and Santa Barbara

1963 *Eduardo Paolozzi* by Michael Middleton published (Methuen)

1964 One-man exhibitions at Robert Fraser Gallery,
Museum of Modern Art, New York
Exhibited in 'Neue Realisten und Pop Art' at Akademie der Kunste, Berlin

1966 Exhibited in 'Blake, Boshier, Caulfield, Hamilton, Paolozzi' at Studio Marconi, Milan

1967 Exhibited in 'Sculpture from Twenty Nations' at Guggenheim Museum, New York and travelling (prizewinner)

1968 Exhibited in 'Britische Kunst heute' at Kunstverein, Hamburg
Received CBE

1968- Lecturer in ceramics at Royal College of Art

1969 Exhibited in 'Pop Art Redefined' at Hayward Gallery
1970 Exhibited in Expo 1970 at Osaka *Eduardo Paolozzi* by Diane Kilpatrick published (Studio Vista)
1971 Retrospective exhibition at Tate Gallery
1972 Exhibited in 'British Sculptors '72' at Royal Academy
Elected Associate of Royal Academy
1975 Retrospective exhibition at Nationalgalerie, Berlin and Karlsruhe and Bremen
1976 One-man exhibitions at Fruit Market Gallery, Edinburgh, Marlborough Fine Art
Exhibited in 'Arte inglese oggi' at Palazzo Reale, Milan
1977 Retrospective exhibition of prints at Victoria and Albert Museum
One-man exhibition at Anthony d'Offay Gallery
Exhibited in 'Hayward Annual' at Hayward Gallery,
Silver Jubilee Contemporary British Sculpture Exhibition in Battersea Park
1977- Professor in ceramics at Fachhochschule, Cologne
1978 One-man exhibition at Kunstverein, Kassel
1979 One-man exhibition 'The Development of an Idea' Glasgow League of Artists travelling exhibition
Elected Royal Academician

Contact 107 Dovehouse Street, London SW3

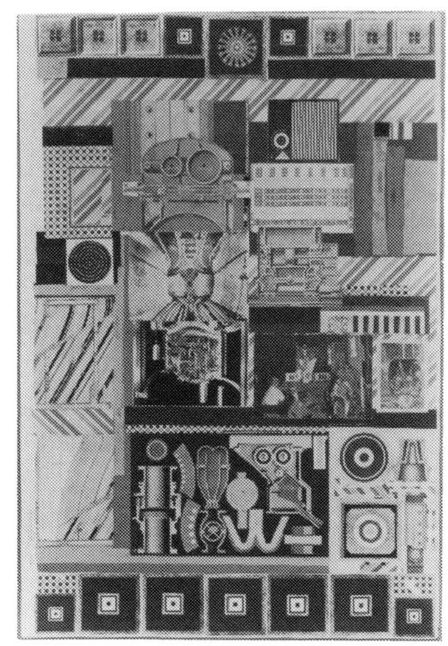
Eduardo Paolozzi *Conjectures to Identity* 1963 Collage for screen print 75.9x51.1cm (29⅞x20⅛in) Tate Gallery

JW: You mentioned the idea of man and machine.

EP: Well, this in a strange way has been a kind of theme of mine from the word go. I don't think one should be too theoretical about these ideas but I feel that man's position in general is his feeling and his attitude towards the machine. You can retreat from it or you can wrestle with it and I think there's a history of successes and failures in both directions.

JW: So you're not turning against the machine?

EP: Well, in a kind of way – I think it hangs like a great big shadow over all our lives. I think you have to define your attitude and not take a kind of dogmatic view like some kind of political, social commentary. It still has to be like great poetry: a series of metaphors.

I use a kind of collage technique of trying to assemble the ideas.

Eduardo Paolozzi 1979
(in conversation with Jim Waugh)

Victor Pasmore 13

1908 Born in Chelsham, Surrey
1927-37 Worked for London County Council Government Service
Influenced by Paris School (Fauvism and Cubism)
1938 Became full-time painter
Formed Euston Road School with William Coldstream and Claude Rogers
1940 One-man exhibition at Redfern Gallery (also 1947/48/50/51/55)
1943-9 Taught at Camberwell School of Art
1948 Turned to independence of painting in purely abstract terms
1949-53 Visiting Professor at Central School of Art and Design
1951-63 Began to work in relief constructions

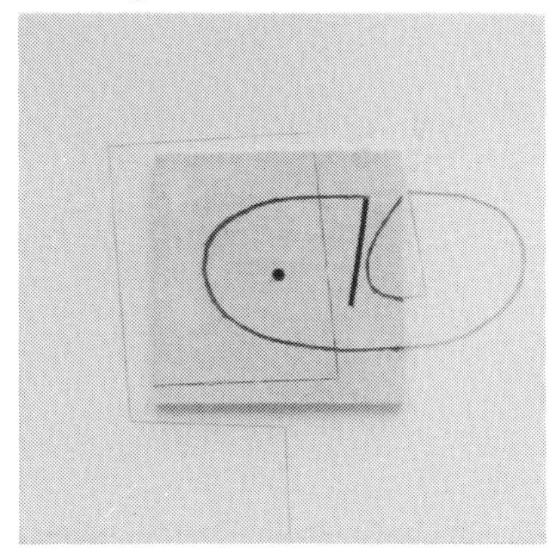
Victor Pasmore *Linear Image* 1976 Relief 40.6x40.6cm (16x16in) Lorenzelli Collection, Milan

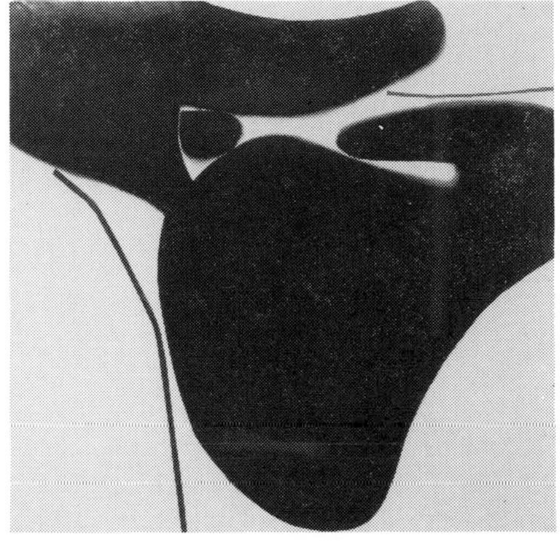
Victor Pasmore *Black Development* 1964 Oil on canvas 205x210cm (6ft8¾inx6ft10¾in) Artist's Collection

1954-61 Director of Painting at Department of Fine Art, University of Newcastle
1954-77 Consulting Director of Urban Design at Peterlee New Town where designed architecture and layout of south west area of town
1960 Exhibited in Venice Biennale (also 1971),
'British Painting 1720-1960' at Pushkin Museum, Moscow
1960-2 Retrospective exhibitions at Musée des Arts Décoratifs, Paris,
Stedelijk Museum, Amsterdam,
Palais des Beaux Arts, Brussels,
Kunsthalle, Berne
1961 One-man exhibition at Marlborough New London Gallery (also 1964/66/69)
1964 Exhibited in 'Painting and Sculpture of a Decade 1954-64' at Tate Gallery,
'Documenta 3' in Kassel,
Carnegie International Exhibition, Pittsburgh (prizewinner),
Ljubljana Biennale (also Prix d'honneur in 1977/78)
Extensive development in graphics
1965 Retrospective exhibition at Tate Gallery and travelling
Exhibited in Sao Paulo Bienal
1967 One-man exhibition at Marlborough-Gerson Gallery, New York
1968 Exhibited in 'Britische Kunst heute' at Kunstverein, Hamburg
1971 One-man exhibition at Arts Club of Chicago
1972 One-man exhibition at Marlborough Fine Art (also 1977/79)
1973 One-man exhibition at Galerie Marlborough, Zurich

▶

Victor Pasmore *Points of Contact (Indigo)* 1974 Oil on curved panel 121.9x50.8cm (48x20in) Private Collection

1974 One-man exhibitions at Marlborough Galleria d'Arte, Rome, Galerie Farber, Brussels (also 1976)
1976 One-man exhibitions at Goodman Gallery, Johannesburg, Fabian Fine Art, Cape Town
1978 Exhibited in International Graphics Biennale, Messina
1980 One-man British Council travelling exhibition

Dealer Marlborough Fine Art

Peter Phillips 116

1939 Born in Birmingham
1955-9 Studied at Birmingham College of Art
1959 Exhibited in 'Young Contemporaries' (also 1960/61/62)
1959-62 Studied at Royal College of Art
1961 Exhibited in John Moores Exhibition, Liverpool
1962 Exhibited in 'British Art Today' in San Francisco, Dallas and Santa Barbara, 'New Realists' at Sidney Janis Gallery, New York
1963 Exhibited in Paris Biennale (also 1977)
1964 Exhibited in 'The New Generation' at Whitechapel Art Gallery, 'Contemporary British Painting' at Albright-Knox Art Gallery, Buffalo, 'Britische Malerei der Gegenwart' travelling exhibition in Germany and Switzerland
Received Harkness Fellowship
1964-6 Lived in New York
1965 First one-man exhibition at Kornblee Gallery, New York (also 1966/68)
Exhibited in 'Pop Art – Nouveau Realisme' at Palais des Beaux Arts, Brussels
1966 Exhibited in 'Pop and Op' American Federation of Arts travelling exhibition
1967 One-man exhibition at Galerie Bischofberger, Zurich (also 1968/69/74)
Exhibited in 'The New Generation' at Museum of Modern Art, New York and travelling, 'Recent British Painting' at Tate Gallery (Peter Stuyvesant Foundation Collection)
1968 One-man exhibition at Galerie der Spiegel, Cologne
Exhibited in 'British Artists: 6 Painters, 6 Sculptors' at Museum of Modern Art and travelling
1968-9 Guest professor at Hochschule für Bildende Kunst, Hamburg
1969 One-man exhibition at Studio d'Arte Condotti, Rome (also 1971)
Exhibited in 'Pop Art Redefined' at Hayward Gallery
1970-9 Travelled extensively in USA, Africa and Far East
1972 Retrospective exhibition at Kunstverein, Munster and Westfalen

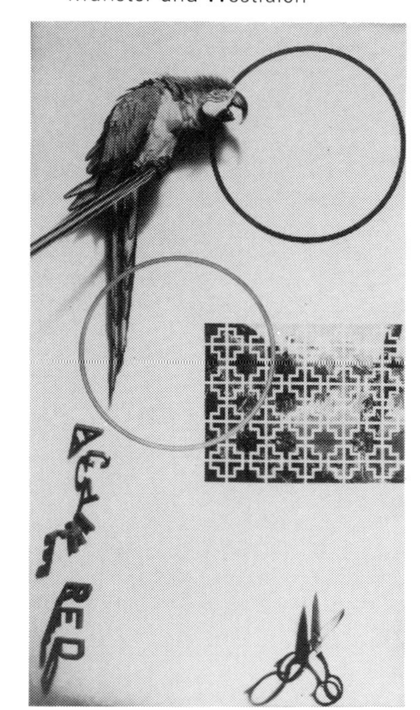

Peter Phillips *No Focus Frame* 1976-7 Oil on canvas 220x120cm (7ft2⅝inx3ft11¼in) Private Collection, Switzerland

1974 Exhibited in 'British Painting '74' at Hayward Gallery
1976 One-man exhibitions (graphics) at Tate Gallery, Waddington Galleries
Exhibited in 'Pop Art Redefined' at Kunstverein, Hamburg
1977 Exhibited in 'British Painting in the 60s' at Tate Gallery, 'Hayward Annual' at Hayward Gallery, 'British Painting 1952-1977' at Royal Academy

Contact Hans Neundorf, Hamburg and New York

Peter Phillips *The Entertainment Machine* 1961 Oil on canvas 182.9x182.9 (6ftx6ft) Tate Gallery

Phillips was the toughest of the English Pop artists who made a reputation in the early 60s, and in many ways the least English, in the whimsical, literary sense. He is also the least known, probably because he has worked abroad since the mid-60s, in New York for two years on a Harkness scholarship, and since then has lived in Zurich and taught in Germany. Yet Phillips was always one of the most impressive English artists of his generation.

There are four large pictures among those in his new exhibition which are very good. They are called *Mosaikbild* although they are not mosaics so much as grids of quite large squares. The pictures are composed of several images, highly realistic, drawn from magazines and advertisements; chocolates, pin-ups and cars predominate, and an image that has recurred throughout Phillips's work, the tiger. These images extend over three or more squares and interlock like a puzzle.

The grid has the effect of flattening out the images by drawing attention to the surface of the painting, so that despite their photographic realism they seem to have hardly any depth or illusionistic space. Each picture resembles a large and very sophisticated multi-screen projection . . .

Paul Overy 1976

Tom Phillips 137

Tom Phillips *The Skin Game* 1974 Acrylic on canvas 101.4x76.2cm (40x30in) Marlborough Fine Art

1937 Born in London
1957-66 Studied at St Catherine's College, Oxford
1961-3 Studied at Camberwell School of Art
1964 Exhibited in 'Young Contemporaries'
1965 One-man exhibition at AIA Gallery
1968 One-man exhibition at Ikon Gallery, Birmingham
1969 Exhibited in John Moores Exhibition, Liverpool
1970 One-man exhibition at Angela Flowers Gallery
Exhibited in 'Critic's Choice' at Arthur Tooth & Sons
Gave performance at Purcell Room with John Tilbury
1971 Exhibited in Venice Biennale
1971-6 Published *A Humument* Vols 1-10
1973 Retrospective exhibition (graphics) at Marlborough Graphics
One-man exhibitions at Hatton Gallery, Newcastle,
Marlborough Fine Art (also 1979),
'A Humument' at Institute of Contemporary Arts
Exhibited in 'La peinture anglaise aujourd'hui' at Musée d'Art Moderne, Paris
World Première of opera 'Irma' at Ceolfrith Arts Centre

Tom Phillips *Dante in his Study with Episodes from the Inferno* 1978 Oil on canvas-board (Polyptych) 63.5x48.3cm +(34x) 10.2x10.2cm (25x19in+(34x) 4x4in) Private Collection

1974 One-man exhibition at Marlborough Gallery, New York
Exhibited in Tokyo Biennale,
'British Painting '74' at Hayward Gallery
1975 Retrospective exhibition at Vaduz Kunsthalle, Basle
One-man exhibitions at Gemeentemuseum, The Hague,
Galerie Bama, Paris (also 1978),
Musée d'Art Moderne, Paris
Exhibited in Sao Paulo Bienal
1976 One-man exhibitions in Cape Town, Durban and Johannesburg
Exhibited in 'Arte inglese oggi' at Palazzo Reale, Milan
1977 One-man exhibition at Kunstverein, Mannheim
Exhibited in 'British Painting 1952-1977' at Royal Academy
1977-8 Dante's *Inferno*: start of book project
1978 One-man exhibition at Lefebre Gallery, New York
Exhibited in 'Art for Society' at Whitechapel Art Gallery
1979 One-man exhibition at Thumb Gallery

Dealer Marlborough Fine Art
Waddington Graphics

Roland Piché 120

1938 Born in London
1956-60 Studied at Hornsey College of Art
1960 Worked with the sculptor, Gaudia, in Montreal
1960-4 Studied at Royal College of Art
1961 Received Walter Neurath Prize
1962-3 Worked as assistant to Henry Moore
1963 Exhibited in 'Young Contemporaries'
1964- Living and working in Essex
Principal lecturer in sculpture at Maidstone College of Art
1965 Exhibited in 'The New Generation' at Whitechapel Art Gallery and Whitworth Art Gallery, Manchester,
Paris Biennale
Received Peter Stuyvesant Foundation Travel Bursary
1966 Exhibited in 'The English Eye' at Marlborough-Gerson Gallery, New York
1967 One-man exhibition at Marlborough New London Gallery
Exhibited in Carnegie International Exhibition, Pittsburgh
1968 Exhibited in 'New Generation' at Whitechapel Art Gallery
Received commission prize in Moorgate Sculpture Competition
1969 One-man exhibitions at Gallery Ad Libitum,
Middelheim Biennale, Antwerp
1970 Exhibited in 'British Sculpture of the 60s' at Institute of Contemporary Art
1972 Exhibited in 'British Sculptors '72' at Royal Academy
1975 One-man exhibition at Cannon Park, Birmingham
1976-8 Member of Fine Art Panel of CNAA
1977 Exhibited in Silver Jubilee Contemporary British Sculpture Exhibition in Battersea Park

Contact Victoria Studios, Tollesbury, Essex ▶

Roland Piché *Orbit* 1977 Fibreglass and resin 200x350x350cm (6ft7inx11ft5¾inx11ft5¾in) Artist's Collection

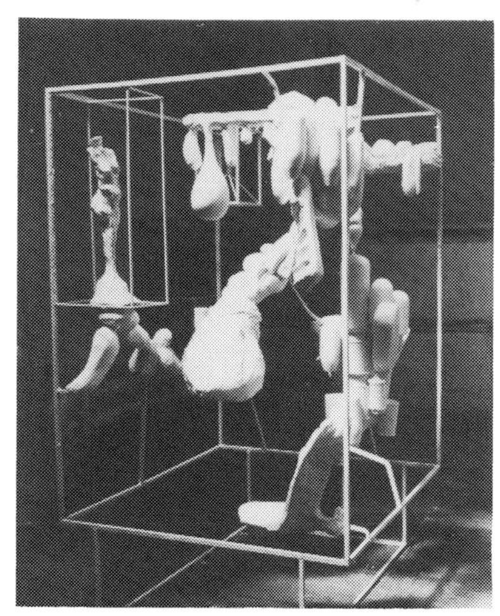

Roland Piché *Spaceframe in White* 1963-4 Plaster and steel 152x137x121.9cm (60x54x48in) No longer in existence

My world is one of contradiction and paradox in which I have begun to be aware of the quality of constancy. Sculpture has this quality in its silence, in its waiting, in its state of eternal presence. In locating this absolute, all things and feelings become transitory and changing. The enormity and limitations of every aspect of experience moves towards this moment, the magic space, the celebration of existence through the making process.

I work with the notion that what appears to be solid is not, to demonstrate that opposites can create an experience of truth. By placing and exploding solids into a relatively fixed state, the parts are extended into space, and collectively assert the total sensation of the original experience. Fragmenting what appears to be solid is a problem that eludes me; occasionally I discover enough in part to continue towards a comprehensive new understanding. The recurring spaceframe and rings provide a means to explore these thoughts and feelings.

The human being as an experience of vulnerability and lifegiving energy has always been central to my working attitudes. The sense of birth in which all living things carry the shadow of their own death and decay: of human violation, of fears and resistance lying uncomfortably with the forces of indifference and the cold universe. In my work space does not equal volume.

Currently my ideas use circles and rings as a centrifugal force to open the figure into a new spatial existence. The spaceframe and rings are the container, the vessel of the soul, the inner space. The container is contained in our comprehension and limitations. The empty shell contains the idea, and the idea contains the shell.

Roland Piché 1979

John Piper 5

John Piper Original study for stage design for *Death in Venice* 1974 Gouache 52.8x100.6cm ($20\frac{3}{4}$x$39\frac{5}{8}$in) Marlborough Fine Art

1903 Born in Epsom
1921-6 Studied law
1926-8 Studied at Richmond College of Art and Royal College of Art
1928-40 Worked as reviewer for *Athenaeum*, *New Statesman*, *Listener* etc
1935-7 Published (with Myfanwy Evans) *Axis* review of abstract art
1936 Exhibited in International Exhibition of Abstract Art travelling in Britain
First of series of illustrated articles for *Architectural Review*
1938- Designing stage sets for opera and ballet at Glyndebourne, Covent Garden and Sadlers Wells
1940 One-man exhibition at Leicester Galleries (also 1945/46/51/57/59)
1940-5 Official War Artist for Ministry of Information and Ministry of War
1941 Exhibited with Henry Moore and Graham Sutherland at Temple Newsam, Leeds
1943 Illustrated volume 1 of Osbert Sitwell's autobiography
1944-53 Trustee of Tate Gallery (also 1954-61)
1948 One-man exhibition at Curt Valentin Gallery, New York (also 1950/51)
1953 Worked at Mourlot's studio in Paris on lithography commission

John Piper *Skeabost, Skye* 1973 Gouache 59.7x78.7cm ($23\frac{1}{2}$x31in) Marlborough Fine Art

John Piper *Shadwell Park, near Thetford* 1977 Gouache 45.8x61cm (18x24in) Marlborough Fine Art

1955 Arranged with Patrick Reyntiens 'Anthology of Modern Stained Glass' Arts Council exhibition
1957 One-man exhibition at Durlacher's, New York (also 1960)
1957-62 Commission for Baptistry window at Coventry Cathedral
1959- Member of Royal Fine Art Commission
1960 One-man exhibition at Arthur Jeffress Gallery (also 1962)
1963 One-man exhibition at Marlborough New London Gallery (also 1964/69)
Commission for windows for Liverpool Roman Catholic Cathedral
1964 Commission for George VI memorial window in St George's Chapel, Windsor
1966 Exhibited with Nolan and Richards at Marlborough New London Gallery
'John Piper: A Film Portrait' directed by John Burder
1967 One-man exhibition at Marlborough Fine Art (also 1972/75/77)
1967-8 Retrospective exhibition travelling throughout Britain
1968 Retrospective exhibitions in Birmingham and Bradford
1969 One-man exhibition at Bear Lane Gallery, Oxford
1970 One-man exhibition at Pieter Wenning Gallery, Johannesburg (also 1973)
Exhibited in International Art Fair, Basle
Commission for windows for Christchurch College Chapel, Oxford
1972 Received CH
1973 One-man exhibition at Marjorie Parr Gallery (also 1975)
1976 One-man exhibition at Kasahara Gallery, Osaka

Dealer Marlborough Fine Art

Roland Vivian Pitchforth RA 16

1895	Born in Wakefield
1913-15	Studied at Leeds School of Art (also 1919-21)
1920-35	Member of 7 + 5 Group
1921-5	Studied at Royal College of Art
1926	Taught at Camberwell School of Art
1926-39	Taught at Clapham College of Art
1928	One-man exhibitions at London Artists Association (also 1929/31) Elected member of London Group and London Artists Association
1930	Taught at St Martin's School of Art
1931	First exhibited in Summer Exhibition at Royal Academy
1937-9	Taught at Royal College of Art
1939	Two-man exhibition (with Buhler) at Leger Galleries
1940-5	War Artist to Ministry of Information and to Admiralty in Burma, India, Ceylon and South Africa
1942	Retrospective exhibition at Wakefield Elected Associate of Royal Academy
1946	One-man exhibition at Maskew Miller Gallery, Cape Town
1948	Taught at Chelsea School of Art
1952	Elected Royal Academician
1954	Exhibited in group show at Leicester Galleries (also 1957)
1963	One-man exhibition at Leicester Galleries

Contact Royal Academy

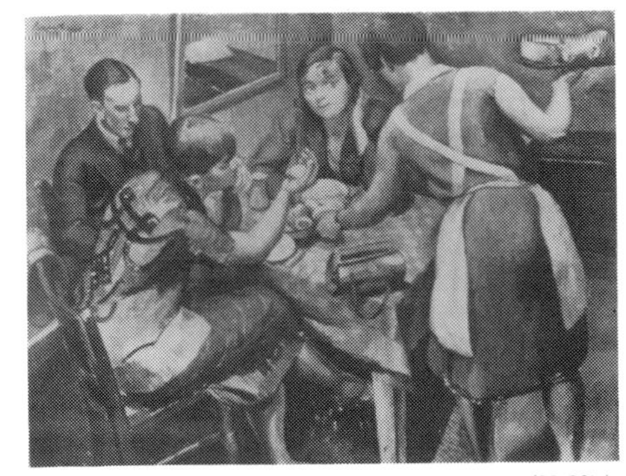

Roland Vivian Pitchforth *Tea* 1925 Oil on canvas 76.2x71.1cm (30x28in) Private Collection

My early work was done under the influence of Cezanne and others, in both oil and watercolour mediums. After the war (1939-45) I concentrated on watercolour, my preference, and in which I have done my best work, I believe. A steady development, particularly in close objective drawing, led towards an interest in space, which now occupies my mind, along with the feel of daylight and fresh air. I am also interested in rain-mists and their subtle differences, and in values, but am also constantly

Roland Vivian Pitchforth *Pembroke Dock* 1958 Watercolour 76.2x71.1cm (30x28in) Private Collection

aware of anything that is happening. However as one grows older, one's eyes deteriorate and one's enthusiasm for closer detailed forms abates and a broader feeling of unity, one's vision and simplicity take over. Enthusiasm and dedication are everything on top of years of hard drawing. However the results of immediate work are nothing but a pain in the neck until a year or two later, when one sees what one has got.

Roland Vivian Pitchforth 1979

Carl Plackman 168

1943	Born in Huddersfield
1959	Apprenticed as architect
1962-7	Studied at West of England College of Art
1967-70	Studied at Royal College of Art
1968	Received Walter Neurath Prize
1969	Exhibited in 'Young Contemporaries' (prizewinner)
1970	Exhibited in 'New Sculpture 1970' Arts Council travelling exhibition
1971-	Teaching at Ravensbourne College of Art
1972	One-man exhibition at Serpentine Gallery Exhibited in 'British Sculptors '72' at Royal Academy, 'Sculpture in the Open Air' in Holland Park
1972-	Teaching at Goldsmiths College
1973	Exhibited in 'Magic and Strong Medicine' at Walker Art Gallery, Paris Biennale
1975	Exhibited in 'British Art of the mid-1970s' in Frankfurt and Cologne, Sao Paulo Bienal, 'New Work 1' at Hayward Gallery
1976	Exhibited in 'Arte inglese oggi' at Palazzo Reale, Milan, Sydney Biennale, 'Recent British Art' British Council exhibition travelling in Europe
1977	One-man exhibition at Felicity Samuel Gallery
1978	One-man exhibition at Arnolfini Gallery, Bristol Exhibited in 'Scale for Sculpture' at Serpentine Gallery
1979	One-man exhibition at Chapter Arts Centre, Cardiff Exhibited in Tolly Cobbold Eastern Arts National Exhibition

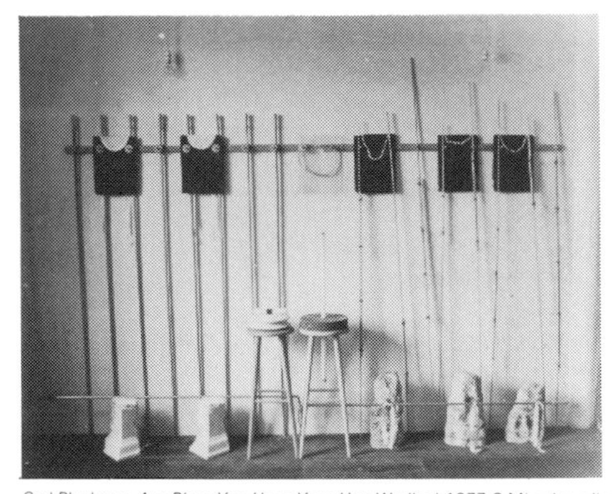

Carl Plackman *Any Place You Hang Your Hat: Wedlock* 1977-8 Mixed media 366x213x45.7cm (12ftx7ftx1ft6in) Arnolfini Gallery, Bristol

Dealer Felicity Samuel Gallery

Carl Plackman *Raft* 1978 Mixed media 10.67mx5.99m (35x19ft) Arts Council of Great Britain

Some people appear to move and act as if they were completely at ease in the world. I have always felt ill at ease; my body fitting as awkwardly as my clothes, the spaces in which I move just that little too empty or too full, the air too hot or too cold. Some people seem to have confidence, others are always uncertain, constantly attempting to find their own space in the world – questioning their very identity. Things are never what they appear to be.

This unknowing, this suspicion, creates a sense of unease which seems to govern the emotional undercurrents of our lives. Outwardly it makes us manufacture seemingly ▶

stable patterns and habits which give us some sense of security. We often gather objects around us to help us to do this. But no objects are neutral. In a sense they are embodiments of value systems which have been decided by others. This is an oblique kind of control which to a large extent means we are in the service of others . . .

Objects seem to exist in the world with more authority than people. If we question this, authority we question the way in which we live. If we attempt to define these objects or give them limits, we often discover that the reverse happens – a whole web of meanings is dredged up which presents more questions than answers. The only situation I can think of where objects are literally tied down by people is on a moving vehicle or a rocking boat floating on the surface of our subconscious.

Carl Plackman 1978

John Plumb 78

John Plumb *Clougy House from the South Garden* 1978 Oil on canvas 71.1x91.4cm (28x36in) Ray Danowski Collection

1927 Born in Luton
1948-50 Studied at Byam Shaw School of Art
1951-4 Studied at Central School of Art and Design
1955-68 Taught part-time at Central School of Art and Design, Luton School of Art and Maidstone College of Art
1957 One-man exhibition at Gallery One
1959 One-man exhibition at New Vision Centre Gallery
1960 Exhibited in 'Situation' at RBA Galleries
1961 One-man exhibition at Molton Gallery
Exhibited in 'New London Situation' at Marlborough New London Gallery
1962 Exhibited in 'British Painting in the 60s' in Dusseldorf,
'British Art Today' in San Francisco, Dallas and Santa Barbara,
'Hoyland, Plumb, Stroud and Turnbull' at Marlborough New London Gallery
1964 One-man exhibition at Galerie Muller, Stuttgart,
New London Gallery
1966 Exhibited in 'New Forms of Shape and Colour' at Stedelijk Museum, Amsterdam
1967 Two-man exhibition at Arnolfini Gallery, Bristol
Exhibited in Tokyo Biennale
1968 One-man exhibition at Axiom Gallery
1968-9 Taught at Bennington College, Vermont
1969- Teaching at Central School of Art and Design
1970 One-man exhibition at London Arts Gallery
1973 One-man exhibition at Commonwealth Institute Art Gallery
1974 Exhibited in John Moores Exhibition, Liverpool,
'British Painting '74' at Hayward Gallery
1977 Exhibited in 'British Painting 1952-1977' at Royal Academy

Contact 2 Kara Lodge, 14 Newton Grove, London W4

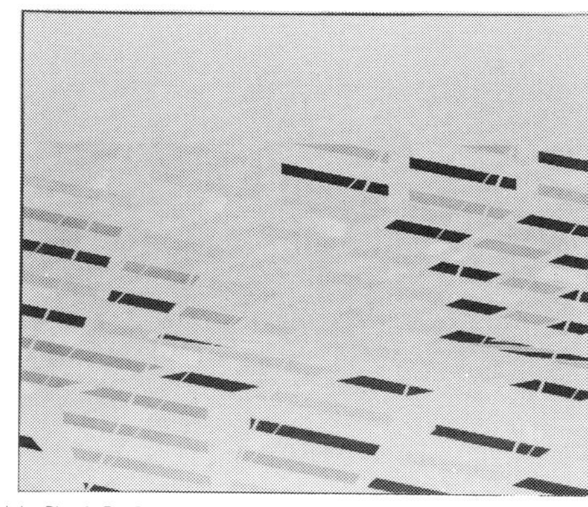

John Plumb *For Bill Basie* 1974 Acrylic on cotton duck 167.6x203.2cm (66x80in) Artist's Collection

Since the summer of 1977 I have been working exclusively in a figurative idiom. This change came about with an increasing need to deal with stimulus from my everyday vision of places, and the way light affects the quality of that vision. Although I have been an abstract painter for 20 years I came to feel that what I was involved with would not contain all that was exciting me in the outside world, so I decided to deal with these phenomena by familiarizing myself through drawings, pastels and water-colours – taking these into the studio and distilling the information so obtained to make oil paintings. This process continues . . .

John Plumb 1979

Nicholas Pope 129

1949 Born in Sydney
1970-3 Studied at Bath Academy of Art
1974 Received Southern Arts Association Bursary
1974-5 Received Rumanian Government Exchange Scholarship
1975 Exhibited in 'The Condition of Sculpture' at Hayward Gallery
1976 One-man exhibitions at Garage Gallery,
Portsmouth Museum and Art Gallery
Exhibited in Arts Council Collection Exhibition at Hayward Gallery,
Group show at Serpentine Gallery
Received Gulbenkian Foundation Award
1977 Two-man exhibition (with Stephanie Bergman) at Southampton Art Gallery,
Mappin Art Gallery, Sheffield
Exhibited in Silver Jubilee British Sculpture Exhibition in Battersea Park,
'On Site' at Arnolfini Gallery, Bristol
British Council Visitor to Rumania
1978 Exhibited in 'Critic's Choice' at Institute of Contemporary Arts,
Group show at Taranman Gallery
Co-organizer of 'Capital Elms' Chelsea School of Art sculpture project in Hyde Park
Commission from Edmonton Commonwealth Games Sculpture Symposium
1979 One-man exhibition at Anthony Stokes

Dealer Anthony Stokes

Nicholas Pope *Stacked Lead* 1976 Lead, Bath stone and wood 120cm (47¼in) high Tate Gallery

Nicholas Pope *Apple Pile* 1979 Apple wood 110cm (43⅜in) high Anthony Stokes Gallery

Terry Pope 170

1941 Born in Cornwall
1959-62 Studied at Bath Academy of Art
1962 Received Royal Netherlands Government Scholarship
1962-3 Studied at Royal Academy of Fine Art, The Hague
1966 Exhibited in 'Constructions '66' at Axiom Gallery
1968- Teaching at University of Reading
1969 Exhibited in John Moores Exhibition, Liverpool
1973 Exhibited in 'Summer Studio' at Institute of Contemporary Arts
1974 One-man exhibition at Lucy Milton Gallery
Received Arts Council Award (also 1976)
1975 Exhibited in 'Constructions' at Bristol University
Received University of Reading Research Grant (also 1977)
1975- Teaching at Chelsea School of Art
1976 Exhibited in 'Space' at Abbot Hall Gallery, Kendal
1977 Exhibited in TELIC Constructionist Exhibition in Kansas City
Received British Council Award
1978 Exhibited in 'Hayward Annual' at Hayward Gallery,
'Arts et informatique' at UNESCO, Paris,
'The Constructivist Context' at Warehouse Gallery and travelling
1980 Exhibited in 'Non-Standard Constructions' at Museum of Modern Art, Oxford

Contact Fine Art Department, University of Reading

All my constructions using large numbers of repetitive elements, in shapes easily recognised by the spectator, have at least two objectives. One is to modify the exact rules of perspective beyond the use of a single projection centre. This is essential in handling stereoscopic information, because formal perspective describes a vision which is both static and monocular. It does, within its limitations, allow certain spatial ambiguities, but these form quite a small repertoire.

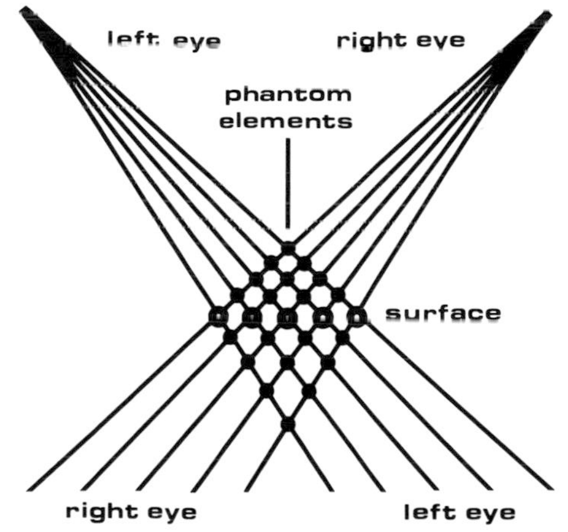

In contrast, the other is a strategy to create, with binocular fusion, perceptual experiences of space and depth invisible through orthodox binocular functions. The accompanying diagram explains how the repetitive elements can be visually reorganised in space by superimposing the images seen by each eye. Depending upon the convergence of vision, phantom elements are seen creating complex depth levels and gradients, either in front of or behind the surface of the object. The muscular convergençe of the eyes involved in this activity, though subtle, is another mechanism for stimulating or suppressing stereoscopic vision.

To extend my experience of space I have invented spectacles which dramatically alter fundamental perceptions of space, transparency, scale and movement.

Normal vision itself is a vigorous and highly developed sense, creating an image which in many ways is in exceptional correspondence with reality. So pervasive have the modes become by which this is achieved, that powerful stimuli are needed to deflect established visual functions into new roles. Not uncharacteristically, these functions themselves in their turn become rapidly established, irrespective of how unusual their stabilized forms may be.

Terry Pope 1979

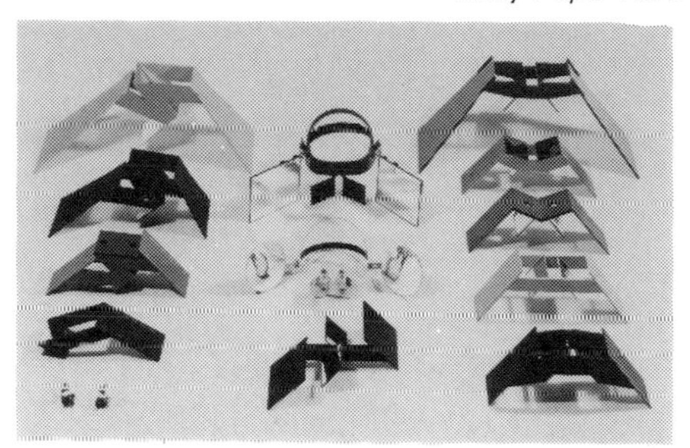
Terry Pope *Experimental Spectacles* 1961-78 Artist's Collection

Douglas Portway 31

1922 Born in Johannesburg
1952 Delegate to Ford Rockefeller Foundation International Art Programme
1956 Exhibited in Venice Biennale
1959 One-man exhibitions at Drian Galleries (also 1960/61/63/64/68), Galeria Vedra, Ibiza (also 1961)
1961 One-man exhibition at Galeria Christa Moering, Germany
Exhibited in John Moores Exhibition, Liverpool
1962 One-man exhibition at Adler Fielding Gallery, Johannesburg
1963 One-man exhibition at Gallery Ivan Spence, Ibiza (also 1964/67)
1964 One-man exhibition at Galerie Synthèse, Paris
Exhibited in group show at Whitworth Art Gallery, Manchester,
Studio International Jubilee Exhibition
1965 One-man exhibition at Wolpe Gallery, Cape Town (also 1967)
Exhibited in group show at Musée d'Art Moderne, Paris
1967 Retrospective exhibition at Pretoria Art Museum
One-man exhibition at Goodman Gallery, Johannesburg (also 1972/74 and in Cape Town /1976/77)

▶

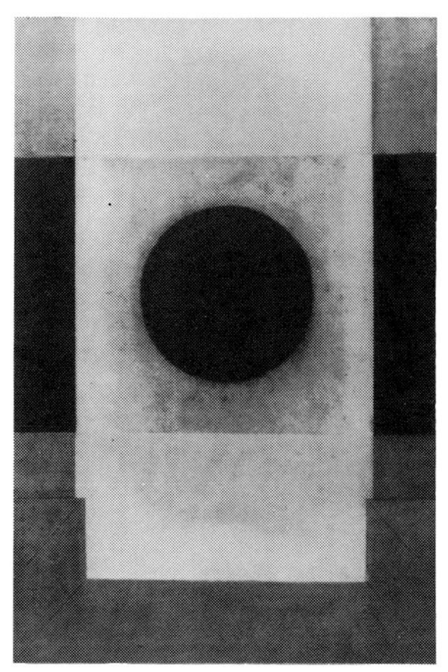
Douglas Portway *Untitled* 1974 Oil on canvas 182.9x121.9cm (6x4ft) Private Collection

1969 Received prize in European Painting Exhibition, Ostend (also 1971)
1970 One-man exhibition at Marjorie Parr Gallery (also 1971/73/75)
1977 One-man exhibitions at Galerie Contemporaine, Geneva, Gilbert Parr Gallery

Dealer Gilbert Parr Gallery
Galerie Contemporaine, Geneva
Goodman Gallery, Johannesburg

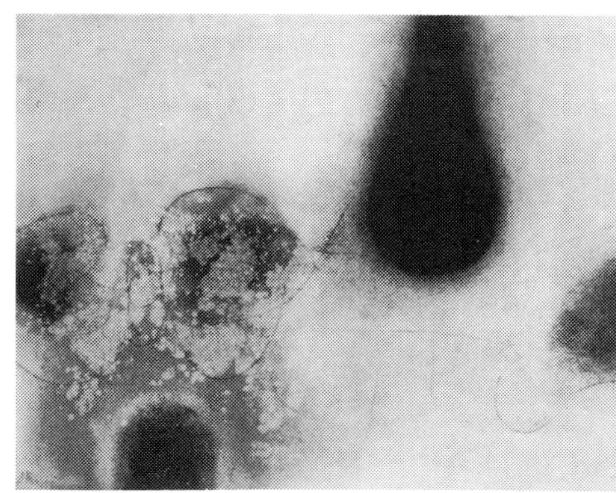
Douglas Portway *Untitled* 1977 Oil on paper 50.8x66cm (20x26in) Private Collection

I began working as a figurative painter around 1940 in South Africa, and evolved through various styles and schools, affected mainly by African sculpture, cave painting and crafts, attempting (unsuccessfully) to find an individual identity within the framework of the existing national culture.

Later, as I worked to broaden my means of expression, I was influenced by Picasso, the German Expressionists, Klee, early Sutherland, Moore, Tamayo and others, whose work – for the most part – I knew only through reproductions.

The turning point for me came in 1952 when, on a trip to the USA, I saw early exhibitions of the Abstract Expressionists. I was bowled over by their freshness and their vigour, and through Kline, Motherwell and Rothko in particular a whole new world of possibilities seemed to have opened up before me.

Feeling that if I was to develop as a painter I must leave the narrow confines of my native African environment, and at odds with the political and social set-up prevailing there, I left for Europe in 1957. Living and working in Spain, and other European countries, I began, in the late 50s, to develop the interests and tendencies which continue to preoccupy me today. Stylistically my work does not belong to any school or movement, and I feel, as I have always done, that this is as it should be . . .

Douglas Portway 1979

Mary Potter 20

1900 Born in Beckenham, Kent
1916-18 Studied at Beckenham School of Art
1918-20 Studied at Slade School of Fine Art
1920 Member of 7 + 5 Group
Exhibited with New English Art Club
1927 Exhibited with London Group
1931 One-man exhibition at Bloomsbury Gallery
1934 One-man exhibition at Redfern Gallery (also 1949)
1939-46 One-man exhibitions at Arthur Tooth & Sons
1951 Exhibited in '60 Paintings for 51' Festival of Britain Exhibition

Mary Potter *Fishing Nets* 1953 Oil on canvas 76.2x101.6cm (30x40in) Peter Pears Collection

1951-63 One-man exhibitions at Leicester Galleries
1951- Living and working in Aldeburgh, Suffolk
1953 Exhibited in 'Figures in their Settings' at Tate Gallery
1958 Exhibited in 'Religious Theme' at Tate Gallery
1961 Retrospective exhibition at The Minories, Colchester
1964 Retrospective exhibition at Whitechapel Art Gallery
1966 Exhibited in 'Painters in East Anglia' Arts Council travelling exhibition
1967 One-man exhibition at New Art Centre (also 1969/72/74/76/78)
1968 One-man exhibition at Oxford Gallery, Oxford
1969 One-man Festival Exhibition at Aldeburgh (also 1976)

Dealer New Art Centre

Mary Potter *Butterfly* 1975 Oil on canvas 55.9x61cm (22x24in) Burnet Pavitt Collection

I work mostly in oil on canvas or board using a beeswax and turpentine medium to make the surface matt. I also use watercolour and chalk. When I was young I was most influenced by Piero della Francesca, and later on by Braque and Paul Klee. I have done a large amount of portrait commissions, but now that I am 78, I have given it up as I find it too exhausting. I have never had any definite period or style. I paint anything that is around me. I now paint less realistically than I once did, but in a not entirely abstract way.

Mary Potter 1979

Patrick Procktor 103

Patrick Procktor *Palazzo Dario* 1978 Oil and pastel on canvas 142x101.6cm (56x40in) Redfern Gallery

1936 Born in Dublin
1958-62 Studied at Slade School of Fine Art
1959-62 Exhibited in 'Young Contemporaries'
1962 Elected member of London Group
1963 First one-man exhibition at Redfern Gallery (also 1965/67/68/70/72/74/76/78)
1964 Exhibited in 'New British Art' in Houston, 'New Generation' at Whitechapel Art Gallery
1965 Designed scenery for 'Saint's Day' at Theatre Royal, Stratford
1967 Exhibited in Darmstadt International Exhibition
Designed scenery and costumes for Western Theatre Ballet at Sadler's Wells Theatre
1968 One-man exhibition at Lee Nordness Gallery, New York
Exhibited in 'Interim' at Whitechapel Art Gallery
Designed scenery and costumes for 'Twelfth Night' at Royal Court Theatre
1969 One-man exhibitions at Alecto Gallery, London and New York
Exhibited in 'Il tempo dell'immagine' in Bologna, '12 Britische Artisten' at Kunstlerhaus Galerie, Vienna
1970 Exhibited in 'Image Dessin' at Musée d'Art Moderne, Paris
1971 One-man exhibition at Studio La Città, Verona
Exhibited in 'Critic's Choice' at Arthur Tooth & Sons
1972 One-man exhibitions at Galleria del Cavallino, Venice, Galleria L'Approdo, Turin, Palazzo Galvani, Bologna
1973 One-man exhibition at Gallery Henze, Basle
1974 One-man exhibition at Gallery 101, Johannesburg and travelling
Published *Ancient Mariner* Suite (Alecto/Redfern)
1977 One-man exhibition at David Paul Gallery, Chichester
1978 Published *Venice* Suite (Alecto/Redfern)
1979 One-man exhibition at Salisbury Festival

Dealer Redfern Gallery
Robert Miller Gallery, New York

Patrick Procktor *Self-portrait as Cadet* 1965 Oil on canvas 40.6x30.5cm (16x12in) Harry Tatlock-Miller Collection

It is sometimes incorrectly supposed that dainty children always make graceful adults. On the contrary the greatest agility is a conquered clumsiness. A clumsy child can learn to be agile. We read that great dancers kept falling over things as children. So in watercolour it becomes our greatest delight as artists not to botch effects we botched as children.

The last watercolour I did as a child was a view of Brighton from the cliffs outside Rottingdean. A breeze blew, the paper flapped and wrinkled making uneven valleys of paint where there should have been sea and smooth horizon, and the green was all wrong, too thin and shrill and too yellow. I blamed my childishness on the childishness of the medium. I raced home to Hove, stopping only to buy a box of oils in a bookshop, and indoors nauseated myself with the mixture of central heating and turpentine. I came back to watercolour recently, discovering as though by magic techniques formerly misunderstood, rediscovering what was then only half understood, completing the circle in which 'memory gives birth to desire'. Childhood memory, the little sables and the jamjar (like the madeleine dipped in tea) giving the illusion of total recall . . .

Patrick Procktor 1967
(from *A Return to Watercolour* in London Magazine)

William Pye 130

William Pye *Quillion* 1970 Stainless steel 305cm (10ft) high Private Collection

1938 Born in London
1958-61 Studied at Wimbledon School of Art
1961-5 Studied at Royal College of Art
1965 Exhibited in 'Towards Art 2' at Arts Council Gallery
1965-70 Taught at Central School of Art and Design
1966 First one-man exhibition at Redfern Gallery (also 1969/73/75)
Exhibited in 'Structure 1966' at National Museum of Wales
1968 First sculptures made with co-operation and sponsorship of industry
Exhibited in Coventry Cathedral Open Air British Sculpture Exhibition, 'British Art' at Palazzo Strozzi, Florence

William Pye *Aeolos* 1973 Steel and stainless steel 9.15m (30ft) high Birmingham

1969 Exhibited in Middelheim Biennale
1970 One-man exhibition at Bertha Schaefer Gallery, New York
1970-5 Taught at Goldsmiths College
1971 Made films 'Reflections' (British Film Institute/Arts Council) and 'From Scrap to Sculpture' documenting making of sculpture *Zemran* (now South Bank)
Exhibited in 'Reflections' at Taft Museum, USA
1972 One-man exhibition at Bear Lane Gallery, Oxford
Exhibited in 'British Sculptors '72' at Royal Academy,
Open Air Sculpture Exhibition in Holland Park
1975 One-man exhibition at Ikon Gallery, Birmingham
1976 One-man exhibition at Morgan Thomas Gallery, Los Angeles
Visiting Professor at California State University
1977 Exhibited in 'Private Images' at Los Angeles County Museum,
Silver Jubilee Contemporary British Sculpture Exhibition in Battersea Park,
Summer Exhibition at Royal Academy (also 1978)
1978 One-man exhibition at Yorkshire Sculpture Park
1979 One-man exhibitions at Photographers Gallery,
Cartwright Hall, Bradford
1979- Working on American commissions for sites at Louisville, Phoenix and Cincinnati

Dealer Redfern Gallery
Tamara B. Thomas' Fine Art Services, Los Angeles

I made my first sculptures when I was 12 years old and it was at that time I decided to become a sculptor. These early tendencies were later reinforced on my first visit to Florence, as a first year student at Wimbledon School of Art. I became aware in the great museums and galleries that my attention was drawn more towards sculpture, than to painting. The following year I went to Greece, where the predominance of sculpture and the experience of the temples combined to hone my sculptural sensibility still further. While at the Royal College of Art I embarked on a series of environmental pieces. Modelled organic forms were placed on or hung from rugged timber structures based on Greek or Japanese temple architecture – the references were undisguised. Later highly reflective surfaces replaced the loosely modelled forms as a means of achieving the sensuality I needed to express, and from this emerged a series of tubular stainless steel tripod pieces.

Also during this period (around 1970) I made my only Kinetic piece *Revolving Tower*, the purpose of which was to pursue my preoccupation with reflection and this was extended still further in my film 'Reflections' which was sponsored by the British Film Institute and the Arts Council of Great Britain. Then followed *Zemran* which is sited on the South Bank of the Thames – this was prompted by the chance to use the hemispheres and dished end forms used in the chemical industry. Since then my work has become less substantial. It is now more illusive and ephemeral, employing curtains and shafts of tensioned steel cables. All my work attempts to combine an architectural experience while retaining the sense of object, of self containment rather than theatrical space. Currently I am working on three large commissions for sites in the USA, all closely related to and integrated with the architecture, while continuing to work on smaller more private work.

William Pye 1979

Alan Reynolds *The Village Fair* 1952 Oil 26x36.2cm (10¼x14¼in) Vona Reynolds Collection

Alan Reynolds 147

Alan Reynolds *Modular Construction* 1978 Painted wood 48.6x81x48.6cm (19⅛x31⅞x19⅛in) Annely Juda Fine Art

1926 Born in Newmarket, Suffolk
1948-52 Studied at Woolwich Polytechnic School of Art
1952 One-man exhibition at Redfern Gallery (also 1953/54/56/60/62/64/69/72/74)
Exhibited in Carnegie International Exhibition, Pittsburgh (also 1955/58/61)
1952-3 Studied at Royal College of Art (received medal for painting)
1954 One-man exhibition at Durlacher Gallery, New York (also 1958)
1954-61 Taught at Central School of Art and Design
1955 Exhibited in group shows at Galleria Nazionale d'Arte Moderna, Rome, Musée d'Art Moderne, Paris
1961- Teaching at St Martin's School of Art
1967 Received Arts Council Purchase Award
1971 Exhibited in 'Art Spectrum' Arts Council travelling exhibition
1977 Exhibited in group show at Galerie Loyse Oppenheim, Nyon, Switzerland, 'British Painting 1952-1977' at Royal Academy
1978 One-man exhibition at Annely Juda Fine Art

Dealer Annely Juda Fine Art
Saidenberg Gallery, New York

I work in the tradition of European Constructivism, and the decisive influences on my work have been De Stijl, Mondrian, Vantongerloo and Swiss Allianz, Sophie Taeuber, Bill and Lohse.

In 1946 in Germany I first encountered 'modern' art, which made a deep and lasting impression on me. I saw the first post-war exhibition of German art of the 20s and 30s, and was influenced particularly by the paintings and writings of Paul Klee. Until 1958 I painted landscape in watercolour and oil.

From 1958 to 1966 my work was of an improvizory nature. The emphasis in abstract paintings and watercolours was on pictorial construction, the use of horizontal/vertical elements and a concern with interval.

In 1969 I produced my first group of reliefs, in painted wood and curvilinear in form. Their structure was intuitive and reflected the influence of Sophie Taeuber. I began to work on Constructional reliefs in 1975, using basic standardized elements and orthogonal form, while subsidiary forms were finalized through intuitive decisions. From then on printmaking, especially wood engraving and lino prints, became particularly important.

By 1976 I was working on free-standing constructions in painted wood, partly standardized in form but again partly of an improvizatory nature. In 1978 I began to work on modular constructions and drawings, working with the cubic module. My recent relief constructions are of a concrete nature, and reflect my concern with the recoverable element or factor as part of the working process.

Alan Reynolds 1979

Bridget Riley 80

1931 Born in London
1949-52 Studied at Goldsmiths College
1952-5 Studied at Royal College of Art
1955 Exhibited in 'Young Contemporaries'
1960-4 Taught part-time at Hornsey College of Art and Croydon College of Art
1962 First one-man exhibition at Gallery One (also 1963)
1963 Exhibited in John Moores Exhibition, Liverpool (prizewinner)
1964 Exhibited in Carnegie International Exhibition, Pittsburgh (also 1967), Tokyo Biennale (also 1972 prizewinner), 'The New Generation' at Whitechapel Art Gallery, 'Nouvelle Tendance' at Musée des Arts Décoratifs, Paris
Received Peter Stuyvesant Foundation Travel Bursary to USA
1965 One-man exhibition at Richard Feigen Gallery, New York (also 1966/67/68)
Exhibited in Paris Biennale des Jeunes, 'The Responsive Eye' at Museum of Modern Art, New York
1966 One-man travelling exhibition of drawings organized by Museum of Modern Art, New York

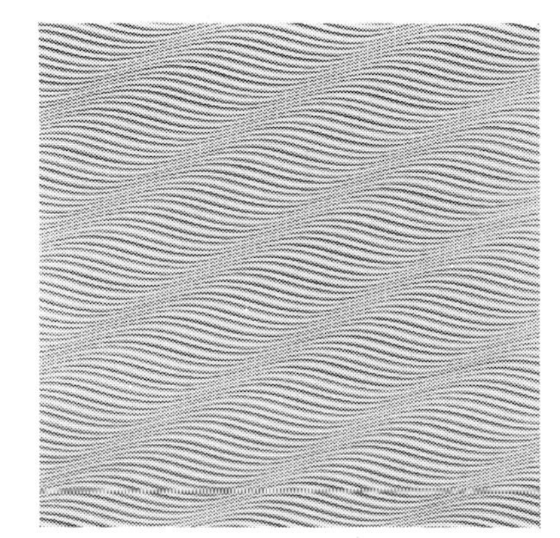

Bridget Riley *Gala* 1974 Acrylic on canvas 159.4x159.4cm ($62\frac{3}{4}$x$62\frac{3}{4}$in) Private Collection

1967 Exhibited in 'Acquisitions of the 60s' at Museum of Modern Art, New York. 'Jeunes peintres anglais' at Palais des Beaux Arts, Brussels
1968 Two-man exhibition (with Phillip King) at Venice Biennale (International Prize for Painting)
Exhibited in 'European Painters of Today' at Musée des Arts Décoratifs, Paris and travelling in USA, '20th-century Art' at Fondation Maeght, St Paul de Vence, 'British Artists: 6 Painters, 6 Sculptors' at Museum of Modern Art, New York and travelling, 'Documenta 4' at Kassel (also in 6 in 1977)
1969 One-man exhibition at Rowan Gallery (also 1971/72/76)
One-man exhibition of drawings travelling in Britain
Exhibited in 'Contemporary Art: Dialogue between East and West' at Museum of Modern Art, Tokyo
1970-1 Retrospective exhibition travelling to Hanover, Berne, Dusseldorf, Turin, London and Prague

Bridget Riley *Descending* 1965-6 Emulsion on board 91.4x91.4cm (36x36in) Sarah Riley Collection

1973 One-man Arts Council travelling exhibition 'Paintings and Drawings 1961-73'
1974 Exhibited in 'British Painting '74' at Hayward Gallery
1975 One-man exhibitions at Galeríe Beyeler, Basle, Sidney Janis Gallery, New York (also 1978)
1976 One-man exhibition at Coventry Gallery, Sydney (also 1979)
1977 One-man exhibition at Minami Gallery, Tokyo
1977-8 Exhibited in 'Recent British Art' British Council Exhibition travelling in Yugoslavia, Greece, Austria, Poland, Sweden, Norway and Finland
1978-9 Retrospective British Council exhibition travelling in USA, Australia and Japan

Dealer Rowan Gallery

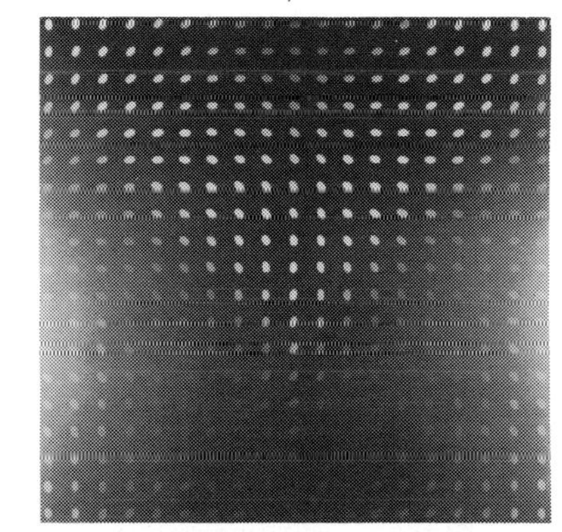

Bridget Riley *Deny 2* 1967 PVA on canvas 217.2x217.2cm (7ft$1\frac{1}{2}$inx7ft$1\frac{1}{2}$in) Tate Gallery

In any painting by Riley, the confluence of precisely stated physical conditions gives place at once to a total presence of etherealized colour and light but the vibrations *behind* that presence change structurally as the eye moves across the surface of the painting from different angles. Formal subtleties, at more than one level, have to be sought out: the potentialities of a Riley painting do not subside at easily defined frontiers. Its presence is imaginatively alive, charged with action and unpredictable flux: constant under stable conditions of lighting and most radiantly discharged in full daylight, which implies that Riley's paintings are as free of artificiality, in a negative or contrived sense, as they are devoid of extraneous factors. At their best, they are like spontaneous acts of nature. Riley is showing us what we did not know before, and here she is an innovator because she brings these 'acts of nature' into existence.

▶

Riley's paintings, like those of the best of her contemporaries, continually ask questions and incessantly probe into the spectator's awareness of the physical world. But in the very act of questioning, the process of interrogation is conducted with such authority that it provides its own answer.

Bryan Robertson 1971

William Roberts RA

1895 Born in London
Studied at St Martin's School of Art and Slade School of Fine Art
1914 Worked at Omega Workshops under Roger Fry
Joined Vorticist Group
1914-18 Official War Artist (also 1939-45)
1915 Elected member of London Group
1958 Elected Associate of Royal Academy
1965 Retrospective exhibition at Tate Gallery
1966 Elected Royal Academician
1969 One-man exhibition at d'Offay Couper Gallery
1971 Retrospective exhibition at Hamet Gallery

Contact 14 St Mark's Crescent, London NW1

Leonard Rosoman RA 41

Leonard Rosoman *The Secretary. New York* 1971 Acrylic on canvas 121.9x121.9cm (48x48in) Private Collection

1913 Born in London
1930-5 Studied at King Edward VII School of Art, University of Durham
1935-6 Studied at Royal Academy Schools
1936-7 Studied at Central School of Art and Design
1943-5 War Artist to the Admiralty
1946-8 Taught at Camberwell School of Art
1948-56 Taught at Edinburgh College of Art
1951 Mural commission for Festival of Britain and Brussels World Fair
1954 One-man exhibition at Roland, Browse & Delbanco (also 1957/59/65/69)
Chief designer of Diaghilev Exhibition in London and Edinburgh
1955 Exhibited in 'Critic's Choice' at Arthur Tooth & Sons
1957-78 Taught at Royal College of Art
1960 Elected Associate of Royal Academy
1960- Exhibited in Summer Exhibition at Royal Academy
1964 Mural commission for Shakespeare Exhibition at Stratford-upon-Avon
1968 One-man exhibition at Lincoln Center, New York
1970 Elected Royal Academician
1971 One-man exhibition at State University of New York
1974 One-man exhibition at Fine Art Society, London and Edinburgh
1975 One-man exhibitions at Touchstone Gallery, New York,
David Paul Gallery, Chichester
1976 One-man exhibition at Octagon Gallery, Belfast
1977 One-man exhibition at Oldham Art Gallery
Exhibited in 'British Painting 1952-1977' at Royal Academy
1978 One-man exhibition at Fine Art Society, London and Edinburgh

Dealer Fine Art Society
Touchstone Gallery, New York

Leonard Rosoman *Portrait of Jill Bennett No 2* 1969 Gouache 30.5x40.6cm (12x16in) Private Collection

My painting has always been figurative but it is not realistic or naturalistic and there are undertones of abstraction in the way the images are organized. In the 1940s and 50s I was linked with a group known as the young English Romantics which included John Minton, Keith Vaughan and Prunella Clough. The influences were Samuel Palmer and Graham Sutherland and there was great emphasis on the problems of figures in landscape. My experiences as an Official War Artist played a very important part in my development at this time and in the early 1950s I was becoming aware of what sort of artist I was. I painted in oils and gouache and the latter has always been a favourite medium. In the middle 1960s I began to experiment with acrylics and now I use them all the time, having given up oils entirely. I have always been interested in the problems of scale and enjoy moving from a book illustration to a large mural.

Now the language of the painting is the same, but the imagery has extended and is more distorted. The source material is basically man's predicament and insecurity and there are elements of fantasy and a strong feeling of menace in the work. The bending and breaking of the rules of perspective (I once taught perspective at the Reimann School) are very evident in some of the works and contribute to an overall feeling of disintegration.

I travel a great deal and draw and paint wherever I go; I also write a lot and bring all the material back to my London studio. I never want to live and work anywhere else.

Leonard Rosoman 1979

Michael Sandle 133

Michael Sandle Drawing for *A 20th-Century Memorial* 1977 Pencil and watercolour 150x100cm (59x39⅜in) Felicity Samuel Collection

1936 Born in Weymouth
1951-4 Studied at Douglas School of Art and Technology
1956-9 Studied at Slade School of Fine Art
1959-60 Worked in Paris as lithographer
1960-3 Taught part-time at Leicester College of Art
Formed Leicester Group
1963 One-man exhibition at Drian Gallery
1963-8 Taught at Coventry College of Art
1966 Exhibited in Paris Biennale
1968 Exhibited in 'Documenta 4' in Kassel (also '6' in 1977)
1970 Exhibited in '6 at the Hayward' at Hayward Gallery

1970-2 Visiting Assistant Professor at Universities of Calgary and Victoria, Canada
1972 Exhibited in 'British Sculptors '72' at Royal Academy
1973 Exhibited in 'Monumente' at Städtische Kunsthalle, Dusseldorf
Elected member of British School at Rome
1973- Pròfessor of Sculpture at Fachhochschule für Gestaltung, Pforzheim
1975 One-man exhibitions in Berlin, Baden Baden and Cologne
1976 One-man exhibitions at Galerie Hecate, Paris, Bernard Jacobson, New York, Felicity Samuel Gallery
1977 One-man exhibition at Galerie 2, Stuttgart
Exhibited in 'Le Dessin' at Musée d'Art Moderne, Paris
1978 Exhibited in 'Hayward Annual' at Hayward Gallery

Dealer Fischer Fine Art

Michael Sandle *Oranges and Lemons* 1966 Fibreglass, perspex, brass and polyurethane lacquer 274x487x182cm (9x16x6ft) Klaus Jurgan-Fischer Collection, Baden-Baden

My theory of art was at one time influenced by what I thought I understood about 'existential phenomenology'. However calloused with scepticism this theory has become, there still remains some belief in the notion that subjective experience can at the same time be public and anonymous. My work therefore, is concerned with examining memory, in the hope that there may be discovered among the paradigms of subjective experience, some that are universal.

Michael Sandle 1979

Tim Scott 83

Tim Scott *Alingana 3* 1979 Steel and forged steel, oiled 83x68x58cm ($32\frac{3}{4}$x26x$22\frac{7}{8}$in) Private Collection

1937 Born in Richmond, Surrey
1954 Studied at Architectural Association
1955-9 Studied part-time at St Martin's School of Art
1958 Exhibited in 'Young Contemporaries' (also 1959)
1959-61 Worked in Paris
1961 Exhibited in '26 Young Sculptors' at Institute of Contemporary Arts
1961- Teaching at St Martin's School of Art and other art schools
1965 Exhibited in 'The New Generation' at Whitechapel Art Gallery, Paris Biennale
1966 One-man exhibition at Waddington Galleries (also 1969/71/73/74/75/77)
1967 Retrospective exhibition at Whitechapel Art Gallery
Exhibited in 'Young British Sculptors' at Kunsthalle, Berne and travelling
1969 Retrospective exhibition at Museum of Modern Art, Oxford
One-man exhibition at Lawrence Rubin Gallery, New York (also 1971/73)
1970 Exhibited in 'Contemporary British Art' at Museum of Modern Art, Tokyo
1971-3 Exhibited in McAlpine Gift Exhibition at Tate Gallery and travelling to Museum of Fine Arts, Boston and Corcoran Museum, Washington DC
1974 One-man exhibition at André Emmerich Gallery, New York
1975 Exhibited in 'The Condition of Sculpture' at Hayward Gallery
1976 Exhibited in 'Arte inglese oggi' at Palazzo Reale, Milan

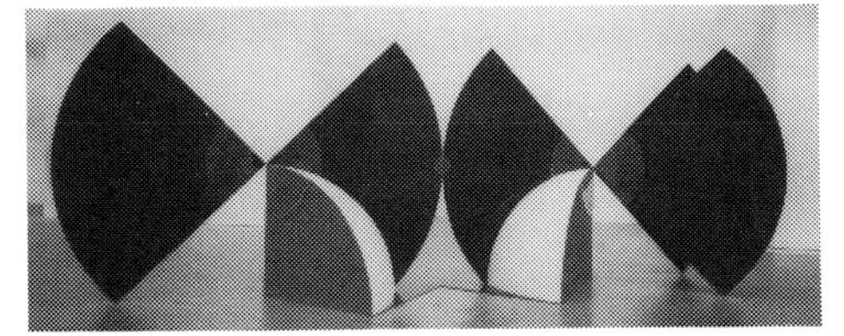

Tim Scott *Quinquereme* 1966 Mixed media 213.3x610x215.9cm (7ftx20ftx7ft1in) Tate Gallery

1977 One-man exhibitions at Tibor de Nagy Gallery, New York, Galerie von Wentzel, Hamburg
1979 Retrospective exhibition at Kunsthalle, Bielefeld
One-man exhibitions at Knoedler Gallery, Tiergarten Gallery, Hanover

Dealer Knoedler Gallery
Meredith Long Contemporary, New York

William Scott ARA 58

1913 Born in Greenock, Scotland
1928-31 Studied at Belfast College of Art
1931-5 Studied at Royal Academy Schools
1942 First one-man exhibition at Leger Gallery
1946-56 Senior Painting Master at Bath Academy of Art
1948 One-man exhibition at Leicester Galleries (also 1951)
1951 Exhibited in Festival of Britain exhibition
1953 One-man exhibition at Hanover Gallery (also 1956/61/62/63/65/67/69/71)
Exhibited in Sao Paulo Bienal (also 1961)

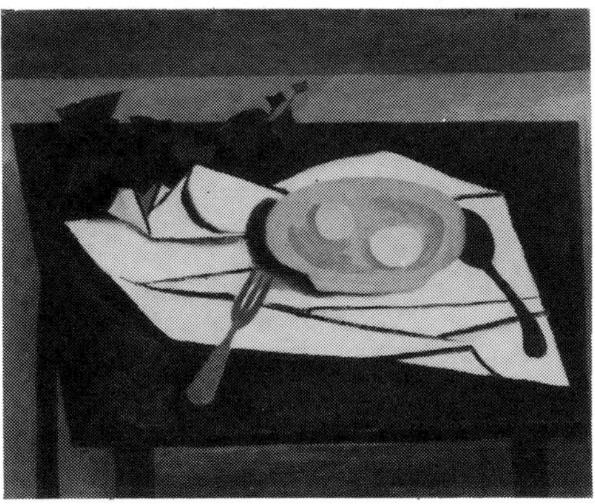

William Scott *Still-life: Lemons on a Plate* 1948 Oil on canvas 50.8x61cm (20x24in) Private Collection

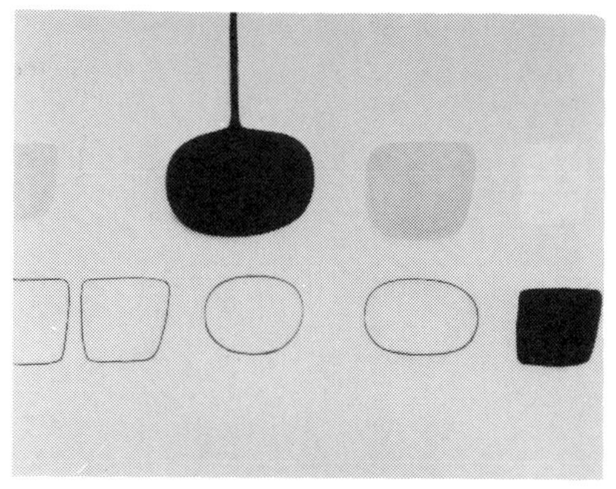

William Scott *Still-life: Nine Forms* 1970 Oil on canvas 154x195cm (61x79in) Private Collection

1954 One-man exhibition at Martha Jackson Gallery, New York (also 1956/59/62/73/75/76)
1955 Exhibited in International Art Exhibition, Tokyo, Carnegie International Exhibition, Pittsburgh
1958 One-man exhibition at Venice Biennale
1959 One-man exhibitions at Galleria Galatea, Turin and Milan, Galerie Charles Leinhard, Zurich
Exhibited in John Moores Exhibition, Liverpool (First Prize)
1960 One-man exhibition at Kestner Gesellschaft, Hanover and travelling
1961 One-man exhibitions at Esther Robles, Gallery, Los Angeles
1963 One-man exhibitions at Kunsthalle, Berne, Galerie Anderson-Mayer, Paris
1964 Exhibited in 'Documenta 3' in Kassel
1966 One-man exhibition at Gimpel-Hanover Gallery, Zurich (also 1974)
Received CBE
1968 One-man exhibition at Dawson Gallery, Dublin
1969 One-man exhibition at Richard Demarco Gallery, Edinburgh
1971 One-man exhibition at Scottish National Gallery of Modern Art, Edinburgh
1972 Retrospective exhibition at Tate Gallery
1974 One-man exhibition at Gimpel Fils Gallery (also 1976/78)
1975 One-man exhibition at Albright-Knox Art Gallery, Buffalo, Santa Barbara Museum
1976 One-man exhibition at Kasahara Gallery, Tokyo (also 1977)
1977 Elected Associate of Royal Academy
1979 One-man Arts Council of Northern Ireland travelling exhibition

Dealer Gimpel Fils
Martha Jackson Gallery, New York

Peter Sedgley 173

1930 Born in London
1944-6 Studied architecture at Brixton Technical School
1965 One-man exhibitions at McRoberts & Tunnard Gallery (also 1966), Howard Wise Gallery, New York (also 1966)
Exhibited in 'The Responsive Eye' at Museum of Modern Art, New York
1966 One-man exhibition at Richard Feigen Gallery, Chicago
Exhibited in Tokyo Biennale (prizewinner)
1968 One-man exhibitions at Galerie Neuendorf, Hamburg, Redfern Gallery
Exhibited in 'British Drawing' at Museum of Modern Art, New York
1969 Exhibited in Kunstmarkt, Cologne
1971 One-man exhibition at Haus am Waldsee, Berlin
1972 One-man exhibition at Forum Kunst, Rottweil
Commission for audio-visual concert at Donaueschingen Music Festival
1973 Retrospective exhibitions at Ikon Gallery, Birmingham, Midland Group Gallery, Nottingham, Arnolfini Gallery, Bristol
Commission for *Light Installation* at Bordeaux Festival

Peter Sedgley *Wind-Sail Structure* 1978 Semi-transparent sheeting on steel structure with 18 colour projection lamps controlled by wind direction and speed 900x300cm (29ft4inx9ft10in) Munich

1974 Commission for *Chain Reactions* at Haus am Waldsee, Berlin
1976 Commission for *Labyrinth* audio-visual environment show in Berlin and Bonn
1978 One-man exhibition at Akademie der Kunst, Berlin
Commission for *Sail Structure* for Munich Culture Week

Dealer Redfern Gallery

Visual art is better seen rather than written about and contemporary art is generally not easy to describe. Perhaps the few pictures accompanying this text will give some indication as to my intentions.

Peter Sedgley 1979

Peter Sedgley *Five Blues* 1977 Slowly rotating panel with inset special filter plates producing changing colour composition 72x72cm (6x6ft) Artist's Collection

Jack Smith 62

1928 Born in Sheffield
1944-6 Studied at Sheffield College of Art
1948-50 Studied at St Martin's School of Art
1950-3 Studied at Royal College of Art
1952 One-man exhibition at Beaux Arts Gallery (also 1953/54/56/58)
1954 Exhibited in 'British Painting and Sculpture' at Whitechapel Art Gallery
1955 Exhibited in Carnegie International Exhibition, Pittsburgh (also 1958/61/63)
1956 Exhibited in Venice Biennale
1957 Exhibited in John Moores Exhibition, Liverpool (1st Prize)
1958 One-man exhibition at Catherine Viviano Gallery, New York (also 1962/63)
1959 Retrospective exhibition at Whitechapel Art Gallery

1960 One-man exhibition at Matthiesen Gallery (also 1963)
Exhibited in Guggenheim International Exhibition, New York (prizewinner)
1963 Exhibited in 'British Painting in the 60s' at Tate Gallery
1963-71 Taught at Hornsey School of Art
1967 Exhibited in 'Aspects of New British Art' travelling exhibition in Australia and New Zealand
1968 One-man exhibition at Marlborough Fine Art
1971 One-man exhibition at Whitechapel Art Gallery
1971- Teaching at Chelsea School of Art
1974 One-man exhibition at Redfern Gallery (also 1976)
Exhibited in 'British Painting '74' at Hayward Gallery
1977 Retrospective exhibition at Sunderland Arts Centre and travelling
1978 One-man exhibition at Serpentine Gallery

Dealer Redfern Gallery
Monika Kinley

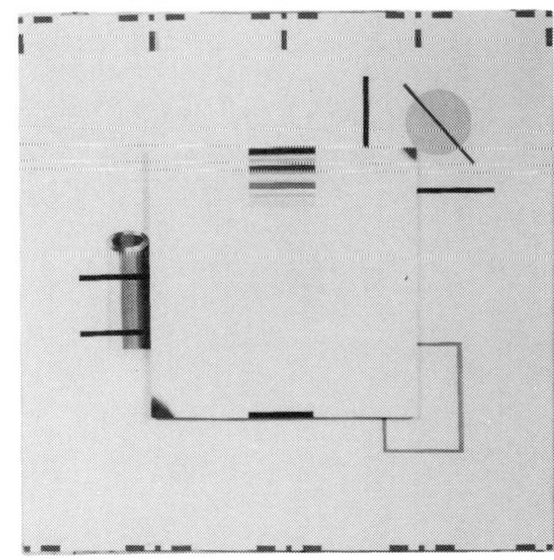

Jack Smith *43 Elements on White* 1977 Oil on board 61x61cm (24x24in) Artist's Collection

I think of my paintings as diagrams of an experience or sensation. The subject is very important. The sound of the subject, its noise or its silence, its intervals and its activity. When I talk about the sound or the music of the subject, I am not always thinking in terms of a symphony, but groups of single notes. The closer the painting is to a diagram or graph, the nearer it is to my intention. I like every mark to establish a fact in the most precise, economical way.

I have been consistently interested in light; between 1952 and 1956 as an outside

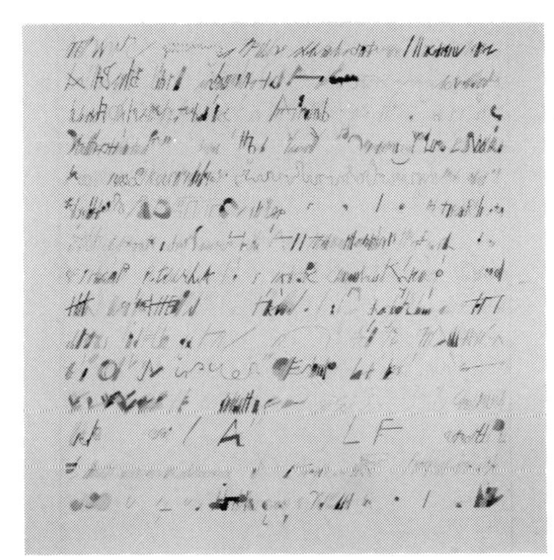

Jack Smith *Various Activities No 5* 1966 Oil on canvas 152.4x152.4cm (60x60in) Goteborg Museum, Sweden

force and since then as a quality within the painting. Light as a subject no longer interests me, but it is still essential that each painting contains it.

The above statement was written in 1965 and is still relevant. The 'written paintings' produced between 1965 and 1970 are to be read from side to side. The marks are a kind of colour short-hand, a visual equivalent of sound and speech, speed and interval.

Jack Smith 1979

Richard Smith 76

Richard Smith *Piano* 1963 Oil on canvas 182.6x277.2x114cm ($71\frac{7}{8}$x$109\frac{1}{8}$x$44\frac{7}{8}$in) Tate Gallery

1931 Born in Hertfordshire
1952-4 Studied at St Albans School of Art
1954 Exhibited in 'Young Contemporaries'
1954-7 Studied at Royal College of Art
1959 Received Harkness Travel Fellowship
1961 One-man exhibition at Green Gallery, New York (also 1963/65)
Exhibited in Carnegie International Exhibition, Pittsburgh

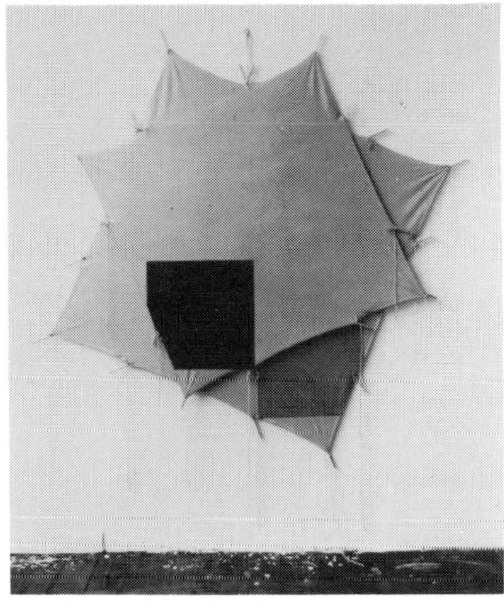

Richard Smith *Both Halves* 1977 Acrylic and oil on canvas, and aluminium poles 140x140cm ($55\frac{1}{8}$x$55\frac{1}{8}$in) Gimpels Fils Gallery

1962 One-man exhibition at Institute of Contemporary Arts
1963 One-man exhibition at Kasmin Gallery (also 1967/69/71/72)
Exhibited in Tokyo Biennale
1964 Exhibited in 'The Shaped Canvas' at Guggenheim Museum, New York
1966 One-man exhibitions at Whitechapel Art Gallery,
Richard Feigen Gallery, New York (also 1967/68/71)
Exhibited in Venice Biennale (prizewinner; also 1970)
1967 Exhibited in 'New Shapes of Colour' at Stedelijk Museum, Amsterdam,
Sao Paulo Bienal (Grand Prize)
1968 Artist in Residence at University of California (also 1976)
1969 One-man exhibition at Galleria dell'Ariete, Milan (also 1972)
1970 Exhibited in 'Contemporary British Art' at Museum of Modern Art, Tokyo
1972 One-man exhibition at Museum of Modern Art, Oxford
Received OBE
1973 One-man exhibition at Waddington Galleries
Exhibited in 'La peinture anglaise aujourd'hui' at Musée d'Art Moderne, Paris
1974 One-man exhibitions at OK Harris Gallery, New York,
Galerie Swart, Amsterdam
Exhibited in 'British Painting '74' at Hayward Gallery

▶

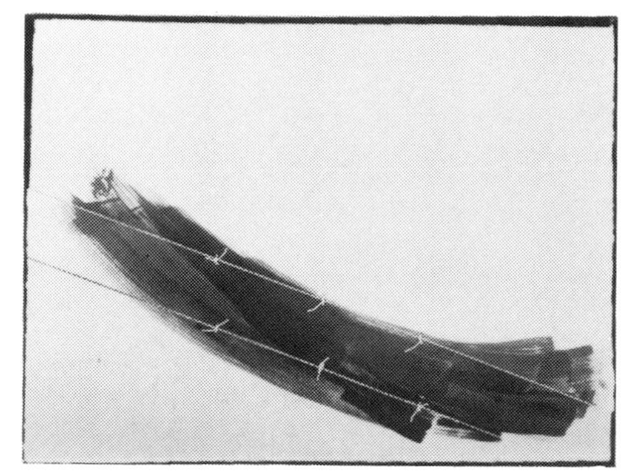

Richard Smith *Lawson Set* (1 of 2) 1973 Litho with string 59x79cm ($23\frac{1}{4}$x$31\frac{1}{8}$in) Edition of 50

1975 Retrospective exhibition at Tate Gallery
One-man exhibition at Gimpel Fils (also 1976)
1976 One-man exhibition at Galleria del Cavallino, Venice
Exhibited in 'Arte inglese oggi' at Palazzo Reale, Milan
1977 One-man exhibition at Gimpel-Hanover Gallery, Zurich
1978 One-man exhibition at Jan Hoffman Gallery, Chicago
1979 One-man exhibition at Hedendaagsekunst, Utrecht

Dealer Gimpel Fils

Willi Soukop RA 26

Willi Soukop *Creative Imagination* 1960 Steel, iron and copper 305cm (10ft) high College of Further Education, Ilkestone, Derbyshire

1907 Born in Vienna
1928-34 Studied at Academy of Fine Art, Vienna
1934-40 Taught sculpture at Dartington Hall
1935- Exhibiting in Summer Exhibitions at Royal Academy
1939 One-man exhibition at Dartington Hall
1947- Teaching at Chelsea School of Art
1949 Exhibited in 'Sculpture in the Open Air' in Battersea Park (also 1950)

Willi Soukop *Tranquillity* 1970-3 Papier maché 243.8cm(8ft) high Artist's Collection

1953-75 Member of Faculty of Sculpture, British School at Rome
1959 Exhibited in Middelheim Biennale (also 1961)
1963 Elected Associate of Royal Academy
1963-6 Examiner for sculpture at Scottish School of Art
1969 Elected Royal Academician
Master of Sculpture at Royal Academy Schools
1979 One-man exhibition at Yehudi Menuhin School, Cobham
Exhibited in group shows at Ashgate Gallery, Farnham and many other locations

Contact Royal Academy

My work is rather catholic and ranges over a wide variety of subject matter as well as materials. The art education I received was traditional, but travelling and making contact with other artists widened my horizons. In particular, teaching in England for many years and meeting other budding artists have both added to my range of interests in different periods and styles. Though I am a Royal Academician, I am not attached to a particular gallery or special group of artists. I am therefore completely free as to the choice of work and the kind of materials I use.

Taking a bird's eye view of my sculpture over many years, I realize that there are basically two modes of expression which alternate – the square, cubic form and the rounded fluid spherical shape. Natural forms, as observed in trees and rocks, often combine with movement to provide the inspiration for my work and, as my preference is for carving rather than modelling, the material used plays an important part. As I enjoy using hard materials, I also work by casting in bronze. When cut, hammered and polished, the metal seems to come to life.

I do not follow a particular style or direction. My ambition is to produce a piece of sculpture in harmony with the material used, and so to capture something of the vitality of life translated into three dimensional form.

Willi Soukop 1979

Ruskin Spear RA 9

Ruskin Spear *Winston Churchill at the Microphone* 1957 Oil 121.9x91.4cm (48x36in) Beaverbrook Collection

1911 Born in London
Studied at Hammersmith School of Art
1931-4 Studied at Royal College of Art
1932 First exhibited in Summer Exhibition at Royal Academy
1942 Elected member of London Group
1944 Elected Associate of Royal Academy
1945-8 Taught at Central School of Art and Design
1948-77 Taught at Royal College of Art
1949-50 President of London Group
1951 One-man exhibition at Leicester Galleries
1954 Elected Royal Academician
1956 Commission for portrait of Sir Laurence Olivier as Macbeth (Stratford)
1957 Exhibited in 'British Painting' at Pushkin Museum, Moscow
1959 Commission for altarpiece for St Clement Danes
1964 Commission for portrait of Dr Ramsay (Magdalen College, Cambridge)
1965 Two-man exhibition (with Carel Weight) at Russell Coates Museum, Bournemouth

Ruskin Spear *Brown Ale* 1951 Oil 35.6x91.4cm (14x36in) 6 versions in Private Collections

1976	Commission for portrait of Sir Hugh Greene (BBC)
1979	Received CBE

Dealer Fieldborne Galleries
New Grafton Gallery

Jean Spencer 98

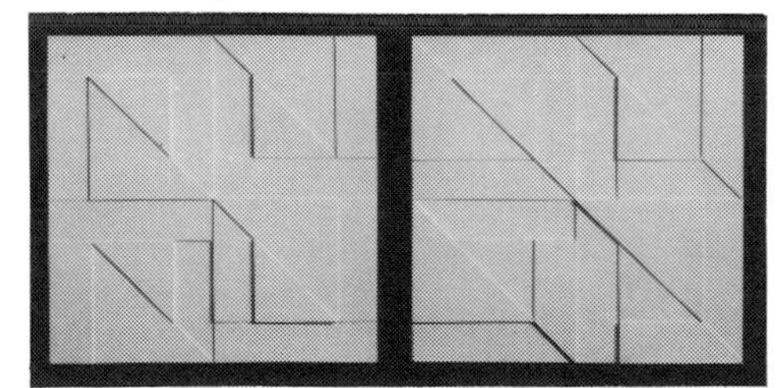

Jean Spencer *Double Cube Relief* 1969 Acrylic on hardboard 61x121.9cm (24x48in) Arts Council of Great Britain

1942	Born in Hampshire
1960-3	Studied at Bath Academy of Art
1965	One-man exhibition at Bear Lane Gallery, Oxford
1967	Exhibited in 'Unit, Series, Progression' Arts Council exhibition
1969	One-man exhibition at University of Sussex Exhibited in 'Systemi' at Amos Anderson Museum, Helsinki Founder member of Systems Group
1969-1971	Teaching at Bulmershe College Exhibited in 'Matrix' at Arnolfini Gallery, Bristol and travelling
1972	Exhibited in 'Systems' at Whitechapel Art Gallery and travelling, 'System' at Lucy Milton Gallery
1973	Two-man exhibition (with Malcolm Hughes) at Plus Kern, Ghent Exhibited in 'Constructive Art' at Leicester Museum and Art Gallery
1974	One-man exhibition at Didsbury College
1975-6	Exhibited in 'Rational Concepts' at Kunstcentrum Badhuis, Gorinchem, Holland
1978	Exhibited in 'Constructive Context' at Warehouse Gallery, 'IAFKG et ses amis' at Galerie Circulus, Bonn, John Moores Exhibition, Liverpool

Contact 37 Haldon Road, London SW18

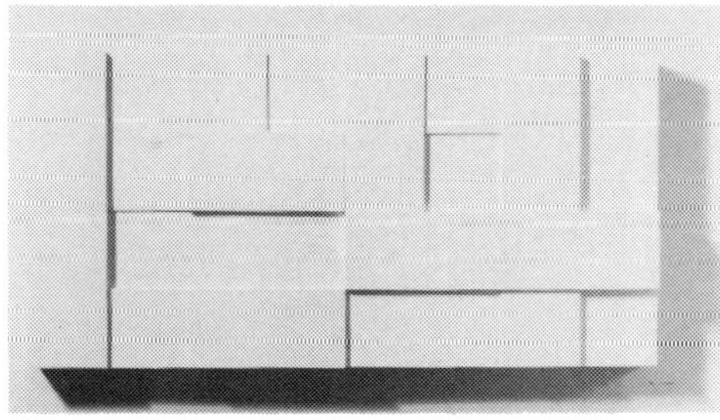

Jean Spencer *4 Reliefs (Varese) No 2* 1977 Acrylic on hardboard 35.6x71.1cm (14x28in) Artist's Collection

Since 1963 I have worked within the European constructivist tradition. Early constructed reliefs were loosely related to the intuitive procedures of, for instance, Mondrian or Nicholson, though their initial stimulus was from mathematics rather than nature. Between 1966 and 1969 the structures became more rigorously mathematical, often involving a series of systematic variations (analogous to the musical invention) of a simple geometric configuration.

Since that time my work has adhered to two fundamental principles, both of which relate to accessibility:

1. Clarity: meanings are conveyed without recourse to private or hermetic codes; determined relations – of opposition, exclusion, reflection, sequence . . . are realized through material, spatial or chromatic equivalents; they demand of the spectator the same skills as does any other sensible, intelligent experience.
2. Recoverability: the structure of the single work may be recovered by reference to a general system through which the work may be related precisely to all other works generated by the same system, and, in a broader sense, to other rationally constructed artefacts and systems . . .

More recently the elements have been reduced to horizontal and vertical binary divisions of the square, and simple combinatory laws. From the exhaustive series the presence and nature of the legislating matrix may be extrapolated: through analysis of the relations which hold between the elements in each unit, between the same element as it appears in different units, and of the overall structural characteristics of the set.

Jean Spencer 1979

Ian Stephenson ARA 164

1934	Born in County Durham
1951-6	Studied at University of Durham
1957	Received John Moores junior prize
1958	One-man exhibition at New Vision
1959	Received Boise Travel Award to Italy
1959-66	Taught at Chelsea School of Art
1960	Received Gulbenkian Purchase Award
1962	One-man exhibition at New Art Centre (also 1964/68)
1963	Exhibited in 'British Painting in the 60s' at Whitechapel Art Gallery
1964	Awarded Marzotto Selection Prize, Italy
1966-70	Director of Foundation Studies in Fine Art at University of Newcastle
1967	Exhibited in Paris Biennale, 'Recent British Painting' at Tate Gallery
1968	Exhibited in 'Junge generation grossbritannien' at Akademie, Berlin
1969	Exhibited in '6 at the Hayward' at Hayward Gallery

Ian Stephenson *Quadrama 4* 1969 Oil and enamel on four canvases 336x458cm (11x15ft) Tate Gallery

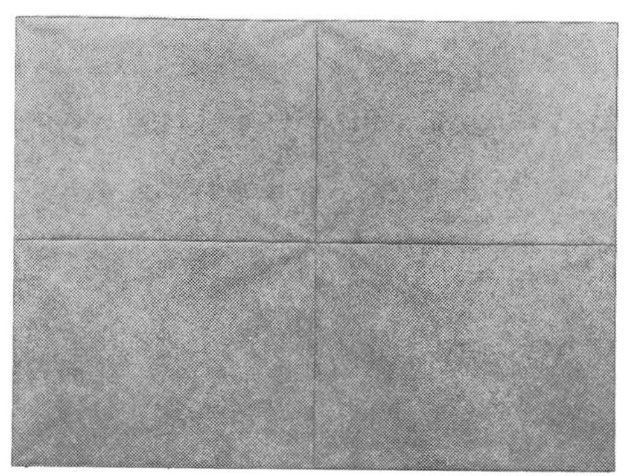

Ian Stephenson *First Easement Series 4* 1976 Acrylic on paper with collage 39x29cm (15¼x11¼in) Birmingham City Art Gallery

1970 Retrospective exhibition at Laing Art Gallery, Newcastle upon Tyne
1970- Principal Lecturer in Painting at Chelsea School of Art
1973 Exhibited in 'Elf englische Zeichner' at Kunsthalles, Baden-Baden and Bremen, 'Recente britse tekenkunst' at Koninklijk Museum, Antwerp, 'La peinture anglaise aujourd'hui' at Musée d'Art Moderne, Paris
1974 Exhibited in 'British Painting '74' at Hayward Gallery
1975 One-man exhibition at Hester van Royen Gallery
Exhibited in Sao Paulo Bienal
1976 Exhibited in 'Arte inglese oggi' at Palazzo Reale, Milan
1977 Retrospective exhibition at Hayward Gallery and travelling
Exhibited in 'British Painting 1952-1977' at Royal Academy, 'Englische Kunst der Gegenwart' at Palais Thurn und Taxis, Bregenz, 'Color en la pintura britanica' at Museu de Arte Moderna, Rio de Janeiro
1978-9 Retrospective exhibition at City Art Gallery, Birmingham and travelling

Contact Chelsea School of Art

Annealing and concealing colour. All of painting is camouflage, not least of all by means of subject matter whatever the sentiment. It is within the freaked skin of camouflage that the art resides. To be blessed with the contradictory nature of things. If there is no alternative to the way things are, then the picture must be more and more of what it is. Neural and neutral, the greyness scintillates. Overlapping and obliterated. Oblivion. Such is the practice of palimpsestial painting. Alas, it is as dilemmic as remembering to forget.

Ian Stephenson 1973

Norman Stevens 162

1937 Born in Yorkshire
1952-7 Studied at Bradford College of Art
1957-60 Studied at Royal College of Art
1960 Received Lloyd Landscape Scholarship and Abbey Minor travelling scholarship
1960-6 Taught at Manchester College of Art
1965 Exhibited in John Moores Exhibition, Liverpool
1966 Two-man exhibition (with Norman Adams) at Bradford City Art Gallery
1966-70 Taught at Maidstone College of Art
1967 Exhibited in 'Contemporary British Art' in Miami
1968 Exhibited in 'Fine Art for Industry' at Royal College of Art
1969 One-man exhibition at Hanover Gallery (also 1971)
Exhibited in 'The English Landscape Tradition in the 20th century' at Camden Art Centre, 'Young and Fantastic' at Institute of Contemporary Arts and travelling in Canada and USA
1970-3 Taught at Hornsey College of Art
1972 Exhibited in Bradford Print Biennale (also 1979 prizewinner), International Art Market, Dusseldorf, Group shows at Studio La Città, Verona and Galleria del Cavallino, Venice
1974 Exhibited in 'Graveurs anglais contemporains' at Musée d'Art et d'Histoire, Geneva
1974-5 Gregory Fellow at University of Leeds
1975 Exhibited in 'Luova Grafikka' at Alvar Aalto Museum, Finland, Chichester Arts Festival (major prizewinner)

Norman Stevens *Repaired Stone and Earthwork, Avebury Stone Circle* 1979 Etching, 3 plates, 3 colours 49.5x53cm (19½x20⅞in) Edition of 150 Printed by J. C. Editions

1976 Exhibited in 'Constable's Stonehenge' at Victoria and Albert Museum, 'Homage to Constable' at Tate Gallery, 'Graphics '76 Britain' at University of Kentucky Art Gallery, Lexington
1977 One-man exhibition at Arnolfini Gallery, Bristol
Exhibited in 'British Painting 1952-1977' at Royal Academy
1978 One-man exhibition at Redfern Gallery

Dealer James Kirkman
Redfern Gallery

Norman Stevens *Flagpoles* 1977 Oil on canvas 182.9x152.4cm (6x5ft) British Council Collection

John Stezaker 185

1949 Born in Worcester
1967-73 Studied at Slade School of Fine Art
1970 One-man exhibition at Sigi Krauss Gallery
1971 Exhibited in 'Lisson Wall Show' at Lisson Gallery
1972 One-man exhibition at Nigel Greenwood Inc (also 1975/76/77)
Exhibited in 'New Air' at Hayward Gallery, 'A Survey of the Avant-garde in Britain' at Gallery House
1973 One-man exhibition at Museum of Modern Art, Oxford
Exhibited in 'Critic's Choice' at Arthur Tooth & Sons

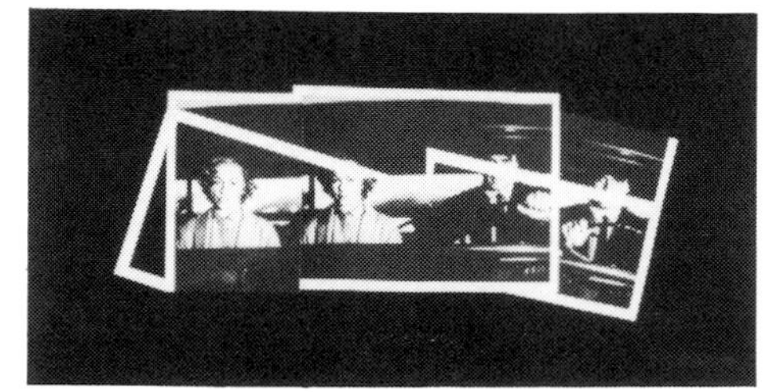

John Stezaker *Psycho Montage 2: The Window* 1978 Photographs 51.5x59.3cm (20¼x23⅜in) Nigel Greenwood Collection

John Stezaker *Psycho Montage 1: The View* 1978 Photographs 51.5x59.3cm ($20\frac{1}{4}$x$23\frac{3}{8}$in) Nigel Greenwood Collection

1974 One-man exhibition at Galerie December, Munster
Exhibited in 'Project '74' at Kunsthalle, Cologne,
'Beyond Painting and Sculpture' Arts Council travelling exhibition

1975 One-man exhibition at Lia Rumma, Rome and Naples
Exhibited in Paris Biennale

1975- Teaching at St Martin's School of Art

1976 One-man exhibition at Eric Fabre, Paris
Exhibited in 'Arte inglese oggi' at Palazzo Reale, Milan

1977 One-man exhibition at Schema Gallery, Florence

1978 One-man exhibitions at Photographers' Gallery, Ikon Gallery, Birmingham, City Museum, Southampton
Exhibited in 'Art into Society' at Whitechapel Art Gallery

1979 One-man exhibition at Kunstmuseum, Lucerne
Exhibited in 'Un certain art anglais' in Paris,
'Hayward Annual' at Hayward Gallery

Dealer Nigel Greenwood Inc

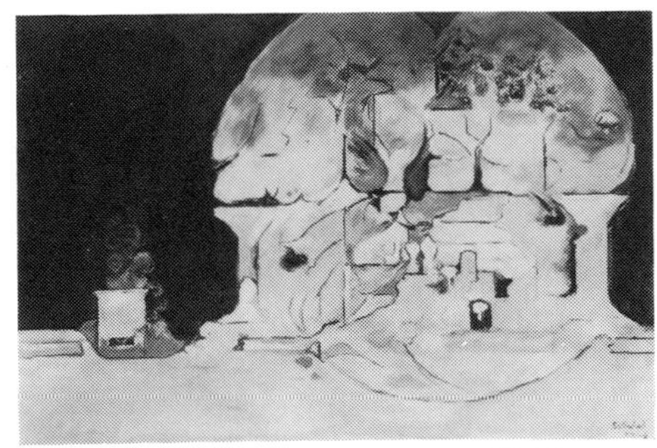

Graham Sutherland *Rock Shelter* 1973-4 Oil on canvas 117x173cm ($46\frac{1}{8}$x68in) Private Collection

Graham Sutherland OM 2

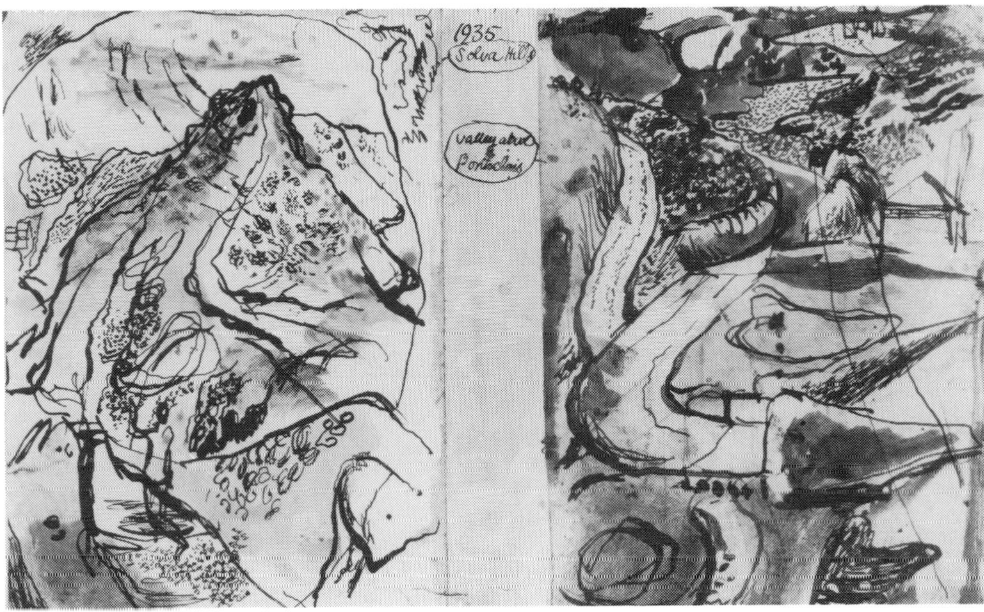

Graham Sutherland *Solva and Valley above Porthclais* 1935 Pen and wash 12.5x21cm ($5\frac{1}{2}$x$8\frac{1}{2}$in) Private Collection

1903 Born in London

1921-6 Studied at Goldsmiths College

1925 First one-man exhibition at XXI Gallery (also 1928)
Elected associate of Royal Society of Painters, Etchers and Engravers

1928-32 Taught engraving at Chelsea School of Art

1932-9 Taught composition and book illustration at Chelsea School of Art

1934 First visit to Pembrokeshire

1938 One-man exhibition at Rosenberg & Holft Gallery

1939 Exhibited in 'Contemporary British Art' at Worlds Fair, New York

1940-5 Official War Artist

1943 *Graham Sutherland* by Edward Sackville-West published (Penguin Modern Painters)

1946 One-man exhibition at Buchholz Gallery, New York (also 1948)

1947 One-man exhibition at Roland, Browse & Delbanco (also 1956/60)
First visit to South of France, where met Picasso and Matisse

1951 Retrospective exhibition at Institute of Contemporary Arts

1950 Exhibited in Carnegie International Exhibition, Pittsburgh (also 1952/58)

1952 Retrospective exhibition at Venice Biennale
One-man exhibition at Redfern Gallery (also 1958/59/64)
Commission for tapestry for new Coventry Cathedral

1953 Retrospective exhibitions at Tate Gallery, Stedelijk Museum, Amsterdam, Kunsthaus, Zurich

1954 One-man exhibition at Akademie der Bildende Kunste, Vienna and travelling in Austria and Germany
Exhibited in Sao Paulo Bienal

1955 Exhibited in 'Documenta 1' in Kassel

1957 Received Foreign Minister's Prize, Tokyo

1959 One-man exhibition at Rosenberg Gallery, New York (also 1964)

1960 Received OM

1962 One-man exhibition at Marlborough Fine Art (also 1966/68/73/74/77/79)
Exhibited in 'British Art Today' in San Francisco, Dallas and Santa Barbara
Received honorary degrees from Oxford and Leicester Universities

1963 One-man Welsh Arts Council exhibition

1965 Retrospective exhibition at Museum of Modern Art, Turin

1966 Retrospective exhibition at Kunsthalle, Basle

1967 Retrospective exhibition at Haus der Kunst, Munich and travelling in Holland and Germany

1968 Published lithograph series *A Bestiary*

1968-9 Visited Wales in connection with Italian television film on his work directed by Pier Paolo Ruggerini

1970 Exhibited in 'Moore, Picasso and Sutherland' at Marlborough Fine Art ▶

Graham Sutherland *Road at Porthclais with Setting Sun* 1975 Oil on canvas 52x50cm (20½x19¾in) Private Collection

1972 Commission from HM The Queen for painting as gift to President Pompidou
Elected honorary member of National Institute of Arts and Letters and American Academy of Arts and Letters, New York
Guest of Honour at Menton Biennale (First Prize)

1973 *Graham Sutherland* by Francesco Arcangeli published (Fratelli Fabbri, Milan)
Named Commandeur des Arts et des Lettres in France and Honorary Fellow of Accademia di San Luca, Rome

1974 *Sutherland Sketchbook* published
Appointed Honorary President of Menton Biennale
Received Shakespeare Prize, Hamburg
Founded Graham and Kathleen Sutherland Foundation/Picton Castle Trust in Pembrokeshire

1979 Retrospective exhibition of war drawings at Palazzo Reale, Milan
One-man exhibition of aquatint illustrations to Apollinaire's *Bestiary* at Bergamini and 2RC Galleries, Milan and travelling in Italy, USA and Britain
Received Honorary Doctorate from Cardiff University

Dealer Marlborough Fine Art, London and New York
Bergamini Gallery, Milan

As for my own procedure – I may go for a walk – for there is, as Croce said . . . 'the need for feeding the eye as well as the other senses'. As I walk I look attentively but casually; I am in a passive state. At this stage I feel often frustrated – 'boxed in', with the will to do something, but not always the means. I could comfort myself with the words of Petrarch 'an enclosed flame burns more fiercely (but) when it grows, be it ever so little, it can in no way be concealed'.

But suddenly – if I am lucky, I see something – some conjunction of forms – which seems to dominate all others. There is a sudden recognition that in what I have been looking at there is contained a unique series of rhythms – a magic equilibrium – a coming together of the elements before me which form a self-contained and moving image.

A shiver down the spine arrives to prove the validity of such an encounter – the nervous system has been touched.

I make notes on the spot, but this preliminary stage must then be ordered by the mind. The difficulty then is to preserve the direct emotion of the first encounter in another form. But by studying and restudying, correcting and recorrecting (anybody who has seen the original score of a work by Beethoven will know what I mean !) I live in the hope that I can make something which will give as direct and as strong an impact as the emotion which originally astonished me.

Graham Sutherland 1974
(Excerpt from speech given by the artist when awarded Shakespeare Prize in Hamburg)

Philip Sutton ARA 60

Philip Sutton *Imogen's Still-life* 1978 Oil on canvas 101x91.4cm (40x36in) Private Collection

1928 Born in Dorset

1950-4 Studied at Slade School of Fine Art
Received travelling scholarship to France and Italy

1956 One-man exhibition at Roland, Browse & Delbanco (also 1958/60/62/63/65/67/69/71/73/75)
Elected member of London Group

Philip Sutton *Homage to Manet* 1975 Oil on canvas 101x101cm (40x40in) Private Collection

1959 One-man exhibition at Geffrye Museum

1960 Retrospective exhibition at Leeds City Art Gallery

1962 One-man exhibitions at Stone Gallery, Newcastle-upon-Tyne,
Lane Gallery, Bradford,
57 Gallery, Edinburgh

1963 One-man exhibitions at David Jones Gallery, Sydney (also 1966/70/73),
Gallery A, Melbourne,
Battersea Central Library (also 1971/72)

1964-5 Travelled to Fiji Islands to paint

1967 One-man exhibition at London Arts Association, Detroit

1970 One-man exhibitions at Arnolfini Gallery, Bristol,
Folkestone Arts Centre

1972 One-man exhibition at Studio Prints

1976 One-man exhibitions in Johannesburg, Durban and Cape Town

1977 One-man exhibitions at Falmouth School of Art,
Royal Academy
Elected Associate of Royal Academy

1979 One-man exhibitions at Browse & Darby,
Bath Festival

Dealer Browse & Darby

All my work is done with the object in front of me – portraits, still-life, landscape, nudes. I try to be simple, direct and with a clear mind but if it should change in the course of doing the drawing or painting, I change with it.

Philip Sutton 1979

Patrick Symons 64

1925 Born in Kent
1946-50 Studied at Camberwell School of Art, with Euston Road School painters and John Dodgson
1953-9 Taught at Camberwell School of Art and St Albans School of Art
1959- Teaching at Chelsea School of Art
1960 One-man exhibition at New Art Centre
1969- Exhibiting in Summer Exhibitions at Royal Academy
1974 Exhibited in 'British Painting '74' at Hayward Gallery, John Moores Exhibition, Liverpool
1975-6 One-man exhibition at William Darby Gallery
Exhibited in 'Drawings of People' at Serpentine Gallery and travelling
1979 Exhibited in 'Hayward Annual' at Hayward Gallery

Dealer Browse & Darby

Patrick Symons *Holly under Oak at Wimbledon* 1972-5 Oil on canvas 57.2x61cm (22½x24in) Private collection

In recent drawings and paintings I have been trying to make settled pictures from things that move a little (like leaves or string players) by working from the subject for a very long time and trying to relate movements in space to some flat pictorial geometry. This normally entails some preliminary unmeasured drawing (which I usually refer to as 'scribbles') in which I try to find the geometrical structure which will serve as a scaffold for the finished work, whether painting or drawing. I draw most often with thin charcoal sharpened by breaking. In recent paintings, colours tend to be separated from each mixture at the edges in an attempt to celebrate radiance and clarity. With the leaf pictures, I find it necessary to work back from the tip of each branch to the balance of the plant so that the climax of the branch has the right emphasis – rather like the fingers or the direction of an eye in the musician pictures. In earlier paintings the paint tends to be thinner and the colour more literal but still often about a complex series of small surfaces. I frequently frame my work with some sort of mount which is a measured extension of geometrical elements in the picture.

Patrick Symons 1979

Wendy Taylor 121

1945 Born in Lincolnshire
1961-6 Studied at St Martin's School of Art
1964 Received Walter Neurath Award
1964- Exhibiting in many group shows in Britain and abroad
1965 Received Pratt Award
1966 Received Sainsbury Award
1970 One-man exhibition at Axiom Gallery
BBC Southern television film 'Sculpture – Wendy Taylor' made
1972 One-man exhibition at Angela Flowers Gallery
1974 One-man exhibitions at World Trade Centre, King's Lynn Festival
1975 One-man exhibition at Annely Juda Fine Art
1976 One-man exhibitions at Oxford Gallery, Oliver Dowling Gallery, Dublin (also 1979)
1977 Exhibited in Listowel Graphics Exhibition (Gold medal)
Received Arts Council Award
1978 Exhibited in 'Hayward Annual' at Hayward Gallery

Contact 69a Nightingale Lane, London SW12

Wendy Taylor *Brick Knot* 1977-8 Mixed media 213x335x236cm (7ftx11ftx7ft9in) Artist's Collection

My early work was greatly influenced by colours and shapes found in a natural landscape. As a student I worked as a gardener and involved myself completely in studying and abstracting from this source. *The Series*, a collection of eight pieces of sculpture, with accompanying drawings and prints, were the main outcome of this period, leading to *Calthae* a large floating sculpture. From *The Series* I then became more involved with the area of balance and illusion over-riding the use of colour. Forms became more simplified, stronger. *Nocturne* used balanced white circles, while *Chevron* and other works of this period had developed into balanced, tensioned tubular forms. Developing from these pieces *The Gazebo*, a commissioned multiple, incorporated the development of these shapes involving the surrounding landscape and the human figure within that landscape. My involvement with the importance of siting sculpture within a natural setting led to commissions such as *The Travellers* and *Triad* and other works such as *Enclave* and *Flight* which created interacting tensions by outline on a large enough scale to enable people to walk through them.

Wendy Taylor *Enclave* 1969 Steel with reflective aluminium finish 16.77m (55ft) long South Hill Park, Bracknell

The theme of balance was emphasized by *Liberation, Restrain* and a large series of sculptures all using welded chain to create stress and apparent movement, appearing to negate gravity. *Timepiece*, the commissioned sundial sculpture beside Tower Bridge, embodied these basics in materials appropriate to the setting. Three-dimensional prints and drawings produced during this period have echoed the motivation of the sculpture and have often clarified the problems associated with its construction.

Recently the use of bricks, exemplified by *Brick Knot, Brick Arch* and *Crossbow* (first shown in the 'Hayward Annual' in 1978), has explored this area further and the larger scale of current work extends the dominant themes of balanced stress and involvement with the landscape into commissions for specific sites.

Wendy Taylor 1979

Harry Thubron 51

1915 Born in County Durham
1933-8 Studied at Sunderland School of Art
1938-40 Studied at Royal College of Art
1950-5 Head of Fine Art at Sunderland College of Art
1955-64 Head of Fine Art at Leeds College of Art
1961 One-man exhibition in Frauenfeld, Switzerland
1963 One-man exhibition at University of Leeds.
1964 One-man exhibition at Lords Gallery Exhibited in 'The Teaching Image' at City Art Gallery, Leeds, Group show at Queen's Square Gallery, Leeds (also 1967)
1965-6 Visiting Professor at University of Illinois
1966 Exhibited in group show at Krannaert Museum, University of Illinois
1966-8 Head of Painting School at Leicester College of Art
1968 Received Arts Council Grant (also 1976)
1971- Teaching part-time at Goldsmiths College
1974 Exhibited in 'British Painting '74' at Hayward Gallery, Group show at Artists Market (also 1976/78)
1975 Exhibited in 'Source and Image' at Camden Arts Centre
1976 One-man exhibition at Peterloo Gallery, Manchester Exhibited in group show at Serpentine Gallery
1977 Exhibited in 'British Painting 1952-1977' at Royal Academy
1978 One-man exhibition at Jordan Gallery Received OBE

Contact 41B Granville Road, London SE13

Harry Thubron *Paloma* 1979 Mixed media 79x120cm (31x47¼in) Artist's Collection

Prior to 1965, I had access to machine shops and the assistance and advice of scientists, chemists, engineers and technicians; at that time much of my work was in wood, spun copper, brass and resins. A visit to America however, made for an enforced break from this way of working, and I returned to the use of paint and collage, (ie rubbish): this has formed a large part of my subsequent activity.

One of the most marvellous things that has ever happened to me was going to Mexico ten years ago. The light was enormous, golden, it unified all the coloured garments that the Indians threw together. I think of the old, golden, crumbling walls of the early Spanish cathedral at Cuernavaca. After returning to this country, this memory took me to Spain looking for the same thing, but Spain was different. Andalusia, in the mountains: Ronda is a great listening dish . . . here the light is different: brilliantly reflected from white walls in narrow streets with a bleached dust covering all. Everything there is hard and harsh. It brings a reality to living, pervading everything from the land to the people. No wonder so many have confronted themselves with this place before, Cervantes and Rilke, Hemingway and Bomberg. This is where I find many of the 'pieces' (that make themselves into collage) along the unmade road which passes the studio to the village. Rubbish, shaped by the passing of people, on foot, mule or by lorry, shapes which man's ingenuity could not fashion, unified by the covering of blond dust . . . pollen so fresh, and which I try to retain . . . Among the Spanish peasant community, living is starkly abrasive in its intensity, enabling the senses to be quick and alert: seeing-finding-doing becomes a total way of life.

Harry Thubron 1979

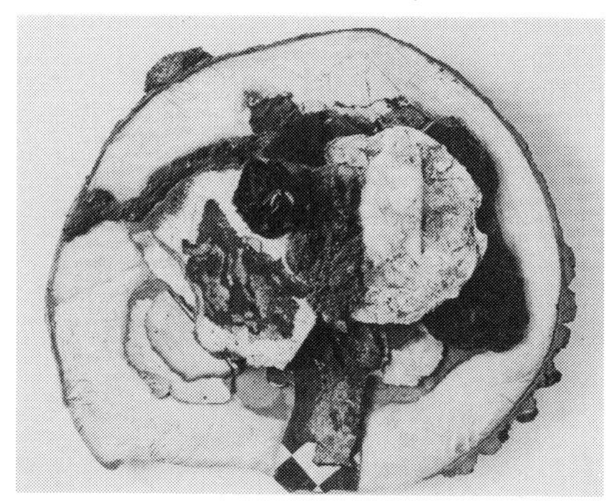
Harry Thubron *Black Rose* 1967 Mixed media 59x66cm (23⅛x26in) Artist's Collection

Joe Tilson 106

Joe Tilson *Labyrinth: Trojan Door* 1974 Elm 239x178x8cm (7ft 8inx5ft 10inx3in) Artist's Collection

1928 Born in London
1949-52 Studied at St Martin's School of Art
1950 Exhibited in 'Young Contemporaries' (also 1951/52/54/55)
1952-5 Studied at Royal College of Art
1955 Received Knapping Foundation Prize and Rome Prize
1957 Exhibited in John Moores Exhibition, Liverpool (also 1963/67)
1958-63 Taught at St Martin's School of Art
1960 Received Gulbenkian Foundation Prize
1961 Exhibited in Paris Biennale, Carnegie International Exhibition, Pittsburgh (also 1967)
1962 One-man exhibition at Marlborough Fine Art (also 1964/66/70) Exhibited in 'British Art Today' in San Francisco, Dallas and Santa Barbara
1963 One-man exhibition at Walker Art Art Gallery, Liverpool Exhibited in Tokyo Biennale (also 1964), San Marino Biennale (Gold Medal)
1964 Exhibited in Venice Biennale (also 1971/76), 'Contemporary British Painting and Sculpture' at Albright-Knox Art Gallery, Buffalo

1965 Exhibited in Ljubljana Biennale (prizewinner and in 1965/67/69/71/75/77), 'The English Eye' at Marlborough Gerson Gallery, New York
1966 Taught at School of Visual Art, New York
1967 One-man exhibitions at Marlborough Gallery, New York, Marlborough Galleria d'Arte, Rome
Exhibited in 'Recent British Painting' at Tate Gallery (Peter Stuyvesant Foundation Collection)
1968 One-man exhibition at Galerie Brusberg, Hanover
Exhibited in 'Britische Kunst heute' in Kunstverein, Hamburg, 'Documenta 4' at Kassel
1969 Exhibited in 'Pop Art' at Hayward Gallery
1970 Two-man exhibition at Haus am Waldsee, Berlin
Exhibited in 'Contemporary British Art' at Museum of Modern Art, Tokyo, Cracow Biennale (also 1974/76)
1971 One-man exhibition at Waddington Galleries (also 1970)
1971-2 Taught at Staatliche Hochschule für Bildende Kunste, Hamburg
1972 One-man exhibition at Galerie René Block, Berlin
1973 Retrospective exhibition at Boymans Van Beuningen Museum, Rotterdam
1974 One-man exhibition at Galerie Van Loeper, Hamburg
1975 One-man exhibition at Galleria del Cavallino, Venice
1976 Exhibited in 'Arte inglese oggi' at Palazzo Reale, Milan
1978 One-man exhibition 'Alchera 1970-7' at Tate Gallery

Dealer Waddington Galleries

Joe Tilson *Four Ladders: Earth, Water, Air, Fire* 1974 Western red cedar Fire: 225x120x7cm (7ft 4inx4ftx2¾in) Air, Water and Earth: 225x120x9cm (7ft 4inx4ftx3½in) Artist's Collection

David Tindle RA 28

1932 Born in Huddersfield
1945-6 Studied at Coventry School of Art
1954 Exhibited in Summer Exhibition at Royal Academy (also 1968/70-6)
1954- Regular one-man exhibitions at Piccadilly Gallery
1957 Retrospective exhibition at Coventry City Art Gallery
One-man exhibition at 57 Gallery, Edinburgh
1958 One-man exhibition at Stone Gallery, Newcastle (also 1959)
1959 Exhibited in John Moores Exhibition, Liverpool (also 1961)
1959-74 Taught at Hornsey College of Art
1961 One-man exhibition at Bear Lane Gallery, Oxford
1964 One-man exhibition at Galerie du Tours, San Francisco and Los Angeles
1967 Exhibited in 'Salon de la jeune peinture' in Paris
1968 One-man exhibitions at Galleria Carbonesi, Bologna, Galleria Vinciana, Milan
1972 Retrospective exhibition at Northampton Art Gallery
1972- Teaching part-time at Royal College of Art
1973 Elected Associate of Royal Academy
1974 One-man exhibition at Galerie XX, Hamburg (also 1977)
Exhibited in 'British Painting '74' at Hayward Gallery
1975 Exhibited in Chichester National Art Exhibition (prizewinner)
1977 Exhibited in 'British Painting 1952-1977' at Royal Academy
1979 Elected Royal Academician

Dealer Piccadilly Gallery

David Tindle *Moth* 1976 Egg tempera 55.7x86.2cm (21⅞x34in) Private Collection

In the early 50s I was influenced by post-war British figurative painting (Minton, Freud and Bacon). The influence of Bacon and some American painters seemed to follow through into the 60s. The paint was very heavy and gestural during this time, but by the late 60s this had worn itself out for me and the paintings became very formal in the selection of subject (mainly still-life) and in the manner in which they were painted.

By 1970 it seemed to me that egg tempera was a more suitable medium for my subject matter, and my interest in tightly-drawn images and textural surfaces. My subject matter is usually that which is closest to me in my environment. It is not so much an exploration of Art but of environment, object or figure.

David Tindle 1979

David Tindle *Taxis – Regent Street* 1960 Oil 111.8x121.9cm (44x48in) Private Collection

Julian Trevelyan

1910 Born in Surrey
1928-30 Studied at Trinity College, Cambridge
1931-4 Studied at SW Hayter's Atelier 17, Paris
1936 One-man exhibition at Lefevre Gallery (also 1942/43/44/46/48)
1950-60 Taught at Chelsea School of Art
1955 One-man exhibition at Zwemmer Gallery (also 1958/60/63/65/66)
1955-63 Senior Tutor in Etching at Royal College
1972 Exhibited in 'Surrealist Retrospective' at Hamet Gallery
1974 One-man exhibition at Printmakers Council, Oxford Press

Contact Durham Wharf, Hammersmith Terrace, London W6

▶

William Tucker

1935 Born in Cairo
1955-8 Studied history at Oxford University
1959-60 Studied sculpture at Central School of Art and Design and St Martin's School of Art
1961 Exhibited in Paris Biennale
1963 Onc-man exhibition at Rowan Gallery (also 1966)
1965 One-man exhibition at Richard Feigen Gallery, New York
1966 Exhibited in International Sculpture Exhibition at Guggenheim Museum, New York
1967 One-man exhibition at Kasmin Gallery (also 1969/70)
1968 Exhibited in 'Documenta 4' in Kassel
1970 Exhibited in 'Contemporary British Painting and Sculpture' at Museum of Modern Art, Tokyo
1972 Exhibited in Venice Biennale
1973 One-man exhibitions at Kunstverein, Hamburg, Serpentine Gallery

Dealer Hester van Royen

William Turnbull 86

William Turnbull *Trestle* 1971 Wood 104.8x121.9x152.4cm (41¼x48x60in) Tate Gallery

1922 Born in Scotland
1946-8 Studied at Slade School of Fine Art
1948-50 Lived in Paris
1950 One-man exhibition at Hanover Gallery (also 1952)
1952 Exhibited in Venice Biennale
1957 One-man exhibition at Institute of Contemporary Arts
Exhibited in Sao Paulo Bienal (also 1967)
1958 Exhibited in Carnegie International Exhibition, Pittsburgh (also 1961)
1960 One-man exhibition at Molton Gallery (also 1961)
Exhibited in 'Sculpture in the Open Air' in Battersea Park

William Turnbull *Woman and Acrobat* 1955 Monoprint 76.2x55.9cm (30x22in) Artist's Collection

1962 Exhibited in Hirshhorn Collection Exhibition at Guggenheim Museum, New York
1963 One-man exhibitions at Marlborough Gerson Gallery, New York, Art Institute, Detroit
1964 Exhibited in Guggenheim International Exhibition at Guggenheim Museum, New York (also 1967), 'Painting and Sculpture of a Decade' at Tate Gallery
1965 One-man exhibition at Galerie Muller, Stuttgart (also 1974)
1966 One-man exhibition at Pavilion Gallery, Balboa, California
1967 One-man exhibition at Waddington Galleries (also 1969/70/76/78)
1968 One-man exhibitions at Hayward Gallery, Museo de Arte Moderna, Rio de Janeiro and travelling in South America
Exhibited in 'Documenta 4' in Kassel
1969 Exhibited in International Sculpture Exhibition at Hakone Open Air Museum, Japan
1973 Retrospective exhibition at Tate Gallery
1974 One man Scottish Arts Council exhibition in Edinburgh

Dealer Waddington Galleries

Euan Uglow 69

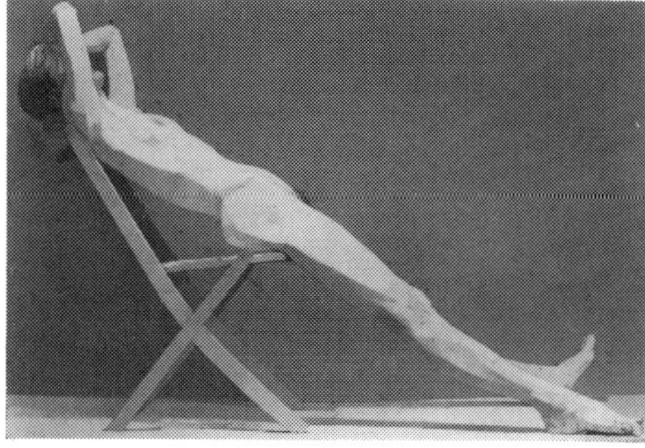
Euan Uglow *The Diagonal* 1977 Oil 118.1x167cm (46½x65¾in) Private Collection

1932 Born in London
1948-51 Studied at Camberwell School of Art
1951 Studied at Slade School of Fine Art (also 1954)
1953 Received Abbey Minor Scholarship
1956 First exhibited with London Group
1960 Elected member of London Group
1961 One-man exhibition at Beaux Arts Gallery
Exhibited in 'Modern British Portraits' Arts Council travelling exhibition,
John Moores Exhibition, Liverpool (prizewinner; also 1972 1st Prize)
1961- Teaching part-time at Slade School of Fine Art and Camberwell School of Art

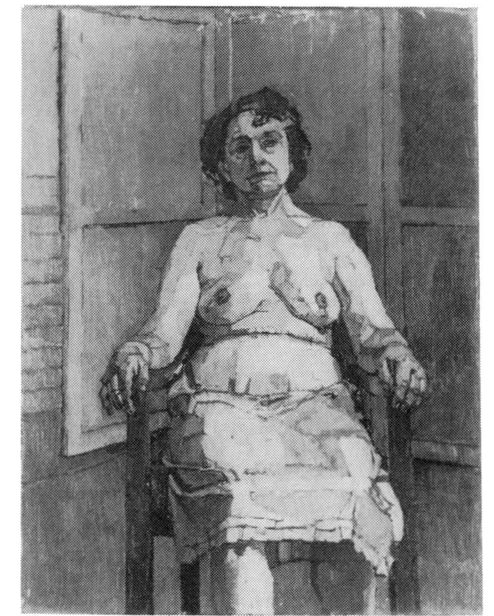
Euan Uglow *Woman with White Skirt* 1953 Oil 94x66cm (37x26in) Artist's Collection

1962 Exhibited in 'Drawing towards Painting 1' Arts Council travelling exhibition
1964 Exhibited in '6 Young Painters' Arts Council travelling exhibition
1968 Exhibited in 'Helen Lessore and the Beaux Arts Gallery' at Marlborough Fine Art
1969 Exhibited in group show at University of Sussex
1971 Exhibited in 'Painting and Perception' at University of Stirling
Received Edwin Austin Abbey Scholarship
1974 One-man exhibition at Whitechapel Art Gallery
1977 One-man exhibition at Browse & Darby
'Aquarius' television film made on his work

Dealer Browse & Darby

Marc Vaux 88

1932 Born in Swindon
1954-7 Studied at Swindon School of Art
1957-60 Studied at Slade School of Fine Art
1960 Received Boise Travel Scholarship
1961 Exhibited in Paris Biennale
1962 Exhibited in Tokyo Biennale
1962-72 Taught at Bath Academy of Art and Hornsey College of Art
1963 One-man exhibition at Grabowski Gallery
Exhibited in International Graphic Art Exhibition, Ljubljana
1965 One-man exhibition at Hamilton Galleries
1966 Exhibited in 'London under 40' at Galleria Milano, Milan,
'Vormen van de Kleur' at Stedelijk Museum, Amsterdam and travelling in Europe
1967 One-man exhibition at Axiom Gallery (also 1970)
Exhibited in International Art Exhibition, Tokyo,
'6 Artists' at Victoria and Albert Museum

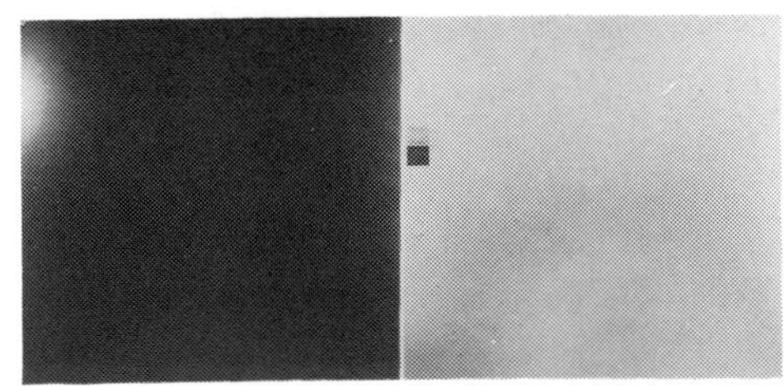

Marc Vaux *Double Painting 2CR/75* 1975 Acrylic on cotton duck 213.4x426.8cm (7x14ft) Artist's Collection

Marc Vaux *Union Brand* 1965 Acrylic on cotton duck 213.4x213.4cm (7x7ft) Artist's Collection

1968 Exhibited in 'British Painting' at Whitechapel Art Gallery
1969 One-man exhibition at Galerie Wilbrand, Cologne
Exhibited in 'Contemporary British Graphics' at Smithsonian Institution, Washington DC and travelling
1970 Exhibited in 'Colour and Structure: Recent British and Australian Painting' at Farmers Blaxland Gallery, Sydney
1973 One man exhibition at Whitechapel Art Gallery
1973- Principal Lecturer in Painting at Central School of Art and Design
1974 Exhibited in 'British Painting '74' at Hayward Gallery,
'Artistas gráphicos británicos de la décade del '60' in Mexico
1976 One-man studio exhibition
1977 Received Arts Council Major Award
1978 Commission for mural from IBM, UK

Contact 45 Tabernacle Street, London EC2

Shelagh Wakely 171

1932 Born in London
1951-62 Studied at Wye College of Agriculture and Chelsea School of Art
1968-71 Research Fellowship at Royal College of Art
1972 Started making sculpture
1975 One-man exhibition at Sheila David Gallery
Exhibited in group shows at AIR Gallery,
Clarendon Graphics
1976 Two-man exhibition (with Alizon Wilding) at AIR Gallery
Received GLAA Visual Arts Award
1977 Exhibited in 'Summer Show 1' at Serpentine Gallery,
Industrial Sponsors Exhibition,
'Miniatures' at Coracle Press,
'British Artists' Prints 1972-7' British Council travelling exhibition,
'Graphics at work' at Institute of Contemporary Arts
1978 Exhibited in 'Foundlings' at Coracle Press,
With London Group
1979 One-man exhibitions at Coracle Press, Institute of Contemporary Arts
Exhibited in Bradford Print Biennale, Cleveland Drawing Biennale
It is so green outside it is difficult to leave the window published (Coracle Press)

Contact 23 Falkland Road, London NW5

Looking at this photograph of me taken in 1975, what can I say. I can describe its form in words, but not what it's about. Similarly thinking about the work I can write about its form only, otherwise I would have written in the first place. I look out of the window I see two people passing in a motorcar, perhaps they are going to the theatre, why have they chosen that particular play. I can only know that by travelling with them, watching the play, trying to sort out their conversation and it's gaps.

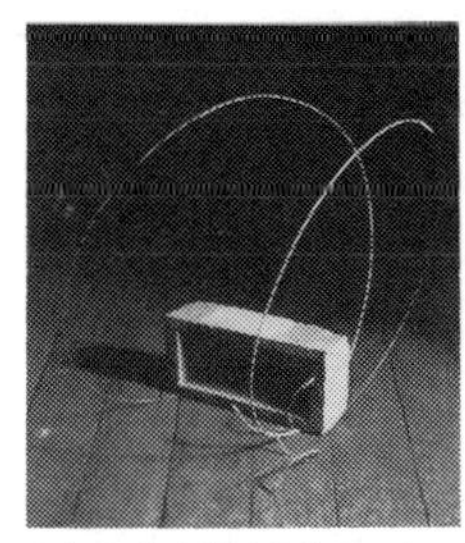

Left: Shelagh Wakely 1 piece from *Some Encounters with Reality* 1977 Steel and woodjewel tied together with string weighted down with a brick Artist's Collection

Right: Shelagh Wakely 1 piece from *Towards the Inside of a Container* 1979 White biscuit fired clay, moulded over a dome. Each mould 22.9cm (9in) diameter

Shelagh Wakely *Towards the Inside of a Container* 1979 Mixed media, clay, paper, paving slabs and steel Artist's Collection

The first group of work, *Walking through a walled garden* came together in 1975. Collections of hand-sized things were placed on any available surface: floor, table, walls, a board leaning against a wall. In 1976 I showed things in loose groups on the floor, many of them were attached to the floor by nails and threads that held them in place. There were also some etchings which dealt with ridding the plate of previous marks and pictures. The last three groups of work I have done: *Some encounters with reality* 1977, *Precisely defined for the moment* 1978 and *Towards the inside of a container* 1979 have been made up of three dimensional pieces. Each piece to be considered by itself but making up part of a larger story. This story emerges as I make the pieces.

In the latest work, *Towards the inside of a container* surfaces of objects are particularly important, like photographs one cannot get behind them, it is to do with memory or possibility. Recently I have begun to deal with many levels of experience using different kinds of drawing, prints, a documentary photographic piece as well as three dimensional pieces and some words of description. The link between these is purposefully loose.

Shelagh Wakely 1979

John Walker 90

John Walker *Juggernaut with Plume – For P Neruda* 1975 Mixed media 305x243.8cm (10x8ft) Artist's Collection

1939 Born in Birmingham
1960 Received Abbey Travelling Scholarship

John Walker *'Numinous' Study X* 1978 Acrylic and charcoal on paper 117.5x97.5cm (46¼x38⅜in) Nigel Greenwood Collection

1965 Exhibited in John Moores Exhibition, Liverpool (prizewinner; also 1974 prizewinner/76 1st Prize)
1966-7 Exhibited in 'European Painters of Today' at Musée des Arts Décoratifs, Paris and travelling in America
1967 One-man exhibition at Axiom Gallery (also 1968)
1967-9 Gregory Fellow at University of Leeds
1968 One-man exhibition at Hayward Gallery
1969 Exhibited in Paris Biennale, Theodoren Foundation Exhibition at Guggenheim Museum, New York (prizewinner)
1970 One-man exhibition at Nigel Greenwood Inc (also 1972/75/78)
Exhibited in 'Contemporary Art in Britain' at Museum of Modern Art, Tokyo,
'British Painting and Sculpture' at National Gallery of Art, Washington DC
Received Harkness Fellowship
1971 One-man exhibition at Reese Palley, New York (also 1972)
1972 One-man exhibition at Studio La Città, Verona
Exhibited in Venice Biennale
1973 One-man exhibitions at Kunstverein, Hamburg,
Cuningham Ward, New York (also 1975/76/78)
1974 Exhibited in 'British Painting '74' at Hayward Gallery
1974-5 One-man exhibitions at Museum of Modern Art, New York,
Galerie Swart, Amsterdam
1974-8 Taught at Royal College of Art
Visiting Artist at Columbia University, New York
1975-7 Visiting Professor at Yale University
1976 Exhibited in 'Arte inglese oggi' at Palazzo Reale, Milan
1977 Exhibited in 'British Painting 1952-1977' at Royal Academy
1977-8 Artist in Residence at St Catherine's College, Oxford
1978 One-man exhibition at Phillips Collection, Washington DC

Dealer Nigel Greenwood Inc
Betty Cuningham, New York

John Ward RA 33

1917 Born in Hereford
1933-6 Studied at Hereford School of Art
1936-9 Studied at Royal College of Art (received travelling scholarship and drawing prize)
1948-52 Taught part-time at Wimbledon School of Art
Worked part-time for *Vogue* magazine
1952- Working as portrait painter and book illustrator (HE Bates' Autobiography, Richard Church's *Little Kingdom* etc)
1956 Elected Associate of Royal Academy
1959 Illustrated *Cider with Rosie* by Laurie Lee (Chatto & Windus)
1964 One-man exhibition at Maas Gallery (also 1967/71/72/73/74/76/78)
1965 Elected Royal Academician

Dealer Maas Gallery

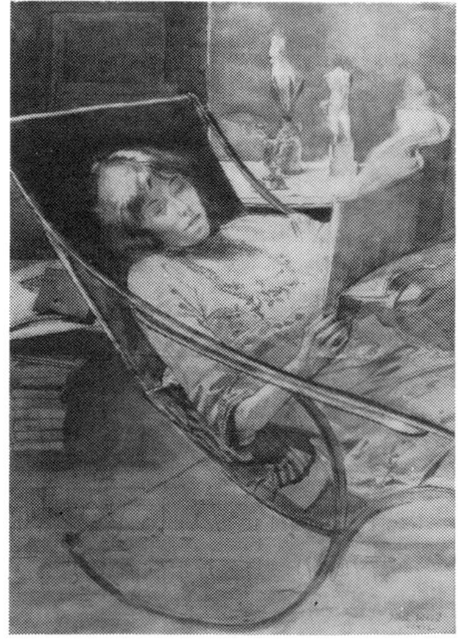

John Ward *Girl in Chair* 1972 Watercolour 48.3x30.5cm (19x12in) Private Collection

I have always loved drawing and painting what I could see and was lucky enough to have had excellent teachers at the Royal College of Art. The skill I acquired has proved to be most rewarding since I have been able to find pleasing employment over a wide field. My time working on *Vogue* magazine was particularly valuable since I worked alongside first-rate photographers who taught me much that hadn't come my way, by Art School training.

I don't think my work falls into any definite periods or styles since my early aim to paint what I see has never become any easier or any less absorbing. It is something which not only needs a lifetime but also constant practice.

Over the years, I have done various figure groups which have presented fascinating problems of design – one such for the Sale Room at Christie's and another for the Society of Dilettantes.

In between portrait work, I do water-colours of landscape and architecture and usually accumulate enough work to have a one-man show every two years.

John Ward 1979

John Ward *Sir Thomas Norrington, President of Trinity College, Oxford* 1967 Oil on canvas 74.9x62.2cm (29½x24½in) Trinity College, Oxford

Carel Weight RA 43

1908 Born in London
1928-30 Studied at Hammersmith College of Art
1930-3 Studied at Goldsmiths College
1937-9 One-man exhibitions at Picture Hire
1938 Exhibited in Carnegie International Exhibition, Pittsburgh

Carel Weight *Despair* 1970 Oil 366x121.9cm (12x4ft) Artist's Collection

1939-45 Official War Artist in Italy, Austria and Greece
1947 One-man exhibition at Leicester Galleries (also 1951)
1947-57 Taught at Royal College of Art
1951 Exhibited in '60 Pictures for 1951' at Tate Gallery
1954 Exhibited in 'Figures in a Setting' at Tate Gallery,
Group show at Zwemmer Gallery (also 1959/61)
1955 Elected Associate of Royal Academy
1956 Exhibited in 'The Seasons' at Tate Gallery
1958 Exhibited in 'Religious Theme' at Tate Gallery,
'British Art' at Pushkin Museum, Moscow
1960 One-man exhibition at Thomas Agnew & Sons
Exhibited in '70 Years of British Painting' in China
1962 Received CBE
1963 Commission for mural for Manchester Cathedral
1964 Received David Cargill Award
1965 Elected Royal Academician
1966 Two-man exhibition (with Roger de Grey) at Nottingham University
1968 Two-man exhibition (with Ruskin Spear) at Leicester Galleries

Contact 33 Spencer Road, London SW18

Carel Weight *Battersea Gardens* 1978 Oil 121.9x121.9cm (48x48in) Private Collection

I aim to create in my painting a world superficially close to the visual one but a world of greater tension and drama. The products of memory, mood and imagination rise upon a foundation of fact. My art is concerned with such things as anger, love, fear, hate and loneliness emphasized by the ordinary landscape in which the dramatic scene is set.

Carel Weight 1979

Karl Weschke 141

1925 Born in Germany
1948 Moved to England
1954-5 Lived in Sweden
1958 One-man exhibition at New Vision Centre Gallery
1959 One-man exhibition at Woodstock Gallery
Exhibited in '11 British Artists' at Jefferson Place Gallery, Washington ▶

Karl Weschke *Figure* 1967 Charcoal on paper 55.9x86.4cm (22x32in) Private Collection

Karl Weschke *Bather Walking on Rocks* 1973 Oil on tempera primed hardboard 154x121.9cm (61x48in) Private Collection

1960 One-man exhibition at Matthiesen Gallery
Exhibited in 'Contemporary British Landscape' Arts Council travelling exhibition
1962 Exhibited in 'Malerei der Gegenwart aus Sudwest England' at Kunstverein, Hanover
1963 Exhibited in 'Contemporary Landscape Painting' at Whitechapel Art Gallery,
'British Painting in the 60s' at Tate Gallery
1964 One-man exhibitions at Grosvenor Gallery,
Arnolfini Gallery, Bristol (also 1968/71)
1971 One-man exhibitions at Bear Lane Gallery, Oxford,
City Art Gallery, Plymouth and travelling
Exhibited in 'Art Spectrum (South)' Arts Council exhibition
1972 One-man exhibition at Park Square Gallery, Leeds
1974 One-man exhibition at Whitechapel Art Gallery
1976 Received Arts Council Major Award
1977 Exhibited in 'Englische Kunst der Gegenwart' in Bregenz
1978 Exhibited in John Moores Exhibition, Liverpool (prizewinner)
Received South West Arts Major Award

Contact Ruston, Cape Cornwall, St Just, Penzance

The simplest and perhaps the most direct statement I can make, is that I paint about life.

I think painting is inherently allegorical. The Oxford Dictionary definition for the word allegory is 'Narrative describing one subject in the guise of another'. One describes life with a visual simile. If I paint a picture of a gale, I make a visual simile of a tangible fact. The gale itself I cannot paint, the gale is !

One sees or experiences aspects of living and these facts are given some degree of visual, or should I say visible, permanency. The word visual is not totally removed from visionary. Perhaps it is the intensity of vision – in the sense of insight – which makes the painter in visual terms a narrator of life. One is always aware of other painters. I appreciate all the good ones, but only affinity dictates influences. At one and the same instant I am aware that the first painter did not go to an Art School, and that art does not come from Art. Art is not a perpetual mobile, it has to be generated by life. I know we can no longer be these first painters but their immediacy of vision, their directness, we can retain. One does not think paintings into existence, one paints them, but this does not mean that painting excludes thought.

My materials are very traditional. Charcoal or pencil on paper for drawing, and oil paint on canvas or board for painting, etc. which does, I suppose, explain my methods.

Karl Weschke 1979

Anthony Whishaw 155

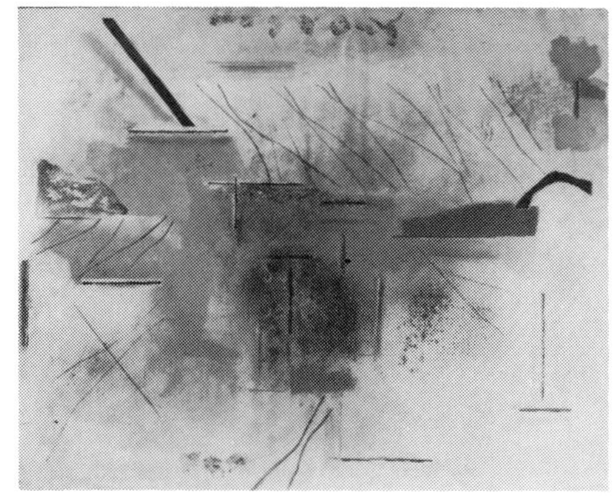

Anthony Whishaw *Garden, Early Spring* 1978 Acrylic on canvas 243.8x305cm (8x10ft) Artist's Collection

1930 Born in London
1948-52 Studied at Chelsea School of Art
1952-5 Studied at Royal College of Art
1960 One-man exhibition at Roland, Browse & Delbanco (also 1961/63/65/68)
1964-5 Exhibited in 'Towards Art' at Royal College of Art
1969 Exhibited in group show at Camden Arts Centre
1971 One-man exhibition at Institute of Contemporary Arts
1972 One-man exhibition at New Art Centre
1973 Exhibited in Middlesbrough Biennale
Received Perth Biennale Prize
1974 One-man exhibitions at Hoya Gallery, Oxford Gallery, Oxford
Exhibited in Summer Exhibition at Royal Academy (also 1975/76/77/78/79)
Received Bayer International Painting Prize
1977 Exhibited in 'British Painting 1952-1977' at Royal Academy
1977-8 Received Greater London Arts Association Grant
1978 One-man exhibition at Acme Gallery
Exhibited in 'A Free Hand' Arts Council travelling exhibition
Elected member of London Group
Received Arts Council Award
1979 One-man exhibition at Newcastle Polytechnic Art Gallery
Exhibited in Tolly Cobbold Eastern Arts National Exhibition
1979- Teaching at St Martin's School of Art and Chelsea School of Art

Dealer Acme Gallery

Anthony Whishaw *Up to Stone Street I* 1978 Acrylic on canvas 167x228cm (5ft 6inx7ft 6in) Wayne Anderson Collection, USA

I have always been poised on a knife edge between abstract and figurative ideas. I am involved with the edge of perception. I have wanted to extract essences of visual experiences – destroy them, amalgamate and then recreate them into a new but parallel order. But – a paradox – how can a painting be autonomous and yet refer even by analogy to something outside itself? This is my permanent conflict and I don't know whether it is a weakness or a strength but it is certainly central to my work.

I am interested in the idea or picture the mind might have at the moment before perception – the idea of the brain about to and in the midst of arranging its incoming imagery and making sense of it. Symbols can be offered by the elements of landscape – fences, fields, furrows, hills – and I should like to think that variations on these themes are used a little as in music – to lead the eye around the painting – to hint at depths, illusions and after-images and then possibly to deny them. Some are intended to loom out and even to cast shadows. Randomness and order in nature find a parallel in the process of painting. Feelings and ideas merge: early morning sunshine, frost, ploughed fields, valleys, space (as in Turner) and shallow space (like looking downwards while gardening). Forms are shattered or, quite the opposite, are trying to materialize.

My paintings are done in acrylic on canvas duck with sand or polyfilla sometimes added.

Anthony Whishaw 1979

Stephen Willats 188

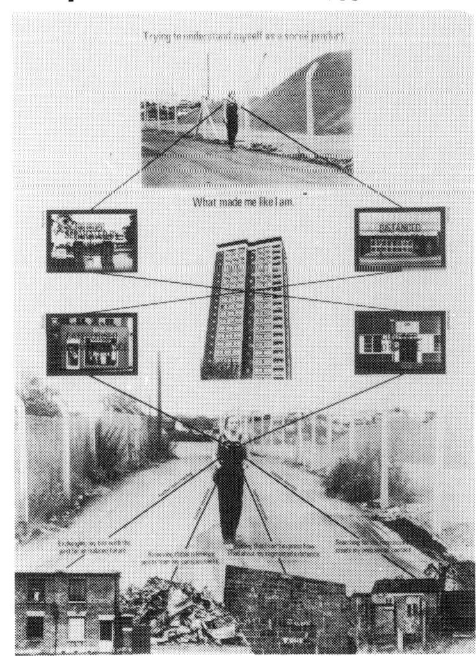

Stephen Willats *What Made Me Like I Am* 1977-8 Photographs, text and ink on board 80x108.5cm (31½x42¾in) Artist's Collection

1943 Born in London
1966 Exhibited in 'Kunst Licht Kunst' at Stedelijk Van Abbe-museum, Eindhoven
1968 One-man exhibition 'Visual Automatics and Visual Transmitters' at Museum of Modern Art, Oxford
1972 Exhibited in 'Survey of the Avant-Garde' at Gallery House
1972-3 Worked on the West London Social Resource Project
1973 One-man exhibition 'The Artist as an Instigator of Changes in Social Cognition and Behaviour' at Gallery House
1974 One-man exhibition 'Life Codes and Behaviour Parameters' at Galerie December, Munster
Exhibited in 'Art as Thought Process' at Serpentine Gallery
1975 One-man exhibition 'Meta Filter' at The Gallery
1976 One-man exhibitions 'Life Codes and Behaviour Parameters' at Midland Group Gallery, Nottingham,
'Social Structures: The Perception of Context' at Galerie Stampa, Basle,
'Attitudes within 4 Relationships' at Lisson Gallery
Art and Social Function published (Latimer New Dimensions)
1977 Exhibited in 'Social Criticism and Art Practice' at San Francisco Art Institute, Paris Biennale
1978 One-man exhibitions 'Questions about Ourselves' at Lisson Gallery,
'Living within Contained Conditions' at Museum of Modern Art, Oxford (also book published)
Exhibited in 'Art for Whom' at Serpentine Gallery
1979 One-man exhibition 'Concerning our Present Way of Living' at Whitechapel Art Gallery
Exhibited in 'Un certain art anglais' at Musée d'Art Moderne, Paris

Dealer Lisson Gallery

Edward Wolfe RA 6

1897 Born in Johannesburg
1917 Studied at Slade School of Fine Art
Invited by Roger Fry to join Omega Workshop
1918 One-man exhibition at Omega Workshop
First exhibited with London Group
1919-21 Returned to South Africa
1920 One-man exhibition at Leon Levson Gallery, Johannesburg
1922-5 Worked in France, Spain and Italy
1923 Exhibited in Venice Biennale
1926 One-man exhibition at Mayor Gallery (also 1938/51/54/73)
1930 One-man exhibition at London Artists Association (also 1934)
1931 Designed costumes and set for Cochrane's Revue
1934-6 Worked in USA and Mexico
1936 One-man exhibition at Lefevre Gallery (also 1948)
1943 Arranged London Group exhibition at City Art Gallery, Bristol
1944 Exhibited in group shows at Redfern Gallery, American Art Centre, New York
1948 Exhibited with Baynes, Grant and du Plessis at Bristol City Art Gallery
1950 One-man exhibitions in Manchester, Salford, Cardiff and Liverpool
1953 One-man exhibition at O'Hara Gallery
Two-man exhibition (with Jane Lane) at Galerie de Seine, Paris
1956 One-man exhibition at Gainsborough Galleries, Johannesburg
1956-8 Worked in South Africa
1964- Exhibiting in Summer Exhibition at Royal Academy
1967 Retrospective exhibition at Arts Council Gallery and travelling
Elected Associate of Royal Academy
1972 Elected Royal Academician
1974 Exhibited in '20th-century Portraits' at Wildenstein Gallery
1977 Exhibited in 'British Painting 1952-1977' at Royal Academy
1979 One-man exhibition at Fieldbourne Gallery

Dealer Fieldborne Galleries

Edward Wolfe *Nude Painted Morocco in Rabat* 1952 pastel 58.4x43.2cm (27x17in) Private Collection

. . . I would say that essentially he is a lyrical painter with a sensuality rare in England; that in his best work a strong constructive logic organizes his sensations into often unexpected and poetic harmonies. He is not the kind of painter who simply sits in front of any delightful little view, attractive figure or delicious corner of the dinner table. His landscapes, for example, are often very full, very various in their light and shade and abundant in linear motifs and changes of perspective; the best of his still lifes are frequently sumptuous in their composition, as rhythmically plump as some Mannerist overmantel. His naturally fluent line is both descriptive ▶

Edward Wolfe *Flowers and Fruit* 1956 Oil on canvas 119.4x86.4cm (47x34in) Private Collection

and decorative, following his formal intuition without being tied to the exigencies of the subject; he can distort, run off at a tangent, deliver an arabesque and yet keep the essential rhythm upon which so much depends. This is seen to advantage in several portraits in which figure and setting are integrated not so much through subtle tonal changes but through a continuously varied line which evokes the spatial situation. Quite a few painters would stop there and fill in with colour as best they could. Not Wolfe, for, from the time he began, it was the colour people noticed; he revels in it, his basic subsistence. It has sent him scurrying all over the world (he is dreaming now of India) and when I see him on a gloomy London day, the grey mattress of a winter sky pressing at the windows, I feel a pang as though some splendid flower was fated to bloom, unseen in an uncongenial air. But he is tough and holds, from old experience, a pack of cards in store, dealing out his yellows, vermilions, curious hot pinks and illumined blues with the confidence of a man who trusts his vision.

Richard Shone 1979

Gary Wragg 199

1946 Born in High Wycombe
1962-6 Studied at High Wycombe School of Art
1966-9 Studied at Camberwell School of Art
1968 Received Rotary Travelling Gift to Italy and Lord Carron Prize
1969 Exhibited in 'Play Orbit' at Institute of Contemporary Arts
1969-71 Studied at Slade School of Fine Art
Received Boise Travel Scholarship to USA and Mexico
1970 Exhibited in 'Young Contemporaries'
1971 Exhibited in Slade Centenary Exhibition at Royal Academy
1971- Teaching at Camberwell School of Art, St Martin's School of Art and Portsmouth Polytechnic
1972 Exhibited in 'Drawing' at Museum of Modern Art, Oxford
1973 One-man studio exhibition (also 1975)
Exhibited in group show at Warehouse Gallery (also 1976/77/78)
1974 Exhibited in 'British Painting' 74' at Hayward Gallery
1975 Received Arts Council Major Grant
1976 One-man exhibition at Acme Gallery (also 1979)
1977 Exhibited in 'British Painting 1952-1977' at Royal Academy
1978 One-man exhibition at Newcastle Polytechnic Art Gallery
Exhibited with London Group at Royal College of Art
Exhibited in Summer Exhibition at Royal Academy (also 1979), 'Recent Acquisitions' at Hayward Gallery
Received Greater London Arts Association Major Grant
1979 Exhibited in 'Hayward Annual' at Hayward Gallery

Dealer Acme Gallery

Gary Wragg *Oracle* 1978 Charcoal and romplex on cotton duck 261x305cm (8ft 7inx10ft) Artist's Collection

As an artist my rejections are motivated by a need to ditch formulas, conventionalized manners, a fashionable 'look', in order to seek out an *essential* relationship with my work, to allow the workings of intuition spontaneity, direct give-and-take. It is a quest for 'natural' painting, total painting.

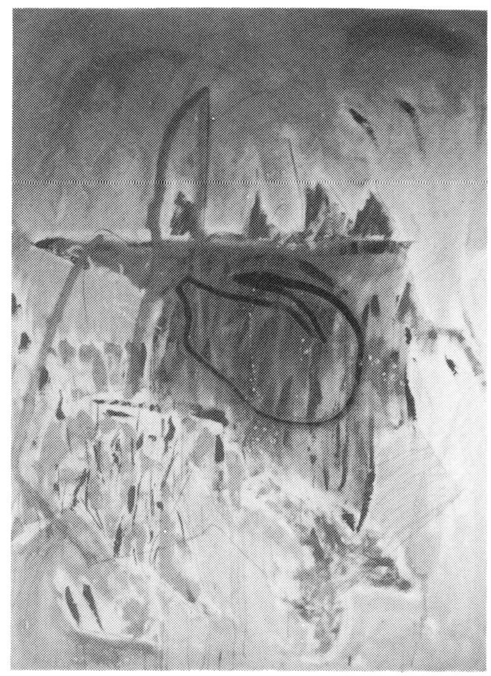

Gary Wragg *Green Snake* 1977 Acrylic, pastel and romplex on cotton duck 241x175.3cm (7ft 11inx5ft 9in) Artist's Collection

'Contact' is the measure: the contact gets finer as the work evolves. I allow the structure to emerge rather than imposing it. I let it develop without forcing its outcome. Creating a picture is a matter of watching linkages, affinities, rhythms, a space, a presence etc, develop. Good painting can't be made without a sensitivity to structure, but consciously imposing a structure will interfere with the emergence of a natural structure (the mind organizes spontaneously), and it breaks the circuit of empathy, emphasizing the ego at the expense of an autonomous image. I like to feel that my painting and I are equally impressionable to one another, that we're equally alive, responsive, open to a greater closeness of rapport.

Modern science tells us that there are many levels of reality. By the variety of elements, their layering, relativity and implicit shuttling in space/time, I try to make my paintings as real as possible to the light of experience. Through painting I try to understand energy, how to achieve a maximum intensity without the employment of force. The more economical the investment of energy, the more sensitive and 'natural' the painting becomes.

Gary Wragg 1979

John Wragg 125

1937 Born in York
1953-6 Studied at York School of Art
1956-60 Studied at Royal College of Art
1959 Exhibited in group show at Lords Gallery
1960 Received Sainsbury Award (also 1966)
1963 One-man exhibition at Hanover Gallery (also 1966/70)
1965-8 Exhibited in 'L'art vivant' at Fondation Maeght, St Paul de Vence
1966 Exhibited in Arts Council group show in Belfast
1967 One-man exhibition at Alexandre Zolas, Paris
Exhibited in Carnegie International Exhibition, Pittsburgh,
Group show at Bath Festival Gallery
1968 Exhibited in 'Britische Kunstlerer' in Hamburg,
Contemporary Art Fair in Florence
1969 One man exhibition at York Festival
1977 Exhibited in group show at Artists Market
Received Arts Council Major Award

Contact 4 Landsdowne Terrace, Morris Lane, Devizes

John Wragg *Squeeze* 1964 Aluminium 61x30.5cm (24x12in) Private Collection

John Wragg *Head of a Man* 1978 Painted resin 61x30.5cm (24x12in) Private Collection

Laetitia Yhap 52

1941 Born in St Albans
1958-62 Studied at Camberwell School of Art
1962-3 Received Leverhulme Travel Scholarship to Italy
1963-5 Studied at Slade School of Fine Art
1965 Exhibited in 'Young Contemporaries', Group show at South London Art Gallery (also 1975/76),
With London Group (also 1967/68/70/72/73)
1968 Individual exhibition at Piccadilly Gallery (also 1970/73)
1969 Exhibited in 'East Anglian Art' at Royal Institute Galleries
1970 Elected member of London Group
1973 Exhibited in group show at Warehouse Gallery
1974 Exhibited in John Moores Exhibition, Liverpool (prizewinner),
National Painting Competition, Chichester
1975 Exhibited in Basle Art Fair,
'9 Painters of the English Landscape' at Piccadilly Gallery,
Middlesbrough Biennale (also 1979),
'Drawings of People' at Serpentine Gallery
1976 Exhibited drawings in group show at Diploma Galleries, Royal Academy
1978 Exhibited in Egg Exhibition at Langton Gallery,
Amnesty International exhibition at Battersea Library
1979 Exhibited in 'Summer Show 1' at Serpentine Gallery

Contact 12 The Croft, Hastings, Sussex

Laetitia Yhap *Leon and Rod under their Boat – Hastings* 1977-8 Oil 62x60cm (24½x23⅝in) Artist's Collection

All is confusion. I struggle to exist in it by painting. A Londoner, I had a Chinese father and a Viennese mother. For years I had felt it too complicated to paint people. Painting was a meditation on fire and water, earth and air – it seemed rather Chinese. I regretted the unpeopled look of my paintings, especially as in Western Art I admired the humanist painters.

On Hastings beach, men and boys who fish live out most of their lives together. It was this communal, continuous, life out-of-doors which made me envious. I wanted a share in it. I went there every day. Often in the discomfort of wind and cold, glare or damp or even at sea I made hundreds of drawings.

I find that in the paintings which I do in my room, I need to determine things more exactly than I do in drawings. The problem is not to lose my experience of actuality by sinking Life in Art.

Laetitia Yhap 1979

Laetitia Yhap *A Boy and a Man Handling Nets – Hastings* 1977-8 Oil 61x69cm (24x27in) Artist's Collection

Gallery Addresses

This section gives the addresses of the artists' dealers mentioned in the directory and of other selected art galleries where the artists included in the book have shown. It is neither a comprehensive list of every gallery exhibiting or dealing in contemporary British art, nor does it include the addresses of public collections in Britain and abroad.

Great Britain

London

Aberbach Fine Art
17 Savile Row
London W1

Acme Gallery
43 Shelton Street
London WC1

Thomas Agnew & Son Ltd
43 Old Bond Street
London W1

Browse & Darby
19 Cork Street
London W1

Anthony d'Offay
9 Dering Street
London W1

Drian Galleries
7 Porchester Place
London W2

Fieldborne Galleries
63 Queens Grove
London NW8

Fine Art Society Ltd
148 New Bond Street
London W1

Fischer Fine Art
30 King Street
London SW1

Angela Flowers Gallery
11 Tottenham Mews
London W1

Furneaux Gallery
23 Church Road
Wimbledon Village
London SW19

Gimpel Fils
30 Davies Street
London W1

Graffiti
44 Great Marlborough Street
London W1

Nigel Greenwood Inc Ltd
41 Sloane Gardens
London SW1

House
62 Regents Park Road
London NW1

J P L Fine Arts
24 Davies Street
London W1

Annely Juda Fine Art
11 Tottenham Mews
London W1

Monika Kinley
54 Digby Mansions
Lower Mall
London W6

Knoedler Gallery
144 New Bond Street
London W1

Lefevre Gallery
Alex Reid & Lefevre Ltd
30 Bruton Street
London W1

Lisson Gallery
66-68 Bell Street
London NW1

J S Maas & Co Ltd
15a Clifford Street
London W1

Marlborough Fine Art
6 Albermarle Street
London W1

Mayor Gallery
22a Cork Street
London W1

Mercury Gallery
26 Cork Street
London W1

New Art Centre
41 Sloane Street
London SW1

New Grafton Gallery
42 Old Bond Street
London W1

Michael Parkin Fine Art Ltd
11 Motcombe Street
London SW1

Gilbert Parr Gallery
285 Kings Road
London SW3

Piccadilly Gallery
16 Cork Street
London W1

Redfern Gallery
20 Cork Street
London W1

Rowan Gallery Ltd
31a Bruton Place
Berkeley Square
London W1

Hester Van Royen
1 Langley Court
London WC2

Rutland Gallery
32 St Georges Street
London W1

Felicity Samuel
16 Savile Row
London W1

Robert Self
9 Cork Street
London W1

Anthony Stokes Ltd
3 Langley Court
London WC2

Taranman
236 Brompton Road
London SW3

Thackeray Gallery
18 Thackeray Street
Kensington Square
London W8

Arthur Tooth & Sons Ltd
33 Cork Street
London W1

Waddington Galleries Ltd
2 Cork Street
London W1

Wildenstein
47 New Bond Street
London W1

Regional Galleries in Britain and Ireland

Birmingham

Ikon Gallery
58-72 John Bright Street
Birmingham B1

Bradford

Cartwright Hall Art Gallery
Lister Park
Bradford, West Yorkshire

Brighton

Gardner Centre Gallery
University of Sussex
Falmer
Brighton, Sussex

Bristol

Arnolfini
Narrow Quay
Bristol BS1

Cambridge

Kettle's Yard
University of Cambridge
Northampton Street
Cambridge

Chichester

David Paul Gallery
St John's Street
Chichester, Sussex

Colchester

The Minories
74 High Street
Colchester, Essex

Dublin

Oliver Dowling Gallery
19 Kildare Street
Dublin 2

Edinburgh

Richard Demarco Gallery
Monteith House
61 High Street
Edinburgh

Fine Art Society Ltd
12 Great King Street
Edinburgh

Fruit Market Gallery
24 Market Street
Edinburgh

New 57 Gallery
29 Market Street
Edinburgh

Farnham

New Ashgate Gallery
Wagon Yard
Farnham, Surrey

Folkstone

The Arts Centre
New Metropole
The Leas
Folkstone, Kent

Glasgow

Third Eye Centre
350 Sauchiehall Street
Glasgow G2

Liverpool

Bluecoat Gallery
School Lane
Liverpool 1

Manchester

Peterloo Gallery
8 Clarence Street
Albert Square
Manchester M2

Newcastle-upon-Tyne

Robert Self Gallery
17 Queen's Lane
Newcastle-upon-Tyne

Stone Gallery
10 St Mary's Place
Newcastle-upon-Tyne

Nottingham

Midland Group Gallery
24-32 Carlton Street
Nottingham

Oxford

Oxford Gallery
23 High Street
Oxford

Sheffield

Philip Francis Gallery
359-361 Ecclesall Road
Sheffield S11

Southampton

Southampton Art Gallery
The Civic Centre
Southampton

St Ives

Penwith Galleries Ltd
Back Road West
St Ives, Cornwall

Sunderland

Sunderland Arts Centre
17 Grange Terrace
Stockton Road
Sunderland

Wakefield

Wakefield Art Gallery
Wentworth Terrace
Wakefield, West Yorkshire

United States of America

Chicago

Richard Feigen & Co Inc
620 North Michigan Avenue
Chicago 60611

Hokin Gallery Inc
200 East Ontario Street
Chicago 60611

Dorothy Rosenthal Gallery
233 East Ontario Street
Chicago 60611

Los Angeles

Ankrum Gallery
657 North La Cienega Boulevard
Los Angeles 90069

Circle Gallery
969 North La Cienega Boulevard
Los Angeles 90069

James Corcoran Galleries
8223 Santa Monica Boulevard
Los Angeles 90045

Feingarten
736 North La Cienega Boulevard
Los Angeles 90069

Charles S Grieve
8229 Santa Monica Boulevard
Los Angeles 90045

Janus Gallery
303 North Sweeter
Los Angeles 90001

Felix Landau
PO Box 49055
Los Angeles 90049

McConnell's
7969 Melrose Avenue
Los Angeles 90046

Herbert B Palmer
2252 Mandev
Canyon Road
Los Angeles 90049

Ruth Schaffner
8406 Melrose Avenue
Los Angeles 90069

Esther Robles Gallery
665 North La Cienega Boulevard
Los Angeles 90069

Tamara B Thomas' Fine Art Services
107 South Irving Boulevard
Los Angeles 90045

Richard Tobey
741 North La Cienega Boulevard
Los Angeles 90069

Nicholas Wilder Gallery
8225 Santa Monica Boulevard
Los Angeles 90046

New York

Aberbach Fine Art
988 Madison Avenue
NYC 10021

Acquavella Inc
18 East 79 Street
NYC 10021

Associated American Artists
663 Fifth Avenue
NYC 10021

Bodley Gallery
1063 Madison Avenue
NYC 10028

Susan Caldwell
383 West Broadway
NYC 10012

Leo Castelli Gallery
4 East 77 Street
NYC 10021
420 West Broadway
NYC 10012

Betty Cunningham
94 Prince Street
NYC 10012

Davis and Long Company
746 Madison Avenue
NYC 10021

Tibor de Nagy Inc
29 West 57 Street
NYC 10019

Terry Dintenfass
50 West 57 Street
NYC 10019

J H Duffy & Sons
157 Spring Street
NYC 10012

Robert Elkon Gallery
1063 Madison Avenue
NYC 10012

André Emmerich Gallery
41 East 57 Street
NYC 10022
420 West Broadway
NYC 10012

Richard Feigen & Co Inc
900 Park Avenue
NYC 10021

Ronald Feldman Fine Arts Inc
33 East 74 Street
NYC 10021

William J Fischer Inc
54 East 13 Street
NYC 10013

Allan Frumkin
50 West 57 Street
NYC 10019

John Gibson
392 West Broadway
NYC 10012

Harriet Griffin
850 Madison Avenue
NYC 10021

Gimpel & Weitzenhoffer Ltd
1040 Madison Avenue
NYC 10028

O K Harris
383 West Broadway
NYC 10013

Nancy Hoffmann Gallery Inc
429 West Broadway
NYC 10012

Brooks Jackson Gallery Iolas
52 East 57 Street
NYC 10019

Martha Jackson Gallery
521 West 57 Street
NYC 10019

Bernard Jacobson
24 West 57 Street
NYC 10019

Sidney Janis Gallery
6 West 57 Street
NYC 10019

M Knoedler & Co Inc
19 East 70 Street
NYC 10021

Kornblee Gallery
20 West 57 Street
NYC 10019

Lefebre Gallery
47 East 77 Street
NYC 10021

Meredith Long Contemporary
7 West 57 Street
NYC 10019

Marlborough Gallery Inc
40 West 57 Street
NYC 10019

Pierre Matisse Gallery
41 East 57 Street
NYC 10022

Elise Meyer Inc
410 West Broadway
NYC 10012

Robert Miller Gallery
724 Fifth Avenue
NYC 10021

William Edward O'Reilly Inc
35 East 67 Street
NYC 10021

Pace Gallery
32 East 57 Street
NYC 10022

Betty Parsons Gallery
24 West 57 Street
NYC 10019

Paul Rosenberg & Co
20 East 79 Street
NYC 10021

Lawrence Rubin Gallery
118 East 61 Street
NYC 10021

Saidenberg Gallery
1 East 79 Street
NYC 10021

Ivy Sky Rutsky
PO Box 215
NYC

Bertha Schaefer Inc
41 East 57 Street
NYC 10022

Sonnabend Gallery
420 West Broadway
NYC 10012

Staempfli Gallery
47 East 77 Street
NYC 10021

Touchstone Gallery Inc
118 East 64 Street
NYC 10021

Catherine Viviano
250 East 65 Street
NYC 10021

John Weber Gallery
420 West Broadway
NYC 10012

Wildenstein
19 East 64 Street
NYC 10021

San Francisco

John Berrgruen Gallery
228 Grant Avenue
San Francisco 94108

Washington

Sidney Micholson Gallery
707 G Street N W
Washington D C

Canada

Montreal

Waddington Galleries Inc
1456 Sherbrooke Street West
Montreal
Quebec

Toronto

Waddington Galleries Inc
33 Hazelton Avenue
Toronto
Ontario

Belgium
Brussels

Delta Gallery
Ernest Allardstraat 21-1000
Brussels

Le Disque Rouge
rue Piers 15
Brussels

Galerie Farber
5 Ravenstein 1000
Brussels

Gallery Anne Van Horenbeeck
Art Actuel
Ch de Charleroi 183
Brussels

France
Paris

Art Vivant
72 boulevard Raspail
75007 Paris

Balcon des Arts
141 rue Saint-Martin
75004 Paris

Craven
4 avenue de Messine
75008 Paris

Jacques Duborg
10 rue Maspéro
750016 Paris

Durrand-Dessert
43 rue de Montmorency
750016 Paris

Fondation Wildenstein
57 rue de La Boetie
75008 Paris

Galerie Bama
80 rue du Bac
75007 Paris

Iolas
8 rue Perronet
75007 Paris

Galerie Maeght
13 rue de Téhéran
75008 Paris

Messine
1 avenue de Messine
75008 Paris

Proscenium
35 rue de Seine
75006 Paris

Rive Gauche
44 rue de Fleuras
75006 Paris

Jacomo Santivieri
104 rue du Bac
75007 Paris

Ileana Sonnabend
12 rue Mazarine
75006 Paris

West Germany
Berlin

René Block
Schapestrasse 11
Berlin

Galerie Mikro
Carmerstrasse 1
Berlin

Folker Skulima
Niebuhrstrasse 2
Berlin

Springer
Fasanenstrasse 13
Berlin

Cologne

Paul Maenz
Lindenstrasse 32
Cologne

Gallery Nuendorf
Lindenstrasse 20
Cologne

Galerie der Spiegel
Richartzstrasse 10
Cologne

Galerie Michael Werner
1 Friesenstrasse 50
Cologne

Galerie Rudolph Zwirner
Albertusstrasse 18
Cologne

Dusseldorf

Galerie Art in Progress
Kasernenstrasse 18
Dusseldorf

Artkontakt
Weizenmuhlenstrasse 16
Dusseldorf

Konrad Fischer
Platanenstrasse 7
Dusseldorf

Galerie December
Schirmerstrasse 23
Dusseldorf

Hamburg

Galerie Wentzel
60 Agnesstrasse 49
Hamburg

Hanover

Kestner-Gesellschaft
Warn Buchenstrasse 13241
Hanover

Stuttgart

Margaret Muller
Hohenheimerstrasse 7
Stuttgart

Holland
Amsterdam

De Appel
Brouwersgraacht 169
Amsterdam

B V D'Eendt
Spuistraat 270-272
Amsterdam

Espace Gallery
Keizer Gr 548
Amsterdam

Galerie Jurka
Vyzelstraat 80
Amsterdam

Mickery Gallery
Rozengarten 117
Amsterdam

Galerie Swart
Van Breestraat 23
Amsterdam

Italy
Florence

Vaccarino Arte Contemporanea
via del Tournabuoni 7/r
Florence

Milan

Ariete
via S. Andre 5
Milan

Galeria Bergamini
Corzo Venezia 16
Milan

Galleria Milano
via Manin 13
Milan

Morone
via Morone 6
Milan

Studio Marconi
via Tadino 15
Milan

Rome

L'Obelisco
via Sistina 146
Rome

Marlborough Galleria d'Arte
via Gregoriana 5
Rome

Primo Piano
via Vittoria 32
Rome

Studio d'Arte Condotti
via Condotti 85
Rome

Turin

Galleria Gian Enzo Sperone
corso San Maurizo 27
Turin

Venice

Galleria del Cavallino
San Marco 1725
Venice

Verona

Studio la Citta
vicolo Samaritana 10
Verona

Portugal

Lisbon

Galeria Judite Dacruz
R Alecrim 72
Lisbon

Modulo
453 Estrada Benf
Lisbon

Spain

Madrid

Galeria Nebli
Serrano 80
Madrid

Galeria Skira
Ortega y Gasset 23
Madrid

Galeria Ynguanzo
Antonio Maura 12
Madrid

Zaragoza

Galeria de Arte Goya
Plaza Ntr Sra Del Pilar 16
Zaragoza 3

Switzerland

Basle

Beyeler
Baumleingasse 9
Basle

Geneva

Galerie Contemporaine
4 Place de Temple
Carouge
Geneva

Nyon

Loyse Oppenheim Galerie
Ruelle de la Tour 1
Nyon

Zurich

Bischofsberger
Buhlstrasse 7
Zurich

Galerie André Emmerich
Todistrasse 40
Zurich

Galerie Paul Facchetti
Speigelgasse 11
Zurich

Galerie Gimpel and Hanover
34 Claridenstrasse
Zurich

Renée Ziegler
Minervastrasse 33
Zurich

Japan

Tokyo

Fuji Television Gallery Co Ltd
Ichigaya-Kawadacho
Shinjuko-Ku
Tokyo

Ginza Art Gallery
8 chome Ginza
Chuo-ku
Tokyo

Minami Gallery
3-7-20 Nihonbashi Chuo-ku
Tokyo

Nantenshi
3-7-13 Kyobashi
Chuo-ku
Tokyo

Nishimura Gallery
Kyobashi Nakadori Building
7 Kyobashi 2-chome
Tokyo

Giza Nisho Building
Giza
Tokyo

Setsu Gatodo Co Ltd
7-9-3 chome
Nihombashi
Chuo-ku
Tokyo

Wildenstein
3-1-1 Maranouchi
Chiyoda-ku
Tokyo

Nagoya

Yamada Kyoto
Gallery Valeur
Nagoya

All the photographs of work reproduced in this book were supplied by the artists or obtained on their behalf. They include photographs by the following:

Jann Anderson; Derek Balmer; Jonathan Bayer; Beedle & Cooper; Brompton Studio; N Collins; David Cornfield; Courtauld Institute of Art; Cremonesi Fine Art Photographers; Harriet Crowder; Prudence Cuming Associates; Chris Davies; John Donat; Crispin Eurich; David Farrell; Robert Fraser Gallery; John R Freeman & Co; Pl Gates Photography Ltd; John Goldblatt; Hugh Gordon; Carlos Granger; Hanover Gallery; Conrad Hafenrichter; Mark Harrison; Leslie D Haslam, Berlin; Robin Hughes; John Hunnex; Brian Hunt; Errol Jackson; K&J Jelley; Peter Kinnear; Martin Koretz; Tiffany Lacey; Patricia Leroux, France; Kim Lim; Ingeborg Lommatzsch, Berlin; Nicholas MacKenzie; Joseph McKenzie; Peter Moore, New York; James Mortimer; Gallery One; Roger Park; Jon Pasmore; Photowork Ltd; Paul Popper Ltd; Royal Academy of Arts; Reijo Ruster, Stockholm; Mickey Slingsby; SNAP; Alexander Von Steiger, Basle; Studio St Ives; John Summerhayes; Michael Sweet; Tate Gallery; Sam Thomas; Eileen Tweedy; John Underwood; Walia; Peter Walser, Stuttgart; John Webb; Stephen Weiss; Todd White; Cumming Wright-Watson Associates Ltd; Rodney Wright-Watson Photography; Fotografie Dick Wolters, Holland.